THE
LAST HURRAH?

THE LAST HURRAH?

*Soft Money and
Issue Advocacy in the
2002 Congressional Elections*

David B. Magleby

J. Quin Monson

editors

Brookings Institution Press
Washington, D.C.

Copyright © 2004
THE BROOKINGS INSTITUTION
1775 Massachusetts Avenue, N.W., Washington, D.C. 20036
www.brookings.edu

Library of Congress Cataloging-in-Publication data
The last hurrah? : soft money and issue advocacy in the 2002 congressional
    elections / David B. Magleby and J. Quin Monson, editors.
    p.   cm.
    Includes bibliographical references and index.
    ISBN 0-8157-5436-1 (cloth : alk. paper)
    ISBN 0-8157-5437-X (pbk. : alk. paper)
    1. Campaign funds—United States. 2. Pressure groups—United States. 3. United
States. Congress—Elections, 2002—Case studies. I. Magleby, David B. II. Monson,
J. Quin. III. Title.
JK1991.L37 2004
324.973'0931—dc22   2004000215

9 8 7 6 5 4 3 2 1
The paper used in this publication meets minimum requirements of the
American National Standard for Information Sciences—Permanence of Paper for
Printed Library Materials: ANSI Z39.48-1992.

Typeset in Sabon

Composition by Betsy Kulamer
Washington, D.C.

Printed by R. R. Donnelley
Harrisonburg, Virginia

Contents

Preface

THIS BOOK EXAMINES campaign finance in federal elections in 2002, the last time campaign financing was governed by the Federal Elections Campaign Act (FECA). The surge in party soft money spending that we document here continued a trend begun in 1996 when parties began using large amounts of soft money for candidate promotion purposes. The day after Election Day 2002, FECA was superseded by the substantially different Bipartisan Campaign Reform Act (BCRA), which bans party soft money, a fact used by both parties to encourage even more soft money contributions in 2002.

Interest groups have also recently expanded their expenditures on federal elections through a device called issue advocacy. As interpreted by the Supreme Court under FECA, communications that did not use words such as *vote for* or *vote against* were determined to be about an issue and not the election or defeat of a candidate. This narrow and unrealistic definition allowed groups to expend unlimited and undisclosed amounts of money in a small set of competitive races with the clear intent of influencing the outcome.

Both soft money and electioneering issue advocacy activities could rely on corporate and union general funds, technically referred to as treasury funds, and allowed corporations or unions to support political parties or candidates in ways that would otherwise be blocked. BCRA restores the longstanding ban on the use of corporate and union treasury funds in electioneering. We titled our book *The Last Hurrah?* because passage of BCRA may mean the 2002 election cycle is the last hurrah of soft money as we know it. We inserted a question mark in the title because it remains to be seen how much soft money finds other outlets in the campaign finance system in 2004 and beyond. The research reported in this book establishes a benchmark against which to compare the changes in interest group and party activity under this new campaign finance law.

Our methodology in monitoring noncandidate electioneering efforts relies on systematic data collection and elite interviewing in a set of competitive congressional races. To establish a frame of reference for the competitive races we also studied a set of control races. In 2002 our sample of competitive races numbered 25, and we also observed campaigns in 17 control races. This book builds on similar studies organized by the Center for the Study of Elections and Democracy (CSED) in 1998 and 2000. Across the three election cycles we have now collected data on all forms of campaign communication in 81 contests. Our research on the 2002 election, as well as the earlier studies in 1998 and 2000, were funded by a grant from the Pew Charitable Trusts, whose support in funding original research in the areas of campaign conduct and campaign finance is extraordinary. We express appreciation to Sean Treglia, a superb program officer at Pew; Michael Delli Carpini, who directed the organization's Public Policy Program; Paul Light, who was the director of the Public Policy Program during our initial project in 1998 and has remained supportive of our work; and Pew President Rebecca Rimel for her continuing trust and confidence.

This kind of systematic coordinated data collection would not be possible without academics in the districts and states in our sample committing significant time and effort to this project. Our association with them on a truly collaborative effort is one of the most rewarding aspects of this research. We gratefully acknowledge the good work of Owen Abbe (University of Maryland); Sandra M. Anglund and Sarah M. Morehouse (University of Connecticut); Lonna Rae Atkeson, Nancy Carrillo, and Margaret C. Toulouse (University of New Mexico); Jay Barth (Hendrix College); Janine Parry (University of Arkansas); David A. Breaux (Mississippi State University); Chris Carman (University of Pittsburgh); William Flanigan, Joanne Miller, and Jennifer Williams (University of Minnesota); Nancy Zingale (University of St. Thomas); Eric S. Heberlig (University of North Carolina–Charlotte); E. Terrence Jones and Matt McLaughlin (University of Missouri–St. Louis); Martha Kropf and Dale Neuman (University of Missouri–Kansas City); Drew

Linzer (University of California–Los Angeles), David Menefee-Libey and Matt Muller (Pomona College); James Meader and John Bart (Augustana College); Stephen K. Medvic and Matthew M. Schousen (Franklin and Marshall College); Kelly Patterson (Brigham Young University); Joseph A. Pika (University of Delaware); David Redlawsk (University of Iowa); Arthur Sanders (Drake University); John Roos and Christopher Rodriguez (University of Notre Dame); Daniel A. Smith (University of Denver, now with University of Florida); Frederic I. Solop and James I. Bowie (Northern Arizona University); Michael W. Traugott (University of Michigan); Craig Wilson (Montana State University–Billings); J. Mark Wrighton (University of New Hampshire). Space did not permit us to include all of these case studies in this book. The initial version of these case studies can be found at http://csed.byu.edu, and updated versions of all case studies were published as an electronic symposium in conjunction with the July 2003 issue of *PS: Political Science and Politics*, available at www.apsanet.org/PS/july03/toc.cfm.

We also acknowledge the hard work and professionalism of our research associates at the Center for the Study of Elections and Democracy (CSED)—Stephanie Perry Curtis, Jennifer Jensen McArthur, Nicole Carlisle Squires, and Jonathan Tanner. Stephanie, Jennifer, Nicole, and Jonathan, all recent Brigham Young University (BYU) graduates, worked full time on the project for a year or more, while Emily Walsh was involved in the project's early planning. The research associates provided assistance to the academics in the field, managed the websites, coordinated database construction, conducted data entry and cleaning, scheduled and accompanied us on interviews, analyzed a variety of data, transcribed interviews, edited the book manuscript, and much more. Their significant contribution to the overall effort is apparent to anyone familiar with the day-to-day operations of CSED. Jennifer Jensen and later Jonathan Tanner worked on our project from space provided us in Washington, D.C., by the Center for Public Integrity (CPI). We are most grateful to Charles Lewis and his associates at CPI for their hospitality and collegiality. BYU undergraduates Analisa Underdown, Jeffrey R. Makin, Susan Christiansen, Eric McArthur, Andrew Jenson, and Elliott D. Wise also provided research assistance. Marianne Holt Viray, Eric Smith, Jason Beal, and Anna Nibley Baker, research associates from the 1998 and 2000 projects, provided timely advice on this project as well. In addition to the able editorial assistance provided by Nicole Carlisle Squires, we are grateful for the editing provided by Elaine Tomlinson,

Luana Uluave Miller, Peter Jasinski, and Anna Nibley Baker. We are also indebted to the Office of Research and Creative Activities at BYU, especially Gary R. Reynolds, Melvin Carr, Kathleen Rugg, and Nancy A. Davis, for helping to coordinate and facilitate our research.

To supplement our data collection directly from broadcast and cable stations, we acquired the Campaign Media Analysis Group (CMAG) data on broadcast television ads when it was available for media markets in our sample races. We gratefully acknowledge the assistance of Ken Goldstein of the University of Wisconsin–Madison and his Wisconsin Advertising Project associates Joel Rivlin, Timothy Wells, and Travis Ridout. As in 1998 and 2000, we contacted members of the League of Women Voters and Common Cause as well as Brigham Young University alumni in each of the contests we monitored. Our academic partners further expanded this reconnaissance network with alumni from their own universities and others with a broad reach of interests and contacts. We express appreciation to Lloyd Leonard and Betsy Lawson of the League of Women Voters and Ed Davis of Common Cause for their assistance in this effort.

In 2002 CSED also organized a panel study of voter opinion about campaign finance in two states, two congressional districts, and a national baseline sample. We gratefully acknowledge the collaboration of Fred Yang, Mark Mellman, Ed Goeas, and Linda DiVall and their colleagues in designing this survey, as well as Western Wats for administering so many interviews in such a timely manner. We also organized a survey in four states in which registered voters recorded their political phone calls and personal contacts and forwarded to us all of their political mail over a three-week period leading up to the election. The staff of the Social and Economic Sciences Research Center at Washington State University was very helpful in this major data collection effort. In particular, Don Dillman gave us sound advice on the design of the survey, and Ashley Grosse worked tirelessly to implement the data collection and coding. Bob Biersack and Paul Clark of the Federal Election Commission were, as always, most helpful in providing and interpreting FEC data.

Our sample selection process identifies competitive contests in which outside groups and party committees are likely to mount campaigns. To help identify these races we use data provided by Charles Cook and Stuart Rothenberg. In addition, we interview party and interest group leaders, and political reporters, often multiple times before, during, and after the campaign. In 2002 our panel of experts involved in helping design the sample included Karen Ackerman, Matt Angle, Damon Ansell, Bob Bennenson, Ed Brookover, Bernadette Budde, Martin Burns, Chuck Cunningham, Greg Giroux, John Guzik, Tom Hofeller, Bill Miller, Scott Stoermer, Deanna White, Derrick Willis, and Sharon Wolff.

We have also been fortunate to have had access to all four congressional campaign committees. We especially thank each of the following for candid and helpful interviews: Michael Matthews (political director, DCCC), Andy Grossman (political director, DSCC), Mike McElwain (political director, NRCC), and Chris LaCivita (political director, NRSC). A list of all of the interest group and party interviews we conducted is found in Appendix B. We are grateful so many leaders of these organizations made time available for us to interview them.

Political scientists John Bibby and David Dulio provided helpful reviews of our overview chapters and the 2002 case studies. More generally we benefited from comments provided by Paul Beck, Janet Box-Steffensmeier, Richard Fenno, Paul Herrnson, Gary Jacobson, Tom Mann, Norm Ornstein, and Frank Sorauf. We also appreciate the anonymous reviewers at Brookings who provided helpful comments and insights.

Steve Rabinowitz, Adam Segal, and Jesse Derris at Rabinowitz Media were of great assistance in organizing our Washington, D.C., press events and with media relations generally.

We are most appreciative of the careful attention and professionalism provided by Chris Kelaher, Janet Walker, and Holly Hammond at the Brookings Institution Press.

A project of this scope would not have been possible without the support of our spouses, Linda Waters Magleby and Kate Monson. We dedicate this book to them.

THE
LAST HURRAH?

ONE

The Importance of Outside Money in the 2002 Congressional Elections

DAVID B. MAGLEBY

 'THE RELATIVE ROLE of candidates, parties, and interest groups in competitive congressional elections has undergone a dramatic transformation since 1996. Before 1996, and in noncompetitive races since, candidates were the primary loci of activity in raising and spending campaign money.[1] The vast majority of congressional contests are not competitive, but those few competitive races have become battlegrounds for control of Congress. The close party balance at all levels of government and in the electorate has also amplified the importance of competitive elections.

We began monitoring competitive races in 1998, in response to the dramatic transformation of individual donors, political parties, and interest groups that began in 1996. The first campaign finance watershed in 1996 was the use of party soft money for candidate promotion or attack. Democratic political consultant Dick Morris, with the approval of party lawyers, developed a strategy that "by the end of the race . . . had spent almost $35 million on issue-advocacy ads (in addition to the $50 million on conventional candidate-oriented media)."[2] The Republicans followed suit, and the widespread use of soft money to attack and promote candidates was in full swing.

 In our 1998 and 2000 studies we documented the surge in party soft money for candidate-specific electioneering purposes. In both election cycles, party campaign committees made the raising and spending of soft money a high priority. Unlike contributions and coordinated spending, soft money can be spent in unlimited amounts. In 2000 the parties went a step further and made it easier for donors to contribute hard and

I

soft money simultaneously by establishing joint fund-raising committees with candidates (sometimes called victory committees). These devices allow donors in a single check to designate contributions to candidates (hard dollars), party committees (hard dollars), and party soft-money accounts. The growth of joint fund-raising committees for candidates and party committees readily permits donors to signal their candidate preferences.[3] Some of the most important advantages of soft money are that it can be raised and spent by the parties in unlimited amounts, and corporations and unions can contribute treasury funds as soft money.[N]

The second campaign finance watershed in 1996 was the use of issue advocacy for specific candidate promotion or attack purposes. The American Federation of Labor–Congress of Industrial Organizations (AFL-CIO) was the first group to mount a large-scale campaign effort, while avoiding disclosure and contribution limits. The Supreme Court in the *Buckley* v. *Valeo* decision defined election-related communications as ads that use words like "vote for," "elect," "support," "cast your ballot for," "Smith for Congress," "vote against," "defeat," and "reject."[4] The AFL-CIO avoided these words but, as the National Republican Congressional Committee (NRCC) contended in a complaint with the Federal Election Commission, the ads advocated "the defeat of a clearly identified candidate in the 1996 congressional election."[5] In 1996 the AFL-CIO spent $35 million, much of it on television, aimed at defeating 105 members of Congress, including 32 heavily targeted Republican freshmen.[6] Labor ran television ads in forty districts, distributed over 11.5 million voter guides in twenty-four districts, and broadcast radio ads in many others.[7]

Following labor's lead, the business community mounted its own unlimited and undisclosed campaign named The Coalition–Americans Working for Real Change. Groups involved in this campaign included the National Federation of Independent Business, the U.S. Chamber of Commerce, the National Association of Wholesaler-Distributors, the National Restaurant Association, and the National Association of Manufacturers. The coalition was active in thirty-seven House races, spent an estimated $5 million on over 13 thousand television and radio ads, and mailed over 2 million letters.[8] Another Republican-leaning group using this tactic in 1996 was Triad Management Services.[9]

The absence of action by the Federal Election Commission to bar issue-advocacy electioneering created the climate for expanded activity by these and other groups, which we have documented in past studies.[10]

In competitive races since 1996, spending by noncandidate entities, or outside money, has grown to rival and sometimes exceed spending by candidates. How that money is spent has also diversified to include a greater emphasis on nonbroadcast communications. We define outside money to include party soft money, election issue advocacy, independent expenditures, and internal communications.

This book documents all forms of campaign communications in competitive congressional elections in 2002, including soft money and issue advocacy. In addition we include observations made while monitoring spending in a set of noncompetitive control races to establish a baseline against which to compare campaign spending in more highly charged environments.[11]

Much of the research in this book is the result of systematic monitoring of campaigns by knowledgeable academics from within the states or districts in our sample. Our common objective was to better understand the dynamics of campaigns and elections in highly contested environments with substantial campaigning not controlled by candidates. Each academic team created a reconnaissance network of individuals who collected mail and logged phone calls and personal contacts about the election.[12] Data on political mail, phone calls, personal contacts, e-mail, and other contacts were systematically gathered. Local academics also gathered ad-buy data from radio and television stations, including cable stations, in all of our sample and control races. As a supplement to our ad-buy data, we purchased the Campaign Media Analysis Group's (CMAG) data for television advertising in our sample and control races.[13] In addition, the participating academics interviewed scores of local experts, campaign staff, party professionals, and interest-group leaders in their states and districts. Likewise we conducted 134 interviews with party officials, interest-group leaders, and other experts in Washington. As a rule, these interviews were "on the record" and are cited in this book. Our 2002 project also measured voters' reactions to highly competitive campaign environments in comparison to a national baseline survey. In a separate survey voters logged their political mail and campaign contacts and provided us with all their political mail. These surveys enabled us to validate the data collection of the reconnaissance networks and to accurately measure the volume of campaign communications with voters as well as to gauge their reactions to the deluge of mail, phone calls, and in-person contacts.[14] Table 1-1 lists the congressional contests included in our 2002 study and notes the four races

Table 1-1. *U.S. Senate and House Races Studied in 2002*[a]

Congressional races	Focus race(s)	Control race(s)	Democrat	Republican
Senate				
Arkansas	x[b, c]		**Mark Pryor**	*Tim Hutchinson*
Delaware		x	***Joseph Biden***	Ray Clatworthy
Iowa	x		***Tom Harkin***	Greg Ganske
Michigan		x	***Carl Levin***	Andrew Raczkowski
Minnesota	x[c]		*Paul Wellstone /* Walter Mondale	**Norm Coleman**
Missouri	x[b]		*Jean Carnahan*	**Jim Talent**
Montana		x	***Max Baucus***	Mike Taylor
New Hampshire	x		Jeanne Shaheen	**John Sununu**
New Mexico		x[b]	Gloria Tristani	***Pete Domenici***
South Dakota	x[c]		***Tim Johnson***	John Thune
House				
Arkansas	4[b, c]		***Mike Ross***	Jay Dickey
		1	***Marion Berry***	Tommy Robinson
Arizona	1		George Cordova	**Rick Renzi**
California		29	***Adam Schiff***	Jim Scileppi
Colorado	7[b]		Mike Feeley	**Bob Beauprez**
		1	***Diana DeGette***	Ken Chlouber
Connecticut	5[b]		*Jim Maloney*	***Nancy Johnson***
		1	***John Larson***	Phil Steele
Iowa	1		Ann Hutchinson	***Jim Nussle***
	2		Julianne Thomas	***Jim Leach***
	3		***Leonard Boswell***	Stan Thompson
	4		John Norris	***Tom Latham***
Indiana	2		Jill Long Thompson	**Chris Chocola**
Maryland	8		**Christopher Van Hollen**	*Connie Morella*
		5	***Steny Hoyer***	Joe Crawford
Minnesota	2[c]		*Bill Luther*	**John Kline**
Mississippi	3		*Ronnie Shows*	***Chip Pickering***
		2	***Bennie Thompson***	Clinton LeSueur
Montana		At-large	Steve Kelly	***Dennis Rehberg***
North Carolina	8		Chris Kouri	***Robin Hayes***
		9	Ed McGuire	***Sue Myrick***
New Hampshire	1		Martha Fuller Clark	**Jeb Bradley**
		2	Katrina Swett	***Charlie Bass***
New Mexico	1[c]		Richard Romero	***Heather Wilson***
	2[c]		John Arthur Smith	**Steve Pearce**
		3[c]	***Tom Udall***	No nominee
Pennsylvania		4	Stevan Drobac Jr.	***Melissa Hart***
	17		***Tim Holden***	*George Gekas*
		6	Dan Wofford	**Jim Gerlach**
South Dakota	At-large[c]		Stephanie Herseth	**Bill Janklow**
Utah	2		***Jim Matheson***	John Swallow
		1	Dave Thomas	**Rob Bishop**
		3	Nancy Jane Woodside	***Chris Cannon***

a. Names in italics are incumbents; those in bold are winners. Numbers denote the congressional district number within the state.

b. Part of a three-wave panel survey. For details, see appendix A.

c. Part of a campaign communication voter log survey. For details, see appendix A.

in which we did polling on public perceptions of the campaign and the four races in which we asked random samples of voters to record their campaign contacts and forward to us their political mail. For a more detailed description of our methodology for the 2002 studies, including the methodology for our public opinion surveys, see appendix A. For a complete list of national-level elites interviewed for this study, see appendix B.

This book builds upon similar collaborative research efforts in 1998 and 2000. In the aggregate we have now monitored eighty-one congressional general elections or presidential primary contests in 1998, 2000, and 2002. Having collected data on the full range of campaign communications over three cycles allows us to identify trends and broader patterns. A systematic monitoring of campaign finance in 2002 was important because the 2002 election marked potentially the last hurrah for soft money and at least some interest-group electioneering before the Bipartisan Campaign Reform Act takes effect in the 2004 election cycle. The extent to which BCRA changes the campaign finance system depends on what parts of the act survive constitutional challenge,[15] how the law is interpreted during the rule-making process at the FEC[16] and FCC, and the ability of interested parties to find ways to circumvent the act.[17] BCRA has the potential to transform campaign finance in ways that are not yet clear to political operatives, candidates, and scholars.

Outside Money in the 2002 Election

Battleground races once again experienced extraordinary levels of spending, especially by the parties. In ten of the twenty-six competitive races we studied in 2002, noncandidate spending exceeded candidate spending; in one case, the Pennsylvania Seventeenth Congressional District, noncandidate spending more than doubled candidate spending. The candidate spending in these contests is already high, creating a campaign environment where voters face a barrage of political communication. In the South Dakota Senate race, for instance, candidates, parties, and interest groups spent over $24 million, which amounted to $70.50 per voter.[18] This made South Dakota in 2002 one of the most expensive elections in dollars per voter in U.S. history.

The convergence of high levels of candidate, party, and interest-group campaigning again meant that voters faced a barrage of TV and radio ads, mail, and phone calls. Based on a survey we commissioned in the

Minnesota Senate race, for example, registered voters received an average of eighteen pieces of mail in the last three weeks of the campaign, and one voter received eighty pieces of political mail.[19]

With outside money, voters often cannot determine the source of the money spent in a race. Party soft-money contributions often come from large donors, many of whom have a vested interest in particular races. Contributing through a political party permits issue activists or interest groups to mask their identity while still targeting money to a particular race. With issue advocacy it is even more difficult to know who is funding the communication.

Noncandidate campaigns are highly professional, using pollsters, field staff, and media, telephone, and mail consultants.[20] Many interest groups and their political action committees have long retained professional pollsters and other campaign professionals. But in 1996, as parties and groups started to mount issue advocacy campaigns, they significantly expanded their investment in consultants of all types.[21]

Tone and Volume of Outside-Money Advertising

In the competitive races where candidates, parties, and interest groups all participate, the tone of the campaign is more likely to be negative. The primary source of this negativity is the outside money because of "an implicit division of labor, with outside money used to attack one candidate or the other in hope of helping the favored candidates."[22] As Kathleen Hall Jamieson has observed, "Candidates don't have to attack because others will do it for them."[23] Mark Mellman, an experienced pollster, concurs that money spent by outside groups "increases the negative tone of races," and in his view "the public blames the candidates."[24] In surveys conducted in cooperation with a bipartisan panel of pollsters, we found that voters in battleground environments blame the parties and interest groups for the greater negativity in campaigns. We review the tone of party and interest-group advertisements in chapters 2 and 3 and the voter survey results in chapter 12.

Mike Lux, who helped design the hate-crimes ad run by the NAACP Voter Fund against George W. Bush in 2000, said that in 2002 both parties started being more "aggressive with the truth," operating on the assumption that campaigns "weren't going to get called on it." Lux believes that the media are playing a less active role in commenting on the accuracy and fairness of ads, including issue ads.[25] However, ads were challenged by opposing candidates and parties in 2002 and some were pulled. In Indiana's Second District in early September 2002, the Indiana Democratic Party ran an ad claiming that Republican candidate Chris Chocola held "Enron values" rather than "Hoosier values" and showing the Enron logo. After Chocola made formal complaints, the television stations decided to pull the ad. Soon thereafter the NRCC ran an ad for Chocola, asserting that "Long Thompson had voted to cut the military, opposed stopping Saddam Hussein, and had taken money from a radical group that opposes the war on terror." Again the television stations pulled the ad. This practice also occurred in 2000.[26] The assertion that groups have broad leeway in their independent communications is not new. In 1980 National Conservative Political Action Committee (NCPAC) founder John Terry Dolan once bragged that his organization "could lie through its teeth and the candidate it helps stays clean."[27]

Absent some assessment as to the truthfulness of party and interest-group ads, voters are left to the constant charges and countercharges of the candidates, parties, and groups about the other side being misleading or untruthful. As discussed in chapter 12, voters have a variety of reactions to these high-intensity campaigns. Their awareness of the campaign is heightened, but this interest does not necessarily lead to higher turnout. When faced with daunting volumes of political communication, voters are more likely to indicate that they have seen too much mail and advertising, are less likely to view the campaigns as "fair" or "accurate," and are more likely to view the campaign as more negative compared to recent political contests. Under these conditions voters turn to trusted sources of information such as family and friends, groups they affiliate with, or objective sources like newspapers or television news.[28]

The Growing Importance of the Ground War

Outside-money campaigns in 1996 were primarily run on television and radio, but since then they have been increasingly diversified to include direct mail, live and recorded telephone calls, personal persuasion (face to face), and get-out-the-vote (GOTV) efforts.[29] This shift to less reliance on broadcast advertising and increased use of ground-war tactics continued in 2002.

The 2002 case studies demonstrate the importance of the ground war, paid for with outside money, to voter activation and mobilization efforts. Both parties and several allied groups waged expanded ground-war campaigns. Republicans, pointing to the successes of the Democrats and their interest-group allies in voter mobilization in 1998 and 2000, invested heavily in voter mobilization in 2002. The Republican National Committee (RNC), under the leadership of the White House, initiated the 72 Hour Task Force, and the Republican leadership in the House initiated the Strategic Taskforce to Organize and Mobilize People (STOMP). A major element of their program included visits by President Bush or other Republican luminaries, including Vice President Dick Cheney, First Lady Laura Bush, or former New York Mayor Rudy Giuliani to energize the paid and volunteer workers and dominate news coverage. The GOP ground war included direct contact with voters, telephone calls, mail, and GOTV activities on Election Day. Interest in voter mobilization on the part of Republican-allied groups such as the Business Industry Political Action Committee (BIPAC), the Chamber of Commerce, the National Federation of Independent Business (NFIB), and the National Rifle Association (NRA) provided significant help for Republican ground-war efforts. Organized labor has long worked side by side with the Democratic Party and Democratic candidates in key races. We examine the ground war in greater detail in chapter 4.

Outside Money Unlimited and Targeted at Competitive Races

Decisions on where to invest soft money and election issue advocacy funds are "driven by the numbers"; races that are competitive see activity, and noncompetitive races do not.[30] Because they are not subject to Federal Election Commission (FEC) contribution limits, interest groups and parties spend their noncandidate campaign funds in much larger chunks, often allocating large amounts to a single race. Since the parties and interest groups control the expenditure of outside money, they can allocate it in contests and at times that suit their strategic purposes. Groups vary in when they allocate their outside money. Some groups that tend to favor particular candidates for ideological or gender reasons, like EMILY's List and the Club for Growth, contribute in primaries. Groups sometimes sequence their investments in the general election to monitor the reaction of voters to their ads and, if the race remains competitive, invest even more. Outside money has the advantage of fungibility; it can be held centrally until late in the campaign and then spent in the most competitive races, where it can have the most impact.

Our research has shown that outside money flows almost exclusively to competitive races. As AFL-CIO political director Steve Rosenthal testified in *McConnell* v. *FEC*, "issue ads work best if they are run in a place where there is a competitive political environment."[31] Most con-

Table 1-2. *Number of Unique Campaign Communications in Sample Races, 2002*

Type of communication	Senate battleground race	Senate control race	House battleground race	House control race
Candidate TV	29[a]	9[a]	9[a]	2[a]
Noncandidate TV[b]	30[a]	3[a]	11[a]	1[a]
Candidate radio	6	17	2	1
Noncandidate radio[b]	13[a]	1[a]	2	1
Candidate mail	13	10	9[a]	1[a]
Noncandidate mail[b]	105[a]	19[a]	42[a]	9[a]

Source: David B. Magleby, J. Quin Monson, and the Center for the Study of Elections and Democracy, CSED 2002 Soft Money and Issue Advocacy Database [dataset] (Center for the Study of Elections and Democracy, Brigham Young University, 2002).

a. Using an *F* test, the difference between battleground and control races is significant at p < .05.

b. Noncandidate includes communications funded by party soft money, interest-group issue advocacy, and independent expenditures.

gressional contests in 2002 did not see outside money activity because they were not competitive. For example, in 2000 the contest in California's Twenty-Seventh Congressional District was among the most intensely fought House races in history, with parties, groups, and candidates spending an estimated $18.5 million. Two years later, in the contest involving Republican incumbent Adam Schiff and much of the same congressional district, David Menefee-Libey found that the "political parties and outside interest groups spent practically nothing to contest this extremely safe seat."[32] In another race that was significantly affected by outside money in 2000, Pennsylvania's Fourth Congressional District, Chris Carman found in 2002 that there was almost a "complete absence of 'outside' money and influence."[33] Carman, having watched the same district across two election cycles, concludes: "We should think of outside organizations as strategic actors that weigh their investment choices and stay out of competitions where they perceive that they cannot influence the outcome."[34]

Evidence of outside money being directed to competitive races is found in table 1-2, which provides a comparison of the average numbers of unique TV ads, radio ads, and mail pieces for candidate and noncandidate groups in sample and control House and Senate races in our 2002 study. A control race is one in which we did not expect significant outside money activity. Control races also establish a baseline against which to compare the contests where outside money is injected.

The difference in the numbers of party and interest-group ads run in battleground races compared to control races is especially large. Except for radio advertisements, all the differences between battleground and control races for noncandidate communications are statistically significant.[35] However, the differences in candidate communications between battleground and control races are less pronounced, and fewer of the differences are statistically significant. For example, there were five times as many pieces of noncandidate mail in battleground Senate races as in control races, while the difference in candidate mail for the Senate was not significant. We found a staggering average of 105 unique noncandidate mail pieces in our battleground races, a sign of the intense ground war, which we explore in more detail in chapter 4. The discrepancy in noncandidate radio ads was even greater in battleground Senate races, with an average of thirteen in battleground races and only one in control races. In sum, even more than among candidates, the noncandidate campaigns focus on the competitive, or battleground, districts.

How Money Is Used in Congressional Elections

The money chase by candidates has been a long-standing element of seeking federal office and a factor in the relative competitiveness of the candidate. Incumbents have long enjoyed advantages in this candidate-centered system.[36] Incumbents also have consistently raised more money than they needed, in hopes that these war chests would scare away challengers.[37]

Federal election law limits the ways in which individuals, political parties, and interest groups can contribute, raise, and spend money on federal elections. Individuals have limits on how much they can contribute to candidates and parties in an election cycle. Candidates are subject to disclosure and limitations on how they raise money. Parties operate with disclosure and limits on their fund-raising and contributions, except for soft money, which can be raised in unlimited amounts. Interest groups have more options, including some that are neither limited nor disclosed. Table 1-3 provides the contribution limits in force during the 2001–02 election cycle.

Hard Money

Under the Federal Election Campaign Act (FECA), individuals and political action committees (PACs) can make limited and disclosed contributions to candidates and political parties. These contributions are

Table 1-3. *Contribution Limits, Election Cycle 2001–02*

		Recipients			
Donors	Candidate committee	PAC	State, district and local party committee	National party committee	Special limits
Individual	$1,000 per election	$5,000 per year	$5,000 per year combined limit	$20,000 per year	$25,000 per year overall
State, district, and local party committee[a]	$5,000 per election combined limit	$5,000 per election combined limit	Unlimited transfers to other party committees		
National party committee (multicandidate)[b]	$5,000 per election	$5,000 per year	Unlimited transfers to other party committees		$17,500 to Senate candidate per campaign[c]
PAC (multi-candidate)	$5,000 per election	$5,000 per year	$5,000 per year combined limit	$15,000 per year	
PAC (not multi-candidate)	$1,000 per election	$5,000 per year	$5,000 per year combined limit	$20,000 per year	

Source: Federal Election Commission, Campaign Guide for Political Party Committees, 1996.

a. State and local party committees share limits unless the local party committee can prove independence.

b. A party's national committee, Senate campaign committee, and House campaign committee are commonly called the national party committees and each has a separate limit. See special limits column for the exception.

c. The Senate campaign committee and the national committee share this limit.

called *hard money* (they are also called *federal money* because they are subject to federal limitations). Individuals can give up to $2,000 and PACs up to $10,000 each election cycle to any one candidate.[38] Individuals have an aggregate contribution limit, while PACs do not. In addition to spending their own funds, federal candidates can only spend hard money on their campaigns. Interest groups may also make in-kind contributions, including providing paid staff to campaigns.[39]

Republicans enjoyed a substantial hard-money advantage over Democrats in 2002, with the three GOP national committees raising $442 million in hard money, compared to $217 million for the Democrats.[40] The gap is smaller for the senatorial campaign committees. The National

Table 1-4. *Contribution Limits under Bipartisan Campaign Reform Act,*
2004

			Recipients		
Donors	*Candidate committee*	*PAC*	*State, district and local party committee*	*National party committee*	*Special limits*
Individual	$2,000 per election	$5,000 per year	$10,000 per year combined limit	$25,000 per year	Biennial limit of $95,000 ($37,500 to all candidates and $57,500 to all PACs and parties)
State, district, and local party committee	$5,000 per election combined limit	$5,000 per election combined limit	Unlimited transfers to other party committees		
National party committee	$5,000 per election	$5,000 per year	Unlimited transfers to other party committees		$35,000 to Senate candidate per campaign
PAC multi-candidate	$5,000 per election	$5,000 per year	$5,000 per year combined limit	$15,000 per year	
PAC not multi-candidate	$2,000 per election	$5,000 per year	$10,000 per year combined limit	$25,000 per year	

Source: "BCRA Campaign Guide Supplement," Federal Election Commission, vol. 29, January 2003.

Republican Senatorial Committee (NRSC) raised $59 million in hard money in 2001–02, compared to $48 million for the Democratic Senatorial Campaign Committee (DSCC).[41] One of the most significant changes of BCRA is the higher individual contribution limits found in table 1-4. Under BCRA an individual can give $95,000 to parties or candidates in the aggregate and $4,000 to each candidate in each election cycle, compared to $50,000 hard plus unlimited soft under FECA.[42] These higher limits, at least in the short run, will benefit the Republicans.

Soft Money

FECA has been amended and interpreted to permit political parties to raise and spend unlimited amounts of money for generic "party building" purposes. These nonfederal funds are also called *soft money*. As is typical of midterm elections, the lack of a presidential contest in 2002 led to a decline in soft-money receipts for the Republican National Committee (RNC) and the Democratic National Committee (DNC). However, soft-money receipts for three of the four congressional campaign committees rose to new highs. The average soft-money growth between 2000 and 2002 for the NRCC, the NRSC, and the DSCC was 47 percent.[43] As we discuss in chapter 2, the Democratic Congressional Campaign Committee (DCCC) did not keep pace in soft-money fundraising with the other congressional campaign committees. BCRA bans soft money contributions and expenditures by national party committees, while permitting state party committees to engage in limited soft-money-funded voter registration and mobilization activities.[44] Yet, even with the enactment of BCRA, it remains to be seen whether soft money may find new avenues through quasi-party interest groups and other entities.[45]

Electioneering Issue Advocacy

Political consultants, like Republican Douglas Bailey, testified in the 2002 *McConnell* v. *FEC* litigation that "it is rarely advisable to use such clumsy words as 'vote for' or 'vote against.'"[46] As we have demonstrated in past research, groups and parties can effectively communicate an election message by showing the image or likeness of a candidate, mentioning the candidate by name, and broadcasting the advertisement during the weeks shortly before an election. The call to action in an issue ad is typically through other action words, like *call, phone,* or *write,* rather than the words of express advocacy. However, in the context of a campaign the content of the message is much more important than the call to action.[47] Election issue advocacy is more likely to oppose than endorse a candidate, partly because it is easier to avoid legal scrutiny for coordination when attacking an opponent than when supporting a candidate of your own party. The timing of ads is often critical, with candidates, parties, and groups often planning from Election Day backward, with the most intense advertising coming at the end of the race. Issue advocacy and soft-money-funded ads again tend to appear late in the election. As Republican National Committee political operations director Terry Nelson testified in *McConnell* v. *FEC*, "issue advocacy is not as effective in August of an election year as it is in October or early November."[48] Voters, especially undecided or swing voters, are presumed not to focus on an election until after Labor Day and for

some not until the last few weeks of the campaign. In addition, as outside money has funded more and more political mail, it is presumed that
direct mail is most effective in the last week or even the last few days of
a campaign.

Some of this activity is conducted by groups called 527 and 501(c)
organizations. These groups are organized under section 527 of the Internal Revenue Code and until July 2000 did not report their activity to any
government regulatory agency. In 2002 disclosure of the activities of these
groups was not timely, complete, or easily available through the Internal
Revenue Service.[49] We explain these groups more fully in chapter 3.

BCRA restores the FECA prohibition on corporations and trade
unions from using treasury funds for electioneering issue advocacy on
broadcast or cable, and from contributing these funds to political parties.[50] Corporate and treasury funds have been a component of party
soft-money receipts and a major source of electioneering issue advocacy
since 1996. Unions and corporations fought hard to overturn BCRA's
ban on using treasury funds for issue ads. In *McConnell* v. *FEC* Judge
Henderson concluded that the PACs "cannot finance more than a small
fraction of the electioneering communications corporations and unions
have been able to fund from their treasury funds."[51]

Occasionally groups, parties, and individuals wish to communicate
about issues without referring to a particular candidate running in a
particular race. Genuine issue ads were run against the Clinton administration health care reforms (the so-called Harry and Louise ads) and
later against the proposed tobacco tax legislation. Generally very little
genuine issue advocacy occurs in the period between Labor Day and
Election Day.[52] This was true in 2002, where in our sample only 5 percent of the ads detected by the researchers between Labor Day and Election Day were genuine issue advocacy.

Independent Expenditures

The Supreme Court ruled in *Buckley* v. *Valeo* that groups and individuals could spend unlimited amounts of money on the election or
defeat of a candidate, as long as those expenditures were not coordinated with the candidate or party campaigns. The Court also held that
the individual or group making the independent expenditure could be
required to disclose its identity, as well as how the money was spent, to
the FEC. With the advent of issue advocacy in the 1990s, some groups
shifted away from independent expenditures because engaging in issue

advocacy does not require disclosure. Groups that continue to engage in independent expenditures tend to be membership organizations, like the National Right to Life, the National Rifle Association (NRA), the League of Conservation Voters (LCV), or the American Medical Association (AMA). We discuss why some groups continue to prefer independent expenditures in chapter 3.

The Supreme Court later ruled in *Colorado Republican Federal Campaign Committee* v. *FEC* that political parties might also engage in independent expenditures.[53] Party independent expenditures must be made with hard dollars and have therefore been used less frequently than soft-money expenditures. We examine party independent expenditure activity in chapter 2 and the more common interest-group independent expenditure activity in chapter 3.

Internal Communications

Membership organizations, like trade unions, teachers' associations, business organizations, and environmental, gun, and other issue groups, communicate with their members about candidates via internal communications.[54] This form of electioneering is rarely noted by the media because it is aimed at members only. Unions and corporations may use general or treasury funds to pay for these communications. Expenditures on internal communications are to be reported to the FEC when the entity making the communication expressly advocates the election or defeat of a candidate, the communication costs exceed $2,000 per election, and the election information is the primary purpose of the communication. Since many internal communications are not primarily about an election or otherwise fail to meet the disclosure requirement, many go unreported to the FEC. We examine the extent and nature of internal communications in chapters 3 and 4. Under BCRA, unions, corporations, and interest groups may still engage in unlimited internal communications with their employees or members.

Candidate Self-Financing

The Supreme Court ruled in *Buckley* v. *Valeo* that candidates may contribute as much personal wealth as they wish to their own campaigns. This is sometimes called the millionaire's exception to contribution limits and has led both parties to actively recruit wealthy candidates willing to finance their own campaigns. Self-financed candidates permit parties to direct their soft- and hard-money resources to other races.

One candidate for the House of Representatives in our sample races, Bob Beauprez, loaned his campaign $455,000.[55] Under BCRA there are no limits to candidate self-financing, but it increases individual contribution limits by 300 to 600 percent for the candidate facing the self-financed candidate, depending on the amount of money the self-financed candidate gives to his or her own campaign.

The 2002 Election in Context

There has been remarkable regularity in midterm elections since the Civil War. With only 1934, 1998, and now 2002 as exceptions, the party of the president has lost seats in the House of Representatives. During this election cycle, public approval of President Bush grew as a result of his leadership after the terrorist attacks of 2001. Before September 11, 2001, President Bush's approval ratings were at about 50 percent, as measured by CBS/*New York Times* and Gallup/CNN/*USA Today* polls. Those ratings rose to unprecedented levels, between 86 and 90 percent, after the attacks; by Election Day his ratings had fallen to between 61 and 63 percent, still relatively high approval ratings.[56] Even with such high popularity, standard political science models based on factors such as the state of the economy, the level of incumbent presidential popularity, and polling questions measuring the "generic" vote for the U.S. House of Representatives predicted that the Democrats should have gained between four and fourteen seats in the House and maintained control of the Senate.[57]

The Role of President Bush

President Bush used his popularity to help Republican candidates in the 2002 elections. In the final five days he visited fifteen states and seventeen cities on behalf of Republican candidates. The tone and feel of the final days were reminiscent of a presidential election, with substantial press coverage of his activities. Table 1-5 summarizes the number of visits between January 21, 2001, and Election Day 2002 by President Bush, Vice President Cheney, Al Gore, Joe Lieberman, Tom Daschle, and Dick Gephardt to our sample races in 2002.

While frequent trips to important fund-raising centers like California and key presidential nomination states like Iowa are not particularly unusual, the frequency of President Bush's visits to the 2002 battleground Senate states is noteworthy. For example, he visited Missouri

Table 1-5. *Visits by National Leaders to Sample Races, 2001-02*[a]

State	Bush	Cheney	Gore	Lieberman	Daschle	Gephardt	Total
California	5	1	9	5	2	13	35
Pennsylvania	17	5	1	3	0	6	32
Iowa	10	1	2	2	4	3	22
Colorado	3	3	4	3	3	3	19
New Hampshire	3	0	2	6	0	6	17
Michigan	3	3	1	4	0	5	16
Minnesota	5	4	2	1	2	1	15
Missouri	7	2	1	1	2	. . .	13
Arizona	4	1	0	3	1	3	12
North Carolina	5	2	1	1	0	2	11
Maryland	2	0	2	3	0	3	10
Arkansas	4	4	0	0	0	1	9
Indiana	3	3	0	2	0	0	8
New Mexico	4	2	1	1	0	0	8
Connecticut	3	1	1	. . .	0	2	7
South Dakota	5	2	0	0	. . .	0	7
Utah	1	2	1	0	1	0	5
Delaware	1	1	1	1	0	0	4
Mississippi	1	1	0	0	0	0	2
Montana	1	1	0	0	0	0	2
Total	87	39	29	36	15	48	254

Source: "White House 2004: Candidate State Visit Tallies," *National Journal,* December 30, 2002 (http://nationaljournal.com/pubs/hotline/extra/wh2004/04statetally.htm [30 December 2002]).

a. These visits were made from January 21, 2001, through November 5, 2002. List does not differentiate between campaign-related visits and "official" visits. This may explain, for example, the high number of visits to Pennsylvania by President Bush.

seven times and South Dakota and Minnesota five times each. These visits generally boosted the standing of Republican candidates, and in the case of Rick Renzi, the GOP candidate in the Arizona First District, his standing in the polls shot up eleven points following President Bush's visit to Flagstaff on September 27, 2002.[58]

The pattern used by the White House and national GOP committees was to send the president in as early as April 2001, but more typically in March and April of 2002, to speak at fund-raisers intended to both help the state party and stimulate fund-raising and positive publicity for the preferred candidate. For example, on March 18, 2002, President Bush visited Missouri for Jim Talent, where he raised $1.3 million.[59] One estimate credits President Bush with raising at least $140 million for Republican Party committees and candidates.[60]

In the critical closing weeks of the campaign, the White House orchestrated high-profile visits by not only President Bush, but also by

First Lady Laura Bush, former New York Mayor Rudy Giuliani, and Vice President Cheney. In the Minnesota Senate race, for example, these four individuals visited the state on successive days at the end of the campaign.[61] This blitz of visits by the White House was seen by several observers as forcing extensive local news coverage and "sucking the oxygen out" of the Democratic candidates.[62] One analysis of local news calculated the number of appearances in a random sample of news stories by prominent political figures during the seven-week period leading up to Election Day. President Bush appeared in more than twice as many (351), compared to Bill Clinton (160), Rudy Giuliani (90), and Dick Cheney (77).[63]

The story of presidential involvement in 2002 started long before Election Day. President Bush, Vice President Cheney, and the White House political operation headed by Karl Rove and Ken Mehlman, together with the NRSC and NRCC, helped recruit candidates for several Senate and House races. For example, in Minnesota a call from Vice President Cheney on the day of the filing deadline convinced Tim Pawlenty, a U.S. Senate hopeful, to run for governor instead, clearing the field for former St. Paul Mayor Norm Coleman.[64] The White House also played a role in recruiting John Thune to run in South Dakota, Saxby Chambliss in Georgia, and Elizabeth Dole in North Carolina. As Ken Mehlman put it, "Once they announce, half your battle is over [because] candidate quality is the most important factor in elections."[65]

Democrats also involved party leaders in candidate recruitment and found success in recruiting incumbent Governor Jeanne Shaheen in New Hampshire and Attorney General Mark Pryor in Arkansas to run for the U.S. Senate. House Minority Leader Dick Gephardt called Mike Feeley to recruit him to run in the new Colorado Seventh Congressional District.[66] Party failures to attract the right candidate to the race are just as important as their successes. In Montana the Republicans' failure to recruit former governor and current RNC chair Marc Racicot to contend the re-election bid of Senator Max Baucus made this race less competitive.[67] Likewise in Oregon the failure of Democrats to recruit former Governor John Kitzhaber to challenge first-term incumbent Republican Senator Gordon Smith made this a less competitive race.

Last-minute Senatorial candidate recruitments were also important in 2002. Democrats not only substituted former Senator Frank Lautenberg for Robert Toricelli in New Jersey but, following the accidental death of Senator Paul Wellstone in Minnesota, also ran former vice president and former U.S. Senator Walter Mondale in Wellstone's place.[68] Lautenberg won, and Mondale lost to Republican Norm Coleman, former mayor of St. Paul. Chapter 5 examines how parties, interest groups, and candidates in Minnesota responded to the late change in nominees.[69]

Participation in 2002

Nationally, voter turnout in 2002 was 39 percent, up slightly from 1998 but well below 2000 levels.[70] With lower rates of participation in midterm elections, the candidate and outside-money-funded campaigns adjust to a more targeted strategy of voter identification and mobilization. Some states with traditionally high turnout rates, like Minnesota and South Dakota, were battlegrounds for control of the U.S. Senate and House and also had competitive gubernatorial elections. In both Minnesota and South Dakota, turnout was over 61 percent, the highest in the country.[71] But not all battleground races had high turnout. Colorado, Arizona, and New Mexico saw record low levels of turnout for a midterm election, despite the intense advertising and mobilization efforts by candidates, parties, and allied groups.[72] We explore voter mobilization in greater detail in chapter 4.[73]

Relatively Few Competitive U.S. House Races

The fact that most congressional seats are safe has made the relatively few competitive contests more important in determining party control in both houses. For the past three election cycles the average number of seats needed to reverse the majority in the House has been seven and in the Senate only four.

The 2002 election was also the first election following the 2000 reapportionment of U.S. House seats and redistricting to accommodate population shifts over the past decade. Typically in the first election after reapportionment and redistricting there is a surge in the number of competitive U.S. House seats, but 2002 was an exception to this pattern.[74] In 1992, for example, there were 151 competitive U.S. House races, more than three times the 44 competitive races in 2002 (see figure 1-1).

Since the ascendancy of outside money in congressional elections in 1996, there have typically been comparatively few competitive U.S. House elections. The number of districts at play influences how outside resources are allocated. If more districts were competitive, parties would have more difficulty allocating their resources, having to decide whether to concentrate most of their resources in a small number of House races

Figure 1-1. *Number of Competitive House Races, 1992–2002*

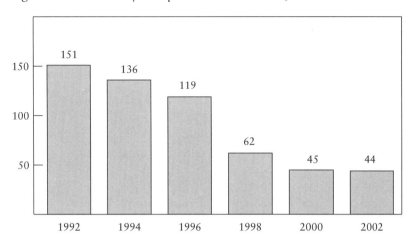

Source: Charlie Cook, "National Overview," *Cook Political Report*, October 4, 2002, p. 6. The numbers of competitive races were tallied in early October of each year and are those classified as toss-ups or leaning toward one party.

or distribute the resources more broadly in hopes of making gains. Similarly interest groups might be able to find more compatible candidates in the larger pool of competitive races. But the reality has been that the numbers of competitive races in 1998, 2000, and 2002 have been very low compared to previous years, which has limited the options for parties and interest groups.

The implications of there being so few competitive districts are widely debated by party and interest-group professionals. Most Democrats and their allies saw 2002 as having too few races at play. To pick up seats, they argued, the Democrats needed more opportunities to compete. Sheila O' Connell of EMILY's List asserted that "redistricting did not provide the kind of opportunities that it had in the past. It was very much an incumbent protection program."[75] This school of thought sees the incumbent protection emphasis in 2001–02 as clearly benefiting Republicans. However, some also contend that, since Democrats and their allies typically have fewer resources, they benefit from fewer races at play. Fewer competitive races, so the argument goes, allow Democrats to spend enough to stay competitive with Republicans in those races.

The narrow field of competitive general election races has meant that interest groups and parties are more likely to invest in primary elections and more inclined to clear the field for a preferred candidate. The consequences of not fielding the best candidate in a competitive race are more severe when there are fewer potential competitive races in an election cycle, as was the case in 2002. One group that pursued an aggressive strategy in the 2002 primaries was the Club for Growth, which successfully backed candidates in at least six primaries.[76] They see primaries as an economic investment of their resources, claiming that "One dollar in a primary carries three times the weight [compared to] one dollar in the general election."[77] EMILY's List also aggressively worked for pro-choice Democratic women in at least nine primaries in 2002 but was unsuccessful in six of them. Despite criticism about injecting themselves into primaries, their involvement is consistent with their goal of "bringing newcomers into politics."[78] The NRCC also injected themselves into primaries in 2002 to an extent that they have not done in previous years, taking sides in the primaries in Ohio's and Kansas's Third Congressional Districts.[79]

It is important to note that, even with this push by groups to get involved early, the bulk of activity still occurs right before the election. In 2002, 60 percent of interest-group electioneering activity came in the last two weeks, slightly more than the 58 percent we observed in 2000.[80]

A Greater Focus on Senate Elections

In 2002 all the key players devoted more time and money to the battle for control of the U.S. Senate than they did to House races. Greater attention to U.S. Senate races is understandable in the context of the evenly divided Senate coming out of the 2000 elections, the subsequent switch in party control of the chamber as a result of Vermont Senator James Jeffords leaving the Republican Party, and the particular constitutional roles the Senate plays, including confirming judicial nominations.

Part of the reason the Senate became the more important battleground was the widely shared perception that a switch in party control was more likely there. Speaking of the Democrats, Linda Lipsen of the Association of Trial Lawyers of America said, "By the last two weeks people had given up on the House,"[81] an assessment shared by Mike Matthews of the DCCC, who felt that the Democrats were challenged throughout the cycle by perceptions that they could not retake the House.[82] Democratic groups have also tended to give more attention to Senate races because they are higher profile and accompanied by additional media attention.[83] The White House also made winning back control of the Senate their highest 2002 election priority.[84]

Issues, Themes, and Messages

Outside money is generally spent to reinforce candidate themes and messages and to help define the campaign agenda.[85] In 1998 the NRCC emphasized a different set of issues than did Republican candidates, a strategy many saw as a failure.[86] Table 1-6 presents the most frequent themes used by candidates, parties, and interest groups in their communications in our sample races.

THE ECONOMY. Past studies found that voters hold the president and his party responsible for the state of the economy.[87] Our panel survey of voters in a national sample and four of our battleground contests found that voters were not pleased with the state of the economy. Roughly three out of four voters said the state of the economy was only fair or poor in the mid-October and post-election waves of our panel survey.[88] Without prompting, respondents consistently volunteered "economy and jobs" as the most important issue, followed by education.

The public saw economic conditions in 1994 in much the same way as they saw them in 2002. In 1994, 69 percent said economic conditions were either fair (49 percent) or poor (20 percent), and in 2002 the number was 71 percent, with 45 percent saying fair and 26 percent saying poor.[89] But in 1994 President Clinton's party lost thirty-four representatives and two senators. How did Republicans avoid such losses in 2002? The popularity of President Bush is part of the answer. They were successful in avoiding blame for the economy and in elevating issues like safety, security, and taxes. In 2002 Republican candidates and party committees both emphasized taxes in their mail and television advertising.

SAFETY AND SECURITY. One factor that militated against Democrats exploiting the economy as an issue was that the public in part blamed the terrorist attacks of September 11, 2001, for the economic problems in 2002.[90] The potential for war also affected the saliency of other issues. Andy Grossman of the DSCC, in the aftermath of September 11, said, "The Republican issue of safety and security was more salient to [voters'] lives . . . [because] facing war supersedes facing some economic pain." Thus the potential for war was not only the most salient issue but also "crowded out time" for competing issues.[91] The security issue was amplified by the perceived threat from Iraq, and the protracted debate in Congress over a resolution on possible war with Iraq served as a backdrop for the election. The series of sniper shootings in the Washing-

Table 1-6. *Themes of Campaign Messages in Sample Races, by Frequency, 2002*

Party	Candidates		Political parties		Interest groups	
	Mail	TV	Mail	TV	Mail	TV
Democrat						
Education	57	42	79	21	106	2
Health care	47	28	63	16	23	1
Social Security	38	41	80	34	41	3
Prescription drugs	37	30	81	27	20	0
Medicare	27	10	33	16	7	1
Environment	25	9	29	1	55	15
Senior citizens	17	15	32	17	6	1
Corporate fraud/Enron	16	32	52	30	12	11
Taxes	16	27	38	24	3	2
Economy/economics	11	20	29	9	8	1
Employment/jobs	16	13	47	11	20	6
Labor/unions	0	0	3	1	51	3
Abortion	6	5	22	4	43	3
Children	16	7	16	1	21	0
Campaign finance reform	3	0	0	2	0	5
International trade globalization	1	0	1	2	11	3
Women's health/rights	1	0	6	1	10	3
Republican						
Taxes	39	40	146	41	50	10
Education	33	39	74	16	4	3
Defense/military/ national security	22	15	65	20	4	0
Social Security	20	46	111	17	33	7
Employment/jobs	16	29	50	15	14	4
Prescription drugs	15	29	75	10	50	20
Environment	14	7	25	1	5	0
Senior citizens	14	28	64	13	38	12
Health care	9	26	50	10	18	12
Medicare	13	21	51	10	42	11
Government ethics/trust	3	10	3	20	0	0
Abortion	3	0	26	0	36	2
Gun control	9	3	24	0	36	0

Source: David B. Magleby, J. Quin Monson, and the Center for the Study of Elections and Democracy, 2002 Soft Money and Issue Advocacy Database (Brigham Young University, 2002).

ton, D.C., area for nearly three weeks in October heightened concern about domestic security.

SOCIAL SECURITY AND PRESCRIPTION DRUGS. The predictable agenda of issues for 2002 included prescription drug benefits for seniors and a proposal by Republicans to allow individuals more say over how their Social Security retirement funds are invested. Seniors' issues have typically advantaged Democrats, but Republicans in recent years have neutralized the impact of Social Security or prescription drug benefits for seniors.

During the 2000 election, President Bush and the Republicans made proposals regarding Social Security reform that included talk of partial privatization. But growth in the stock market, which seemed a constant in the 1990s, dropped sharply in 2001 and 2002, affecting many Americans. Democrats and their allied interest groups, including labor unions, attacked Republicans for advocating privatization. Republicans quickly responded by claiming that the privatization term was inaccurate and instead candidates should describe their proposal as "personal accounts."[92] Republicans also worked aggressively and successfully to get Democratic Party ads on this issue pulled. The success of the GOP and allied groups in redefining the Social Security issue was not lost on other interest groups. As Jack Polidori of the National Education Association (NEA) said, "The way they buried the president's recommendation on Social Security, I mean Houdini would have been proud."[93] In our panel study, where respondents in the national sample indicated the most important issue influencing their vote, only 4 percent of respondents said Social Security in the postelection wave, and prescription drugs were mentioned by only 2 percent of respondents.

House Republicans skillfully defused the prescription drug issue in June 2002 by passing legislation providing for limited benefits.[94] In many of our campaigns, Republicans like Nancy Johnson in Connecticut's Fifth District race claimed credit for enacting prescription drug benefits for seniors. Democrats countered that the legislation was only a limited benefit and that it was meaningless because the Senate had not acted. This then gave Republicans the chance to blame the Democratic-controlled Senate for inaction. Later the Senate passed a bill expediting the approval time for generic drugs, giving Senate Republicans a claim to action in this area, even though nothing was signed into law.[95]

An ally in this effort to neutralize the Democrats' claim on seniors' issues has been the pharmaceutical industry, which campaigned through groups like Citizens for Better Medicare (CBM) in 2000,[96] and the United Seniors Association in 2002.[97] In some House races United Seniors spent over $500,000.[98] Using a catchy name like United Seniors is an effective way to dodge negative fallout, because voters infer different agendas from "pharmaceutical and drug companies" than from the "United Seniors Association." In our panel survey, 58 percent of respondents across the nation had an unfavorable view of pharmaceutical or drug companies, while only 5 percent had a negative impression of the United Seniors Association.[99]

EDUCATION. Republicans worked to at least neutralize the long-standing Democratic advantage on issues like education, as well.[100] Enactment of the No Child Left Behind legislation in 2001 helped Republicans neutralize the Democrats' claim to the education issue.[101] This legislation tied increased funding, especially for early childhood education, to reaching predetermined targets as measured in standardized tests. Speaking more generally about the emphasis on Social Security, prescription benefits, and education, DNC political director Gail Stoltz said, "If you had closed your eyes you would have thought all the ads on the air were for Democratic issues."[102]

Plan for the Book

To help set the stage for our case studies and to emphasize our major findings, we begin by looking at party activity. In chapter 2, Nicole Carlisle Squires and I document party hard- and soft-money activity in the 2002 election cycle. The party committees in the aggregate fought to a draw in total soft money receipts. The RNC and House Republicans raised and spent more than their Democratic counterparts, while the reverse was true for the DSCC and NRSC. Republican committees raised much more hard money than Democratic committees, again with the exception of the DSCC. As we demonstrate, however, the story becomes more complicated and interesting when we examine party hard- and soft-money spending at the level of individual races.

In chapter 3 Jonathan Tanner and I examine interest-group behavior in 2002. Groups have a wide array of ways they can seek to influence the outcome of competitive congressional races, including PAC contributions, independent expenditures, internal communications, and issue advocacy. Although interest groups remained important in competitive races in 2002, they were not as visible as, nor did they keep pace with spending by, the parties. Some liberal groups spent significantly less overall in 2002 than in 2000. Several factors, including the recession, party soft money's last hurrah, and an economy that reduced the willingness or ability of large donors to spend heavily, may account for interest groups' failure to keep pace with the party soft-money spending.

Quin Monson examines the 2002 ground war in chapter 4. Democrats and their allies, especially the AFL-CIO, continued to make voter registration and mobilization a major emphasis. The GOP invested heavily in its 72 Hour Task Force and related voter mobilization efforts. Both sides placed a major emphasis on the ground war. The growth in 2002 is especially evident among the political parties. Which voters were targeted and how they were activated are important parts of the outside money story in 2002.

In chapters 5 through 11 we present several of our most important and interesting case studies from 2002. In chapter 5 William Flanigan and colleagues examine the hotly contested Minnesota Senate race between Democratic incumbent Paul Wellstone and Republican challenger Norm Coleman. Both parties and allied interest groups made this a high-priority race. The contest took a tragic turn when Wellstone died in an airplane accident and former Vice President Walter Mondale replaced Wellstone in the closing days of the campaign. Both sides of the Minnesota race drew on the Missouri experience in 2000, where Missouri Governor Mel Carnahan also died in an airplane accident. His widow, Jean, was appointed to the Senate after Mel Carnahan posthumously received more votes than his opponent, John Ashcroft.[103] Just as it did in 2000, the 2002 Missouri Senate race between Jean Carnahan and Republican Jim Talent involved substantial noncandidate activity. Martha Kropf, Terry Jones, Matt McLaughlin, and Dale Neuman, largely the same team who monitored Missouri in 2000, present the 2002 Missouri case study in chapter 6.[104] The South Dakota Senate race in 2002 was not only a battle between Democratic incumbent Tim Johnson and Republican Congressman John Thune, but it was a battle between South Dakota's other Democratic senator, then Majority Leader Tom Daschle, and President George W. Bush, who visited sparsely populated South Dakota five times to campaign for Thune. Jim Meader and John Bart examine this contest in chapter 7.

We then turn to competitive contests for the House of Representatives. The closest race in 2002, decided by just 121 votes, took place in a new Colorado district between Republican Bob Beauprez and Democrat Mike

Feeley, is analyzed by Daniel Smith in chapter 8. Our next two case studies pitted incumbents against each other because of reapportionment and redistricting. In chapter 9 Sandra Anglund and Sarah Morehouse examine the Connecticut Fifth Congressional District race between Nancy Johnson (R) and Jim Maloney (D). We have examined this district for three consecutive election cycles, with party and outside groups consistently involved in the race.[105] Connecticut's state ban on soft money makes this race doubly interesting because parties had to adapt their strategies. In chapter 10 Stephen K. Medvic and Matthew M. Schousen examine another incumbent matchup between George Gekas (R) and Tim Holden (D). This is a case where party money clearly dominated the campaigns. In chapter 11 Kelly D. Patterson examines a contest between Jim Matheson (D) and John Swallow (R), which involved a Democratic incumbent running in a redrawn district with a larger Republican majority. This district, like Connecticut's Fifth, was the focus of intense issue advocacy for three cycles. After intense opposition from both the NRA and U.S. Chamber of Commerce in his 2000 contest, Matheson successfully defused issue-advocacy opposition from both groups in 2002. An example of the policy implications of issue advocacy, Utah's Second Congressional District was also one of the few contests in 2002 where a party committee mistakenly failed to invest enough soft money and perhaps missed an opportunity to gain an additional seat.

Finally Quin Monson and I examine the implications of our findings for congressional elections and the institution of Congress. Our 2002 study includes substantial measurement of how voters perceive campaigns with extensive party and interest-group campaigning. We summarize these data in chapter 12. Enactment of BCRA made the dynamic world of congressional campaign finance even more uncertain. We explore the implications of BCRA on future elections in this concluding chapter.

Notes

1. See David B. Magleby and Candice J. Nelson, *The Money Chase: Congressional Campaign Finance Reform* (Brookings, 1990); and Gary C. Jacobson, *Money in Congressional Elections* (Yale University Press, 1980). See also Frank J. Sorauf, *Inside Campaign Finance: Myths and Realities* (Yale University Press, 1992).

2. Dick Morris, *Behind the Oval Office: Getting Reelected against All Odds* (Los Angeles: Renaissance Books, 1999), pp. 141, 624.

3. David B. Magleby, ed., *The Other Campaign: Soft Money and Issue Advocacy in the 2000 Congressional Elections* (Lanham, Md.: Rowman and Littlefield, 2003), p. 3. See also Paul S. Herrnson and Kelly D. Patterson, "Financing the 2000 Congressional Elections," in David B. Magleby, ed., *Financing the 2000 Election* (Brookings, 2002), p. 112.

4. *Buckley* v. *Valeo*, 424 U.S. 1, 44 n. 52 (1976).

5. See *In the Matter of AFL-CIO Project '95* (complaint filed with the Federal Election Commission, February 13, 1996). The FEC did not pursue this complaint.

6. Deborah Beck and others, "Issue Advocacy Advertising during the 1996 Campaign: A Catalog," Report 16, Annenberg Public Policy Center, September 1997, p. 10. See also Paul Herrnson, *Congressional Elections: Campaigning at Home and in Washington* (Congressional Quarterly, 1998), p. 123.

7. "Labor Targets," *Congressional Quarterly Weekly Report* 26, October 1996, p. 3084; Jeanne I. Dugan, "Washington Ain't Seen Nothing Yet," *Business Week Report*, May 13, 1996, p. 3

8. Paul Herrnson, "Parties and Interest Groups in Postreform Congressional Elections," in Allan Cigler and Burdette A. Loomis, eds. *Interest Group Politics* (Congressional Quarterly, 1998), pp. 160–61.

9. Center for Public Integrity, "The 'Black Hole' Groups," *The Public-I*, February 9, 2001 (www.publicintegrity.org/adwatch_02_033000.htm [July 15, 2002]).

10. David B. Magleby, ed., *Outside Money: Soft Money and Issue Advocacy in the 1998 Congressional Elections* (Lanham, Md.: Rowman and Littlefield, 2000); Magleby, *The Other Campaign*; and David B. Magleby, ed., *Getting Inside the Outside Campaign: Issue Advocacy in the 2000 Presidential Primaries* (Center for the Study of Elections and Democracy, Brigham Young University, 2000).

11. For a discussion of how the sample of competitive and control races was drawn, see appendix A of this book.

12. We are grateful for the help of the League of Women Voters and Common Cause, whose local membership helped with this data collection effort.

13. We acquired the CMAG data through the Wisconsin Advertising Project at the University of Wisconsin–Madison, and acknowledge the assistance of Ken Goldstein, Joel Rivlin, Travis Ridout, and Timothy Wells. For a discussion of our methodology in using the CMAG data, see appendix A.

14. See appendix A for descriptions of the methodology of these surveys.

15. For briefs, expert reports, and other materials relating to *McConnell* v. *FEC,* see the Campaign Legal Center website (www.campaignlegalcenter.org).

16. See the Campaign Legal Center website for information on the FEC's rule-making on BCRA (www.campaignlegalcenter.org).

17. Examples of efforts at circumvention are abundant in the ongoing process by the FEC to implement BCRA. See Editorial, "Overhauling the FEC," *Washington Post,* July 11, 2003, p. A20.

18. See chapter 7 of this volume.

19. J. Quin Monson and David B. Magleby, 2002 Campaign Communication Study [dataset] (Center for the Study of Elections and Democracy, Brigham Young University, 2002). See chapter 12 for more discussion of these data. This number is in line with findings from our earlier studies. In 2000, for example, voters received over twelve pieces of mail a day in the Washington Second Congressional District race. See Todd Donovan and Charles Morrow, "The 2000 Washington Second Congressional District Race," in Magleby, *The Other Campaign*, pp. 220.

20. Groups that have done independent polling in past election cycles include the NEA, AFL-CIO, Trial Lawyers, NAACP, NRA, Chamber of Commerce, and all four congressional campaign committees. See David B. Magleby, "The Impact of Issue Advocacy and Party Soft Money Electioneering," in Kenneth Goldstein, ed., *The Message and the Medium* (Prentice Hall, forthcoming).

21. Paul S. Herrnson, "Hired Guns and House Races: Campaign Professionals in House Elections," in James A. Thurber and Candice J. Nelson, eds., *Campaign Warriors: Political Consultants in Elections* (Brookings, 2000), pp. 65–90.

22. Magleby, *The Other Campaign*, p. 49.

23. Remarks by Kathleen Hall Jamieson, CQ Post Elections Conference, Washington, D.C., November 2, 1998.

24. Mark Mellman, phone interview by Marianne Holt, March 23, 1999.

25. Mike Lux, president, Progressive Strategies, telephone interview by David Magleby and Quin Monson, January 9, 2003.

26. John Roos and Christopher Rodriguez, "The Indiana 2nd Congressional District Race," in David B. Magleby and J. Quin Monson, eds., *The Last Hurrah: Soft Money and Issue Advocacy in the 2002 Congressional Elections*, monograph version (Center for the Study of Elections and Democracy, Brigham Young University, 2003), pp. 223–35.

27. Penny M. Miller and Donald A. Gross, "The 2000 Kentucky Sixth Congressional District Race," in Magleby, *The Other Campaign*, p. 177; and Adam J. Berinsky and Susan S. Lederman, "The 2000 New Jersey Twelfth Congressional District Race," in David B. Magleby, ed., *Election Advocacy: Soft Money and Issue Advocacy in the 2000 Congressional Elections* (Center for the Study of Elections and Democracy, Brigham Young University, 2001), pp. 217–18.

28. Myra MacPherson, "The New Right Brigade: John Terry Dolan's NCPAC Targets Liberals and the Federal Election Commission," *Washington Post*, August 10, 1980, p. F1; see also Magleby, *Outside Money*, p. 45.

29. For further details, see chapter 12 of this volume; and David B. Magleby and J. Quin Monson, "Campaign 2002: 'The Perfect Storm' " (Center for the Study of Elections and Democracy, Brigham Young University, November 13, 2003).

30. This shift first occurred in 1998 by the labor unions. See David B. Magleby and Marianne Holt, eds., *Outside Money: Soft Money and Issue Ads in*

Competitive 1998 Congressional Elections (Center for the Study of Elections and Democracy, Brigham Young University, 2001); and Magleby, *Outside Money*.

31. Diana Dwyre and Robin Kolodny, "Throwing Out the Rule Book: Party Financing of the 2000 Elections," in Magleby, *Financing the 2000 Election*, pp. 153–55.

32. Karen L. Henderson, Memorandum Opinion in *McConnell v. FEC*, Civ. No. 02-581, p. 119.

33 Drew A. Linzer, David Menefee-Libey, and Matt Muller, "The 2002 California Twenty-Ninth Congressional District Race," in Magleby and Monson, *The Last Hurrah*, monograph version, p. 321.

34. Christopher J. Carman, "The 2002 Pennsylvania Fourth Congressional District," in Magleby and Monson, *The Last Hurrah*, monograph version, p. 355.

35. Ibid.

36. To test for statistical significance, we conducted F tests for each difference between battleground and control races. In all cases these were significant (p < .05).

37. See Magleby and Nelson, *The Money Chase*; and Magleby, *Financing the 2000 Election*. See also Frank J. Sorauf, *Money in American Elections* (Glenview, Ill.: Scott, Foresman, 1988); and Paul Herrnson, *Congressional Elections: Campaigning at Home and in Washington,* 3d ed. (Congressional Quarterly, 2000).

38. There is a debate in the literature on the impact of war chests. For a summary of the view that war chests matter, see Janet M. Box-Steffensmeier, "A Dynamic Analysis of the Role of War Chests in Campaign Strategy," *American Journal of Political Science,* vol. 40 (1996), pp. 352–71. For a more recent article critical of the war chests theory, see Jay Goodliffe, "The Effect of War Chests on Challenger Entry in U.S. House Elections," *American Journal of Political Science, v*ol. 45 (2001), pp. 830–44.

39. The actual individual contribution limit to candidates is $1,000 per election. Primaries, general, runoff, and special elections each count as one election. The limit for PACs is $5,000 per election.

40. Allan J. Cigler, "Interest Groups and Financing the 2000 Elections," in Magleby, *Financing the 2000 Election*, p. 171.

41. Federal Election Commission, "Party Committees Raise More than $1 Billion in 2001–2002," press release, March 20, 2003 (www.fec.gov/press/20030320party/20030103party.html [April 29, 2003]).

42. Ibid.

43. Under FECA, individuals could give unlimited amounts of nonfederal or soft money.

44. Federal Election Commission, "Party Committees Raise More than $1 Billion." Adjusted by CPI (ftp://ftp.bls.gov/pub/special.requests/cpi/cpiai.txt [January 15, 2003]).

45. This exception to the soft money ban is called the Levin Amendment.

46. See Anthony Corrado, Thomas E. Mann, and Trevor Potter, eds., *Inside the Campaign Finance Battle: Court Testimony on the New Reforms* (Brookings, 2003); Michael J. Malbin, ed., *Life after Reform: When the Bipartisan Campaign Reform Act Meets Politics* (Lanham, Md.: Rowman and Littlefield, forthcoming); prepublication draft available at www.cfinst.org/studies/bcra-book/index.html.

47. Henderson opinion in *McConnell v. FEC*, p. 82.

48. Magleby, *The Other Campaign*; David B. Magleby, *Dictum without Data: The Myth of Issue Advocacy and Party Building* (Center for the Study of Elections and Democracy, Brigham Young University, 2000).

49. Henderson opinion in *McConnell v. FEC*, p. 85.

50 For a discussion of legal regulations for groups like this, see Elizabeth Garrett and Daniel A. Smith, "Veiled Political Actors: The Real Threat to Campaign Disclosure Statutes," working paper (USC-Caltech Center for the Study of Law and Politics, 2003) (http://lawweb.usc.edu/cslp/pages/papers.html [July 21, 2003]).

51. Federal election law has long prohibited unions and corporations from using treasury funds for electioneering purposes (express advocacy).

52. Henderson opinion in *McConnell v. FEC*, p. 111.

53. Jonathan S. Krasno and Daniel E. Seltz, *Buying Time: Television Advertising in the 1998 Congressional Elections* (New York: Brennan Center for Justice, 2000), p. 22; see also Craig B. Holman and Luke P. McLaughlin, *Buying Time 2000: Television Advertising in the 2000 Federal Elections* (New York: Brennan Center for Justice, 2001), p. 56.

54. *Colorado Republican Federal Campaign Committee v. Federal Election Commission*, 116 S.Ct. 2309 (1996).

55. Cigler, "Interest Groups and Financing the 2000 Elections," p. 175.

56. See chapter 8 of this volume.

57. AEI Election Watch, "2002 Evaluation of President Bush," November 7, 2002, (www.aeipoliticalcorner.org/KB%20Articles/EW_Handout_November.pdf [May 16, 2003]).

58. For a collection of these models that were assembled just before the 2002 election, see "Elections, Public Opinion, and Voting Behavior Archives," American Political Science Association, January 4, 2003 (www.apsanet.net/~elections/archives.html [January 21, 2003]).

59. Renzi and Cordova were each tied with 37 percent of the vote in a poll conducted just after the primary election. But in a poll taken October 17–20, Rienzi's lead had grown to 48 to 36 percent. See "Arizona CD 1 Election: Cordova and Renzi Tied in Support," press release, Northern Arizona University Social Research Laboratory, September 17, 2002 (www.nau.edu/srl/09-17-02.pdf [April 29, 2003]); and "Renzi Surges ahead of Cordova," press release, Northern Arizona University Social Research Laboratory, October 21, 2002 (www.nau.edu/srl/10-21-02.pdf [April 29, 2003]).

60. Judy Keen, "Bush Isn't on the Ballot, but His Influence Is," *USA Today,* April 28, 2002, p. 7A.

61. Eric M. Appleman, "President Bush on the Money Trail," Democracy in Action, January 16, 2003 (www.gwu.edu/~action/2004/money/bushmoney.html [January 21, 2003]).

62. Patricia Lopez, "Coleman Edges Mondale; Pawlenty Rides GOP Wave," *Minneapolis Star Tribune,* November 6, 2002, p. 1A.

63. Mike McElwain, political director, NRCC, interview by David Magleby and Jonathan Tanner, Washington, D.C., December 2, 2002; and Karen Acker-man, political director, Mike Podhorzier, political department assistant director, David Boundy, political department assistant director, James Chiong, analyst, and Ellen Moran, campaign operation analyst, AFL-CIO, interview by David Magleby and Jonathan Tanner, Washington, D.C., December 2, 2002.

64. The Lear Center Local News Archive, "Local TV Coverage of the 2002 General Election," The Norman Lear Center at the University of Southern Cali-fornia Annenberg School and the Wisconsin News Lab at the University of Wis-consin, Madison (www.localnewsarchive.org/pdf/LocalTV2002.pdf [July 29, 2003]), p. 15.

65. Judy Keen, "GOP Strategy Charted in Early '01," *USA Today,* November 8, 2002, p. 5A.

66. Kenneth B. Mehlman, deputy assistant to the president and director of political affairs, interview with David Magleby and Jonathan Tanner, Washing-ton, D.C., November 15, 2002.

67. See chapter 8 of this volume.

68. Baucus instead faced Republican candidate Mike Taylor, who withdrew from the race after the state Democratic Party ran an attack ad funded by the DSCC but then reconsidered and returned to the race twelve days later. Craig Wilson, "The Montana Senate and At-Large Congressional District Races," in Magleby and Monson, *The Last Hurrah*, monograph version, pp. 342–43; see also David B. Magleby and J. Quin Monson, "The Noncandidate Campaign: Soft Money and Issue Advocacy in the 2002 Congressional Elections," *PS: Polit-ical Science and Politics* online e-symposium, July 2003 (www.apsanet.org/PS/July03/toc.cfm [July 30, 2003]).

69. Toricelli, under an ethical cloud and having been "severely admonished" by the Senate, dropped out of the race. See Jim VandeHei and Helen Dewar, "Senate Ethics Panel Rebukes Torricelli: Reprimand over Gifts Could Have Political Consequences for N.J. Democrat," *Washington Post,* July 31, 2002, p. A1.

70. For a discussion of this same phenomenon in the 2000 election, see Martha E. Kropf and others, "The 2000 Missouri Senate Race," in Magleby, *Election Advocacy,* pp. 75–91.

71. Edward Walsh, "Election Turnout Rose Slightly to 39.3%; GOP Mobilization Credited; Participation Was Down in Some Democratic Areas," *Washington Post*, November 8, 2002, p. A10.

72. Ibid.

73. See Curtis Gans, "Turnout Mostly Higher, Democrats in Deep Doo Doo, Many Questions Emerge," press release, Center for the Study of the American Electorate, November 8, 2002 (www.fairvote.org/turnout/csae2002.htm [May 16, 2003]).

74. For a discussion of how campaign spending increases information and turnout, see Bradley Smith, *Unfree Speech: The Folly of Campaign Finance Reform* (Princeton University Press, 2001). Others, like Curtis Gans of the Center for the Study of the American Electorate, dispute this claim. Curtis Gans, interview by David Magleby and Jonathan Tanner, Washington, D.C., May 7, 2003.

75. Herrnson, *Congressional Elections*, 3d ed., p. 26.

76. Sheila O'Connell, political director, EMILY's List, interview by Quin Monson and Jonathan Tanner, Washington, D.C., December 11, 2002.

77. Stephen Moore and David Keating, "Election Results Review," memorandum to Club for Growth Members, November 15, 2002 (www.clubforgrowth.org/members-only/021115.php [January 21, 2003]).

78. Stephen Moore, president, Club for Growth, interview by David Magleby and Jonathan Tanner, Washington, D.C., December 2, 2002.

79. Amy Schatz, "Men Cry Foul over EMILY; Despite Critics, Group Expects Big Win Nov. 5," *Atlanta Journal-Constitution*, September 15, 2002, p. 4C.

80. Richard L. Berke, "G.O.P. Gives Help to House Hopefuls," *New York Times*, March 3, 2002, p. A26.

81. David B. Magleby, Election Advocacy Database 2000 [dataset] (Center for the Study of Elections and Democracy, Brigham Young University, 2000); Monson and Magleby, 2002 Campaign Communication Study [dataset].

82. Linda Lipsen, senior director of public affairs, Association of Trial Lawyers of America, telephone interview by David Magleby and Quin Monson, December 19, 2002.

83. Mike Matthews, political director, DCCC, interview by David Magleby and Nicole Carlisle Squires, Washington, D.C., November 12, 2002.

84. Lipsen interview, December 19, 2002.

85. Jim VandeHei and Dan Balz, "In GOP Win, a Lesson in Money, Muscle, Planning," *Washington Post*, November 10, 2002, p. A1.

86. On the issue agenda in congressional elections more generally, see Owen Abbe and others, "Agenda Setting in Congressional Elections: The Impact of Issues and Campaigns on Voting Behavior," *Political Research Quarterly* (forthcoming). See also John Petrocik, "Issue Ownership in Presidential Elections, with a 1980 Case Study," *American Journal of Political Science*, vol. 40 (August

1996), pp. 825–50; Jon K. Daloger, "Voters, Issues, and Elections: Are the Candidates' Messages Getting Through?" *Journal of Politics,* vol. 58 (May 1996): pp. 486–515; and Constantine J. Spiliotes and Lynn Vavreck, "Campaign Advertising: Partisan Convergence or Divergence," *Journal of Politics,* vol. 64 (Winter 2002), pp. 249–61.

87. Speaker-elect Gingrich said, "We underestimated the degree to which people would get sick of the scandal through repetition. . . . We did what we thought would be effective, but our expectations did not fit with what happened on Election Day." See Marc Birtel, "Democrats' Victories Buck History of Midterm Elections," *Congressional Quarterly* 5 (November 1998), p. 7.

88. Gary C. Jacobson, *The Politics of Congressional Elections,* 5th ed. (Addison-Wesley Longman, 2001), p. 142.

89. Monson and Magleby, 2002 Campaign Communication Study [dataset]. A brief description of the panel survey methodology is included in appendix A.

90. These data are drawn from the Gallup/CNN/*USA Today* poll, as provided by the AEI Election Watch. The Gallup percentages are quite consistent with surveys done by ABC News in the same years. "AEI Election Watch," press release, November 7, 2002.

91. David E. Rosenbaum, "But It's Not the Economy, So Far," *New York Times,* October 11, 2002, p. A17.

92. Andy Grossman, political director, DSCC, interview by David Magleby, Quin Monson, and Jonathan Tanner, Washington, D.C., November 8, 2002.

93. Steve Schmidt and Carl Forti, "Words Matter in the Social Security Debate," NRCC Communications Office memorandum to GOP incumbents and candidates, August 26, 2002.

94. Jack Polidori, political affairs specialist, NEA, interview by David Magleby and Jonathan Tanner, Washington, D.C., November 15, 2002.

95. Robert Pear, "House Votes to Place Prescription Drugs under Coverage by Medicare," *New York Times,* June 28, 2002, p. A16.

96. See Robert Pear, "Democrats Start Petition to Force Vote on Drug Bill," *New York Times,* September 19, 2002, p. A30.

97. See discussion of Citizens for Better Medicare as well as the California Twenty-Seventh District case study in Magleby, *The Other Campaign,* p. 158; and Magleby, *Election Advocacy,* p. 139.

98. Robin Toner, "The 2002 Campaign: The Drug Industry: Democrats See a Stealthy Drive by Drug Industry to Help Republicans," *New York Times,* October 19, 2002, p. A20.

99. See chapter 9 of this volume.

100. Magleby and Monson, "Campaign 2002: 'The Perfect Storm.' "

101. Thomas B. Edsall, "The Sum of Its Parts No Longer Works for the Democratic Party," *Washington Post,* November 24, 2002, p. B4.

102. Mike Allen, "Bush Steps into the Classroom to Tout New Education Law," *Washington Post*, May 7, 2002, p. A4.

103. Gail Stoltz, political director, DNC, interview by David Magleby and Jonathan Tanner, Washington, D.C., November 13, 2002.

104. Kropf and others, "The 2000 Missouri Senate Race."

105. Sandra M. Anglund and Clyde McKee, "The 1998 Connecticut Fifth Congressional District Race," in Magleby, *Outside Money*; and Sandra M. Anglund and Joanne M. Miller, "Interest Group and Party Election Activity: A Report on the 2000 Connecticut Fifth Congressional District Race," in David B. Magleby, ed., "Outside Money," *PS: Political Science and Politics,* online e-symposium, June 2001 (www.apsanet.org/PS/june01/anglund.cfm [May 15, 2003]).

TWO

Party Money in the 2002 Congressional Elections

DAVID B. MAGLEBY

NICOLE CARLISLE SQUIRES

ON MARCH 27, 2002, President Bush signed into law the Bipartisan Campaign Reform Act (BCRA). BCRA is comprehensive: It raises individual contribution limits, redefines issue advocacy, mandates greater disclosure, and bans soft money. But BCRA's centerpiece is the abolition of party soft money after the 2002 election cycle, with the sole exception of limited contributions to state and local party committees for voter registration and get-out-the-vote (GOTV) activities.[1] The political parties stressed to soft-money donors that 2002 would be the last year soft money was legal, providing donors with additional incentive to make generous contributions. The parties also emphasized the slim margins of party control in both houses of Congress and that 2002, as the first election after redistricting, could set in place incumbents who would reap the advantages of incumbency in the future. Both parties also emphasized the pending soft-money ban to raise money for other projects, with the Democrats raising $30 million to renovate their old party headquarters.[2]

This chapter examines how political parties raise and spend hard and soft money, especially in 2002. We find that parties focus on a few competitive races and demand that the hard and soft dollars they target at these races be invested at their direction. Party-funded campaigns are more negative than the candidates' messages. We conclude that channeling more campaign spending through the parties has enhanced the power of the national party committees vis-à-vis state parties but has not made parties significantly stronger as institutions, because so much of the soft money is spent on candidate-specific advertisements and con-test-specific voter mobilization efforts.

During the 1980s and early 1990s, advocates of federal campaign finance reform pointed to problems like declining electoral competition, underfunded challengers, candidate dependence on political action com-mittee (PAC) money, the exorbitant time candidates spent fund-raising, and the ability of self-financed candidates to spend unlimited amounts of money in their own campaigns as reasons to overhaul the system.[3] These concerns were superseded in the 1990s by soft money, which came to be effectively used to promote or attack particular candidates.[4] Indeed, more than any other factor, soft money came to be seen as the largest problem with campaign finance.[5] This fact is evidenced by the rhetoric of the sponsors of the reform legislation and their interest-group allies and by the editorial page and media coverage given to the topic.[6]

During this same period the parties became more active in providing campaign services—assisting candidates with such things as public opin-ion polling, opposition research, and training seminars.[7] These were funded through contributions, including soft money. Originally intended for generic party-building purposes to the national and congressional campaign committees, the strategic uses of soft money were dramati-cally transformed in 1996 by the Clinton-Gore campaign.[8] On the advice of their pollster, Dick Morris, they used soft money early in the 1996 cycle to tout Clinton's record in office, with ads coming at a time when the Dole-Kemp campaign was largely absent from the airwaves.[9] Republicans quickly followed suit, spending money promoting their own candidates. Quickly thereafter, both parties also shifted to using soft money to attack opponents more than to communicate positive messages about their own nominees. The 1996 election marked a dra-matic change in how soft money could be spent. Because neither regula-tory agencies nor courts were going to stop this expanded use, both par-ties exploited the opportunity to spend large amounts of unlimited soft money in competitive races. Party donors, both individuals and groups, also expanded their party soft-money contributions, responding to the appeal that party control of the White House and Congress was up for grabs. Party soft money in congressional elections surged in 1998 and again in 2000.[10]

Soft money has at least four distinct advantages for party committees, especially in competitive races. First, party committees can avoid the constraints of contribution and coordinated expenditure limits. As we demonstrate, party committees behave strategically, allocating their soft money in large amounts to only a few competitive races. In Michigan in 2000, for example, the two parties' senatorial campaign committees transferred more than $11 million of hard and soft money to the state parties in the race between Spence Abraham (R) and Debbie Stabenow (D).[11] In 2002 the Democrats transferred a fraction of this amount ($1.4 million) to support the incumbent, Carl Levin, in a much less competitive race. In this noncompetitive environment, the Republicans transferred next to nothing ($11,000) to challenger Andrew "Rocky" Raczkowski.[12]

Second, soft money is widely seen by party leaders as easier to raise than hard money. In response to the question, "What is the allure of soft money?" Dave Hansen, the former political director of the National Republican Senatorial Committee (NRSC) said, "It's easier to get. You can get it in bigger chunks."[13] Those bigger chunks include corporate and union treasury funds that cannot be given to candidates or parties for election purposes but can be given as soft money. The ease of raising soft money has been enhanced with the advent of joint fund-raising committees, or "victory funds."[14] These operations permit parties and candidates or interest groups to combine their hard and soft money fund-raising efforts. Before the advent of joint fund-raising committees in the 1990s, a donor wishing to donate hard and soft money to both a candidate and the party had to write separate checks to the candidate (hard money), party federal (hard money), and party nonfederal (soft money). But with joint fund-raising committees a donor can write a single check, and the funds are presumably allocated according to the donor's wishes and applicable legal limits. Joint fund-raising committees also allow the party committees to tabulate the fund-raising efforts of individual candidates, especially incumbents, and assess their overall impact on party fund-raising.

Third, parties have found ways to deliver candidate-specific election messages with soft money. In the early days of soft money, the parties ran generic "vote Republican" or "vote Democratic" ads, or concentrated on promoting the entire party slate. But since the 1996 cycle they have refined the use of soft money to primarily contrast candidates or attack the opposing party's candidate.[15] Our survey data in 2000 found that four out of five voters perceive party ads as attempts to persuade them to vote against a candidate.[16] Moreover, party committees have more control over how their soft money is spent, even when it is transferred to state parties, than when they make contributions to candidates or coordinated expenditures.

Fourth, soft- and hard-money resources are spent in amounts proportional to the perceived competitiveness of a race. This provides additional evidence that soft money is about electing or defeating particular candidates and not primarily about party building. It appears to be well understood by all the players—donors, candidates, party committees—that soft money has become a means to connect large donors to key races and to concentrate party resources in those battleground races.

Hard Money: A Persistent Republican Party Advantage

Nearly thirty years ago the Republican Party, under the leadership of former Republican National Committee (RNC) Chairman Bill Brock, launched an aggressive campaign to cultivate a small donor base. "[Brock] showed the skeptics in a few short years that a political party could raise substantial amounts of money in relatively small sums." Brock took party receipts from $8.9 million in 1975 to $37 million in 1980, and by the late 1970s 75 percent of these receipts came from direct mail solicitations.[17] At the same time, the GOP also courted PACs who could contribute closer to the legal maximum of $30,000 per cycle.[18] Because of this early prospecting and the Republicans' natural fund-raising advantage, a result of party demographics, Republicans have developed a persistent advantage in hard-money receipts. Figure 2-1 provides the hard-money receipts (in 2002 dollars) for party committees for 1992–2002.

The Republican hard-money advantage is greatest for the RNC and National Republican Congressional Committee (NRCC), where Republicans raise between two and three times as much hard money as the Democratic National Committee (DNC) and Democratic Congressional Campaign Committee (DCCC). As figure 2-1 demonstrates, this hard-money fund-raising advantage is not new. Republican committees combined had a $130 million to $140 million (in 2002 dollars) hard-money advantage in 1992, 1994, and 1998, and a $190 million to $230 million advantage in 1996, 2000, and 2002. Republicans should have a clear hard-money advantage as the parties shift to a post-soft-money world under BCRA—an irony, given disproportionate Democratic support for BCRA.

Figure 2-1. *Hard-Money (Federal) Receipts, 1992–2002*

Millions of 2002 dollars

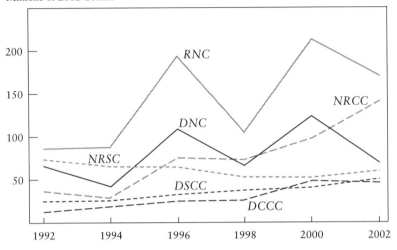

Source: FEC, "Party Committees Raise More than $1 Billion in 2001–2002." Adjusted by CPI (ftp://ftp.bls.gov/ pub/special.requests/cpi/cpiai.txt [January 15, 2003]).

When we examine the 1998, 2000, and 2002 election cycles in hard-money receipts, we find that the DNC had about the same amount of hard money in real terms in 2002 as in 1998, but the DNC spending in both midterms was roughly half of what it was in 2000. The DNC focuses most of its energy on presidential elections and has long seen a surge in hard money in presidential years, followed by a decline in hard-money receipts in the midterm year.[19] Spending by Democratic and Republican state and local parties was up substantially in 2002 as compared to 1998 but below the 2000 figure.

In hard-money receipts, the biggest gains were made by the NRCC, where the amount climbed to $141 million in 2002, up almost $40 million over 2000 and exceeding the 2002 hard-money receipts for the Democratic Senatorial Campaign Committee (DSCC) and DCCC combined. Also noteworthy is the surge in hard-money receipts by the NRCC over previous midterm election cycles. The NRCC raised $32 million in hard money in 1994, $80 million in 1998, and $141 million in 2002, all in 2002 dollars. Party hard money is also used for contributions to candidates, in coordinated expenditures with candidate committees, and can be traded with other party committees for soft money. In addition, parties can spend hard money as independent expenditures.

A Shift toward Soft Money

The shift in both parties from hard money to soft money is remarkable. In 1992 the Democrats raised more than four hard dollars for every soft dollar, and total Democratic Party hard-money fund-raising, including state and local parties, was $209 million, compared to $46 million in soft money. For Republicans in 1992 the difference was even larger, with all GOP committees combined raising $339 million in hard money, compared to $64 million in soft. And in 2002 for the first time, all Democratic committees collectively raised more in soft money ($246 million) than they did in hard money ($217 million). The gap between hard and soft money narrowed for Republicans between 1992 and 2002 but not to the same degree as for Democrats, with hard money at $442 million and soft money at $250 million.

Given the greater emphasis placed on soft-money fund-raising since 1996, the level of party spending by party committees on candidates has shifted. While parties formerly gave contributions to or made coordinated expenditures with candidates, parties now lean toward hard-money transfers to state parties with competitive races. This is because spending soft money requires a hard-money match, with state parties having a more favorable ratio for expending soft money than national parties do. Soft money accounted for anywhere from 26 percent of total DSCC transfers in New Hampshire, to 100 percent in Michigan and New Mexico, but the average for the DSCC was 71 percent, compared to 77 percent for the NRSC.[20] However, if the national party committees spent the soft money centrally, they had to provide 60 percent hard money against 40 percent soft money.[21]

Contributions to Candidates

Evidence of the shift in party priorities from funding many candidates with campaign contributions to directing more hard money to match soft money transfers is found in table 2-1.

Party contributions to candidates have fallen in recent election cycles for all congressional campaign committees, despite the increased hard-money resources available to the parties. As the data in table 2-1 demonstrate, in 1986 the four national congressional campaign committees contributed a combined $7.9 million to House and Senate candidates. In 2002 these same four committees contributed a combined $2.3 million, a 72 percent drop. This is part of a broader trend of focusing hard- and soft-money resources on the few competitive races. To maximize the impact of soft money, the parties need hard money to match it, and so hard-money contributions to uncompetitive challengers or safe seat incumbents have declined.[22] One consequence of the shift to a soft-money strategy in the 1990s is that parties invest less in most races and much more in a few races. Another indicator of the lessening of party support for most congressional candidates is found when we examine the number of candidates receiving $5,000 or less from their national party committee as a contribution. As recently as 1996, 328 House and Senate candidates received $5,000 or more in contributions from their party committee. In 2002 the number of House and Senate candidates receiving $5,000 or more had dropped to 166, a drop of nearly 50 percent in six years.[23]

Coordinated Expenditures

Another way that party committees can assist candidates is through making coordinated expenditures with them. This occurs when parties spend hard money jointly with a candidate's campaign. Table 2-2 provides the level of coordinated expenditure activity by congressional campaign committee for the period 1986–2002.

The decline in party committee spending via coordinated expenditures has dropped even more precipitously than hard-money contributions to candidates. The NRSC was the first to cut coordinated expenditures, reducing them by almost half between 1992 and 1994, and then by over 97 percent in 1996. Total coordinated expenditures in 2002 for all four congressional campaign committees was just over $3 million, compared to over $47 million in 1992. Clearly, for the strategic reasons discussed above, the party committees now aim their hard dollars at purposes other than direct contributions or coordinated expenditures.

Independent Expenditures

As a result of the Supreme Court decision in *Colorado Republican Federal Campaign Committee* v. *Federal Election Commission,* parties are allowed to spend unlimited amounts of hard money in independent expenditures, just as individuals and PACs can.[24] This first became an option for the parties during the 1995–96 cycle. Table 2-3 provides the

Table 2-1. *Hard-Money Contributions to Candidates by Party Committees, 1986–2002*
In 2002 dollars

Committee	1986	1988	1990	1992	1994	1996	1998	2000	2002
DSCC	1,019,048	653,422	594,472	761,017	649,437	619,159	331,656	303,521	409,900
NRSC	1,197,454	1,152,073	958,011	887,569	754,171	798,600	305,012	399,430	455,977
DCCC	1,590,396	1,018,502	616,274	1,074,307	1,202,962	1,187,584	468,823	600,466	640,860
NRCC	4,136,843	2,389,198	1,303,025	934,049	956,482	1,444,503	863,897	730,015	792,947

Source: Federal Election Commission, "Party Committees Raise More than $1 Billion in 2001–2002," press release, March 20, 2002 (www.fec.gov/press/20030320party/20030103party.html [April 29, 2001]). Adjusted by CPI (ftp://ftp.bls.gov/pub/special.requests/cpi/cpiai.txt [January 15, 2003]); and Norman J. Ornstein, Thomas E. Mann, Michael J. Malbin, *Vital Statistics on Congress: 1991–92* (Congressional Quarterly, 1992), p. 94.

Table 2-2. *Coordinated Expenditures by Party Committees, 1986–2002*
In 2002 dollars

Committee	1986	1988	1990	1992	1994	1996	1998	2000	2002
DSCC	10,925,783	10,024,922	7,148,041	14,463,411	15,235,027	9,718,794	9,297	132,843	181,789
NRSC	16,542,104	15,603,398	10,627,937	21,237,673	10,255,193	672,128	31,469	180	553,206
DCCC	3,014,003	4,396,604	4,497,444	5,336,970	9,367,636	6,870,172	3,271,304	2,713,481	1,719,582
NRCC	6,748,669	6,329,510	4,130,160	6,329,300	4,804,419	8,483,382	5,716,958	3,846,480	439,231

Source: See table 2-1.

Table 2-3. *Independent Expenditures by Party Committees, 1996–2002*
In 2002 dollars

Committee	1996	1998	2000	2002
DSCC	1,589,199	1,466,792	138,947	0
NRSC	11,161,419	239,360	279,566	0
DCCC	0	0	2,019,692	1,187,649
NRCC	0	0	573,340	1,321,880

Source: See table 2-1.

independent expenditure activity of the four congressional campaign committees.

In the 1996 cycle, neither House committee used independent expenditures, and the Senate Republicans, who had brought the Colorado case to the Supreme Court, outspent the Democrats ten to one in independent expenditures. Both Senate committees scaled back their independent expenditures in 2000, and neither Senate committee made independent expenditures in 2002. The two House committees spent over $2.5 million in independent expenditures in 2002. Independent expenditures are one way that parties, particularly the Republicans, might exploit their hard-money advantage in the future under BCRA.

Soft Money

While the parties have seen substantial growth in hard money over time, a much greater surge occurred in soft money. Soft-money receipts accounted for 17 percent of total party committee receipts in 1992, and ten years later, in 2002, soft-money receipts made up 49 percent of the total. For the Democrats, soft-money receipts exceeded hard money for the first time in 2002. In 2002 the six national party committees broke fund-raising records for a midterm election cycle, by raising over $1 billion. This is especially impressive, considering that during the first year of this cycle fund-raising activity was distracted by the *Bush* v. *Gore* battle taking place in the Supreme Court, and then after the September 11, 2001, terrorist attacks, fund-raising came to a halt for several weeks.

Soft Money over Time: Democrats Reach Parity
in 2000 and 2002

The RNC and DNC emphasized soft-money activity sooner than the congressional campaign committees. In 1992, for example, the DNC

Figure 2-2. *Soft-Money (Nonfederal) Receipts, 1992–2002*

Millions of 2002 dollars

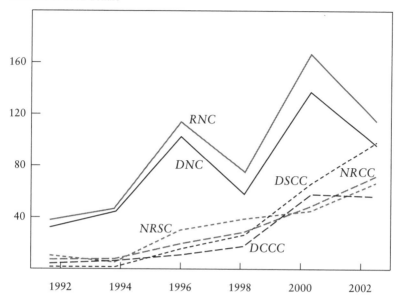

Source: FEC, "Party Committees Raise More than $1 Billion in 2001–2002."

raised just under $40 million, compared to $5.6 million by the DCCC and less than $750,000 by the DSCC. Republican congressional campaign committees were more active in soft money early on; in 1992 the NRSC and NRCC collectively raised $19 million in 2002 dollars, compared to nearly $40 million by the RNC. Figure 2-2 plots the growth in soft money, adjusting for inflation, since 1992.

The four party congressional campaign committees saw dramatic growth in soft-money activity between 1992 and 2002. For example, soft-money receipts climbed from over $6 million for the DSCC and DCCC in 1994 to $151 million in 2002. Democratic Party congressional campaign committee soft-money activity thus experienced a fourfold increase between 1996 and 2002. The NRCC saw a threefold increase over the same period.

The Democratic congressional campaign committees raised more soft money than the Republican congressional campaign committees for the first time in 2000. The NRCC reclaimed their soft-money advantage over House Democrats in 2002, raising just under $70 million, compared to $56 million for the DCCC. But the Senate Democrats, who started with the lowest level of soft money raised by any party committee in 1994, raised the most soft money of any congressional campaign committee in 2000 and 2002. In 2002 the DSCC raised $95 million in soft money, compared to $66 million for the NRSC.

Targeting Soft Money into Competitive U.S. Senate Races

Instead of spending centrally, national party committees often transfer soft and hard money they want to spend on particular races to state parties because of the more favorable soft-to-hard-money matching ratio that state parties enjoy.[25] Exceptions to this practice seem to arise when the national party distrusts the state party.

As documented in table 2-4, in 2002 the DSCC transferred about $8 million more soft money to state parties for U.S. Senate races than did the NRSC, and in the six Senate races we monitored the difference was almost $5 million. In terms of party transfers, the DSCC transferred more than the NRSC to Arkansas, Iowa, Minnesota, Missouri, and South Dakota. The NRSC transferred more hard and soft money than the DSCC in New Hampshire. On the Democratic side, the transfers are the total DSCC effort in each Senate race. In 2002 the NRSC preferred to spend some of its soft money on Senate races from the national level. An advantage in hard-money receipts allowed Republicans to do this more easily than Democrats. The NRSC centrally spent $10 million in issue advocacy and maybe more.[26] Chris LaCivita, political director of the NRSC, provided us with total NRSC spending figures, which include transfers to state parties, for our races. These are provided in table 2-4. When we compare the LaCivita figures to the DSCC transfers, the Republicans achieved rough parity with the Democrats in Arkansas, Minnesota, and Missouri. For both parties, the Minnesota Senate race was the highest priority in 2002. Republicans spent a total of $8.3 million on this race, compared to $8.7 million for the Democrats.

Democrats also made South Dakota a high priority. Overall the DSCC transferred $5.1 million in soft money and $1.4 million in hard money to the South Dakota Democratic Party. The NRSC transferred $3.3 million in soft money and nearly $900,000 in hard money to South Dakota.[27] Chris LaCivita of the NRSC also reported that his committee spent another $200,000 in South Dakota through the NRSC centrally.[28]

New Hampshire, another small state, was a major priority for Republicans. The NRSC transferred a total of $4.5 million, compared to

Table 2-4. Senatorial Committee Transfers to State Parties and NRSC Total Spending in Sample Competitive Races, 2002

In 2002 dollars

| | Senatorial committee transfers[a] | | | | | | | | NRSC total spending[a] |
| | DSCC transfers | | | | NRSC transfers | | | | |
State	Hard	Soft	Soft (%)	Total	Hard	Soft	Soft (%)	Total	
Arkansas	1,333,802	4,289,425	76	5,623,227	1,441,283	2,926,242	67	4,367,525	5,200,000
Iowa	1,279,041	4,315,485	77	5,594,526	541,850	1,824,021	77	2,365,871	3,500,000
Minnesota	2,138,828	6,566,451	75	8,705,279	1,484,998	5,360,994	78	6,845,992	8,300,000
Missouri	2,873,980	5,770,298	67	8,644,278	2,180,067	5,567,365	72	7,747,432	8,100,000
New Hampshire	2,190,576	770,642	26	2,961,218	1,300,643	3,250,736	71	4,551,379	6,600,000
South Dakota	1,445,148	5,123,526	78	6,568,674	853,397	3,260,996	79	4,114,393	4,300,000
Total spent in sample competitive races	11,261,375	26,835,827	70	38,097,202	7,802,238	22,190,354	74	29,992,592	36,000,000
Total spent in all races	21,945,255	52,484,276	71	74,429,531	12,843,004	44,041,837	77	56,884,841	
Percent of total spent in sample competitive races	51	51		51	61	50		53	

Source: FEC, "Party Committees Raise More than $1 Billion in 2001–2002"; and personal e-mail communication from Chris LaCivita.

a. Party transfers reflect the total amount transferred to a given state and not necessarily the amount spent in our sample races, whereas the NRSC amount reflects total spending by the NRSC in each of the sample Senate races.

a DSCC transfer of $3 million. LaCivita of the NRSC also reports that the committee spent an additional $2.1 million on the New Hampshire Senate race, for a total of $6.6 million.

The DSCC transferred more money to Arkansas (overall $5.6 million, soft and hard) than did the NRSC ($4.4 million)—a surprise, given the high priority both parties place on protecting vulnerable incumbents. The NRSC spent another $800,000 on Hutchison in Arkansas, bringing the race closer to parity in party spending. The DSCC outspent the NRSC in Iowa, where they expended a combined $6 million in soft and hard money defending Tom Harkin. The NRSC total expenditure in Iowa was almost half that of the DSCC, at $3.5 million, of which $2.4 million was transferred to the state party.

We also examined spending in the less competitive control races. One surprise in our control races was the Democrats' transfer of $1.4 million to Michigan, where incumbent Carl Levin was seeking his fifth term. The Republicans, in contrast, did not see this seat in play and transferred only $11,000 in soft money to Michigan.[29] Montana is an example of a race in which both parties invested early but then scaled back their spending. Democrats transferred nearly $1.5 million to the Montana Democratic Party to help defend incumbent Max Baucus. One party-funded advertisement generated controversy, when Republican challenger Mike Taylor reacted to an ad that he thought portrayed him as a homosexual by briefly dropping out of the race.[30] The intent of the ad was to "knock Taylor out" of the race.[31] The Baucus campaign asked the DSCC to stop running the ad. The party committee refused, instead hoping that the early attack would mean that they would not have to invest more defending their candidate later in the election. The success of the early attack meant that the DSCC could target its remaining soft money toward other races.

Targeting Soft Money into Competitive U.S. House Races

Tracking the transfer of hard and soft money for expenditures for and against particular U.S. House candidates is often more difficult, because most states have multiple House districts and some have multiple competitive House contests. Table 2-5 presents the House party committee transfers to state parties. And as a supplement to the FEC data, the table also presents the total spending by the NRCC in our sample of competitive races, as obtained from Mike McElwain, political director of the NRCC.[32]

Table 2-5. House Committee Transfers to State Parties and National Republican Congressional Committee Total Spending in Sample Races, 2002

In 2002 dollars

| State | House committee transfers[a] | | | | | | | | NRCC total spending[a] |
| | DCCC transfers | | | | NRCC transfers | | | | |
	Hard	Soft	Soft (%)	Total	Hard	Soft	Soft (%)	Total	
Arkansas (4)	122,339	585,873	83	708,212	117,314	415,920	78	533,234	0
Arizona (1)	105,341	521,744	83	627,085	149,096	378,370	72	527,466	1,900,000
Colorado (7)	666,980	2,006,458	75	2,673,438	645,094	1,523,114	70	2,168,208	2,400,000
Connecticut (5)	0	0	..[b]	0	25,000	0	0	25,000	1,100,000
Iowa	894,055	2,860,795	76	3,754,850	210,709	507,798	71	718,507	
Iowa (1)									1,400,000
Iowa (2)									1,500,000
Iowa (3)									300,000
Iowa (4)									1,100,000
Indiana (2)	312,314	1,867,289	86	2,179,603	74,147	236,055	76	310,202	1,500,000
Maryland (8)	811,426	1,176,294	59	1,987,720	0	0	..[b]	0	800,000
Minnesota (2)	423,543	1,952,134	82	2,375,677	437,916	1,390,752	76	1,828,668	2,300,000
Mississippi (3)	228,441	262,113	53	490,554	277,000	28,000	9	305,000	400,000
North Carolina (8)	310,223	655,636	68	965,859	170,960	718,940	81	889,900	900,000
New Hampshire (1)	648,456	1,649,914	72	2,298,370	609,359	1,397,629	70	2,006,988	2,500,000
New Mexico	643,107	1,757,327	73	2,400,434	340,915	671,513	66	1,012,428	
New Mexico (1)									1,000,000
New Mexico (2)									2,000,000
Pennsylvania (17)	610,653	2,650,814	81	3,261,467	1,284,130	2,100,226	62	3,384,356	2,600,000
South Dakota (at-large)	140,127	408,463	74	548,590	25,001	120,000	83	145,001	1,900,000
Utah (2)	78,991	355,968	82	434,959	105,000	122,500	54	227,500	400,000
Total	5,995,996	18,710,822	76	24,706,818	4,471,641	9,610,817	68	14,082,458	26,000,000

Sources: FEC, "Party Committees Raise More than $1 Billion in 2001-2002"; NRCC spending data (Mike McElwain, NRCC political director, interview by David Magleby and Jonathan Tanner, Washington, D.C., December 2, 2002).

a. Party transfers reflect the total amount transferred to a given state and not necessarily the amount spent in sample races, whereas the NRCC amount reflects total spending by the NRCC in each of the individual districts.

b. Absence of collected data.

House races in Colorado, Pennsylvania, New Hampshire, and Minnesota saw party soft-money transfers in excess of $2 million, along with the requisite hard-money match. Iowa, Indiana, New Mexico, South Dakota, and Maryland saw substantially more Democratic Party committee transfers for House races. One major surprise was the lack of party transfers for Connie Morella in Maryland. The NRCC did not transfer any money to Maryland in 2001–02, while the DCCC transferred nearly $2 million. However, NRCC political director Mike McElwain reports that his committee spent $800,000 on Maryland's Eighth District race. In some races with overall lower levels of spending, Democrats still outpaced Republicans. In Utah's Second District, for example, the DCCC transferred $435,000, compared to $228,000 for the NRCC, and in the South Dakota at-large race, the DCCC transferred $549,000, compared to only $145,000 by the NRCC. However, again according to data provided by the NRCC, the party spent a total of $400,000 on Utah's Second District and $1.9 million on South Dakota's at-large district. Republicans transferred less money in Arizona, with the NRCC transferring $527,000, compared to $627,000 for the DCCC, but total spending by the NRCC in Arizona's First District was $1.9 million. Combined Democratic and Republican soft-money transfers to the six competitive Senate races in our sample averaged $11.3 million, while combined soft-money transfers to our control Senate races averaged only $1 million.[33]

How Soft Money Is Spent

As we have demonstrated, soft money is spent strategically on the most competitive House and Senate elections. Another factor the party committees use is incumbency. For example, the NRCC ranked their priorities as incumbents, open seats, and then challengers.[34]

Overall, both parties targeted their resources into relatively few races. In our sample of six competitive Senate races, we captured over half of all soft money expended by the congressional committees: NRSC (50 percent) and DSCC (51 percent), and between one-half and two-thirds of the hard money transferred by the NRSC (61 percent) and DSCC (51 percent). These proportions suggest that our sample of Senate races were high-priority races for both parties. Both parties transferred a great deal (over $4.8 million) to Colorado, where the Seventh District race was decided by just 121 votes. However, both the Democrats and Republi-

Table 2-6. *States outside Sample That Received Large Transfers from National Senate Party Committees*
Dollars

State	Democratic Senatorial Campaign Committee			National Republican Senatorial Committee		
	Hard	Soft	Soft (%)	Hard	Soft)	Soft
Colorado	1,197,287	4,028,350	77	1,078,160	3,894,573	78
Texas	2,465,059	5,325,165	68	257,943	2,814,526	92
Georgia	1,626,206	2,624,480	62	733,190	2,751,237	79
Florida	26,827	53,738	67	0	5,990,750	100
South Carolina	866,675	2,874,086	77	367,552	1,102,657	75
Louisiana	1,559,875	471,826	23	1,339,235	1,339,235	50

Source: FEC, "Party Committees Raise More than $1 Billion."

cans missed opportunities. In Utah's Second District, the Republicans did not get involved because the race fell into their lowest-priority category—a Republican challenger—and polling data showed that Republican candidate Swallow was down by twelve points in late August and down eighteen points closer to the election.[35] On Election Day Swallow lost by less than 1 percent of the 200,000 votes cast.[36] However, Republicans were not the only party to misallocate money. The DSCC appears to have made a mistake in transferring almost $7.8 million to the Senate race in Texas. Despite the DSCC's approximately doubling the NRSC's spending in Texas, Republican John Cornyn still won, with 55 percent of the vote.

Both parties continue to invest most of their soft money resources on broadcast advertising. According to NRCC political director Mike McElwain, "TV is the best way to communicate" and the cheapest way to make an impression on a lot of people.[37] The numbers indicate that both the candidates and party organizations share McElwain's opinion. Overall, candidates and parties seem to spend similar amounts of money on television advertising. However, in states like South Dakota and Colorado in 2002, party spending on television exceeded candidate levels. Party organizations in South Dakota spent over $6.5 million on TV, while candidates running for both the House and Senate spent only $4.2 million.[38] And in Colorado's Seventh District, Feeley and Beauprez combined to spend nearly $1.2 million, while the national political parties spent or transferred over $2.6 million for this race.[39]

In 2002 both parties built on a strategy used on a more limited basis in 2000. They challenged the truthfulness of the advertisements of the opposing party or allied interest groups, in an effort to have the ads pulled. Once a station pulled an ad, the party pressed other stations in the same media market to follow suit. Mike Matthews of the DCCC said, "When you get an ad pulled, your message has a better chance to come through. It is like the Domino Effect—one station pulls the ad and others follow, or one station keeps the ad, and the others put the ad back up."[40] The final prong in the strategy of challenging advertisements is to attack the candidate of the opposing party for the untruthful nature of his or her campaign. Ned Monroe of the Associated Builders and Contractors observed, "There were a heck of a lot more TV and radio commercials pulled off the air probably than in any other cycle I'm familiar with."[41] For example, in North Carolina's Eighth District, Republican candidate Robin Hayes challenged what he called "misrepresentations" made in a DCCC ad linking his vote for fast-track trade authority to job losses in the textile industry. Several television stations subsequently decided to pull the ad.[42]

Candidates occasionally disavow ads run by their political parties or interest group allies. In the Iowa Second Congressional District in 2002, Jim Leach asked his party and other Republican-allied groups to stop running ads because they were misleading.[43] And in South Dakota, House candidate Bill Janklow publicly criticized an ad run by the Republican Party accusing Stephanie Herseth of carpetbagging. Janklow denied any prior knowledge of the ad and even asked the party to stop running it.[44] More typically, however, the soft-money transfers provided competitive campaigns with a substantial volume of additional campaign communications. They were usually aimed at attacking the opposing party's candidate and included all forms of communication.

The use of soft money to fund such campaign activities as mail, phone banks, personal contacts, and get-out-the-vote efforts is explored in greater detail in chapter 4. These ground-war expenditures have become increasingly important to the parties in recent cycles.

Does Soft Money Strengthen the Parties?

The goal of stronger political parties is an article of faith for political scientists, dating at least from a report written in the 1950s by the American Political Science Association Committee on Political Parties titled, "Toward a More Responsible Two-Party System."[45] Political scientists differ over whether soft money has strengthened the political parties, an assessment that first requires us to explore the definition of a strong party.[46] There are numerous ways to define party strength, including (but not limited to): the size of party staff and infrastructure and the ability to deliver a party message, to recruit, nominate, and elect candidates, and to register and mobilize voters. Our assessment of whether the surge in soft money has strengthened parties is limited to an examination of national party campaign committees and the election activities of state parties. These committees are not typically as concerned with the ability to push legislation through Congress as they are with winning elections and achieving or maintaining majority status in both houses of Congress.[47]

With the advent of skyrocketing soft-money fund-raising and spending by the national party campaign committees has come an increasingly heated debate about whether soft money strengthens or weakens the parties. Those who perceive soft money strengthening parties emphasize that soft money provides more resources to devote to party building, leading to greater integration between national and state parties.[48] They claim that soft money strengthens parties in relation to interest groups, because the case can be made that the campaign finance reforms of the 1970s empowered interest groups and candidate-centered campaigns at the expense of parties.[49] Advocates of this thesis also believe that soft money fosters greater competition. Our data on 2002 confirm the conventional wisdom that PACs are much more likely to give only to incumbents.[50] Parties, on the other hand, can and do invest in challengers.[51] Soft money may also further insulate candidates from donors by allowing the parties to act as "a protective layer of decisionmakers" between the two, thereby actually reducing corruption and its appearance.[52] In addition to all of this, those who perceive soft money as strengthening parties point to higher levels of party-line voting since the 1970s[53] and increased levels of soft money going to mobilization.[54] Finally, some political scientists even claim a causal link between soft money and turnout and that "eliminating all current 'soft-money' expenditures . . .would lead to a 2 percent decline in voter turnout—without soft money, approximately 2 million fewer Americans would have gone to the polls in 1996."[55]

Those who challenge the thesis that soft money strengthens parties point to the small percentage of total soft money that actually goes to grassroots party building.[56] Instead, a vast majority of soft money goes to broadcast ads, most of which (93 percent in 2000) never even mention the words *Republican* or *Democrat,* except in the "paid for by" tagline at the end of the ad.[57] Opponents emphasize the role candidates play in raising money. "People do not give to be close to party chairs."[58] Both parties have created joint fund-raising committees, or victory funds, in select states to effectively permit large donors to earmark their soft-money donations to particular races.[59] Campaign committees even keep tallies of how much soft money candidates are responsible for having raised, thereby allowing the committee to direct monies appropriately.[60] Furthermore, opponents view state parties as merely check writers and not actual players.[61] Parties also target only competitive races, neglecting the majority of citizens.[62] They focus on candidates, whose short-term goal of winning conflicts with building lasting state and local infrastructures.[63] By focusing on one candidate at a time, no permanent assets are left behind for the party.[64] Finally, opponents also point to lower or static levels of turnout and a lack of evidence suggesting greater partisan identification.[65]

Though not able to resolve the debate, our research sheds light on several issues important to the discussion. Soft money has largely been about electing or defeating particular candidates. Most soft money is spent on candidate-specific electioneering and is indistinguishable from the ads, mail, or phone calls coming from the candidates and interest groups. In Indiana's Second District, for example, only one in seven mailers "prominently displayed party labels." The others limited mention of the party to the return address and the "paid for" tag line.[66] Most campaign mail by political parties is aimed at persuading voters to vote against the opposing party candidate, followed by mail that seeks to persuade voters to vote for the candidate from the party funding the mail. Some late party-funded mail is about getting out to vote, but it is not the modal party message. Further evidence of soft money being primarily about electioneering comes from the congruence we find in party and candidate messages. As we demonstrate, the tone of the advertisements occasionally prompts candidates to criticize their own party ads, but rarely do the parties run on themes different from the candidates. This suggests that, even with large amounts of soft money, the focus remains on the candidates.

Our research indicates that state parties are less independent as a result of soft money, with national parties clearly taking the lead in how the soft-money funds and matching hard dollars are expended. National party committees have substantial say over how and when the money is spent, including which consultants will be used in particular races. For example, after assessing the Colorado Seventh District early on, the DCCC assigned Erik Greathouse to take the place of Beth Minahan, Feeley's longtime confidante.[67] The NRCC not only spent a substantial amount in Pennsylvania's Seventeenth District, they also sent one of their election specialists, Jerry Morgan, to control how the money was spent and to run George W. Gekas's ground war.[68] According to a Harrisburg *Patriot-News* article, "[he] work[ed] out of Gekas' headquarters and over[saw] all aspects of his campaign."[69] This indicates that, while national parties have increased control over campaigns, state parties have become relatively weaker.

In terms of whether soft money contributes to electoral competitiveness, soft money has made at least a handful of races much more competitive than if only hard money were allowed. Examples from 2002 where soft money made challengers more viable against an incumbent include Republican Jim Leach's Democratic opponent, Julianne Thomas, in Iowa's Second Congressional District; Missouri Senate Republican candidate Jim Talent; and Indiana's Second Congressional District Democratic candidate, Jill Long Thompson.

Our research also lends support to the idea that soft money does not result in a stronger party apparatus in the long term. Interviews with party leaders demonstrate that they are focused on winning elections in the present and not worrying about the long term.

Finally, our research shows an increased move to the ground war. In 1998 the Republican strategy consisted mainly of broadcast ads focusing on national, instead of local, issues specific to individual races. Republicans admitted this was a tactical mistake and have since moved toward greater ground war efforts as evidenced by their STOMP (Strategic Task Force for Organizing and Mobilizing People), ROMP (Retain Our Majority Project), and 72 Hour Task Force programs in 2002. Democrats, too, have placed greater emphasis on the ground war at least since 1998. This phenomenon is discussed more fully in chapter 4.

Ray La Raja has undertaken the tedious task of coding FEC expenditure data to assess how party committees actually spend soft money. He estimates that "between the 1992 and 2000 election cycles the combined nonfederal spending by 100 major state parties to mobilize voters increased from $8.6 to $41.8 million."[70] But La Raja is limited by the lack of precision of state and federal party committees in how they report expenditures and by the fact that he includes direct mail and telephone bank activity as voter mobilization. Parties also utilize phone banks for both persuasion and mobilization, reinforcing our concern about La Raja's assumptions. Jonathan Krasno and Frank Sorauf, in research done for the *Colorado Republican Federal Campaign Committee* v. *Federal Election Commission* and *Missouri Republican Party* v. *Lamb* cases in 2000, found that between $1.2 million and $2.2 million was spent canvassing voters, with the rest spent on purchasing voter lists, phone banks, or direct mail.[71] While there is clearly some benefit to the parties from these grassroots activities, they clearly do not constitute expenditures as significant as broadcast advertising or direct mail for persuasion purposes. Moreover, there is no compelling evidence that much of the party soft-money expenditure, even at the grassroots level, has an enduring benefit to the parties. One enduring benefit of party soft-money spending is more registered voters who at one time supported the party.

In the end, deciding whether soft money strengthens parties depends on how one defines a strong party. In the vast majority of contests, parties have not become stronger since the advent of soft money. As we document in this chapter, they are spending significantly less money on contributions to candidates and through coordinated expenditures. In 2002, compared to other recent elections, parties invested smaller amounts on most candidates. However, in the competitive races parties are heavily involved, including in candidate recruitment, voter mobilization, and direct voter communication aimed at persuading voters to vote against or for a particular candidate.

Soft money has both strengthened and weakened parties. National party organizations are strengthened through having money to spend on targeted races with the aim of winning control of the House or Senate. With the additional funds has come increased power for those who allocate the money, notably the national party committees and their leadership. Party committees clearly exercise substantial control over soft money, even when it is transferred to the state parties.

Conclusion

While the courts will ultimately determine whether 2002 was the last hurrah for soft money, both parties and especially soft-money donors behaved as if it were. The four congressional campaign committees set new records in soft-money receipts, up $64 million over 2000. Only the

DCCC saw a decline in 2002. The overall levels of soft-money activity in 2002, including in the DNC and RNC, far exceeded any previous nonpresidential year and came close to the level of the 2000 presidential election year in soft-money receipts and expenditures.

Democrats rely more heavily on soft money than do Republicans. Should the soft-money ban in BCRA be upheld, Republicans will have a substantial advantage, at least in the short run. This advantage is amplified by the fact that BCRA doubled the hard-money contribution limits for individuals.

As we have documented and as is greatly substantiated by the evidentiary record in *McConnell* v. *FEC*, soft money has changed the ways party committees operate. National party committees became the conduit for large amounts of money from interested donors who wanted money spent on particular congressional races. These resources have been concentrated in a small set of races, and the money has primarily gone to state parties in those states. While party efforts in voter registration and mobilization have been crucial in competitive races, much greater amounts of soft money have been invested in efforts to persuade voters to vote against or for a particular candidate. Soft money has essentially funded parallel campaign structures in competitive races.

Yet, even with the enactment of BCRA, it is not clear how much soft money is going away. Some soft money will likely find new avenues through quasi-party interest groups and other entities, a topic we explore in chapter 3.

Notes

1. This provision, known as the Levin Amendment, allows state and local parties to raise up to $10,000 per calendar year ($20,000 per election cycle). These funds may be used for voter registration or GOTV, but if the ballot also contains federal candidates, federal funds (hard money) must be used for 15 to 36 percent of the expenditure. Levin monies may not be used for advertising or for paying salaries of federal campaign workers.

2. Guillermo Meneses, DNC spokesperson, telephone conversation with Nicole Carlisle Squires, May 13, 2003.

3. Gary C. Jacobsen, *Money in Congressional Elections* (Yale University Press, 1980); Gary C. Jacobsen and Samuel Kernell, *Strategy and Choice in Congressional Elections,* 2d ed. (Yale University Press, 1983); and David B. Magleby and Candice J. Nelson, *The Money Chase: Congressional Campaign Finance Reform* (Brookings, 1990).

4. Marianne Holt, "The Surge in Party Money in Competitive 1998 Congressional Elections," in David B. Magleby, ed., *Outside Money: Soft Money and Issue Advocacy in the 1998 Congressional Elections* (Lanham, Md.: Rowman and Littlefield, 2000), pp. 17–40; David B. Magleby and Eric Smith, "Party Soft Money in the 2000 Congressional Elections," in David B. Magleby, ed., *The Other Campaign: Soft Money and Issue Advocacy in the 2000 Congressional Elections* (Lanham, Md.: Rowman and Littlefield, 2003), pp. 43–44; Candice J. Nelson, "Spending in the 2000 Elections," in David B. Magleby, ed., *Financing the 2000 Election* (Brookings, 2002), p. 23.

5. Robert Biersack and Melanie Haskell, "Spitting on the Umpire: Political Parties, the Federal Election Campaign Act, and the 1996 Campaigns," in John C. Greed, ed., *Financing the 1996 Election* (Armonk, N.Y.: M.E. Sharp, 1999), pp. 155–86.

6. John McCain, "Only One Bill Means Reform," *Washington Post,* February 13, 2002, p. A27; Common Cause, "The End of Soft Money in Politics: Common Cause Welcomes the Ban on Soft Money, Vows to Fight for Enforcement," November 5, 2002 (www.commoncause.org/news/default.cfm?ArtID=39 [July 23, 2003]); "Campaign Reform on Trial," *New York Times,* December 4, 2002, p. A30.

7. Paul Allen Beck and Marjorie Randon Hershey, *Party Politics in America,* 9th ed. (Addison-Wesley Longman, 2001), pp. 83–85; Paul S. Herrnson, "Hired Guns and House Races: Campaign Professionals in House Elections," in James A. Thurber and Candice J. Nelson, eds., *Campaign Warriors: Political Consultants in Elections* (Brookings, 2000), p. 65–90.

8. Diana Dwyre and Robin Kolodny, "Throwing Out the Rule Book: Party Financing of the 2000 Elections," in Magleby, *Financing the 2000 Election,* p. 133–35.

9. Dick Morris, *Winning the Presidency in the 90s: Behind the Oval Office* (Random House, 1997), p. 139.

10. Holt, "Surge in Party Money"; Magleby and Smith, "Party Soft Money"; Dwyre and Kolodny, "Throwing Out the Rule Book."

11. Magleby and Smith, "Party Soft Money," p. 40.

12. Federal Election Commission, "Party Committees Raise More than $1 Billion in 2001–2002," press release, March 20, 2003 (http://fecweb1.fec.gov/press/20030320party/20030103party.html [April 29, 2003]); and Chris LaCivita, political director, NRSC, personal e-mail communication to Jonathan Tanner, January 3, 2003.

13. Dave Hansen, former executive director, NRSC, telephone interview by David Magleby, Jason Beal, Anna Nibley Baker, and Emily Walsh, July 2, 2001.

14. Magleby and Smith, "Party Soft Money," p. 39.

15. Jonathan Krasno and Kenneth Goldstein, "The Facts about Television Advertising and the McCain-Feingold Bill," *PS: Political Science and Politics,* vol. 96 (June 2002), p. 10.

16. David B. Magleby, *Dictum without Data: The Myth of Issue Advocacy and Party Building* (Center for the Study of Elections and Democracy, Brigham Young University, 2000).

17. Frank J. Sorauf, *Money in American Politics* (Glenview, Ill.: Scott, Foresman, 1988), pp. 128–30.

18. For contribution limits under FECA, see "Contribution Limits—Hard Money and Soft Money," Campaign Finance Institute, 2002 (www.cfinst.org/eguide/contrib.html [April 29, 2002]).

19. Frank J. Sorauf, *Inside Campaign Finance: Myths and Realities* (Yale University Press, 1992), p. 33.

20. FEC, "Party Committees Raise More than $1 Billion in 2001–2002"; and LaCivita, e-mail communication, January 3, 2003.

21. Dwyre and Kolodny, "Throwing Out the Rule Book" p. 145–46.

22. Ibid., p. 146.

23. Data provided by Robert Biersack, FEC, personal e-mail communication to Jonathan Tanner, May 17, 2003.

24. *Colorado Republican Federal Campaign Committee* v. *Federal Election Commission*, 116 S.Ct. 2309 (1996).

25. During a midterm year, the ratio of hard to soft dollars for the national parties is 60 percent hard to 40 percent soft. This ratio changes at the state level to allow for a higher proportion of soft money to be used. The ratio varies from state to state, depending on the state campaign finance laws and the number of federal races or the state ballot. See Dwyre and Kolodny, "Throwing Out the Rule Book," pp. 145–46.

26. Robert Biersack, FEC, personal e-mail communication to Jonathan Tanner, January 2, 2003. The $10 million comes from voluntary line item descriptions of expenditures by the NRSC. They may have done additional issue advocacy spending without specifically describing it as such.

27. Note that the two parties transferred identical percentages of soft money, 79 percent, to South Dakota. This is because the ratio of hard and soft money in South Dakota in 2002 was 22 percent hard and 78 percent soft by the state party.

28. Note that the two parties transferred nearly the same percentages of soft money to Montana, Iowa, and Minnesota as well.

29. In New Mexico, for example, neither party invested very heavily, although the nearly $200,000 in soft money exceeded the hard money contribution and coordinated expenditure money spent on Democrat Gloria Tristani. In Delaware both parties transferred either no money (Republicans) or under $10,000 (Democrats).

30. Craig Wilson, "The Montana Senate and At-Large Congressional District Races," in David B. Magleby and J. Quin Monson, eds., *The Last Hurrah: Soft Money and Issue Advocacy in the 2002 Congressional Elections,* monograph version (Center for the Study of Elections and Democracy, Brigham Young University, 2003), pp. 342–43.

31. Jim Messina, campaign manager for Max Baucus, telephone interview by Craig Wilson, November 25, 2002.

32. Mike McElwain, political director, NRCC, interview by David Magleby and Jonathan Tanner, Washington, D.C., December 2, 2002.

33. FEC, "Party Committees Raise More than $1 Billion."

34. McElwain interview, December 2, 2002.

35. See chapter 11 of this volume.

36. Ibid.

37. McElwain interview, December 2, 2002.

38. See chapter 7 of this volume for more information on TV spending data.

39. See chapter 8 of this volume for more information on TV spending data.

40. Mike Matthews, political director, DCCC, interview by David Magleby and Nicole Carlisle Squires, Washington, D.C., November 12, 2002.

41. Ned Monroe, director of political affairs, Associated Builders and Contractors, interview by Quin Monson and Jonathan Tanner, Washington, D.C., December 9, 2002.

42. Eric S. Heberlig, "The North Carolina Eighth Congressional District Race," in Magleby and Monson, *The Last Hurrah*, monograph version, p. 259; see also John Roos and Christopher Rodriguez, "The Indiana Second Congressional District Race," in Magleby and Monson, *The Last Hurrah*, monograph version, pp. 230–31.

43. David Redlawsk and Arthur Sanders, "The Iowa Senate and First, Second, Third, and Fourth Congressional District Races," in Magleby and Monson, *The Last Hurrah*, monograph version, p. 84.

44. See chapter 7 of this volume.

45. American Political Science Association Committee on Political Parties, "Toward a More Responsible Two-Party System," *American Political Science Review,* vol. 44 (1950), Supplement. See also E. E. Schattschneider, *Party Government* (Rinehart, 1942); and John C. Green and Paul S. Herrnson, eds., *Responsible Partisanship? The Evolution of American Political Parties since 1950* (University Press of Kansas, 2002), pp. 101–19.

46. As Kelly Patterson has argued, our conceptualization of weak or strong parties is in part based on what notions of democracy we hold. See Kelly Patterson, *Political Parties and the Maintenance of Liberal Democracy* (Columbia University Press, 1996), pp. 117–33.

47. John H. Aldrich, *Why Parties? The Origin and Transformation of Party Politics in America* (University of Chicago Press, 1995); Joseph A. Schlesinger, *Political Parties and the Winning of Office* (University of Michigan Press, 1991).

48. Raymond J. La Raja, "Why Soft Money Has Strengthened Parties," in Anthony Corrado, Thomas E. Mann, and Trevor Potter, eds., *Inside the Campaign Finance Battle: Court Testimony on the New Reforms* (Brookings, 2003), p. 72.

49. Sidney M. Milkis, "Parties versus Interest Groups," in Corrado, Mann, and Potter, *Inside the Campaign Finance Battle*, p. 40.

50. Stephen Ansolabehere and James M. Snyder Jr., "Soft Money, Hard Money, Strong Parties," *Columbia Law Review*, vol. 100, no. 3 (April 2000). See also chapter 3 of this volume."

51. Milkis, "Parties versus Interest Groups," p. 44.

52. Ibid.

53. See Norman Ornstein, Thomas E. Mann, and Michael J. Malbin, *Vital Statistics on Congress, 1997–1998* (Congressional Quarterly, 1998), pp. 11–13.

54. Raymond La Raja estimates that "between the 1992 and 2000 election cycles, spending on voter mobilization increased steadily from $9.6 to $53.1 million." See Raymond J. La Raja, "Why Soft Money Has Strengthened Parties," in Corrado, Mann, and Potter, *Inside the Campaign Finance Battle*, p. 75. This estimate is greatly inflated because of the lack of precision of state and federal party committees in how they report expenditures and by the fact that La Raja classifies all direct mail and telephone bank activity as voter mobilization. As we have shown, the parties have expanded their use of mail, telephone, and personal contact in recent cycles and especially in 2002. But most of this activity is about persuading voters to vote against or for a candidate and not about voter mobilization.

55. Ansolabehere and Snyder, "Soft Money, Hard Money," p. 619.

56. $20 million out of $520 million between 1992 and 1998. See Jonathan S. Krasno and Frank Sorauf, "Why Soft Money Has Not Strengthened Parties," in Corrado, Mann, and Potter, *Inside the Campaign Finance Battle*, p. 54.

57. See Jonathan Krasno and Kenneth Goldstein, "The Facts about Television Advertising and the McCain-Feingold Bill," *PS: Political Science*, vol. 96 (June 2002), pp. 207–12.

58. Robert Rozen, "Large Contributions Provide Unequal Access," in Corrado, Mann, and Potter, *Inside the Campaign Finance Battle*, p. 298.

59. State parties are also important in fund-raising. As Sarah M. Morehouse and Malcolm E. Jewell have found, "the average state party raises 60 percent to 80 percent of all hard money and 37 percent of all soft money." See Morehouse and Jewell, "State Parties: Independent Partners in the Money Relationship," in John C. Green and Rick Farmer, eds., *The State of the Parties*, 4th ed. (Lanham, Md.: Rowman and Littlefield, 2003) pp. 155–66.

60. David Boren, "A Senate Democrat's Perspective,' in Corrado, Mann, and Potter, *Inside the Campaign Finance Battle*, p. 116.

61. Krasno and Sorauf, "Why Soft Money Has Not Strengthened Parties," p. 53.

62. Ibid., p. 55.

63. Ibid., p. 49.

64. Statement by John C. Green, Campaign Finance Institute, "Cyber-Forum: How Would McCain-Feingold Affect the Parties?" (www.cfinst.org/parties/mf_responses.html [July 18, 2003]).

65. See U.S. Bureau of the Census, *Statistical Abstract of the United States: 2001* (Government Printing Office, 2001), p. 253. See also "Party Identification 7-Point Scale 1952–2000," National Election Studies (www.umich.edu/~nes/nes-guide/toptable/tab2a_1.htm [July 18, 2003]).

66. Roos and Rodriguez, "The Indiana Second Congressional District Race," p. 227.

67. See chapter 8 of this volume.

68. See chapter 10 of this volume.

69. Brett Lieberman, "Election-Bureau Visits by GOP Draw Flak," *Patriot-News*, October 31, 2002 (www.pennlive.com [October 31, 2002]).

70. See La Raja, "Why Soft Money Has Strengthened Parties," p. 80.

71. Donald Green, "The Need for Federal Regulation of State Party Activity," in Corrado, Mann, and Potter, *Inside the Campaign Finance Battle*, p. 110.

THREE　　*Interest-Group*
Electioneering in the 2002
Congressional Elections

DAVID B. MAGLEBY

JONATHAN W. TANNER

THE UNITED STATES has a wide array of interest groups, many of which seek to influence the outcome of congressional elections. Our representative democracy lends itself, by its very nature, to being influenced by factions of its citizens. Citizens form groups to influence government policies on ideological and economic issues about which they feel passionate. The need of candidates to fund their election campaigns provides groups with an opportunity to not only influence who holds office but to curry favor with them on policy issues as well. This mutual benefit provides the opportunity for quid pro quo corruption cited by the courts as a reason to uphold campaign finance legislation.[1] Early in our history, James Madison recognized the possibility that groups could exercise influence on the government that would be detrimental to the interests of society as a whole. The view that government should, to use Madison's words, "break and control the violence of factions" is long-standing, and laws regulating money in politics have existed for more than a century.[2]

Around the turn of the century, President Theodore Roosevelt saw a particular need to control political contributions from corporations and sought to limit the influence of corporate special interests on federal elections.[3] Congress subsequently passed the Tilman Act of 1907, which banned corporations from contributing their treasury funds to candidates running for federal office. Several decades later, union treasury funds were similarly banned in the Smith-Connally Act of 1943, which was later included in the Taft-Hartley Act of 1947.[4]

Interest Groups Today

Our current system of campaign laws has become vastly more complex, but it has these same concerns and principles at heart. The system contains regulations designed to remove politicians from the potentially corrupting influence of large donations and to shed light on the groups that give money through a system of disclosure of contributions and expenditures. As noted in chapter 1, by 2002 the Federal Election Campaign Act (FECA) was easily circumvented both as to contribution limits and disclosure.

The relative weakening of parties has created a vacuum, which interest groups have rushed to fill, causing increased complexity in the political landscape.[5] Unlike the largely bimodal party system, there are numerous interest groups, each with its own agenda. Some broadly defined types of interest groups include corporate, trade, labor, and ideological groups.[6] Each of these groups acts in a strategic context created by the interaction of the interest group's internal goals and resources with the broader legal and regulatory environment in which it operates.[7]

Interest Group Activity in 2002

Outside groups once again played a significant role in influencing competitive elections in 2002. In several of our sample races, we estimate that interest groups spent an equal or greater amount of money to help elect a candidate than did the candidates themselves. Although interest groups were still a major factor in many of our sample races, the amount of money they spent overall was probably down, relative to the last few election cycles. In this chapter we examine five types of interest group activities—disclosed and limited activities, soft-money contributions to parties, independent expenditures, internal communications, and issue advocacy—in the 2002 election.

PACs: Disclosed and Limited Activity

Until the mid-1990s, groups most commonly played the electoral game by making contributions to candidates. These came primarily from political action committees (PACs) associated with the group.[8] PACs can contribute up to $5,000 a year ($10,000 per election cycle) directly to candidates.[9] PACs may also make in-kind contributions, including sharing polling data, letting campaigns use their phone bank facilities, and providing paid staff to campaigns. While these in-kind contributions are disclosed, the impact they have on elections is probably underestimated. Friendly interest groups may give services and data to candidates at well below the fair market value.[10]

PAC money in congressional elections tends to go much more to incumbents. In 2002, 76 percent of PAC contributions went to incumbents.[11] This is largely because many PACs have a strategy oriented toward legislative access. These PACs give to members of Congress in order to strengthen their relationship with lawmakers and gain votes on legislation they support.[12]

In one of our control races, Republican Mike Taylor tried to make a competitive bid for the Montana Senate seat by raising a total of $1.8 million, much of which was his own money. This figure was dwarfed, however, by the $5.9 million raised by incumbent Max Baucus. Most of the difference can be explained by PAC contributions. Baucus raised $2.6 million from PACs, while Taylor managed to raise only $77,000.[13] In another of our 2002 control races, for the Senate seat from Michigan, incumbent Carl Levin raised over $800,000 from PACs, while challenger Andrew Raczkowski raised nothing.[14]

Members of Congress have found another way to exploit the tendency of interest groups to give to incumbents by creating committees affiliated with themselves, called leadership PACs, to both receive and expend funds. In 2002 nearly 80 percent of leadership PAC money came from other PACs.[15] Contributions to these leadership PACs has grown tenfold in the past decade, totaling $2.8 million in 1992 and $33.7 million in 2002. These PACs historically favor Republicans, as evidenced again in 2002, when 57 percent of their contributions went to support Republican candidates.[16] Contributions from members of Congress to parties are a significant source of party committee hard money. One study shows that members of Congress contributed 15 percent of the Democratic Congressional Campaign Committee's (DCCC's) and the National Republican Congressional Committee's (NRCC's) hard money through their PAC and principal campaign committees.[17]

While many groups give only to gain favor with incumbent members of Congress, there are also groups that pursue an ideological strategy, similar to that of parties. These groups attempt to influence policy through elections and are therefore likely to support challengers as well as incumbents who are proponents of issues that are important to the group.[18]

One way that groups maximize their importance to candidates is by bundling contributions from many individuals. Members write checks to a candidate that the interest group has endorsed, and the group gives these checks to the candidate all at once.[19] Interest groups that bundle individual contributions are able to circumvent the contribution limits on PACs and thereby increase their influence on the election outcome.[20] Ideological groups with large membership bases tend to find bundling effective. Members of such groups want to elect candidates that support their issues, even if it involves contributing outside of their district. The League of Conservation Voters (LCV), EMILY's List, and the Club for Growth all used extensive bundling efforts in our sample races. Sheila O'Connell, political director for EMILY's List, said, "Nobody's better than us at getting the money [to the candidates]. It is a morale booster for the candidate that women all over the country support her candidacy."[21]

Interest-Group Soft-Money Contributions to Parties

Interest groups also seek to influence elections indirectly through their contributions to political parties. They do this by not only giving the maximum legal PAC contribution of $15,000 per cycle but also by giving soft money to the parties. As noted in chapter 2, soft-money contributions are unlimited. Giving soft money to the parties has an additional advantage for corporations and unions; they can give money to parties from their treasury funds, a practice that has otherwise long been prohibited.[22]

In 2002 fifty-six groups each gave more than $1 million in soft money to national parties.[23] This list of large soft-money donors includes corporations, unions, and trade associations. These large donations go to both parties, but a majority of the groups who give over $1 million give more to Democrats than to Republicans. The top donor, a private venture capital firm called Saban Capital, gave over $12 million to Democrats. Clearly the law to prevent large donations from corporation and union treasuries is no longer effective. While it is true that these donations go to national parties, the parties can easily target these unlimited donations on a few competitive races, often by transferring the money to state parties.

Independent Expenditures

Interest groups and individuals can also make unlimited independent expenditures. In *Buckley* v. *Valeo,* the Court affirmed the First Amend-

Table 3-1. *Independent Expenditures for and against Candidates, 2002*[a]
Dollars

Group	For	Against	Total
LCV Action Fund and LCV	1,645,211	739,767	2,384,978
NARAL PAC and NARAL Pro-Choice America	. . .	2,368,617	2,368,617
American Medical Association PAC	. . .	1,957,100	1,957,100
National Right to Life PAC	46,474	1,800,135	1,846,609
Service Employees International Union PAC	. . .	1,811,242	1,811,242
NRCC Expenditures	. . .	1,604,417	1,604,417
NEA Fund for Children and Public Education	. . .	1,558,357	1,558,357
NRA Political Victory Fund	14,824	1,292,058	1,306,882
DCCC Expenditures	. . .	1,187,645	1,187,645
National Association of Realtors PAC	. . .	1,023,783	1,023,783
Republican National Committee	. . .	500,000	500,000
Democratic Party of Oklahoma	. . .	289,283	289,283
Sierra Club Political Committee	133,215	133,196	266,411
Associated Builders and Contractors PAC (ABC/PAC)	12,844	158,656	171,500
National Committee to Preserve Social Security and Medicare PAC	. . .	163,052	163,052
American Society of Anesthesiologists PAC	129,191	. . .	129,191
Other	220,536	1,511,854	1,732,390
Total	2,202,295	18,099,162	20,301,457

Source: Federal Election Commission (ftp://ftp.fec.gov/FEC/ [July 14, 2003]).

a. We combined expenditures for all national affiliates of an organization but excluded expenditures for the state affiliates.

ment right of groups to expressly advocate the election or defeat a federal candidate, so long as they do not coordinate their efforts with the candidate's campaign. However, the Court also affirmed the right of the government to require disclosure of the entity making the expenditure and the amount expended. Some groups continue to make independent expenditures rather than conduct issue advocacy, even though they could avoid the required disclosure of independent expenditures. Examples of groups who continue to use independent expenditures include the National Right to Life, National Rifle Association (NRA), National Education Association (NEA), American Medical Association (AMA), and the LCV. Table 3-1 provides a summary of the independent expenditure activity by interest groups in the 2002 election cycle.

The LCV, through two entities, made the most independent expenditures in 2002. National Right to Life and NARAL Pro-Choice America also made independent expenditures in excess of $2 million in 2002. Overall, more than $20 million in independent expenditure activity was reported in 2002, down slightly from the $22 million spent in 2000, but well above the $13 million spent in 1998, the last midterm.[24] As in the past, these expenditures favored Democrats by more than two to one in our sample races. Independent expenditures are the communications process of choice for relatively few groups. Most of the top groups doing independent expenditures have pursued this same strategy in previous cycles. However, the Service Employees International Union, which had not made independent expenditures previously, spent $1.8 million independently in 2002.

One reason why groups choose not to mask their identity and campaign through independent expenditures is because they want to appeal to their membership and increase their branding more broadly. These groups want the attention they get from their electioneering activities. However, disclosure requirements may also limit the races in which groups who use independent expenditures can be effective. The NEA does polling early on in areas that they may potentially target during the election. They use the results of these surveys to determine if they are a "good messenger." The NEA will run independent expenditure ads only if their name is viewed positively within the district they are targeting.[25]

Groups that are more sensitive about publicity from electioneering activities often use issue advocacy to avoid the public disclosure requirements of independent expenditures. Unions and corporations also use issue advocacy because it allows them to expend general treasury funds, something they could not do via independent expenditures.

Occasionally independent expenditure groups come to own an issue. For example, in the Arkansas Senate race Republicans counted on the NRA and not the party to do the heavy lifting on the guns issue.[26] One voter-activation tool used by the NRA is an orange postcard reminding people to vote and of the NRA endorsement of a particular candidate. In 2002 several other party and interest groups sent out NRA look-alike postcards, making it appear that candidates had the NRA endorsement when they did not.

Internal Communications

Another way interest groups can attempt to influence the outcome of an election is through internal communications. Both FECA and the Bipartisan Campaign Reform Act (BCRA) permit groups like unions and corporations to communicate express advocacy messages without limita-

Table 3-2. *Internal Communications for and against Candidates, 2002*[a]
Dollars

Group	For	Against	Total
AFL-CIO COPE Political Contributions			
Committee	4,457,816	. . .	4,457,816
National Education Association	3,034,187	. . .	3,034,187
National Association of Realtors	794,896	. . .	794,896
American Federation of Teachers	435,653	. . .	435,653
NFIB Save America's Free Enterprise Trust	336,180	. . .	336,180
American Medical Association	310,244	. . .	310,244
National Rifle Association (Institute for			
Legislative Action)	222,475	2,078	224,553
Other	955,088	116,542	1,071,630
Total	10,546,539	118,620	10,665,159

Source: See table 3-1.

a. We combined expenditures for all national affiliates of an organization but excluded expenditures for the state affiliates.

tion, if the communication is directed only to group members, or so long as it remains an internal communication. As noted in chapter 1, a communication is reported to the Federal Election Commission (FEC) when it meets three requirements: Its primary purpose is to influence the election, it includes express advocacy, and expenditures exceed $2,000 per election cycle.[27] Because of the strict definition of an internal communication, many of these activities go unreported.

Some groups, such as labor unions, corporations, and associations, make extensive use of internal communications, and spending on internal communications has risen over time. In 1978 groups reported spending only $318,000 (or $912,000 in 2002 dollars) on internal communications.[28] In 2002 that figure had risen to $10.7 million. Table 3-2 lists the top groups reporting internal communications in 2002.

The two groups reporting the most expensive internal communications campaigns by far are the AFL-CIO at $4.5 million and the NEA at $3.0 million. These data almost certainly exclude many communications that do not meet the disclosure test described above. The NRA, for example, conducts a large-scale communications effort with its members by inserting customized pages in the magazines sent to its members, but since the election information is only a small proportion of the magazine, the NRA does not need to report it. This is also probably true of other groups who use internal communications, including business groups.

There are several reasons why internal communications are likely to become even more important in the future. First, they are well suited to the Internet and e-mail, which are inexpensive and can be carefully targeted. Second, the message comes from a trusted source. Finally, by constraining groups' soft-money and issue advocacy activity, BCRA will likely lead to more internal communication activity. Personal contact from someone the voter already knows is the most effective way of communicating. The Business Industry Political Action Committee's 2002 Prosperity Project tried to help businesses use internal communications advantageously. Bernadette Budde of BIPAC said that the most effective businesses recognize "that they can only talk to their affinity group."[29]

As we discuss more fully in chapter 4, communications from work associates or employers can be highly effective. Labor unions have discovered that shop stewards who work side by side with members daily have a relationship of trust with associates that is important in conveying information about elections. Employers have a different relationship with workers, but when a business communicates with its employees about why a particular candidate is better for that company, business leaders believe that that communication can be effective as well. BIPAC and others have also created websites that make it easy for companies to create candidate scorecards, absentee ballot request forms, and other election-related items. In 2002 BIPAC contacted over 11 million voters through its Prosperity Project and was responsible for 350,000 voter registrations and absentee ballots requests. The total cost of the program was only $600,000, or about five cents per voter contact.

Election Issue Advocacy

The array of ways that interest groups can seek to influence federal elections grew dramatically in the 1996 election, through what is called election issue advocacy. The AFL-CIO ran substantial candidate-specific advertisements, asserting that they fell outside FECA limitations because they avoided the express advocacy language provided in the *Buckley v. Valeo* decision.[30] The AFL-CIO expended roughly $35 million in an unsuccessful effort to help Democrats regain control of Congress.[31] Not surprisingly, business and other groups copied the AFL-CIO tactic, doing their own issue ads. The FEC failed to intervene and stop the process, and the era of large-scale issue advocacy in federal elections began.

Our past research has demonstrated that groups can effectively deliver an election message through election issue advocacy.[32] An indication of the confidence that groups and individuals place in the effectiveness of election issue advocacy is the large investment they make in it.

Issue advocacy has important advantages for interest groups and individuals. First, unlike independent expenditures, election issue advocacy allows them to avoid disclosure. FECA was interpreted by the courts to apply only to communications that use the "magic words" of express advocacy. Communications by groups or individuals that do not meet this strict definition of electioneering fall outside FECA disclosure requirements. Of the radio ads we monitored in 2002, only 19 percent contained the magic words. One group that was active early in 2002, the Club for Growth, explained that they sometimes serve as a conduit for a donor wishing to influence a particular election. Steve Moore, the Club for Growth president, said, "We'll get a call from somebody saying, 'I want to do issue ads in this particular district.' And I'll say, 'Look, you got the money, we'll run the ads.' "[33]

Second, groups can further mask their identity by communicating through a group with an innocuous name. Groups like the Council for Better Government, Americans for Job Security, and the United Seniors Association have been active in recent elections. As Mike Lux, who has advised liberal groups, stated regarding 2002, "What the Republicans have figured out is that they can set up front groups with good-sounding names that relate to a particular swing constituency and then get their allies in industry to move massive dollars into those front groups to do ads. That is a great strategy for mushing the issues."[34] Democratic allies also use benign names, such as Campaign for America's Future and People for the American Way.

Political science research has demonstrated that voters assess not only the content of political communications but also the source.[35] Issue advocacy permits groups to campaign behind an innocuous name like the United Seniors Association. The pharmaceutical companies spent millions of dollars through the United Seniors Association. Our survey data demonstrate that voters respond differently to the words *pharmaceutical or drug companies* than to *United Seniors Association*. Fifty-eight percent of respondents across the nation had an unfavorable view of pharmaceutical or drug companies, while only 5 percent had a negative impression of the United Seniors Association.[36]

Third, interest groups and individuals are limited in how much money they can contribute to candidates and party committees in hard money but can spend unlimited amounts of money on election issue advocacy and in soft-money contributions to political parties. In North Carolina's Eighth Congressional District, interest-group spending on broadcast advertising was more than the combined candidate spending. The United Seniors Association alone spent more than double the amount spent by Democrat Chris Kouri's campaign.[37] Spending by these groups can be consequential. Andy Grossman of the Democratic Senatorial Campaign Committee (DSCC) stated, "What caused us great harm, all our campaigns great harm, were the conservative issue advocacy groups coming in with fairly heavy [ad] buys over the last couple of weeks, with us not really having an organized presence to do the same."[38]

Fourth, election issue advocacy is not subject to the source limitations applicable to hard-money contributions to candidates or parties. Federal law has long banned corporations and labor unions from spending treasury funds on campaign communications other than communications to their stockholders, employees, or membership. Yet corporations and unions are free to spend their treasury funds on election issue advocacy.

In several respects, issue advocacy resembles soft money. They both constitute what we have previously called outside money because they constitute a means for large amounts of money to be spent on a race by groups outside the formal campaign, without the same spending and disclosure requirements that candidates have.[39] Interest groups, like parties, target their issue advocacy campaigns. This results in large-scale group expenditures in a few selected contests, as our sample races in Connecticut, North Carolina, and Pennsylvania illustrate. In contrast, in noncompetitive races issue advocacy is typically nonexistent, as was the case in our control races.

Interest-group leaders made clear to us in our interviews with them the criteria on which they allocate money. They target issue advocacy dollars in races that are competitive and in ways that advance their larger legislative agenda. This kind of overall strategic thinking is similar to the way national parties view elections. Scott Stoermer of LCV confessed that the "dirty dozen" were targeted for their vulnerability: "[They are] not the twelve worst environmental candidates running in a particular cycle, because that gives us a whole bunch of people who[m] we would just be wasting our money trying to defeat, but the twelve most vulnerable . . . anti-environmental candidates running."[40]

Issue Advocacy in 2002

Most groups involved in issue advocacy in 1998 and 2000 were also active in 2002. In 2002 we observed an average of 10.1 distinct interest groups active in each of our twenty-five competitive races. In 2000 the average number of groups active in a race was 17.1; in 1998 it was 6.9.[41] Several new groups conducted issue advocacy for the first time in 2001–02. Examples of such groups are the Alliance for Retired Americans, the United Seniors Association, Main Street USA, and the Council for Better Government. Among the groups that informed us they expended fewer resources in issue advocacy in 2002 than in 2000 were Citizens for Better Medicare, the Sierra Club, NARAL Pro-Choice America, and the National Association for the Advancement of Colored People (NAACP) Voter Fund. Other groups, like the League of Conservation Voters, the Human Rights Campaign, and the Association of Trial Lawyers of America, reported doing about the same amount of issue advocacy in 2002 as in 2000. Finally, some groups, like the Club for Growth and the National Federation for Independent Business (NFIB), were more active in 2002. Again in 2002 there was a paucity of genuine issue advocacy during the general election period. By genuine issue advocacy we mean advertisements that did not mention a candidate's name, show the image or likeness of a candidate, or mention the pending election.

Interest-group issue advocacy spending has now become a staple of competitive elections. Candidates have come to expect help from these outside groups; they factor it into their campaign plans and are actually surprised if it fails to come. In the highly competitive Minnesota Second Congressional District, both sides expressed dismay that the much-anticipated interest-group money that was supposed to flow into the race never appeared.[42] In the 2002 Montana Senate race, only seven groups were active, compared to thirty-four in 2000. Republican candidate Mike Taylor expressed frustration at the lack of outside help from parties and interest groups in the face of attacks by the DSCC and others.[43] While candidates often rely on outside groups to help them stay competitive in expensive races, the help is not always welcome. Even groups who support a candidate often hijack the candidate's agenda. They raise issues in an untimely manner or attack the candidate's opponent in a way that the candidate does not wish to do. This can subject the candidate to negative backlash from the constituents, who end up blaming the candidate for all election-related communications. The unpredictable nature of outside help causes some candidates to try to refuse all outside help. In the Iowa Second Congressional District, Republican candidate Jim Leach asked all Republican-allied groups to stop running ads because they were misleading.[44]

Issue ads have become an important way to counter an opposing party's or candidate's major themes. Going into 2002, for example, Republicans and their interest-group allies were concerned about prescription drug benefits for seniors. Both the Republican Party and groups like the United Seniors Association took the offensive, praising those who voted for the plan passed by the House and criticizing the Senate for its failure to act. A conservative group, the Seniors Coalition, mailed a flyer to New Mexico's First Congressional District, which read, "While the liberals were talking, Congresswoman Heather Wilson was helping to pass the first comprehensive Medicare prescription drug benefit."[45]

More generally, issue ads oppose a candidate more often than they support one, or they may criticize one candidate while praising the other. Interest groups like the League of Conservation Voters, with their well-known environmental "dirty dozen," consciously seek to put candidates on the defensive and define them in negative terms. Groups use negative and contrast ads in part because of the widespread belief that "negative ads work."[46] In Connecticut's Fifth Congressional District, negative ads backfired when Republican Nancy Johnson used the AFL-CIO's negative attack against her to brand her Democratic opponent, Jim Maloney, as a negative campaigner, a brand that stuck to him for the rest of the race.[47]

At other times, candidates feel they benefit from a group's endorsement. The NRA endorsement has become increasingly valued. The NRA gives a letter grade to every candidate, based on the candidate's past voting record or, in the case of a candidate with no voting record, a survey of the candidate's views on gun-related issues. They then support candidates with "good" grades and oppose those who are "bad" on their issues.[48] Finally, for some interest groups, setting the electoral agenda is their primary concern, with electing or defeating a particular candidate a secondary concern. Groups favoring term limits have been active in past cycles. We found little of this type of activity in 2002.

Issue Advocacy Strategy

Interest groups pursue a range of strategies in communicating with voters. The choice of strategies varies by type of group, the resources they have available to them, whether or not the group has a large, easy-to-mobilize membership, the desire of the group to promote itself or mask its identity, and whether the group wants to influence the entire race or emphasize the final days of the campaign. What has been consistently true in all of our studies is that interest groups only mount issue advocacy campaigns in targeted competitive races. Not all groups target the same competitive races, but significant levels of issue advocacy spending rarely occur in noncompetitive races. This is a strong indicator that issue advocacy is about electing or defeating specific candidates and not about issues.

As documented more fully in chapter 4, much of the campaign in 2002 was waged through the mail, telephone, Internet, and personal contacts. Groups and parties invested a higher share of their resources in these ground-war activities. But issue advocacy broadcast advertising by interest groups remained an important part of the 2002 campaign in several races. The United Seniors Association was clearly the leader in issue advocacy in 2002, spending an estimated $4.5 million in ads in the races we examined. Other groups who also spent significant amounts of money on issue ads include the AFL-CIO, Americans for Job Security, and the Reform Voter Project. (See table 3-3.)

In 2002, as in previous years, the air war was so intense that groups could not buy time in the closing days of the campaign. Some groups, like the AFL-CIO, chose to air television advertisements early. Denise Mitchell of the AFL-CIO said the organization "historically doesn't run ads past Labor Day." It runs ads early to shape the debate and then concentrates on ground efforts with union members later in the cycle. Mitchell took exception to the claim that labor altered its strategy in 2002 and unexpectedly went off the air.[49] If the provision of BCRA that bans political advertising sixty days before an election survives the court challenge, then the AFL-CIO has proved ex ante, by self-imposed restrictions, that they can be effective in influencing a campaign without running ads during the forbidden window. Other groups may follow this same strategy of defining themselves and their candidates early on the air and then following up with mail and phone during the last sixty days. Issue advocacy in 2002 was marked by some early activity by other groups as well. For example EMILY's List and the Club for Growth both targeted candidates in primary elections.

However, as we have demonstrated in previous studies, most issue advocacy occurs in the final three weeks of a campaign, rising to a crescendo in the days before the election. In 2002, 60 percent of interest group electioneering activity came in the last two weeks, slightly more than the 58 percent we observed in 2000.[50] Consultants and interest-

Table 3-3. *The Air War: Television and Radio Advertising Expenditures, Sample Races, 2002*[a]

Dollars

Type and organization	TV	Radio	Total spent	CMAG TV
	Democratic allies[b]			
Candidates				
Democratic Senatorial candidates	20,110,467	1,132,437	21,242,904	14,061,651
Democratic Congressional candidates	14,097,209	537,596	14,634,805	13,258,784
Political parties				
State Democratic parties	24,724,370	780,190	25,504,560	21,583,344
Democratic Congressional Campaign Committee	1,537,320	. . .	1,537,320	1,468,906
Democratic Senatorial Campaign Committee	500,000	520,550	1,020,550	. . .
Local Democratic parties	173,790	508	174,298	. . .
Interest groups				
AFL–CIO	2,131,998	. . .	2,131,998	1,882,072
League of Conservation Voters	770,911	. . .	770,911	271,781
Reform Voter Project	740,795	9,030	749,825	279,975
National Education Assn.	472,517	3,850	476,367	254,336
Sierra Club	333,687	47,700	381,387	444,901
Service Employees International Union	283,429	42,330	325,759	. . .
Campaign for America's Future	258,699	. . .	258,699	66,283
NARAL Pro-Choice America	154,800	. . .	154,800	79,370
America's Future Workers	117,900	. . .	117,900	. . .
Save Our Environment	56,625	. . .	56,625	. . .
People for the American Way	50,800	. . .	50,800	19,904
Law Enforcement Alliance of America	45,225	. . .	45,225	. . .
National Committee to Preserve Social Security and Medicare	. . .	23,288	23,288	. . .
Natural Resources Defense Council	18,700	3,900	22,600	. . .
United Food and Commercial Workers Union	. . .	19,627	19,627	. . .
Planned Parenthood	3,468	. . .	3,468	. . .
Coalition for Affordable Healthcare	. . .	2,250	2,250	. . .
NAACP	. . .	1,628	1,628	. . .
	Republican allies[b]			
Candidates				
Republican Senatorial candidates	14,165,738	1,853,018	16,018,756	9,478,471
Republican Congressional candidates	13,732,848	576,435	14,309,283	12,406,587
Political parties				
State Republican parties	25,484,449	1,403,443	26,887,892	14,334,638

continued on next page

Table 3-3. *The Air War: Television and Radio Advertising Expenditures, Sample Races, 2002*[a] *(continued)*
Dollars

Type and organization	TV	Radio	Total spent	CMAG TV
National Republican Congressional Committee	3,228,523	4,055	3,232,578	6,096,920
National Republican Senatorial Committee	425,500	200,000	625,500	6,649,060
Republican National Committee	447,610	54,522	502,132	792,244
Interest groups				
United Seniors Association	4,508,644	. . .	4,508,644	3,042,950
Americans for Job Security	776,443	42,645	819,088	835,575
Club for Growth	270,558	11,000	281,558	130,554
U.S. Chamber of Commerce	185,000	36,960	221,960	. . .
American Medical Association	169,466	30,565	200,031	175,020
COMPASS	192,074	. . .	192,074	. . .
Council for Better Government	74,920	105,760	180,680	. . .
Republican Leadership Council	148,078	17,999	166,077	. . .
60 Plus Association	. . .	148,197	148,197	. . .
Business Roundtable	141,419	. . .	141,419	56,693
Alliance for Quality Nursing Home Care	96,247	. . .	96,247	. . .
American Society of Anesthesiologists	27,400	22,500	49,900	. . .
National Right to Life	10,000	35,885	45,885	. . .
Seniors Coalition	41,320	. . .	41,320	. . .
Senate Majority Fund	33,974	. . .	33,974	. . .
National Association of Homebuilders	31,588	. . .	31,588	17,383
National Coalition of Ergonomics	. . .	22,350	22,350	. . .
GOPAC	12,800	9,300	22,100	. . .
National Rifle Association	. . .	18,000	18,000	. . .
Associated Builders and Contractors	. . .	. . .	. . .	75,284
Nonpartisan				
Interest group				
AARP	43,200	33,750	76,950	. . .

Source: Data compiled from David B. Magleby, J. Quin Monson, and the Center for the Study of Elections and Democracy, 2002 Soft Money and Issue Advocacy Database (Brigham Young University, 2002); and Campaign Media Analysis Group data.

a. See appendix A for a more detailed data explanation. The ad-buy data collected for this study may contain extraneous data because of the difficulty of determining the content of the ads. The parties or interest groups that purchased the ad buys possibly ran some ads promoting House or Senate candidates or ballot propositions not in the study's sample but still within that media market. Unless the researchers were able to determine the exact content of the ad buy from the limited information given by the station, the data may contain observations that do not pertain to the study's relevant House or Senate races.

For comparison purpose, the CMAG data are included in the table. Because of the number of television and radio stations and varying degrees of compliance in providing ad-buy information, data on spending by various groups might be incomplete. This table is not intended to represent comprehensive organization spending or activity within the sample races. A more complete picture can be obtained by examining this table with table 4-2.

In blank cells, ". . ." reflects absence of collected data and does not imply the organization was inactive in that medium.

b. Certain organizations that maintained neutrality were categorized according to which candidates their ads supported or backed or whether the organization was openly anti- or pro-conservative or liberal.

group professionals indicate that this is because they assume the end of the race to be the most important time to persuade voters.

In 2002 both sides, including candidates, parties, and interest groups, challenged the veracity of their opponent's ads. When they were successful in getting an ad pulled, they attacked the truthfulness of the opposing candidate's campaign, even if the ad came from an interest group.

To protect themselves, groups with solid images and bipartisan memberships are often cautious about how and how much they participate in political activities. Bill Miller, political director of the U.S. Chamber of Commerce, said, "We can't afford to put all our eggs into one particular partisan basket."[51] To protect their bipartisan appeal, they often use alternative forms of communication, such as voter guides, where they can communicate more specifically on the issues. In 2002 the AARP straddled the line between election and genuine issue advocacy. Their ads were clearly about the election and raised issues such as prescription drugs and Social Security but did not mention candidates by name or show their image or likeness—they simply asked voters to "know where the candidates stand and vote." Still, most interest groups and individuals who funded issue advocacy in 2002 expended money in ways that most voters would have seen as communicating about candidates in specific electoral contests.[52]

A Study in Contrasts: What Control Races Teach Us about Issue Advocacy

Election issue advocacy takes place almost exclusively in competitive races. Issue advocacy is expensive and requires a major investment by the interest group, particularly if they want to do broadcast ads. We tested our hypothesis that groups would involve themselves only in competitive settings by studying a number of noncompetitive 2002 races that were competitive in 2000. In 2000, California's Twenty-Seventh Congressional District was home to the most expensive House race ever, with a total price tag of $18.5 million.[53] In 2000, outside groups spent over $2 million on mail and ads and contributed another $1.8 million in PAC contributions to the candidates. In contrast, the same district (the California Twenty-Ninth Congressional District after redistricting) experienced almost no outside involvement in 2002. No one ran broadcast issue ads, but there were a few get-out-the-vote calls from union members on election day, and a couple of groups passed out voter guides. Adam Schiff received slightly over $400,000 in PAC contributions, much less than the $750,000 he received in 2000.[54] The Michigan Senate race tells a similar story, with groups spending over $6 million on broadcast advertising, whereas in 2002 only one group was active, spending slightly more than $268,000 on television ads.[55] We also observed similar discrepancies in the mail. In Pennsylvania's Fourth Congressional District in 2000 we collected seventeen discrete mailings from nine discrete groups; in 2002 there were none.[56]

Falling between the Cracks: 527 and 501(c) Organizations

Interest groups are also subject to more or less regulation, depending on how they choose to organize themselves. Groups that wish to give directly to campaigns form PACs. The FEC strictly limits PAC receipts and expenditures and requires full disclosure. Groups that wish to influence elections indirectly often create entities under the Internal Revenue Service tax code for nonprofit organizations, Sections 527 and 501(c). Until July 2000 interest groups that engaged only in issue advocacy and did not invest their money in interest-bearing accounts were not required to make detailed reports to the IRS. These groups are commonly referred to as 527s. An example of such a group is Republicans for Clean Air, which ran ads attacking Senator John McCain's environmental record in the New York, California, and Ohio 2000 presidential primaries.

In part because of the controversy surrounding Republicans for Clean Air ads in 2000, Congress passed legislation in July 2000 to compel any group organized under Section 527 to register with the IRS within twenty-four hours of its inception and to report monthly spending of amounts over $500 and receipts over $200 if the group plans to spend more than $25,000 to affect the election of any candidate. During the 2002 election cycle and continuing into 2003, the disclosure mechanism at the IRS made these groups difficult to track systematically. The IRS database was not searchable; to get any useful aggregate information about who gave to a certain candidate or party required opening the files for more than 14,800 groups.[57] Congress addressed this problem with legislation mandating that the IRS revamp its system by the end of June 2003.[58] This should result in a more complete and accessible database for most of the 2003–04 election cycle.

Some interest groups also conduct electioneering through entities organized under section 501(c)(4) of the U.S. tax code. The primary purpose of 501(c)(4) groups is "the promotion of social welfare"; they have some limited ability to participate in activities to influence elections, as long as it is not their primary purpose.[59] Because they are not primarily involved in election-related activities, 501(c)(4) groups file only an annual report (Form 990) with the IRS. The form does not require disclosure of the source of the group's receipts, nor the specific details of their expenditures, and is therefore insufficient to provide any meaningful disclosure of election activities.

Some 501(c)(4) organizations have become increasingly aggressive in pursuit of electioneering activities. Although this class of organization includes groups that do not participate in elections, no system of regulation exists to prevent these groups from engaging in extensive amounts of issue advocacy. For example, the United Seniors Association, which spent the most of any outside group in our sample races, perhaps as much as $13 million nationwide, is organized under section 501(c)(4).[60]

The tax code that governs these groups is complex but sufficiently malleable to allow them to remain obscure and avoid most forms of disclosure by using different branches for various activities.[61] Many groups, such as the United Seniors Association, have both PACs and nonprofit 501(c) or 527 branches associated with the same parent organization. Additional groups may consider subdividing if the money to fund issue advocacy activities is available. In the past, donors gave money to the parties because they knew what the party stood for. If the ban on party soft money stands, money that used to go to parties may flow to groups with a good track record and respected name. The National Education Association currently relies solely on hard-money contributions to fund its election activities, but NEA political affairs specialist Jack Polidori responded to a question about a hypothetical $10 million donation by saying, "Now if somebody posed that question and asked us if we wanted to form a 501(c)(4) or 527 organization or something of that ilk, folks would have to take a look at it. That's serious money."[62]

Nonprofit groups can organize quickly and can often blindside candidate campaigns. Because many of them are new each election cycle and the disclosure mechanisms at the IRS are not transparent, these groups often go unnoticed until they start spending large amounts of money. In the Arkansas Senate race, Mark Pryor's biggest ally was the Reform Voter Project (RVP), a Boston-based 527 organization, which spent nearly $700,000 in support of Pryor. A Pryor strategist said he had never even heard of the RVP until they started running ads in mid-July. The RVP focused their efforts on just a few races to make sure they would "make a difference."[63]

If BCRA's ban on party soft money holds, the party committees may also try to exploit the 527 and 501(c) regulations by setting up quasi-party groups that will continue raising and spending unlimited sums of money. In general, parties did not experiment with setting up quasi-party interest groups during the 2002 cycle because there was too much at stake in the election. They concentrated all their effort on winning under the rules as they were in 2002 and let the future take care of itself. When asked point-blank if the parties had experimented with setting up shadow interest groups, Gail Stoltz, political director for the Democratic National Committee, said, "No. There was too much pressure to win this time, and rightly so."[64] However, parties did leave the door open by creating such entities as the Democratic State Parties Organization (DSPO), a group whose origins come from the Association of State Democratic Chairs and the DNC.[65] Another group with intentional connections to a national party committee is the National Committee for a Responsible Senate (NCRS), a name strikingly similar to the National Republican Senatorial Committee (NRSC).[66]

Decreased Issue Advocacy Spending in 2002

Overall in 2002 interest-group activity was somewhat less than it has been in recent election cycles. PAC contributions were up $10 million over 2000—$282 million in 2002, compared to $271.4 million in 2000.[67] However, we observe less issue advocacy by interest groups this cycle. In 2000 the pharmaceutical companies spent an estimated $65 million through a group called Citizens for Better Medicare (CBM).[68] In 2002 the pharmaceutical companies funded the United Seniors Association, which spent between $9 million and $13 million.[69] Newspapers also reported that the Chamber of Commerce planned on investing up to $30 million to influence races across the country; they ended up doing less in several races because of their "inability to meet fund-raising expectations."[70] Progressive interest groups also had less money available in 2002.

Our interviews with interest-group leaders and campaign professionals pointed to several reasons for this. First, the state of the economy meant that resources available to groups and individuals had declined.

The drop in the stock market meant that some individuals could not contribute to groups for issue advocacy as they had previously. For example, in 2000 Jane Fonda contributed $11.7 million to a 527 organization, which then turned her money around and funneled issue advocacy through several progressive groups. The largest beneficiary of Fonda's donation was Planned Parenthood. They received a contribution of $6.3 million from Fonda's fund in 2000, but in 2002 Fonda did not contribute.[71] Planned Parenthood cited the absence of key large donors as one of the reasons they could not participate in 2002 the same way they had in 2000. In 2002 Planned Parenthood raised only about $2 million, compared to over $10 million in 2000. [72]

Another reason issue advocacy declined in total volume in 2002 is that more of the outside money went to parties than in any previous midterm election. Both parties and interest groups compete for resources from the same sources. Parties may have secured some of the money that in the past went to interest groups. One of the reasons for this was that 2002 may have been the last time parties could expend soft money. The parties clearly exploited the pending elimination of soft money in their 2001–02 fund-raising. They also used compelling messengers such as President Bush, who sponsored an unprecedented number of fund-raising events. With the increased competition for funds, issue advocacy came up short.

Interest groups have also shifted their strategy from one that was heavily broadcast-centered in 1996 to one that increasingly invests in nonbroadcast communication strategies. These include mail, phone, personal contact, and Internet communications, as we have discussed in this chapter and as demonstrated in the case studies in this book. Many of these tactics are also less expensive than broadcast advertising and can be targeted to improve effectiveness.

Impact on Candidates, Voters, and Democracy

The political world is more complex for candidates now than it was when issue groups were less involved. Some even feel the trend is moving to the point that issue groups will establish themselves as the primary contact with voters.[73] Candidates can no longer focus solely on their own agenda or campaign plan; instead they must inoculate themselves on multiple issues to gain the vote of constituents who belong to special-interest groups. Candidates in some of our 2002 sample races took steps to avoid attacks from groups with the potential to spend millions of dollars against them. Jim Matheson, a Democrat, won election to Utah's Second Congressional District seat in 2000 in the face of a $1 million campaign by several conservative groups, including the NRA and the Chamber of Commerce.[74] Although Matheson is a Democrat, in his first term in office he cosponsored a bill on gun rights supported by the NRA and voted for many pro-business measures. In 2002 neither the NRA nor the Chamber spent any money against Matheson in his bid for reelection. In fact the Chamber actually endorsed him. In our interviews with these groups, both indicated that Matheson's voting record kept them from supporting his opponent.[75]

Interest group activity in independent expenditures and issue advocacy could expand should the Supreme Court uphold BCRA's ban on party soft money. Some academics suggest that political money may resemble a hydraulic system, in that money, like water, can be diverted but will never disappear.[76] Political elites that we interviewed differ in the extent to which they believe this theory, but none of them believe that the inclination of large soft-money donors evident in recent election cycles will disappear completely under any of the conceivable systems created by BCRA.

A forthcoming book from the Campaign Finance Institute suggests a dichotomy of responses to the new legislation by categorizing each type of interest group by its commitment to influencing elections. Under the old system, some groups had money pulled from them into the political arena, while other groups had an agenda served by pushing money into the system.[77] Groups that had money pulled from them include some corporate interests that bowed to pressure from politicians to contribute in order to maintain influence in Washington. BCRA may be effective in reducing the amount of money that was pulled into the system by banning candidates and officeholders from soliciting soft money.[78] In contrast, groups that are primarily ideological try to push money into elections.[79] As we have shown, these groups have multiple ways of influencing elections under the current system. Many of these channels will remain open to interest groups after BCRA takes effect, and soft money that used to flow to parties may be channeled to interest groups.

We explore the impact of issue advocacy and more broadly outside money in our concluding chapter. In brief, one of the consequences of the surge in issue advocacy is that candidate campaign agendas are only partially determined by the candidates. Outside groups, through issue advocacy, now help define candidates and campaign agendas. They do so through their advertising and in ways for which the groups are often not held accountable. As we have demonstrated, another consequence of issue advocacy is greater negativity in campaigns. Finally, the uncertainty of needing to campaign against not only a well-funded opponent but allied party and interest groups has increased the cost of campaigns and fostered an "arms race" mentality in candidate and party finance.

Notes

1. "[T]he primary interest served by the limitations and, indeed, by the Act as a whole, is the prevention of corruption and the appearance of corruption spawned by the real or imagined coercive influence of large financial contributions on candidates' positions and on their actions if elected to office." *Buckley v. Valeo*, 424 U.S. 1 (1976), p. 26

2. James Madison, "The Federalist No. 10," in Garry Willis, ed., *The Federalist Papers* (Bantam Books, 1982), p. 42.

3. Federal Election Commission, "The FEC and Federal Campaign Finance Law," 1996 (www.fec.gov/pages/brochures/fecfeca.htm [April 15, 2003]).

4. For a more detailed history see Anthony Corrado, "A History of Federal Campaign Finance Law," in Anthony Corrado and others, eds., *Campaign Finance Reform: A Sourcebook* (Brookings, 1997).

5. Allan Cigler and Burdett Loomis, eds., *Interest Group Politics*, 6th ed. (Congressional Quarterly, 2002), p. 21.

6. Paul S. Herrnson and Clyde Wilcox, "Not So Risky Business: PAC Activity in 1992," in Robert Biersack, Paul S. Herrnson, and Clyde Wilcox, eds., *Risky Business?* (American Enterprise Institute, 1994), pp. 239–40.

7. Mark J. Rozell and Clyde Wilcox, *Interest Groups in American Campaigns* (Congressional Quarterly, 1999), p. 2.

8. In 2002 there were 4,594 political action committees registered with the Federal Election Commission. Of these, only 256 made contributions in excess of $500,000. FEC, "PAC Activity Increases for 2002 Elections," press release, March 27, 2003 (www.fec.gov/press/20030327pac/20030327pac.html [April 22, 2003]).

9. See table 1-3.

10. Allan J. Cigler, "Interest Groups and Financing the 2000 Elections," in David B. Magleby, ed., *Financing the 2000 Election* (Brookings, 2002), p. 171.

11. FEC, "PAC Activity Increases for 2002 Elections."

12. Paul S. Herrnson and Kelly D. Patterson, "Financing the 2000 Congressional Elections," in Magleby, *Financing the 2000 Election*, pp. 116–17.

13. David B. Magleby and J. Quin Monson, eds., *The Last Hurrah: Soft Money and Issue Advocacy in the 2002 Congressional Elections*, monograph

version (Center for the Study of Elections and Democracy, Brigham Young University, 2003), p. 344.

14. Ibid., p. 340.

15. Center for Responsive Politics, "Leadership PACs: Long-Term Contribution Trends" (www.opensecrets.org/industries/indus.asp?Ind=Q03 [April 16, 2003]).

16. Ibid.

17. Michael J. Malbin and Anne H. Bedlington, "Members of Congress as Contributors: When Every Race Counts," Campaign Finance Institute, May 16, 2003 (www.cfinst.org/studies/pdf/when_every_race_counts.pdf [May 16, 2003]).

18. Herrnson and Patterson, "Financing the 2000 Congressional Elections," pp. 116–17.

19. See Brooks Jackson, *Honest Graft: Big Money and the American Political Process* (Knopf, 1988), p. 131; and David B. Magleby and Candice J. Nelson, *The Money Chase: Congressional Campaign Finance Reform* (Brookings, 1990), p. 20.

20. Groups are also exempt from reporting bundling of donations of less than $200, so much of this activity goes unreported. EMILY's List encourages their members to send donations of at least $100 through them to the candidates they endorse. See Rozell and Wilcox, *Interest Groups in American Campaigns,* pp. 98–99.

21. Sheila O'Connell, political director, EMILY's List, interview by Quin Monson and Jonathan Tanner, Washington, D.C., December 11, 2002.

22. The Tilman Act of 1907 banned banks and corporations from making contributions to federal candidates from corporate accounts. In 1946 the Taft-Hartley Act made permanent the Smith-Connally Act of 1943, prohibiting unions from using treasury funds for political campaigns.

23. Center for Responsive Politics, "Soft Money to National Parties" (www.opensecrets.org/softmoney/softtop.asp?txtCycle=2002&txtSort=amnt [April 16, 2003]).

24. Federal Election Commission, "Disclosure Database," (ftp.fec.gov [September 26, 2001]). Adjusted for inflation. See also Cigler, "Interest Groups and Financing the 2000 Elections," p. 174.

25. Jack Polidori, political affairs specialist, National Education Association, interview by David Magleby and Jonathan Tanner, Washington, D.C., September 17, 2002.

26. Jay Barth and Janine Parry, "Provincialism, Personalism, and Politics," in Magleby and Monson, *The Last Hurrah,* monograph version, pp. 63–64.

27. Corrado and others, *Campaign Finance Reform,* p. 11.

28. David B. Magleby and Jason Beal, "Independent Expenditures and Internal Communications in the 2000 Congressional Elections," in David B. Magleby, ed., *The Other Campaign: Soft Money and Issue Advocacy in the 2000 Congressional Elections* (Lanham, Md.: Rowman and Littlefield, 2003), p. 86.

29. Bernadette Budde, senior vice president, BIPAC, interview by Quin Monson, Jonathan Tanner, and Nicole Carlisle Squires, Washington, D.C., November 6, 2002.

30. *Buckley* v. *Valeo*, 424 U.S. 1 (1976), n. 52, which reads: "This construction would restrict the application of §§ 608 (e)(1) to communications containing express words of advocacy of election or defeat, such as 'vote for,' 'elect,' 'support,' 'cast your ballot for,' 'Smith for Congress,' 'vote against,' 'defeat,' 'reject.'"

31. Cigler, "Interest Groups and Financing the 2000 Elections," p. 166.

32. Over 80 percent of respondents in a national WebTV survey conducted during the 2000 general election campaign said the purpose of the election issue ads they were shown was to urge them to vote against a particular candidate. Respondents saw the purpose of candidate, party, and election issue ads as primarily about electing or defeating a candidate. In contrast, over 70 percent of respondents in the same study saw the pure issue ads they were shown as primarily about an issue. Respondents in focus groups that were part of this same project drew the same distinctions between pure and election issue ads; they also saw clear differences between pure issue advocacy mail and mail that had a clear candidate referent but that qualified as issue advocacy because it avoided the "magic words" of express advocacy. See David B. Magleby, *Dictum without Data: The Myth of Issue Advocacy and Party Building* (Center for the Study of Elections and Democracy, Brigham Young University, 2000) (http://csed.byu.edu).

33. Steve Moore, president, Club for Growth, interview by David Magleby and Jonathan Tanner, Washington, D.C., December 2, 2002.

34. Michael Lux, president, Progressive Strategies, telephone interview by David Magleby and Quin Monson, January 9, 2003.

35. David B. Magleby, *Direct Legislation: Voting on Ballot Propositions in the United States* (Johns Hopkins University Press, 1984), p. 145. For a fuller discussion of this issue, see Arthur Lupia and Mathew D. McCubbins, *Democratic Dilemma: Can Citizens Learn What They Need to Know?* (Cambridge University Press, 1998); and Elizabeth Garrett and Daniel A. Smith, "Veiled Political Actors: The Real Threat to Campaign Disclosure Statutes," working paper (USC-Caltech Center for the Study of Law and Politics, 2003) (http://lawweb.usc.edu/cslp/pages/papers.html [July 22, 2003]).

36. David B. Magleby and J. Quin Monson, "Campaign 2002: 'The Perfect Storm,' " (Center for the Study of Elections and Democracy, Brigham Young University, November 13, 2002) (http://csed.byu.edu)

37. Eric S. Heberlig, "The North Carolina 8th Congressional District," in Magleby and Monson, *The Last Hurrah,* monograph version, p. 265.

38. Andy Grossman, political director, DSCC, interview by David Magleby, Quin Monson, and Jonathan Tanner, Washington, D.C., November 8, 2002.

39. Soft money has disclosure of the source of funds and limited disclosure of how the money is spent. Tracking how soft money is spent is made even more difficult because it is sometimes transferred from state party to state party.

40. Scott Stoermer, communications director, League of Conservation Voters, press event, "The Last Hurrah: Soft Money and Issue Advocacy in the 2002 Congressional Elections," Center for the Study of Elections and Democracy, National Press Club, Washington, D.C., February 3, 2003.

41. In 2000 we monitored seventeen competitive House and Senate races; in 1998 the number of competitive races monitored was sixteen.

42. William H. Flanigan and others, "The Minnesota U.S. Senate Race," in Magleby and Monson, eds., *The Last Hurrah,* monograph version, p. 114.

43. Craig Wilson, "The Montana Senate and At-Large Congressional District Races," in Magleby and Monson, *The Last Hurrah,* monograph version, pp. 342–43.

44. David Redlawsk and Arthur Sanders, "The Iowa Senate and 1st, 2nd, 3rd, and 4th Congressional District Races," in Magleby and Monson, *The Last Hurrah,* monograph version, p. 84.

45. Lonna Rae Atkeson, Nancy Carrillo, and Margaret C. Toulouse, "The New Mexico 1st and 2nd Congressional District Races," in Magleby and Monson, *The Last Hurrah,* monograph version, p. 277.

46. Judith S. Trent and Robert V. Friedenberg, *Political Campaign Communication: Principles and Practices,* 4th ed. (Westport, Conn.: Praeger, 2000), pp. 94–96.

47. See chapter 9 of this volume.

48. Chuck Cunningham, director for federal affairs, Institute for Legislative Action, National Rifle Association, interview by David Magleby, Quin Monson, Jonathan Tanner, and Nicole Carlisle Squires, Washington, D.C., November 7, 2002.

49. Denise Mitchell, assistant to the president for public affairs, AFL-CIO, interview by Quin Monson and Jonathan Tanner, Washington, D.C., December 10, 2002.

50. David B. Magleby and the Center for the Study of Elections and Democracy, Election Advocacy Database 2000 (Brigham Young University, 2000); David B. Magleby, J. Quin Monson, and the Center for the Study of Elections and Democracy, Election Advocacy Database 2002 (Brigham Young University, 2002).

51. Bill Miller, political director, U.S. Chamber of Commerce, press event, "The Last Hurrah? Soft Money and Issue Advocacy in the 2002 Congressional Elections," Center for the Study of Elections and Democracy, National Press Club, Washington, D.C., February 3, 2003.

52. Magleby, *Dictum without Data.*

53. David B. Magleby, ed., *Election Advocacy: Soft Money and Issue Advocacy in the 2000 Congressional Elections* (Center for the Study of Elections and Democracy, Brigham Young University, 2001), p. 131.

54. Drew Linzer, David Menefee-Libey, and Matt Muller, "The California 29th Congressional District Race," in Magleby and Monson, *The Last Hurrah,* monograph version, p. 323.

55. Michael Traugott, "The Michigan Senate Race," in Magleby and Monson, *The Last Hurrah*, monograph version, p. 336.

56. Christopher J. Carman, "The Pennsylvania 4th Congressional District Race," in Magleby and Monson, *The Last Hurrah*, monograph version, p. 358.

57. "Déjà vu Soft Money: Outlawed Contributions Likely to Flow to Shadowy 527 Groups That Skirt Flawed Disclosure Law," Public Citizen, 2002 (www.citizen.org/documents/ACF8D5.PDF [April 7, 2003]), p. ii.

58. See complete text for new law H.R. 4762: "To amend the Internal Revenue Code of 1986 to require 527 organizations to disclose their political activities" (http://thomas.loc.gov/).

59. Internal Revenue Service, "Social Welfare Orgs: Exemption Requirements" (www.irs.gov/charities/welfare/article/0,,id=96178,00.html [May 13, 2003]).

60. Robin Toner, "The 2002 Campaign: The Drug Industry; Democrats See a Stealthy Drive by Drug Industry to Help Republicans," *New York Times*, October 20, 2002, p. A20.

61. Elizabeth Garrett and Daniel A. Smith, "Veiled Political Actors: The Real Threat to Campaign Disclosure Statutes," working paper (USC-Caltech Center for the Study of Law and Politics, 2003) (http://lawweb.usc.edu/cslp/pages/papers.html [July 22, 2003]).

62. Jack Polidori, political affairs specialist, National Education Association, press event, "The Last Hurrah? Soft Money and Issue Advocacy in the 2002 Congressional Elections," Center for the Study of Elections and Democracy, National Press Club, Washington, D.C., February 3, 2003.

63. Jay Barth and Janine Parry, "Provincialism, Personalism, and Politics," in Magleby and Monson, *The Last Hurrah*, monograph version, p. 59.

64. Gail Stoltz, political director, DNC, interview by David Magleby and Jonathan Tanner, Washington, D.C., November 13, 2002.

65. Thomas B. Edsall, "New Ways to Harness Soft Money in Works: Political Groups Poised to Take Huge Donations," *Washington Post*, August 25, 2002, p. A1.

66. Thomas B. Edsall, "Soft Money Ban Evasion Alleged," *Washington Post*, November 22, 2002 (www.camlc.org/press-374.html) [May 13, 2003])

67. Federal Election Commission, "PAC Activity Increases for 2002 Elections," press release, March 27, 2003 (www.fec.gov/press/20030327pac/sumhistory.xls [April 17, 2003]).

68. Magleby, *Election Advocacy*, pp. 26–27.

69. Toner, "The 2002 Campaign."

70. Dick Castner, western field coordinator, U.S. Chamber of Commerce, interview by Fred Solop, Flagstaff, Ariz., October 18, 2002.

71. "Déjà vu Soft Money," p. 11.

72. David Williams, director of Action Fund and PAC, Planned Parenthood, interview by David Magleby and Nicole Carlisle Squires, Washington, D.C., November 8, 2002.

73. For further discussion see Rozell and Wilcox, *Interest Groups in American Campaigns*, pp. 45; and Cigler and Loomis, *Interest Group Politics*, pp. 20–21.

74. Robert Gehrke, "Despite Differences, McCain Endorses Smith," Associated Press, October 31, 2000.

75. Cunningham interview; and Bill Miller, press event.

76. Samuel Issacharoff and Pamela Karlan, "The Hydraulics of Campaign Finance Reform," *Texas Law Review,* vol. 77 (June 1999), p. 1705.

77. Robert Boatright and others, "BCRA's Impact on Interest Groups and Advocacy Organizations," in Michael J. Malbin, ed., *Life after Reform* (Lanham, Md.: Rowman & Littlefield, 2003), pp. 55–82 (www.cfinst.org/studies/bcrabook/index.html [April 7, 2003]).

78. Federal Election Commission, "BCRA Campaign Guide Supplement," *Record*, vol. 29 (January 2003), p. 7.

79. Boatright and others, "BCRA's Impact on Interest Groups."

FOUR

Get On TeleVision vs. Get On The Van: GOTV and the Ground War in 2002

J. QUIN MONSON

GROUND-WAR EFFORTS played a critical role in competitive contests in the 2002 election. The ground war refers to non-broadcast campaign communications, such as telephone calls, direct mail, and person-to-person contacts, which are often designed to increase voter turnout. Other elements of the ground war include voter registration and early and absentee voting. While it is often used synonymously with fieldwork or get-out-the-vote (GOTV) operations, as used here the ground war includes any nonbroadcast campaign activity, regardless of its primary purpose.[1]

The ground war, in contrast to the air war, concerns campaign communications that are below the radar screen.[2] That is, they are communications that most people never see or hear about and are typically not reported in the media. For this reason they are also more difficult to track and study. A strength of the case studies in this book is their ability to effectively track ground-war communications. In addition, because they are less noticeable, ground-war communications are often quite hard-hitting, using messages and images that would not play well to a large television audience.

The various components of a ground-war strategy are often integrated and use the same theme and message; each contact serves to reinforce previous attempts to persuade and mobilize the potential supporter. For example, over a period of several weeks a potential voter might receive multiple contacts from a campaign in which the various communications would use the same theme and message, through personal contacts, telephone calls, and direct mail.

Without the presidential election campaigns to command media attention and spark voter interest, midterm elections suffer from lower turnout. Thus, in a midterm election, voter mobilization efforts operate in a different context than in a presidential election year. More effort is required to get out the vote, especially among voters with irregular voting habits. In midterm elections, candidates, groups, and parties target their messages even more to particular subgroups of voters, hoping to motivate them to vote. The low stimulus and low turnout context of a midterm election means that a good ground-war effort can have a disproportionate impact on the outcome, compared to a presidential election.

As discussed in chapter 1, the growth of soft money and issue advocacy spending in the 1996 election was focused mostly on broadcast communications, although both parties dedicated some of their resources to fund voter mobilization efforts.[3] However, in 1998, voter mobilization became a significant part of the story, especially for Democrats and their interest-group allies. Turnout among union households and African Americans was high and helped propel higher-than-expected Democratic gains.[4] Going into the 2002 midterm election, there was a growing feeling among some professionals that the ground war was gaining in importance.[5] Ground-war methods were seen by some groups as a more cost-effective way of communicating their message.

Political parties and allied interest groups waged expanded ground-war campaigns in 2002. In the 1998 and 2000 elections, interest groups produced more direct mail, print and radio advertisements, and phone banks than did the political parties; the parties focused more on television advertisements.[6] However, in 2002, while maintaining their presence on television, the parties also expanded their ground-war efforts to exceed those of the interest groups. This happened even while several interest groups expanded their ground-war efforts. In short, the emphasis on grassroots political mobilization has been increasing over time by both parties and interest groups across the political spectrum. The increase in the ground war by parties and interest groups has occurred primarily because these techniques are increasingly seen as effective at increasing turnout of targeted groups. This continues a trend among Democrats and their allies that began in 1998. For Republicans it is a fundamental shift in tactics that grew out of much smaller efforts in the 2000 Bush campaign.

In 2002, as they have done for several elections now, Democrats and their allies, especially labor unions, made extensive mail and phone drives and GOTV efforts a major priority. Republicans and their allies, especially business groups and the National Rifle Association (NRA), pointing to the voter mobilization successes of Democrats and labor unions in 1998 and 2000, also invested heavily in voter mobilization in 2002. The Republican National Committee (RNC), backed by the leadership of the White House, initiated the 72 Hour Task Force, and Republican leadership in the House initiated the Strategic Taskforce to Organize and Mobilize People (STOMP).

This chapter describes the ground-war activities in 2002 and contrasts them with other recent elections. Ground-war activity increased in 2002. For Democrats and their labor union allies, ground-war activities in 2002 followed a similar strategy to the successes of 1998 and 2000. Republicans placed a new, and by most accounts largely successful, emphasis on the ground war in 2002. Given the shift in resources to the ground war in 2002, the chapter explores some possible explanations for this shift and what may lie ahead in 2004 and beyond.

The Growing Importance of the Ground War

This heightened emphasis on the ground war is often spoken of as a "back to basics" approach, but this does not mean that ground-war efforts today are the same as techniques used in the past. In fact, to be effective, "all of the basic principles of new-style campaigning apply" to the ground war.[7] Ground-war tactics are often quite sophisticated; they use messages derived from polling data, narrowly target these tailored messages to specific subgroups, use the latest technology, such as database software that allows for sophisticated targeting and message customization, and are driven by consultants who specialize in each tactic.

Scholars have found that ground-war tactics can be successful in mobilizing voters. The consensus is that mobilization efforts by candidates, political parties, and interest groups have a positive and measurable impact on voter turnout. Rosenstone and Hansen's seminal research demonstrates that, in addition to the well-known sociodemographic predictors of political participation, the strategic actions of politicians, political parties, and interest groups help determine if, when, and to what extent individuals participate in politics.[8] They argue that campaigns can dramatically reduce the costs of participation for citizens and that the interaction of direct mobilization of individuals, together with political contact within their social networks, produces an effect positively related to political participation. In other words, political elites directly mobilize other elites who are at the center of social groups, and those people in turn mobilize their associates. Rosenstone and Hansen further assert that political leaders know the individual characteristics that lead to increased participation and strategically contact citizens most likely to participate.

While the size of the effect and method of inquiry differ, a spate of recent work in political science has largely confirmed the findings of Rosenstone and Hansen on the significance of political mobilization as a positive predictor of political participation.[9] The work of Gerber and Green has been especially influential. They pioneered the use of experimental techniques to test the effects of mobilization efforts and find positive effects on turnout from person-to-person contacting. They suggest that a decline in these personal techniques in favor of automated phone calls and mass advertising may be among the culprits to blame for the steady decline in voter turnout in the United States over time.[10]

The Continued Shift to the Ground in 2002

Beginning with the ground-war activities of the AFL-CIO in 1998, these tactics have reemerged in recent elections. Until 2002 Democratic-allied interest groups and the Democratic Party focused more effort on the ground war in competitive races. These efforts have been particularly effective among African Americans and union members and clearly benefited the Democrats in 1998.[11] Democrats and allied interest groups continued to emphasize the ground war in 2002 at levels comparable to 1998 and 2000. Republicans and allied interest groups placed new emphasis on their ground war in 2002. The continued shift to the ground war is evident in our case studies, comparing data from 1998, 2000, and 2002. It was also discussed in our interviews with party committee and interest group officials, many of whom indicated that they shifted more emphasis to direct mail as well as recruitment and training of volunteers, even sending paid staff to work on campaigns for extended periods. Finally, survey data we collected indicate that voters perceive an increase in ground-war tactics in 2002 as compared to recent past elections.

Table 4-1. *Unique Mail Pieces by Partisan Groups, Sample Races, 2002*

	Democratic	%	Republican	%
Candidate	226	24	126	15
Political party	387	41	521	61
Interest group	336	35	212	25
Total	949	100	859	101

Source: David B. Magleby, J. Quin Monson, and the Center for the Study of Elections and Democracy, 2002 Soft Money and Issue Advocacy Database (Brigham Young University, 2002). See appendix A for a detailed explanation of the data.

Table 4-1 presents the total number of unique mail pieces by parties, interest groups, and candidates that we observed in our 2002 sample races. It is important to note that each distinct mail piece may have been sent to hundreds or thousands of potential voters and does not represent the total amount of mail sent by campaigns and groups. All told, we collected 1,482 unique pieces of party and interest-group mail and 352 unique pieces of candidate mail. Most of these were collected by the academics studying each race, with a few obtained in our postelection interviews. (See appendix A for a detailed explanation of the methodology.) Clearly, noncandidate money funded most of the campaign mail in the House and Senate races we monitored in 2002. Of the mail sent by Republican candidates, parties, and allied interest groups, only 15 percent of the mail pieces were sent by the candidates. Among Democrats, the candidates accounted for only 24 percent of mail pieces. Overall, four of every five mail pieces detected in our 2002 study came from political parties or interest groups and not candidates. On both sides of the partisan spectrum, political parties had the highest share of mail pieces. On the Republican side, the party sent 61 percent of all the unique mail pieces in our races, while on the Democratic side the party sent 41 percent of the unique mail pieces. Interest groups sent 25 percent of mail in support of Republicans (or attacking Democrats) and 35 percent of the mail on the Democratic side.

Not all groups participated equally in the ground war, of which mail is only a part of the total effort. Table 4-2 contrasts the candidates, groups, and parties in all modes of communicating with voters in competitive contests in 2002. The table again refers to the number of unique or distinctive communications we collected from each organization. State party committees were responsible for the most phone and mail activity. Academics in our sample races learned of forty-nine Democratic

Table 4-2. Number of Unique Campaign Communications by Organizations, Sample Races, 2002[a]

Type and organization	Internet banner ads	E-mail messages	Surface mail pieces	Newspaper or magazine ads	Personal contacts	Phone calls	Radio ads	TV ads	Total
				Democratic allies[b]					
Candidates									
Democratic candidates	1	90	227	30	13	69	55	206	691
Political parties									
State Democratic parties	...	18	354	8	10	49	23	131	593
Democratic National Committee	...	27	8	...	...	4	...	1	40
Democratic Congressional Campaign Committee	...	...	5	1	1	4	1	12	24
Local Democratic parties	...	1	12	3	...	...	1	...	17
Democratic Senatorial Campaign Committee	...	...	8	...	...	1	1	...	10
Interest groups									
National Education Association	...	...	72	3	...	10	1	2	88
AFL–CIO	...	2	55	2	1	8	1	14	83
Sierra Club	...	...	29	2	1	7	1	9	49
Planned Parenthood	...	4	23	...	...	5	...	...	32
League of Conservation Voters	...	2	19	1	1	2	...	7	32
Alliance for Retired Americans	...	...	13	...	4	10	3	...	30
NARAL Pro-Choice America	...	4	15	1	1	4	...	2	27
Service Employees International Union	...	...	6	1	3	1	1	1	13

Type of campaign communication

continued on next page

Table 4-2. *Number of Unique Campaign Communications by Organizations, Sample Races, 2002*[a] *(continued)*

				Type of campaign communication					
Type and organization	Internet banner ads	E-mail messages	Surface mail pieces	Newspaper or magazine ads	Personal contacts	Phone calls	Radio ads	TV ads	Total
National Women's Political Caucus	...	10	1	...	...	...	...	...	11
Human Rights Campaign	...	...	4	...	1	4	1	...	10
Iowa Federation of Labor	...	...	9	...	...	...	...	1	10
American Federation of Teachers	...	...	9	...	...	...	...	...	9
United Brotherhood of Carpenters and Joiners of America	...	...	8	...	...	...	...	...	8
NAACP	...	...	2	2	1	1	1	1	8
Republican allies[b]									
Candidates									
Republican candidates	1	98	127	42	20	40	73	220	621
Political parties									
State Republican parties	...	9	340	2	9	30	9	98	497
National Republican Congressional Committee	...	...	129	...	...	2	1	30	162
Republican National Committee	1	15	41	...	3	3	2	10	75
Local Republican parties	...	...	6	5	...	2	...	...	13
National Republican Senatorial Committee	...	1	...	...	...	2	1	7	11

Interest groups

	1	2	3	4	5	6	7	Total
Council for Better Government	...	...	...	1	...	15	25	41
60 Plus Association	...	...	31	2	2	5	...	40
National Rifle Association	...	...	20	1	9	10	...	40
United Seniors Association	...	...	1	...	2	...	31	34
National Right To Life	...	...	20	3	3	6	1	33
U.S. Chamber of Commerce	...	...	15	1	6	...	1	23
America 21	...	...	20	...	2	...	...	22
Seniors Coalition	...	...	16	...	2	...	...	18
National Federation of Independent Business	...	...	14	...	...	2	...	16
Club for Growth	...	...	...	...	...	5	6	11
National Right to Work Committee	...	...	10	1	...	...	...	11
Americans for Job Security	...	...	2	...	...	4	4	10
Business Roundtable	...	...	1	...	...	...	8	9

Nonpartisan

Interest groups

	1	2	3	4	5	6	7	Total
AARP	...	...	7	4	6	1	4	23

Source: David B. Magleby, J. Quin Monson, and the Center for the Study of Elections and Democracy, 2002 Soft Money and Issue Advocacy Database (Brigham Young University, 2002).

a. See appendix A for a more detailed explanation of data. This table is not intended to portray comprehensive organization activity within the sample races. A more complete picture can be obtained by examining this table together with table 3-3. Data represent the number of unique or distinct pieces or ads by the group and do not represent a count of total items sent or made. In blank cells, "..." reflects absence of collected data and does not imply that the organization was inactive in that medium.

b. Certain organizations that maintained partisan neutrality were categorized according to which candidates their ads supported or attacked or whether the organization was anti- or pro-conservative or liberal.

state party–sponsored telephone banks and collected 354 distinct mail
pieces sent by state Democratic parties. State Republican parties
accounted for 340 discrete mail pieces, with the National Republican
Congressional Committee (NRCC) sending another 129. Republican
Party phone banks were somewhat less common than Democratic ones.
On the Democratic side, state political parties are the dominant source
of mail, with national parties and interest groups less active. On the
Republican side, state party committees are almost as active as state
Democratic parties, but the NRCC mounted its own significant effort.
Table 4-2 shows that Democratic candidates sent out 100 more mail
pieces than Republican candidates. Overall, the number of ground-war
activities sponsored by noncandidate groups far outnumbered the
efforts made by candidates. It is important to note that the table
includes all of our sample races in 2002 but that there are big differences between competitive races and control races in our sample. For
example, in table 1-2, the average number of mail pieces for a Senate
battleground race was 105, compared to 19 for a control race.

One method of comparing the overall levels of ground-war activity in
2002 to previous elections is to compute an average level of activity per
competitive race. Figure 4-1 presents the average number of unique or
distinct mail pieces by competitive race by source and party from our
databases in 2000 and 2002. In the aggregate, the average number of
unique mail pieces per competitive race increased from 67 in 2000 to 72
in 2002.[12] Breaking these figures down by party and source demonstrates where the changes occurred. In 2002 the aggregate increase in
mail can be attributed to the parties, especially Republicans. The average number of mail pieces per campaign increased among the political
parties, going from an average of 12.0 per race in 2000 to 13.4 in 2002
for Democrats, and from 13.2 in 2000 to 18.9 in 2002 for Republicans.
Among Republican-allied interest groups, the average declines slightly
from 8.7 in 2000 to 7.8 in 2002, while the average for Democratic-
allied interest groups declines from 17.6 in 2000 to 12.1 in 2002. The
averages also decrease slightly among candidates of both parties. The
most dramatic changes are the large increase in the Republican Party
and the large decrease in Democratic-allied interest groups. The causes
for these dramatic shifts are discussed in further detail below. In sum,
the decreases in the mail among candidates and interest groups (all relatively small, except among liberal interest groups) are offset in the

Figure 4-1. *Average Number of Unique Mail Pieces, by Source, Sample Races, 2000 and 2002*[a]

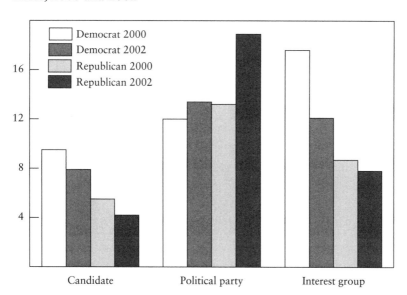

Sources: David B. Magleby and CSED, 2000 Soft Money and Issue Advocacy Database (Brigham Young University, 2000); Magleby, Monson, and CSED, 2002 Soft Money and Issue Advocacy Database.

a. To compare the number of unique mail pieces collected in 2000 and 2002 required computing a standardized average number of unique mail pieces for each year. Making the comparison fair required dropping the eighteen control races (four Senate and fourteen House) from our 2002 sample; there were no control races in the 2000 sample. This left twenty-five competitive races (six Senate and nineteen House) for 2002, compared with seventeen competitive races (five Senate and twelve House) for 2000. Appendix A contains a more detailed explanation of the 2002 data.

aggregate by the large increase in the Republican Party average and the modest increase in the Democratic Party average.

One potential problem with the data in figure 4-1 is that, while the numbers are limited to competitive races only, some of the changes could possibly be attributed to differences in the methods used by the academics to collect the data in 2000 versus 2002. Despite using common methodology, there may be some variation in establishing the network for collecting campaign communications. Thus it is informative to compare the data collected in 2002 and 2000 in a single location. Missouri saw a competitive U.S. Senate election in both years, with roughly comparable spending levels by both candidates and outside groups and with the same group of researchers studying both races.[13] However, in terms of unique mailings, telephone calls, and personal contacts, there

Figure 4-2. *Number of Unique Mail Pieces by Source, Missouri Senate Races, 2000 and 2002*

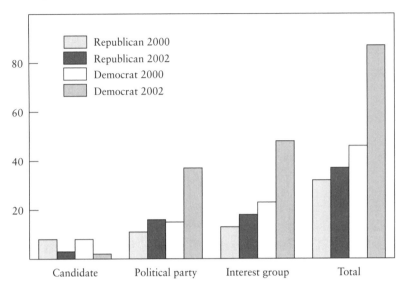

Sources: Magleby and CSED, 2000 Soft Money and Issue Advocacy Database; Magleby, Monson, and CSED, 2002 Soft Money and Issue Advocacy Database. Data summarized from detailed tables in chapter 6 of this volume; and Martha E. Kropf and others, "The 2000 Missouri Senate Race," in David B. Magleby, ed., *Election Advocacy: Soft Money and Issue Advocacy in the 2000 Congressional Elections* (Center for the Study of Elections and Democracy, Brigham Young University, 2001).

was dramatic growth in Missouri between 2000 and 2002, particularly among outside groups.

Figure 4-2 contains a comparison of the number of mail pieces sent by candidates, parties, and interest groups in the 2000 and 2002 Missouri U.S. Senate elections. In both elections the candidates sent the smallest number of unique mail pieces. For Democratic candidates, it declined from eight in 2000 to two in 2002. For Republican candidates, it went from eight in 2000 to three in 2002. However, these declines were more than compensated for by a dramatic increase in mailings by the political parties and interest groups. On the Republican side, the number of mailings by the party increased from eleven in 2000 to sixteen in 2002. The increase for Democrats was much more dramatic, going from fifteen in 2000 to thirty-seven in 2002. Among interest groups the pattern is similar. For Republican-allied groups, the increase was modest, from thirteen in 2000 to eighteen in 2002; for Democratic-allied groups, the increase was again dramatic, from twenty-three in

2000 to forty-eight in 2002. Similar patterns also exist for telephone and in-person contacts. So the level of ground-war activity by the candidates remained constant or slightly declined, with modest to dramatic increases in the ground war by the parties and interest groups.

Another piece of evidence attesting to the increase in the ground war in 2002 is contained in the panel surveys conducted in four competitive states and with a national baseline sample. (See appendix A for a description of the surveys.) By the third wave, conducted just after Election Day, respondents located in the four battleground races typically reported receiving more or about the same amount of mail compared to previous elections, while the proportions among the national sample were about the same or less.[14] In Colorado's Seventh District, for example, 53 percent said they received more mail compared to previous elections, 45 percent reported about the same, and only 5 percent reported less. In Arkansas the proportion receiving more was 37 percent, in Connecticut's Fifth District it was 35 percent, and in Missouri it was 46 percent. However, among the national sample, only 18 percent reported more, while 61 percent reported receiving about the same amount, and 20 percent reported less. It is important to remember that each battleground district experienced competitive races in 2000. The presidential contest was competitive in Missouri, Arkansas, and Colorado. Missouri also had an extremely competitive Senate race in 2000. The Connecticut Fifth Congressional District, while not a presidential battleground, had competitive races with considerable amounts of noncandidate activity in both 1998 and 2000.[15] The survey data thus show that the increased ground war by parties and interest groups noted in our database from competitive races in 2002 was also perceived by voters.

The Importance of Personal Contact and the Shift to the Ground

The growing emphasis on ground-war tactics has its roots in several places, including the adaptation of successful techniques, numerous independent research efforts conducted by the parties and several interest groups on both sides, and a changing campaign environment that requires different techniques to connect with voters. Interest groups and parties observe and adapt the election campaign successes of the other side. With the success of labor unions in 1998, other groups began to experiment with ground-war techniques in a similar fashion.[16]

The AFL-CIO is an example of a group that conducted extensive research of its own, including sophisticated controlled experiments.[17] The early rumblings of an increased emphasis on ground-war tactics by Republicans in 2002 came as an outgrowth of the voter mobilization efforts in the 2000 George W. Bush campaign by Karl Rove and Kenneth Mehlman and some consternation within the Republican Party in the aftermath that they did not do better in the closing days of the campaign.[18] This shift to emphasizing person-to-person contact by the GOP was described by Mehlman as fundamental to campaigning. He called it the "blocking and tackling of politics" and stated that increased attention to mobilizing voters has become more important "because we live in a place where this wealth of information creates a poverty of attention."[19] After the 2000 election and with Bush's campaign operatives firmly in control at the Republican National Committee, the RNC launched a large-scale research effort during the 2001 elections to investigate the effectiveness of various techniques to increase turnout among targeted groups. The purpose of the task force was to investigate what Republicans could do to improve performance in the closing days of the election. Rove and Mehlman believed the Democrats and their allies had outperformed Republicans in this aspect of the 2000 election. To reiterate the importance of the closing days, the effort was called the 72 Hour Task Force and involved leaders of all three party campaign committees, the White House, the Republican Governors' Association, state parties, congressional leadership, Republican-allied interest groups, and consultants.[20] The task force conducted more than fifty experimental tests in 2001 in New Jersey, Virginia, Pennsylvania, South Carolina, and Missouri.[21]

For example, one test measured the effectiveness of paid versus volunteer telephone calls and found that volunteer callers stimulated turnout that was 5 percentage points higher.[22] These research efforts largely confirmed what the AFL-CIO and others had already known—personalized contact about the election from a source known to the voter is the most effective way of increasing their likelihood of voting.[23]

Republican-allied interest groups were also involved in research as part of their own evolution toward the ground war. For example, the National Federation of Independent Business (NFIB) conducted a $100,000 research effort in the 2001 Virginia Fourth Congressional District special election.[24] This included outreach to their 850 members living in the district as well as to an additional 11,000 small-business owners. In a postelection survey of 1,500 small-business owners in the district, they found that 64 percent of respondents could recall receiving information about the candidates from the NFIB, whereas only 47 percent could recall an NFIB radio advertisement.[25]

Ground war communications are also "personalized," because they allow for narrowly targeted messages to be delivered to sympathetic voters. For example, of the sixty-eight unique mailers sent by Republicans in the 2002 South Dakota U.S. Senate race, thirteen were on the topic of abortion. Each of these mailings narrowly targeted voters most likely to respond positively to the message.[26] This kind of targeting is used in part to avoid antagonizing opponents with a polarizing message on topics like abortion or guns. In 2002 the NRA went to extraordinary efforts to target their messages to sympathetic voters. In addition to contacting their membership, the NRA built mailing and phone lists of voters with hunting licenses, subscribers to hunting magazines, gun show attendees, holders of concealed weapon permits, and local shooting and hunting club members in several competitive races in an effort to reach gun-friendly voters on behalf of pro-gun candidates.[27]

A final reason for a growing emphasis on the ground war may be that, in order to gain cooperation from allied interest groups, political parties must devote resources where the groups are willing to spend them. Speaking of the Republicans' newfound interest in the ground war in 2002, Greg Casey, president of the Business Industry Political Action Committee (BIPAC), noted that a primary reason Democrats shifted to the ground war in 1998 was that their labor union allies put limits on how they were willing to spend their resources, essentially forcing a greater emphasis on voter mobilization by Democrats. Casey referred to some Republicans as "reluctant revolutionaries," in reference to their 2002 ground-war efforts, and suggested that business groups could help force the same kind of shift to the ground war among Republicans that he thought the unions had forced on Democrats.[28] While interest groups are thought to learn from each other, the influence of interest groups on party committee strategy has not been previously noted in the literature.[29]

The shift to ground-war tactics seems to be an extension of what groups have found to be effective among their own members. Person-to-person contacts provide an ideal strategy for membership-based organizations such as the AFL-CIO, the NFIB, and the NRA because they are effective and cheap communications from a trusted source. Democrats have an advantage on this point, because their labor union allies are large membership organizations in which members make daily face-to-face contact at the workplace. The same advantage applies to teachers' organizations and African American churches, which have long been more politicized than their white Evangelical counterparts.[30] Republicans, without the same level of support from membership-based organizations, have had to rely on contact people who have no relationship with the voter, sometimes even using "paid volunteers." For example, in the Colorado Seventh Congressional District race, $250,000 from the RNC was used to pay $200 each to some of the "volunteers" in the state party's ninety-six-hour program.[31] This means that Republicans have to make more effort to succeed at personal contacting and may also be more apt to rely on broadcast advertising as well as on less personal forms of the ground war, such as direct mail and automated phone calls.

The Democrats and Their Allies in 2002

In 2002 the Democratic Party and its allies again made the ground war a major priority. Going back several elections, the Democratic Party has run its ground-war efforts through what they call the "coordinated campaign."[32] This consists of a division of labor and resources among the candidates, state and national party organizations, and several allied interest groups, especially the AFL-CIO. Much of the funding is supplied by the candidates and national party committees, with the organization usually coming from the state party level. The planning is approved at the national level. As Gail Stoltz, former political director of the Democratic National Committee, explained, "Typically, the various state parties draft a coordinated campaign plan, which is then approved by the political staff at the DNC. The DNC's outside political consultants and donors to the coordinated campaign, such as labor unions and other interest groups, also sometimes review the coordinated campaign plan."[33] In addition to funding the coordinated campaign, mostly using soft money, the national party committees provide a great deal of strategic guidance and personnel.[34]

Arkansas in 2002 provides an excellent example of how a strong coordinated campaign effort works. In 2001, months before the election, the Arkansas Democratic Party combined efforts with the Democratic Senatorial Campaign Committee, the DNC, the Democratic Governors' Association, the National Education Association, and other unions to put $300,000 toward a unified field operation. By Election Day in 2002, the operation had twelve offices and seventy-five full-time paid employees around the state. The Democratic candidates and even statewide Democratic officials who were not up for reelection also became involved, sharing their mailing and telephone lists. The statewide Democratic ticket, labeled Team Arkansas, benefited greatly from this organized effort.[35]

The Iowa Democratic Party put together a comprehensive coordinated campaign that included an innovative absentee ballot drive. Beginning over the summer, 100 paid canvassers with Palm Pilots in hand contacted Democratic and independent voters and collected pertinent information. Those who appeared inclined to vote Democratic were asked to complete absentee ballot requests, which were then given to the county auditor. By Election Day the coordinated campaign had satellite offices in forty-nine of ninety-nine counties. In the end these efforts appear to have been a tremendous success. In one case, Johnson County, 40 percent of all votes were cast by absentee ballot, with Democrat Tom Harkin taking 71 percent of the early vote.[36]

Labor Unions

The most important Democratic allies in the coordinated campaign ground efforts are labor unions, particularly the AFL-CIO. In 2002 the AFL-CIO touted its "thousands of volunteers, 750 released staff from the AFL-CIO and its affiliate unions, and 4,000 field coordinators."[37] The labor program departed very little from what we observed in the 1998 and 2000 campaigns. As Mike Lux, an experienced observer of liberal politics, observed:

> The union mobilization has stayed pretty consistent election to election, because the AFL-CIO and the big unions that always play in politics really do have it down to a science. They work very, very hard. They tend to spend the same amount of money or close to the same amount of money year after year. So you don't see much drop-off on the union side in terms of intensity.[38]

In 2002 labor union mobilization efforts were particularly notable in our case studies of Senate races in Iowa and Missouri, as well as in congressional district races in the Maryland Eighth, Connecticut Fifth, and Pennsylvania Seventeenth districts. Labor union mobilization followed a successful recipe of carefully targeted communications delivered in person or on the telephone by fellow union members. As Steve Rosenthal, the AFL-CIO's political director in 2002, explained:

> There was a situation in Cleveland at one point where I was doing phone calls with some union members. The guy in the cubicle next to me leaned over and said, "If you're calling operating engineers, don't say you're calling from the union, say you're calling on behalf of the union." I said, "Why?" and he said, "We all know each other." I said, "How many members are there in your union?" He said, "About 2,200." I said, "And you all know each other?" He said, "Pretty much." I listened to his next two or three calls, and it was, "Hi, Mr. Smith, this is Joe Dugan. I work with your sons Tommy and Mike." Each call he would personalize like that. It was so much more valuable than most of the other contacts that campaigns make. We see that all the time.[39]

This level of personalization is facilitated largely by union volunteers. Sometimes the volunteers are funded by the union. These "lost timers" take an unpaid leave from their employer and are then compensated at their regular wage for their political work.[40]

In addition to the AFL-CIO, other unions provide contributions to the coordinated campaign efforts. In 2002 the NEA deployed over twenty staff to a combination of state and local races.[41] The Service Employees International Union (SEIU) and the American Federation of State, County and Municipal Employees (AFSCME) also provide volunteers and other resources to the ground war.

Union-sponsored ground-war tactics were effective in 2002. The AFL-CIO sponsored a postelection survey of AFL-CIO-affiliated households. Of these households, 93 percent had received some information from a union source and, when asked how they got information from the union, the survey respondents mostly listed ground-war sources—a flyer mailed to their home (79 percent), a telephone call (36 percent), a flyer at work (30 percent), and contact at work (16 percent). Only 33 percent named a union television advertisement, while 81 percent listed a newspaper or magazine. Among union households, the Democratic vote was 68 percent for House races and 70 percent for Senate races. Union households that received a high level of union information were even more likely to support the Democratic candidate (76 percent).[42] Turnout by union households in 2002 was comparable to 1998. Voter News Service (VNS) data show that union households composed 22 percent of the electorate in 1998.[43] In 2002 this rose slightly, to 23 percent.[44]

Other Liberal Groups

As noted in chapter 3, liberal groups generally had less money available to spend in 2002 than in 2000. However, these groups still made the ground war a high priority. Trial lawyers, who had previously used mostly television, did not in 2002, in part because they perceived a great deal of competition on the airwaves and were unsure of the effectiveness of broadcast ads in this saturated environment.[45] EMILY's List asked its members in seven states to join the Democratic coordinated campaign; overall about 1,000 members volunteered.[46] Groups such as the Sierra Club, NARAL Pro-Choice America, and Planned Parenthood, which had less money to work with in 2002, invested a greater proportion of their resources in ground-war activities.

African American turnout appeared to be down slightly in 2002. Compared to 1998, when African Americans made up 10 percent of the electorate, they composed 9 percent of voters in 2002.[47] The coordinated campaign also made some significant efforts to mobilize Native Americans. As discussed in chapter 7, this was particularly important in the 2002 South Dakota Senate race.

The GOP and Their Allies in 2002

In recent years Republicans have developed "ground-war envy" of Democrats and especially their labor union allies. Curt Anderson, former RNC political director and a consultant on the 72 Hour Task Force, said, "We spent a lot of time studying what it is the Democrats do and the unions do to get their vote out."[48] In a self-deprecating pre-election comparison, the RNC referred to GOTV for Republicans as "Get On TeleVision" and GOTV for Democrats and labor unions as "Get On The Van."[49] The 72 Hour Task Force was jointly funded by the RNC and state party committee victory programs.[50] While Republicans decline to disclose how much they spent on the 2002 ground war, it is clear that the program was largely funded by soft money transferred to state parties with the required hard-money match. In 2002 Republicans invested a much higher level of resources in the ground war than in previous elections.[51]

Unlike labor unions, Republicans do not have a readily identifiable source of grassroots volunteers and must make greater efforts to identify and recruit their volunteers from a variety of sources. The effectiveness of the Christian Coalition has diminished in recent years, making recruitment of religious conservatives more difficult. In 2002 many were recruited from conservative Christian churches, home school networks, college campuses, and the ranks of interest-group allies. Another source of volunteers was the Strategic Task Force to Organize and Mobilize People (STOMP), an effort begun by Representative Tom DeLay, then House Republican whip, to help supply campaign volunteers for the Republican ground war.[52] An important component of STOMP was more than 1,500 congressional staff members and others from Washington.[53]

The increased attention to the ground war was also true of Republican-allied interest groups. The National Rifle Association has replaced the Christian Coalition as the major interest-group ally of the Republican Party in terms of grassroots organizing. The NRA's focus on the ground war started well before 2002, and it has a long history of targeting its members and other gun owners in competitive races. Beginning in 1994 the NRA instituted a grassroots training program aimed at providing election volunteer coordinators and other trained volunteers for competitive congressional campaigns. According Glen Caroline of the NRA's Institute for Legislative Action, the goal was to educate a corps of volunteers "so that the entire calendar year of 2002 could be dedicated to activation, not education."[54] These volunteers were then turned over to the campaigns to use at their discretion. The NRA also organized training programs in 331 congressional districts and recruited 311 election volunteer coordinators. In 2002 the NRA also sent trademark orange postcards to potential voters in numerous competitive U.S. House and Senate races.[55]

The National Federation of Independent Business also modeled its approach after labor unions. Dennis Whitfield of the NFIB concluded that, "We were effective having business owners going door-to-door, business-to-business, saying here are the facts, saying who's better for business."[56] Another example of an interest group that made the ground war a higher priority in 2002 was the U.S. Chamber of Commerce. Bill Miller of that organization told us, "We concentrated on educating our members and putting people on the ground. I had fifty people on the ground in thirty-two states the last week of the election, compared to only fifteen [people] in 2000."[57]

Business groups especially focused efforts on technology, using the Internet and e-mail to help businesses construct customized websites and contact their employees with customized messages regarding voter registration and the voting records of elected officials. The model for these efforts was created by BIPAC and was called the Prosperity Project. This effort began in 2000 but grew significantly in scope for 2002.[58] This web-based approach was also adopted by the U.S. Chamber of Commerce.

In the immediate aftermath of the 2002 election, the Republican ground war effort was given a lot of credit for the narrow victories in several competitive races.[59] Clearly the 72 Hour Task Force and the efforts of Republican-allied groups deserve a fair amount of credit. Bernadette Budde, of BIPAC, summed it up this way:

> If they were on the field and we were on the sidelines, they were going to beat the crap out of us every single time. If they were on the field and we were tiptoeing on the field, they were probably still going to beat the crap out of us every single time. But if we were both playing with an experienced team, and they field their team and we field our team, why wouldn't we be able to beat them?[60]

The success of the 72 Hour Task Force appears to have varied significantly across states. The RNC cites the South Dakota Senate race, even though they were narrowly defeated, as an example of an especially successful 72 Hour Task Force effort. They had precinct captains in all 844 voting precincts statewide and also claim a total of 5,986 Election Day volunteers. They also cite as examples of particularly successful efforts the voter identification program in the Iowa Second Congressional District race, the absentee vote program in the Colorado Seventh Congressional District race, voter identification and targeting in the North Carolina Senate race, and the final seventy-two hours in both the Indiana Second Congressional District race and the Georgia Senate race.[61]

2004 and Beyond

The broadcast-dominated strategies practiced by parties and interest groups as they made their first major forays into competitive congressional elections through soft money and issue advocacy in 1996 did not bear the kind of fruit they wanted. In the midst of campaigns with high volumes of television and with disinterested, if not disenchanted, citizens, parties and interest groups began to discover more effective ways of connecting with voters and mobilizing their supporters. In 2002 Republicans finally achieved a level of effort and sophistication in their ground-war strategy that neutralized the electoral advantage Democrats had enjoyed as a result of their efforts in 1998 and 2000. Both parties and their allied groups are not likely to ever completely abandon television as a tool to communicate with voters, but both will likely continue to give added emphasis to the ground war, particularly to the person-to-person tactics that have proven so effective.

The growth in ground-war activities in 2002 was particularly evident among political party committees, most notably Republicans. With BCRA in effect for 2004, growth in the ground war is likely to continue because of restrictions the new law places on broadcast advertising and the ban on soft money for party committees. These changes mean that the ground war in 2004 and beyond is likely to grow, especially among interest groups.

The extensive interaction and cooperation between parties and interest groups on ground-war activities justifies a rethinking of our conceptualization of political parties. In the competitive election context, at least, a political party can now more accurately be thought of as a network composed of the traditional party organization, consultants, and allied interest groups. This team approach is especially evident in the ground-war efforts of both sides; it includes not only the coordinated campaign on the Democratic side or the state-level 72 Hour Task Forces on the Republican side but interest groups with the clout to influence party election strategy. The Republican Party depends on business groups for election-related activity, just as the Democratic Party depends on labor unions. Thus, when these groups suggest a shift in election strategy to the party, the party must pay attention.

Ground-war tactics are driven by resources available to each partisan coalition. The Democratic coalition can draw upon a large base of volunteers from labor union allies, which gives them a natural advantage in person-to-person contacting. The Republican reliance on religious conservatives for ground-war efforts is made more difficult by the lack of a centralized membership-based organization from which to draw volunteers. Because the Republican coalition must work harder to find ground-war troops, they are more likely to shift their resources to direct mail and other forms of ground-war communication that do not require a large volunteer force.

Ironically both party coalitions have finally succeeded at dedicating substantial resources toward their ground war and voter mobilization efforts, many of which could be classified as party-building activities, as the 1979 FECA amendments intended for soft money, but this transformation did not occur until the eve of BCRA's soft-money ban. However, because of the much-touted successes on both sides, it is likely that substantial ground-war efforts will continue into the future, even if soft money is no longer available to fund these efforts.

Early indications for 2004 and beyond suggest that both sides will emphasize the ground war more than ever before. With ample resources available from the fund-raising prowess of President Bush, Republicans will likely continue to dedicate significant resources to effective ground war and voter mobilization efforts. Corporate America will also continue to move in this direction, placing more emphasis on mobilizing employees in competitive contests. For example, BIPAC, which contacted 1.5 million employee voters in 2000 and 11 million in 2002, has announced plans to contact at least 20 million in 2004.[62] Democrats will continue to rely on labor unions for their ground war, and these efforts will expand beyond the mobilization of union members and their families. Steve Rosenthal, political director of the AFL-CIO from 1995 through 2002, is now heading up two newly formed 527 organizations called the Partnership for America's Families and America Coming Together, which aim to use the techniques perfected at the AFL-CIO to reach beyond union members to other likely Democratic voters.

The shift to the ground war in 2002 and beyond also has implications for successfully tracking the activities of noncandidate groups in future congressional elections. Broadcast communications are easier to track and assess. When one sees a payment to a television station for $500 of political advertising, it is relatively straightforward to figure out what occurred as a result of that expenditure. It is more difficult to track and assess the impact of ground-war activity. How does one assess the impact of an unpaid volunteer recruited to work on a candidate campaign by an interest group? It is activity that may not even be revealed on disclosure forms. And when it is disclosed, sometimes the only expense listed is the minuscule cost associated with recruiting the volunteer in the first place. As discussed in detail in chapter 3, the same point can be made about internal communications. When an internal communication is sent to group members only and is not primarily political in nature, disclosure is not required. Our research can begin to systematically describe and understand these below-the-radar efforts.

Notes

1. This use of the term *ground war* is consistent with David B. Magleby, "Outside Money and the Ground War in 1998," in David B. Magleby, ed., *Outside Money: Soft Money and Issue Advocacy in the 1998 Congressional Elections* (Lanham, Md.: Rowman and Littlefield, 2000).

2. Darrell M. West, *Air Wars: Television Advertising in Election Campaigns, 1952–2000*, 3d ed. (Congressional Quarterly, 2001).

3. Paul S. Herrnson, "Parties and Interest Groups in Postreform Congressional Elections," in Allan J. Cigler and Burdett A. Loomis, eds., *Interest Group Politics*, 5th ed. (Congressional Quarterly, 1998); Robin Gerber, "Building to Win, Building to Last: The AFL-CIO COPE Takes on the Republican Congress," in Robert Biersack, Paul S. Herrnson, and Clyde Wilcox, eds., *After the Revolution: PACs and Lobbies in the Republican Congress* (Boston: Allyn and Bacon, 1998).

4. Magleby, *Outside Money*, p. 4.

5. Adam Nagourney, "TV's Tight Grip on Campaigns Is Weakening," *New York Times*, September 5, 2002, p. A1.

6. Magleby, *Outside Money*; and David B. Magleby, ed., *The Other Campaign: Soft Money and Issue Advocacy in the 2000 Congressional Elections* (Lanham, Md.: Rowman and Littlefield, 2003).

7. Daniel M. Shea and Michael John Burton, *Campaign Craft: The Strategies, Tactics, and Art of Political Campaign Management* (Westport, Conn.: Praeger, 2001), p. 184.

8. Steven J. Rosenstone and John Mark Hansen, *Mobilization, Participation, and Democracy in America* (Macmillan, 1993).

9. Kenneth M. Goldstein and Travis N. Ridout, "The Politics of Participation: Mobilization and Turnout over Time," *Political Behavior*, vol. 24 (March 2002), pp. 3–29; Michael T. Hannahan, "Campaign Strategy and Direct Voter Contact," in Paul S. Herrnson, ed., *Playing Hardball: Campaigning for the U.S. Congress* (Upper Saddle River, N.J.: Prentice-Hall, 2001); Jan E. Leighley, *Strength in Numbers? The Political Mobilization of Racial and Ethnic Minorities* (Princeton University Press, 2001); David Niven, "The Limits of Mobilization: Turnout Evidence from State House Primaries," *Political Behavior*, vol. 23 (December 2001), pp. 335–50; David Niven, "The Mobilization Calendar: The Time-Dependent Effects of Personal Contact on Turnout," *American Politics Research*, vol. 30 (May 2002), pp. 307–22; Peter W. Wielhouwer, "The Mobilization of Campaign Activists by the Party Canvass," *American Politics Quarterly*, vol. 27 (April 1999), pp. 177–200; Peter W. Wielhouwer, "Releasing the

Fetters: Parties and the Mobilization of the African-American Electorate," *Journal of Politics,* vol. 62 (February 2000), pp. 206–22; Peter W. Wielhouwer and Brad Lockerbie, "Party Contacting and Political Participation, 1952–90," *American Journal of Political Science,* vol. 38 (February 1994), pp. 211–29.

10. Alan S. Gerber and Donald P. Green, "The Effects of Canvassing, Telephone Calls, and Direct Mail on Voter Turnout: A Field Experiment," *American Political Science Review,* vol. 94 (September 2000), pp. 653–63; Alan S. Gerber and Donald P. Green, "Do Phone Calls Increase Voter Turnout: A Field Experiment," *Public Opinion Quarterly,* vol. 65 (2001), pp. 75–85.

11. Magleby, "Outside Money."

12. The averages are compared for the competitive races only—twenty-five (six Senate and nineteen House) in 2002 and seventeen (five Senate and twelve House) in 2000.

13. In Missouri in 2002 the candidates spent about $20 million, the parties $5.7 million, and the interest groups $1.2 million. In 2000 the candidates spent $18 million and the parties at least $10 million, while the interest groups levels are difficult to estimate because of the presidential race. See chapter 6 of this volume." See also Martha E. Kropf and others, "The 2000 Missouri Senate Race," in David B. Magleby, ed., *Election Advocacy: Soft Money and Issue Advocacy in the 2000 Congressional Elections* (Center for the Study of Elections and Democracy, Brigham Young University, 2001).

14. After being asked how many pieces of mail they had received on an average day during the past week, the respondent was asked, "How does this compare to previous elections? Is it more, less, or about the same?"

15. Sandra Anglund and Clyde McKee, "Connecticut Fifth District," in David B. Magleby, ed. *Outside Money: Soft Money and Issue Ads in Competitive 1998 Congressional Elections,* monograph version, Center for the Study of Elections and Democracy, Brigham Young University, 1999; Sandra Anglund and Joanne Miller, "The 2000 Connecticut Fifth Congressional District Race," in Magleby, *Election Advocacy.*

16. Michael J. Malbin and others, "New Interest Group Strategies—A Preview of Post McCain-Feingold Politics?" (www.cfinst.org/studies/pdf/int_groups_CFIpaper.pdf [May 15, 2003]).

17. Ibid.

18. James Dyke, press secretary, RNC, telephone interview by Quin Monson, January 23, 2003.

19. Kenneth B. Mehlman, deputy assistant to the president and director of political affairs, White House, interview by David Magleby and Jonathan Tanner, Washington, D.C., November 15, 2002.

20. Republican National Committee, "72 Hour Task Force," preelection 2002 version, PowerPoint presentation, obtained from James Dyke, RNC press secretary, January 23, 2003.

21. Curt Anderson, The Anderson Group, and Blaise Hazelwood, RNC political director, interview by David Magleby and Jonathan Tanner, Washington, D.C., May 8, 2003.

22. RNC, "72 Hour Task Force," preelection 2002 version. See also Stuart Rothenberg, "Will State Parties Buy What RNC Is Selling on GOTV Efforts?" *Roll Call*, June 24, 2002 (www.rollcall.com/pages/columns/rothenberg/00/2002/roth0624.html [December 20, 2002]).

23. These findings are also generally supported in academic research. See Gerber and Green, "The Effects of Canvassing."

24. Dennis Whitfield, senior vice president, NFIB, interview by David Magleby and Quin Monson, Washington, D.C., November 8, 2002.

25. National Federation of Independent Business, "NFIB, A Case Study: VA-4 Special Election," obtained from Dennis Whitfield, November 8, 2002.

26. See chapter 7 of this volume.

27. Chuck Cunningham, federal affairs director, NRA Institute for Legislative Action, interview by David Magleby, Quin Monson, Jonathan Tanner, and Nicole Carlisle Squires, November 7, 2002.

28. Greg Casey, president, and Darrell Shull, political operations vice president, BIPAC, interview by Quin Monson and Jonathan Tanner, Washington, D.C., November 11, 2002.

29. For a review of the literature on interest group learning with some examples from recent elections, see Malbin and others, "New Interest Group Strategies."

30. Fredrick C. Harris, *Something Within: Religion in African-American Political Activism* (Oxford University Press, 1999).

31. See chapter 8 of this volume.

32. The coordinated campaign organized by each state Democratic Party is not the same as coordinated expenditures, which are shared expenditures between a party and a candidate. Coordinated expenditures are described in detail in chapter 2.

33. Gail Stoltz, "Mobilizing Voters: The Coordinated Campaign," in Anthony Corrado, Thomas E. Mann, and Trevor Potter, eds., *Inside the Campaign Finance Battle: Court Testimony on the New Reforms* (Brookings, 2003), p. 122.

34. Laurie Moskowitz, principal, FieldWorks, interview by David Magleby, Quin Monson, and Jennifer Jensen, Washington, D.C., February 21, 2002; Andy Grossman, political director, and Mike Gehrke, research director, DSCC, interview by David Magleby, Quin Monson, and Jonathan Tanner, Washington, D.C., November 8, 2002.

35. Jay Barth and Janine Parry, "Provincialism, Personalism, and Politics: Campaign Spending and the 2002 U.S. Senate Race in Arkansas," in David B. Magleby and J. Quin Monson, eds., "The Noncandidate Campaign," *PS: Politi-*

cal Science online e-symposium, July 2003 (www.apsanet.org/PS/july03/barth.pdf [July 30, 2003]).

36. David Redlawsk and Arthur Sanders, "The 2002 Iowa House and Senate Elections: The More Things Change . . . ," in Magleby and Monson, "The Non-candidate Campaign."

37. "The 2002 Union Vote," survey by Peter D. Hart Research for the AFL-CIO among 1,020 voting union members, November 5, 2002, AFL-CIO, November 6, 2002 (www.afl-cio.org/mediacenter/prsptm/upload/show6843final_1.ppt [November 20, 2002]).

38. Mike Lux, president, Progressive Strategies, telephone interview by David Magleby and Jonathan Tanner, January 9, 2003.

39. Steve Rosenthal, political director, AFL-CIO, press event, "The Last Hurrah? Soft Money and Issue Advocacy in the 2002 Elections," Center for the Study of Elections and Democracy, National Press Club, Washington, D.C., February 3, 2003.

40. In 2002 we found "lost timers" in the First and Second Congressional District races of New Mexico as well as in the Maryland Eighth Congressional District race. See Lonna Atkeson, "The New Mexico 1st and 2nd Congressional District Races," in Magleby and Monson, monograph version, *The Last Hurrah?* See also Owen Abbe, "The Maryland 8th Congressional District Race," in Magleby and Monson, monograph version, *The Last Hurrah?*

41. Jack Polidori, political affairs specialist, NEA, interview by David Magleby and Jonathan Tanner, Washington, D.C., November 15, 2002.

42. Geoff Garin, Garin-Hart-Yang Research, presentation at AFL-CIO post-election briefing, November 6, 2002, videotape (C-SPAN, tape 173707).

43. Stanley Greenberg, "RE: 2002 Vote by Demographic Groups," memorandum to interested parties, November 12, 2002 (www.greenbergresearch.com/publications/reports/02Vote.pdf [May 19, 2003]), p. 5.

44. Voter News Service General Election Exit Poll, 2002 [computer file], ICPSR version, New York, 2002 (Ann Arbor, Mich.: Inter-University Consortium for Political and Social Research, 2003).

45. Linda Lipsen, senior director of public affairs, Association of Trial Lawyers of America, interview by David Magleby and Jonathan Tanner, Washington, D.C., December 19, 2002.

46. Sheila O'Connell, political director, EMILY's List, interview by Quin Monson and Jonathan Tanner, Washington, D.C., December 11, 2002.

47. Stanley Greenberg, "RE: 2002 Vote by Demographic Groups," p. 2; Voter News Service General Election Exit Poll 2002.

48. Curt Anderson, The Anderson Group, press event, "The Last Hurrah? Soft Money and Issue Advocacy in the 2002 Elections," Center for the Study of Elections and Democracy, National Press Club, Washington, D.C., February 3, 2003.

49. RNC, "72 Hour Task Force," preelection 2002 version.

50. Blaise Hazelwood, RNC political director, telephone interview by David Magleby, Quin Monson, and Jonathan Tanner, January 17, 2003.

51. Anderson and Hazelwood interview, May 8, 2003.

52. Susan Crabtree, "DeLay Steps Up Call for Volunteers," *Roll Call*, October 17, 2002, p. 3.

53. RNC, "72 Hour Task Force," postelection 2003 version.

54. Glen Caroline, Grassroots Division director, NRA Institute for Legislative Action, interview by David Magleby, Quin Monson, Jonathan Tanner, Nicole Carlisle Squires, and Stephanie Curtis, Washington, D.C., November 14, 2002.

55. Ibid. See also Glen Caroline, "Maximizing Campaign Volunteers: The NRA Way," *Campaigns & Elections*, vol. 24 (April 2003), pp. 26–29.

56. Whitfield interview, November 8, 2002.

57. Bill Miller, political director, U.S. Chamber of Commerce, interview by David Magleby and Quin Monson, Washington, D.C., November 7, 2002.

58. Bernadette Budde, senior vice president, BIPAC, interview by Quin Monson, Jonathan Tanner, and Nicole Carlisle Squires, Washington, D.C., November 6, 2002.

59. Edward Walsh, "Election Turnout Rose Slightly, to 39.3%; GOP Mobilization Credited; Participation Was Down in Some Democratic Areas," *Washington Post*, November 8, 2002, p. A10; Todd S. Purdam and David E. Rosenbaum, "The 2002 Elections: The Campaign; Bush's Stumping for Candidates Is Seen as a Critical Factor in Republican Victories," *New York Times*, November 7, 2002, p. B1.

60. Budde interview, November 6, 2002.

61. RNC, "72 Hour Task Force," postelection 2003 version.

62. Brody Mullins, "Business Changes Course: Turnout Becomes Focus," *Roll Call*, July 9, 2003, p. 1.

FIVE   *From Intensity to*
             Tragedy: The Minnesota
             U.S. Senate Race

WILLIAM H. FLANIGAN
JOANNE M. MILLER
JENNIFER L. WILLIAMS
NANCY H. ZINGALE

THE TRAGIC DEATH of Senator Paul Wellstone
(D-Minn.) eleven days before the 2002 election created shock waves
throughout Minnesota. On Friday, October 25, Senator Wellstone was
killed in a plane crash in northern Minnesota. A moratorium on campaigning immediately went into effect in all election races, lasting for
five days, until after the public memorial service on Tuesday night. This
service, held in a sports arena on the University of Minnesota campus
and attracting a crowd of 20,000, was televised for over three hours on
all the major network affiliates in the state. It reflected both the anguish
of the senator's supporters and the passion of his political convictions,
turning, perhaps inevitably, into a foot-stamping, fist-pumping partisan
rally. The backlash was immediate, with callers to the television stations
complaining about the coverage and donors going online or telephoning
the Republican Party to give money.[1] Governor Jesse Ventura (of the
Independence Party) walked out in the middle of the service and thereafter publicly lambasted the Democratic Party for orchestrating it. The
day after the memorial service, the Democratic-Farmer-Labor Party
selected Walter F. Mondale to fill the vacancy on the ticket created by
Wellstone's death. An abbreviated six-day campaign between Mondale
and Republican Senate candidate Norm Coleman ensued.

We want to thank Kali Frederick, Haley Gilman, Shawn Niehaus, and Abby
Pontzer for their research assistance. We would also like to thank Dan Hofren-
ning for sharing information and insights on the Senate race.

The aftermath of the memorial service was felt in many Minnesota races. Strategies were undercut, money went unspent, and attention was diverted. We should not be misled, however, by these dramatic events into thinking that the Minnesota Senate campaign was unique throughout. Our analysis takes into account three phases: first, the long period of campaigning before the plane crash; second, the five-day moratorium after the crash; and third, the six days of campaigning before Election Day. Generalizations and comparisons with other races are necessarily limited to the period before the crash.

The Minnesota Senate race began conventionally enough, with incumbent Democratic Senator Paul Wellstone facing Republican Norm Coleman, former mayor of St. Paul. Wellstone was seen as vulnerable, and the race was expected to be highly competitive, with plenty of outside money. Early polls indicated that the race was not only close, but that relatively few voters were undecided and that voter sentiment changed little throughout the summer and early fall. Ultimately Coleman's victory was attributed to the uproar over the memorial service, the unexpected energizing of Republicans, and the mobilization of independent voters against Democrats. Turnout was over 60 percent, high in an off-year election, even by Minnesota standards.[2]

Minnesota's Political History and Geography

Minnesota was settled in the nineteenth century by Scandinavians, Germans, and Irish. It remains predominantly Caucasian (89.4 percent), with small populations of African Americans (3.5 percent), Hispanics (2.9 percent), Asian Americans (2.9 percent), and Native Americans (1.1 percent).[3] Since the 1980s Minnesota has seen substantial immigration of Southeast Asians, primarily Hmong, and more recently, Somalis. Lutheranism and Catholicism are the largest religious denominations.

According to the 2000 U.S. census, Minnesota's population is 4,919,479 and has remained fairly steady.[4] Within the state, the rural population is declining, and the suburban population growing. Approximately 60 percent of the state's population now resides within the seven-county metropolitan area.[5]

Minnesota is often characterized as one of the most liberal states in the nation, voting Democratic in every presidential election since 1960, save 1972, and twice electing Wellstone, arguably the most liberal member of the Senate. This characterization is something of an exaggeration, ignoring the fact that one or another Minnesota favorite son was on the ballot in five of those presidential races, and for six of his twelve years in the Senate, Wellstone's colleague from Minnesota was one of the more conservative members of that body. Nonetheless Minnesota is heir to a progressive tradition. Populism found fertile soil in the rural areas of the state in the late nineteenth century; the left-leaning Farmer-Labor Party outpolled the Democrats and became the state's second largest party in the 1930s. It merged with the Democrats in 1944, giving Minnesota's Democratic Party its distinctive name—the Democratic-Farmer-Labor Party (DFL).

Minnesota poll data show the electorate to be 44 percent DFL party identifiers and 33 percent Republican.[6] At 23 percent, independents hold the balance of power. Recently DFL numbers have declined, but Republican identifiers have not increased. Democratic strength in Minnesota is concentrated in the Twin Cities of Minneapolis and St. Paul and in the northeastern Iron Range.[7] This Democratic base is supplemented by pockets of strength in the agricultural north and west, with their remnants of populist tradition. The DFL suffers from a bit of schizophrenia, however. The Twin Cities is solidly pro-choice, antigun, and "green." The Iron Range loves its guns, sees tourist development of its wilderness areas as economic salvation after the demise of open-pit mining, and often supports pro-life candidates. It is not easy to hold this coalition together, and urban liberals, especially women candidates, have often been unable to do so.

Minnesota's reputation for progressivism also comes from its Republican Party, historically internationalist and liberal on civil rights and social issues. Since the 1973 decision in *Roe* v. *Wade*, however, Minnesota precinct caucuses, endorsing conventions, and legislative races have been the sites of fierce battles over abortion. As partisans have sorted themselves out over the abortion issue, the Republican Party has become increasingly dominated by the religious right. Republican strength lies in the "Republican L," a band of rural farming communities and small towns and cities running across southern Minnesota and then north through the western half of the state.

The Senate Candidates

Prior to his death, Senator Paul Wellstone was running for his third term in the U.S. Senate, having reconsidered his promise of twelve years before to serve only two terms. A former professor of political science at Carleton College, he was a fiery orator and effective grassroots organizer. His first electoral victory in 1990 was something of a fluke, made possible by a major blunder by his opponent but facilitated by a series of charmingly quirky and self-deprecating TV commercials. Throughout his tenure, Wellstone was seen as a little too liberal and a little too confrontational for Minnesota, and his approval ratings were never high. Yet he navigated the waters of DFL politics with considerable skill. When his airplane crashed eleven days before the election, it was widely believed that he had pulled ahead of his challenger and would hold his Senate seat.[8]

Wellstone's successor candidate was Walter F. Mondale, former Minnesota attorney general, U.S. senator, vice president of the United States, and 1984 Democratic presidential candidate—a true icon of Minnesota politics. He was also seventy-four years old. Voters under forty had never had the opportunity to vote for him, and supporters wondered if he would be able to connect with the new generation. In the single debate between Mondale and Coleman, Mondale demonstrated a command of the issues and a breadth of experience but still presented a stark contrast to his younger and more vigorous opponent.

Republican Norm Coleman began his career as a Democrat, working in the office of Attorney General Hubert H. (Skip) Humphrey III. Although he had competed for and been denied the endorsement of the Democratic Party, he was elected mayor of St. Paul in 1993 in an officially nonpartisan race. In 1996 he supported the re-election of Senator Wellstone and President Clinton in a speech to the DFL State Convention, an appearance that provided an interesting vignette for a Wellstone television ad in 2002. Shortly after the 1996 election, Coleman officially announced his conversion to the Republican Party and received the Republican endorsement for his re-election race as mayor of St. Paul in 1997. Having just been re-elected mayor, he sought and received the Republican endorsement for governor in 1998, ultimately facing his old boss, Skip Humphrey, in the general election. While Coleman and Humphrey concentrated their attacks on each other, Jesse Ventura surprised virtually everyone by winning the governorship. Coleman finished his term as mayor, winning accolades from business for holding the line on taxes and for bringing major league hockey back to Minnesota. He served as chair of the Bush campaign in Minnesota in 2000 and quickly received a payback when Vice President Cheney persuaded a potential

Republican rival for the Senate nomination to opt for the governor's race instead. This was a precursor to the four visits President Bush paid to Minnesota during the course of the 2002 Senate campaign.[9]

As the first phase of the campaign developed, Coleman emphasized his experience and success as mayor of St. Paul, and Wellstone focused on his experience working for Minnesotans in the Senate. Both candidates talked about education and argued about who would protect Social Security and provide low-cost drugs for seniors. Wellstone campaigned against tax breaks for the rich and was in turn attacked for voting to retain the estate tax. Wellstone was criticized for breaking his pledge to serve only two terms, as was Coleman for converting from Democrat to Republican. Although the candidates worked hard and were visible through public appearances and television advertising, political news coverage during this stage of the election year paid more attention to the three-way race to succeed Jesse Ventura as governor.[10]

When Walter Mondale accepted the mantle of Democratic candidacy, he also accepted the Wellstone legacy. In his short campaign, Mondale emphasized his desire to promote the issues that were important to Wellstone and serve the same people and interests as Wellstone. Coleman, for his part, began emphasizing his relative youth and energy.

Money

By Minnesota standards, an enormous amount of money was available and spent in the Senate race. Neither side could claim they had inadequate resources. Even the brief Mondale campaign raised more money than it could spend. The Minnesota Senate race was one of those races in which the candidates outspent the parties and the interest groups.

Candidates' Funds

The candidates raised roughly $25 million, which established a new record for non-self-financed races in Minnesota (see table 5-1). Although much of the money was raised during the general election campaign, Mondale raised his $2.7 million in less than eleven days. Wellstone took in over $2.5 million after the mid-September primary, and the Coleman campaign raised over $1.5 million in the same period. Wellstone accepted very little money from political action committees (PACs), about 7 percent in 2001–02.[11] Coleman received PAC funds amounting to 17 percent of his contributions.

Table 5-1. *Candidate Receipts and Expenditures, 2001–02*
Dollars

Source	Wellstone (D)	Mondale (D)	Coleman(R)
From PACs	781,887	380,004	1,801,287
From individuals	11,699,925	2,129721	6,372,650
From party	26,648	100,467	150,200
From candidate	0	0	0
Other contributions	123,148	116,718	1,882,374
Total receipts	12,631,608	2,726,910	10,206,511
Total expenditures	12,617,876	1,833,029	10,035,279
Cash on hand 12/31/02	13,732	893,880	173,470

Source: Federal Election Commission, "2001–02 U.S. House and U.S. Senate Candidate Info," December 31, 2002 (www.fecinfo.com/cgi-win/x_statedis.exe [June 8, 2003]).

Wellstone raised substantial amounts of money out of state; 58 percent of his individual contributions over $200 were from outside Minnesota. Coleman did well for a challenger, with 37 percent of his funds coming from out of state. The apparent advantage in funding held by Wellstone over Coleman is somewhat misleading because Wellstone, who relied heavily on small donations, spent $3.6 million on fundraising, including $2.8 million in direct mail and telemarketing which brought in contributions from 90,000 people nationwide.[12] This differential in fund-raising costs meant that Wellstone had only about $1 million more than Coleman to spend on the campaign.

Mondale faced a seemingly impossible task when he was approached by Wellstone's surviving sons and campaign manager to take the senator's place on the DFL ticket, on the Saturday morning after the plane crash. In the next ten days a national campaign raised over $2.5 million for Mondale. Although the Wellstone campaign gave the DFL $450,000, under campaign finance regulations only $1,000 could go from the Wellstone campaign to the Mondale campaign. The state DFL Party announced an ad buy of $500,000 to support Mondale, but the campaign needed its own ads and had to finance his whirlwind campaign around the state, nicknamed the Fritz Blitz.

The Democratic National Committee (DNC) helped raise $100,000 for Mondale from state Democratic committees and Senate leadership PACs. Labor PACs contributed as well. Tens of thousands of dollars arrived from Hollywood. In all, almost $1 million arrived in donations of over $1,000. One local fund-raising event took in approximately $200,000. Earlier in the campaign, the fund-raising website MoveOn-

Table 5-2. *National Party Contributions to Minnesota State Parties, 2001–02*

Dollars

Committee	Amount
Contribution to Democratic-Farmer-Labor Party	
Democratic National Committee	564,563
Democratic Senatorial Campaign Committee	8,705,279
Democratic Congressional Campaign Committee	2,375,677
Contribution to Republican Party	
Republican National Committee	3,517,270
National Republican Senatorial Committee	8,300,000
National Republican Congressional Committee	2,300,000

Source: Federal Election Commission, "Party Committees Raise More than $1 Billion in 2001–2002," press release, March 20, 2002 (www.fec.gov/press/20030320party/20030103party.html [April 29, 2003]); NRSC spending data from Chris LaCivita, NRSC political director, personal e-mail communication to Jonathan Tanner, January 3, 2003; NRCC spending data from Mike McElwain, NRCC political director, interview by David Magleby and Jonathan Tanner, Washington, D.C., December 2, 2002.

Pac.org had raised $600,000 for Wellstone from people opposed to war with Iraq. That same website took in $700,000 for Mondale in five days.[13]

Political Party Funds

Both the DFL and the Republican Party had large amounts of money to spend in the Senate race. Each is estimated to have spent over $8 million on behalf of their candidates. Most of this money came from the national parties. In each party the Senate campaign committees were the main source of funds. The bulk of this soft money was spent on issue advocacy television advertising (see table 5-2).

The Impact of Money

The money raised and spent by the candidates, parties, and interest groups was spent overwhelmingly on the air war, mainly television. In Minnesota this may be somewhat misleading, because all candidates, especially Wellstone and Mondale, relied heavily on volunteer activities to wage the ground war.

The Air War

Before the plane crash, Minnesotans might have said that the most memorable characteristic of the 2002 election was the barrage of television ads. Over 25,000 political spots ran on open-air channels in the Twin Cities media market alone.[14] Half of these were for the Senate race. Between $20 million and $25 million was spent on the air war, almost all of which was spent on broadcast television. Each side spent roughly equal amounts on the air war, and expenditures on each side were divided fairly evenly between the candidates and the parties (see table 5-3).

The Wellstone campaign produced twelve ads, and the DFL funded eleven ads on his behalf. The Coleman campaign produced seventeen ads, and Republicans added ten. The AFL-CIO provided one ad for Wellstone, and the Sierra Club contributed three on his behalf. Americans for Job Security and the United Seniors Association both produced attack ads against Wellstone. Pro-Wellstone spots aired a total of 6,535 times between January 1 and October 25, 2002, the day of the plane crash, while pro-Coleman (or anti-Wellstone) spots aired 5,902 times during this period.[15]

Surprisingly the tone of the campaign was more positive than negative, if we consider the kinds of ads produced and the total number of times positive ads versus negative ads aired.[16] The majority of the ads produced by the campaigns and the parties were positive.[17] Seventy percent of the spots aired on Wellstone's behalf were positive, 15 percent were negative ads about Coleman, and 15 percent compared Wellstone and Coleman to emphasize Wellstone's strengths. Although both campaign and DFL Party ads for Wellstone were more positive than negative, a higher percentage of the DFL ads were positive than the campaign's. On the Coleman side, two-thirds of the spots aired were positive, and about one quarter were negative. After the election Chris LaCivita, political director of the National Republican Senatorial Committee (NRSC) commented, "We ran positive ads that were driving me batty."[18] His Democratic counterpart, Andrew Grossman said, "It was giving me butterflies."[19] With regard to interest groups, the ads aired by the Sierra Club and AFL-CIO supporting Wellstone were positive, while the ads from Americans for Job Security and United Seniors Association attacked Wellstone.

Both campaigns began positively and remained so for a considerable period of time. The Wellstone ads, which began airing in June, and the DFL ads on Wellstone's behalf, which began in March, were entirely positive until mid-September. For the remainder of the campaign, the DFL aired only negative or comparison ads, while the Wellstone campaign ran a mix of all three types of ads.[20] The ad deemed most negative

Table 5-3. *The Air War: Television and Radio Advertising Expenditures, Minnesota Senate Race, 2002*[a]
Dollars

Type and organization	TV	Radio	Total spent	CMAG TV
Democratic allies[b]				
Candidates				
Wellstone for Senate	4,775,000	225,000	5,000,000[c]	2,672,665
Mondale for Senate	1,000,000	. . .	1,000,000[c]	. . .
Political parties				
Minnesota DFL	6,000,000	250,000	6,250,000[d]	3,340,220
Interest groups				
AFL–CIO	. . .	. . .	. . .	657,345
North Star Chapter of the Sierra Club	. . .	. . .	. . .	286,469
Sierra Club	45,242	. . .	45,242	279,878
National Education Association	7,587	. . .	7,587	. . .
Planned Parenthood of Minnesota	3,468	. . .	3,468	. . .
Republican allies[b]				
Candidates				
Coleman for U.S. Senate	?	?	5,000,000[e]	1,946,022
Political parties				
Republican Party of Minnesota	?	?	5,000,000[f]	4,055,679
National Republican Senatorial Committee	?	. . .	?	467,764
Republican National Committee	. . .	. . .	. . .	308,686
Interest groups				
United Seniors Association	144,974	. . .	144,974	687,334
Americans for Job Security	10,468	. . .	10,468	426,144

Source: Data compiled from: David B. Magleby, J. Quin Monson, and the Center for the Study of Elections and Democracy, 2002 Soft Money and Issue Advocacy Database (Brigham Young University, 2002); Campaign Media Analysis Group (CMAG) data.

a. See appendix A for a more detailed explanation of data. The ad-buy data collected for this study may contain extraneous data due to the difficulty in determining the content of the ads. Parties or interest groups that purchased ads possibly ran some ads promoting House or Senatorial candidates or ballot propositions not in the study's sample but still within that media market. Unless the researchers were able to determine the exact content of the ad buy from the limited information given by the station, the data may contain observations that do not pertain to the study's relevant House or Senate races.

For comparison purposes, CMAG data are included in the table. Because of the sheer volume of television and radio stations and varying degrees of compliance in providing ad-buy information, data on spending by various groups might be incomplete. This table is not intended to represent comprehensive organization spending or activity within the sample races. A more complete picture can be obtained by examining this table with table 5-4.

In blank cells, ". . ." reflects the absence of collected data and does not imply the organization was inactive in that medium. A "?" indicates money was spent, but specific amounts are unknown.

b. Certain organizations that maintained neutrality were categorized according to which candidates their ads supported or attacked or whether the organization was openly anti- or pro-conservative or liberal.

c. Estimate provided by Jeff Blodgett, campaign manager, Wellstone for Senate.

d. Estimate provided by Bill Amberg, communications and research director, Minnesota DFL.

e. Estimate based on CMAG data, Twin Cities ad-buy data, and inferences from partial ad-buy data from outstate Minnesota.

f. Estimate based on CMAG data, limited ad-buy data from television stations in the Twin Cities and outstate Minnesota.

featured film coverage of the 1996 DFL state convention showing Coleman, then a DFL member, endorsing Wellstone with statements like "Join me today in common bond and unity as Democrats to ensure the reelection of Bill Clinton and Senator Paul Wellstone." The brief Mondale television campaign consisted only of positive ads.

The Coleman campaign ran positive ads from February to the end of July, went off the air for a month to save money, and returned with positive ads through the end of September.[21] There was a second break of one week, and then the campaign ran a mix of positive and negative ads until the plane crash. After the moratorium there were only positive Coleman ads on television, including two ads that featured his young daughter extolling her dad's virtues.

Party ads supporting Coleman ran in April and May, and then there was a break until the end of the summer. For two weeks the state Republican Party ran positive ads, but in mid-September the pattern shifted to mainly negative attacks on Wellstone. This pattern continued until the plane crash. After the moratorium all the spots were positive. A lot of attention was given to an ad that never aired. The NRSC prepared an ad criticizing Mondale by reminding voters of his association with the policies of the Carter administration and made the ad buys to run it. Coleman found out about the ad from the television stations and asked the party to withdraw it.[22]

Coleman made much more use of cable television than did Wellstone or Mondale. The political parties ran radio ads, but these activities did not represent major expenditures. A radio ad attacking Coleman for supporting the North American Free Trade Agreement was pulled by the state AFL-CIO late in the campaign from stations on the Iron Range in northern Minnesota, because Mondale shared this position with Coleman.

Most interest groups stayed off television during the campaign. Those who came into Minnesota, like the Sierra Club and Americans for Job Security, ran their ads both early and late in the campaign. Americans for Job Security made a $1 million anti-Wellstone ad buy for the end of the campaign but pulled the ad after the plane crash.

Why did the interest groups stay out of Minnesota? Several possible answers must be excluded. The race was so close for so long that the groups had to realize that either candidate could win. It would have been extremely odd for Democrats and liberals to give up on Wellstone and equally odd for Republicans and conservatives not to go after him.

Given the candidates' positions, no interest group was likely to conclude that it did not matter who won. Minnesota would appear to have been the perfect place to spend on a campaign. It is possible that interest groups shared the view of informed observers in Minnesota that large amounts of money would come in, and each group calculated that their additional impact would be modest and they should go elsewhere.[23] A final possibility is that the unexpectedly positive tone of the campaign deterred other groups from coming in with their negative ads.

The Senate race also illustrated how bad and inexpensive political advertising can be. A two-man corporation named CORAD, Citizens Opposed to Racism and Discrimination, produced an anti-Wellstone ad that included express advocacy for Coleman.[24] The ad ran twenty-five times on MSNBC in part of the Twin Cities during the middle two weeks of August at a total cost of $500. At one point the image of the Chinese Communist flag appears over Wellstone's forehead.[25] Several stations refused to run the ad, and various Republicans urged CORAD not to air it.[26] CORAD ran a second ad of similar quality in northern Minnesota, but this ad did not include express advocacy.

Overall the candidates held their own on television. Their ads were not outnumbered by issue advocacy party spots or interest-group buys. During much of the year, ads in the Senate race were entirely positive, with both candidates and parties bringing out negative ads toward the end of the campaign. Only the Wellstone tragedy turned the last week positive.

The Ground War

Judging from the elements of the ground war that came to our attention, the candidates' campaigns and the political party organizations accounted for the bulk of the activity (see table 5-4). The Wellstone campaign produced 750,000 pieces of literature.[27] The state Republican Party produced 1 million pieces of literature for Coleman.[28] The state parties paid for the mailing of all literature. The state Republican Party mailed 1 million absentee ballot applications; then they mailed a reminder and phoned the recipients. They also mailed 750,000 sample ballots.

Mondale's late entry into the race precluded much of the traditional ground war activity, so e-mail was used extensively on his behalf. Virtually all the e-mails in the Democratic half of table 5-4 were sent by the DFL and interest groups supporting Mondale. Most of the rest of the e-mails in table 5-4 were newsletters or similar types of communication.

Table 5-4. Number of Unique Campaign Communications by Organizations, Minnesota Senate Race, 2002[a]

Type and organization[b]	Type of campaign communication							Total
	E-mail messages	Surface mail pieces	Newspaper or magazine ads	Personal contacts	Phone calls	Radio ads	TV ads	
Democratic allies[c]								
Candidates								
Wellstone for Senate	3	18	...	...	1	...	12	34
Mondale for Senate	1	...	...	...	...	...	...	1
Political parties								
Minnesota Democratic-Farmer-Labor	1	16	...	...	5	1	11	34
Democratic National Committee	13	1	...	...	...	...	...	14
Democratic Senatorial Campaign Committee	...	3	...	...	...	...	...	3
Interest groups								
Labor[d]	...	17	...	...	2	...	1[e]	20
Sierra Club	...	6	1	...	...	...	3	10
American Federation of Teachers	...	6	...	...	...	...	...	6
Planned Parenthood	1	4	...	...	1[f]	...	...	6
League of Conservation Voters	1	3	...	...	1[g]	...	...	5
Education Minnesota PAC	2	2	...	...	...	...	...	4
NARAL Pro-Choice America	...	2	...	...	1	...	...	3
Alliance for Retired Americans	...	2[h]	...	...	...	...	...	2
Human Rights Campaign	...	1[i]	...	...	1[i]	...	...	2
MoveOn.org	2	...	...	...	...	...	...	2
National Education Association	...	1	...	...	1[j]	...	...	2
Association of Trial Lawyers of America	1[k]	...	...	...	...	...	...	1
Progressive Majority	1	...	...	...	...	...	...	1
Republican allies[c]								
Candidates								
Coleman for U.S. Senate	16	10	1	...	3	4	17	51
Political parties								
Republican Party of Minnesota	3	22	...	...	3	...	10	38

Interest groups

Interest groups					
Minnesota Citizens Concerned for Life	4	...	...	...	4
National Rifle Association	1[l]	1[l]	2	...	4
Americans for Job Security	...	1	2	...	3
U.S. Chamber of Commerce	1[m]	...	...	1	2
60 Plus Association	1	...	...	...	1
America 21	1	...	...	...	1
Associated Builders and Contractors	1[n]	...	...	...	1
Citizens Opposing Racism and Discrimination	...	2	...	...	2
Hunting and Shooting Sports Heritage Foundation	...	2	...	...	2
Minnesota Family Institute Council	1	...	...	...	1
Minnesota Republican Organized Labor Federation	1	...	...	...	1
National Pro-Life Alliance	...	...	...	1	1
National Federation of Independent Business	1	...	...	...	1
People's Advocate	1	...	...	...	1
United Seniors Association	...	1	...	...	1

Source: Magleby, Monson, and the CSED, 2002 Soft Money and Issue Advocacy Database.

a. See appendix A for a more detailed data explanation. This table is not intended to portray comprehensive organization activity within the sample races. A more complete picture can be obtained by examining this table together with table 5-3. Data represent the number of unique pieces or ads by the group and not a count of total items sent or made.

In blank cells, "..." reflects the absence of collected data and does not imply that the organization was inactive in that medium.

b. All state and local chapters or affiliates have been combined with their national affiliate to better render the picture of the organization's activity. For instance, Planned Parenthood of Minnesota data have been included in the Planned Parenthood totals.

c. Certain organizations that maintained neutrality were categorized according to which candidates their ads supported or attacked or whether the organization was anti- or pro-conservative or liberal.

d. The Labor category includes the AFL-CIO and all labor groups not explicitly affiliated with the AFL-CIO, including such groups as the Service Employees International Union and the International Brotherhood of Teamsters.

e. Denise Mitchell, assistant to the president of public affairs, AFL-CIO, interview by Quin Monson and Jonathan Tanner, Washington, D.C., December 10, 2002.

f. David Williams, director of Action Fund and PAC, Planned Parenthood, interview by David Magleby and Nicole Carlisle Squires, Washington, D.C., November 8, 2002.

g. Scott Stoermer, communications director, and Amy Kurtz, campaign director, LCV, interview by David Magleby and Jonathan Tanner, Washington, D.C., November 15, 2002.

h. Ed Coyle, executive director, Alliance for Retired Americans, telephone interview by David Magleby and Quin Monson, December 20, 2002.

i. Mark Perriello, PAC manager, Human Rights Campaign, telephone interview by David Magleby and Jonathan Tanner, January 17, 2003.

j. Jack Polidori, political affairs specialist, NEA, interview by David Magleby and Jonathan Tanner, Washington, D.C., November 15, 2002.

k. Linda Lipsen, senior director of public affairs, Association of Trial Lawyers of America, telephone interview by David Magleby and Quin Monson, December 19, 2002.

l. Glen Caroline, director, NRA Institute for Legislative Action, Grassroots Division, interview by David Magleby, Quin Monson, Jonathan Tanner, Nicole Carlisle Squires, and Stephanie Curtis, Washington, D.C., November 14, 2002

m. Bill Miller, political director, U.S. Chamber of Commerce, interview by David Magleby and Quin Monson, Washington, D.C., November 7, 2002.

n. Ned Monroe, director of political affairs, Associated Builders and Contractors, interview by Quin Monson and Jonathan Tanner, Washington, D.C., December 9, 2002.

The state DFL Party spent $500,000 on persuasive phone calls for Mondale.

Several interest groups were attracted to the Minnesota Senate race, but no one group or set of groups dominated the ground war. The League of Conservation Voters (LCV) spent $400,000 on mail and phone calls in support of Wellstone.[29] The LCV targeted the Twin Cities suburbs with, among other things, a "clean water" flier to independents with a fishing license. The National Education Association backed Wellstone, with $400,000 spent on direct mail and phones. Planned Parenthood mailed 200,000 pieces of literature in support of Wellstone to households in the Twin Cities suburbs; 190,000 of these households were phoned as well. Planned Parenthood also sent 200,000 e-mail messages in support of Mondale. The American Federation of Teachers, Planned Parenthood, and the Sierra Club all sent out mailings supporting Mondale before the election.

Wellstone was also targeted by anti-abortion groups, the National Rifle Association, and business groups. One piece of literature from the National Federation of Independent Businesses (NFIB) attracted attention in the media. On the weekend before the plane crash, the NFIB mailed 30,000 fliers to nonmember small businesses in Minnesota. (Cookie-cutter versions of the piece went to other targeted Senate races.) The flier contained a fairly conventional attack on Wellstone for not supporting the repeal of the estate tax ("taxing the dead") on one side and a large tombstone by an open grave on the other. This flier began arriving the day Wellstone was killed. Two-thirds of the mailing was retrieved from post offices, so presumably only about 10,000 were delivered to Minnesota businesses. The NFIB launched an automatic phone call to everyone on the mailing list. A letter, an e-mail, and a fax from the president of the NFIB went to every member, apologizing and explaining that they had suspended the mailing.

Wellstone's vote to retain the estate tax produced another novel element in the ground war (or perhaps the air war). During Minnesota's well-attended state fair, Americans for Job Security flew an airplane over the fairgrounds, pulling a banner that read, "Wellstone—Stop Taxing the Dead."

Given that turnout in 2002 equaled the unusually high turnout of 1998 in Minnesota, it is reasonable to ask, which candidate benefited? Both sides believed they had outdone the other in getting out their vote. Statewide, the turnout patterns appeared indistinguishable from 1998, so it is difficult to detect any special 2002 effect. It may be that the anti-party reaction that was called the "Ventura factor" in 1998 appeared as the antiparty "memorial service factor" in 2002.

Like state parties across the country, the Minnesota Republican Party launched a get-out-the-vote (GOTV) initiative during the summer, with guidance and money from the national party. It is impossible to disentangle the eventual impact of the 72 Hour Task Force from the effects of the memorial service. Turnout was not unusually high in Republican areas of the state, but in comparison with earlier years the Republicans greatly increased their effort. Because of his convictions, and because in earlier campaigns he had so little money, Wellstone mounted an extensive GOTV effort, and in 2002 his organization remained in place to work for Mondale.

Discussion

Commentary around the nation suggested that Democratic and Republican candidates in Senate and House races had blurred their differences so completely that Democrats seemed to be running as Republicans, and Republicans as Democrats. Nothing of the kind happened in the Senate race in Minnesota. Wellstone and Coleman offered the electorate stark contrasts on every issue raised during the campaign. Wellstone was the only Democratic Senator up for re-election to vote against the Iraq resolution; Coleman was completely supportive of President Bush. There were similar unmistakable differences on NAFTA and a wide range of domestic issues, including tax cuts and prescription drugs for seniors.

From the earliest polling in 2002, the race was extremely close (see table 5-5).[30] The clear choices on issues and the sharp partisan tone on both sides made it easy for most Minnesotans to decide their candidate preference early in the race—and stick with it. When the public absorbed the news of the plane crash, much changed in the public mood but not vote choice. Those voters already committed to Coleman had no reason to abandon their choice. Those who had decided to vote for Wellstone found Mondale an acceptable replacement and saw no reason to switch to Coleman, whom they had already rejected. Table 5-5 shows that on the Monday following Wellstone's death Mondale had picked up Wellstone's support intact.[31]

On Tuesday night the public memorial service brought another major disturbance of the public mood. There were two reactions to the memo-

Table 5-5. *Poll Results, Minnesota Senate Race,*
February–November 2002

Percent

Candidate	February	June	September 13–17	October 28	October 30– November 1	November 3–4
Wellstone-Mondale	45	47	46	47	46	45
Coleman	44	43	42	39	41	45
Other	6	5	7	4	4	3
None[a]	5	5	5	11	9	7
N	?	?	?	639	929	754

Source: Minnesota Poll data handout, Minnesota Political Science Association meeting, St. Paul, Minn., November 9, 2002.

a. No opinion, undecided.

rial service, one partisan and one nonpartisan. The partisan reaction was most obvious: Republicans in and outside of Minnesota responded strongly to what they saw on television. As the memorial service entered its third hour, money began to pour into Coleman headquarters, and for the remainder of the campaign Republican volunteers and crowds at rallies appeared in unprecedented numbers.[32] The Democratic base was also aroused by the plane crash, but widespread Democratic activism was not so unprecedented. This extraordinary level of partisan enthusiasm, however, did not change votes, as the Wednesday to Friday poll numbers show in table 5-5.[33]

Because the memorial service was carried by all the major television and radio stations, it drew a large audience, including many nonpartisans who were little concerned with, or attuned to, politics. Their reaction to the memorial service was antipartisan as well as anti-Democratic. They called stations and newspapers complaining about the strident partisanship they had viewed.

Once campaigning resumed and Mondale was formally nominated by the DFL to replace Wellstone on the ticket, the state was saturated with ten days' worth of advertising in five days.[34] Then there was a Friday visit by Vice President Cheney, a Saturday visit by Laura Bush, and a Sunday visit by President Bush. These events undoubtedly further energized the Republican base, but they did not play well with the nonpartisan, undecided voter. Reportedly, internal Republican polling showed that the visits hurt rather than helped Coleman among nonpartisan voters.[35]

The final column in table 5-5 shows the Sunday-Monday Minnesota Poll with the race dead even, a slight loss for Mondale and a slight gain for Coleman. Combining the two days conceals a sharp break in the support for the two candidates, which occurred after midday on Monday. The interviews conducted later Monday show much stronger support for Coleman. This raises the question of what happened to cause votes to move in Coleman's favor. If we accept the argument that Bush's visit did not sway nonpartisans to Coleman, there appear to be two possibilities.

One obvious possibility is the televised debate between Coleman and Mondale on Monday morning. It is conceivable that the debate made some difference. After all, we are trying to explain a change of only a few percentage points. The debate, however, was not widely viewed, and the most unlikely members of the television audience were nonpartisans not much interested in politics.

The one remaining possibility is the impact of Governor Jesse Ventura. He took some media attention away from the debate by holding a press conference naming Dean Barkley to serve out Wellstone's term in office. This was made somewhat more newsworthy by Ventura's previous threat to name his trash collector to the position ("At least he knows garbage when he sees it."). Ventura denounced both parties, as was his custom, but saved his strongest remarks for Democrats. On Election Day, Coleman did exceptionally well in "Ventura country," and the polls show that he did well among "Ventura voters." This account overinterprets the existing data but is the most plausible explanation.

The extraordinary events of the last days of the race should not overshadow the conventional nature of the campaign prior to the plane crash. While other events conspired to determine the outcome, the Wellstone-Coleman contest was fought with roughly equal amounts of hard and soft money and was controlled by the candidates. Both sides anticipated that huge amounts of interest-group money would influence the race, but those resources for the most part never appeared. Neither the largely positive and expensive campaign up to the middle of September nor the more negative and expensive campaign after that had much impact on the vote preferences of the Minnesota electorate.

Notes

1. Chris LaCivita, political director, NRSC, interview by David Magleby, Quin Monson, Jonathan Tanner, and Nicole Carlisle Squires, Washington, D.C., November 7, 2002.

2. Turnout was almost exactly the same as in 1998, but that was also an unusually high turnout year. Minnesota Secretary of State, "Minnesota General Election Statistics 1950–2000," (www.sos.state.mn.us/election/elstat94.pdf [January 2, 2003]).

3. U.S. Bureau of the Census, "Population," *Statistical Abstract of the United States 2001* (www.census.gov/prod/2002pubs/01statab/pop.pdf [January 2, 2003]).

4. Ibid.

5. Ibid.

6. Bob von Sternberg and Eric Black, "Et Cetera: Bits and Pieces from the Campaign Trail," *Minneapolis Star Tribune*, September 27, 2002, p. 20A. The Minnesota poll includes leaning independents with party identifiers.

7. Ibid.

8. Panel discussion at the Minnesota Political Science Association meeting, November 9, 2002.

9. Two other candidates were on the Senate ballot—Independence Party candidate James Moore and Green Party candidate Ray Tricomo. Moore's candidacy may have had some impact on the race when the League of Women Voters opted to exclude Moore from the one and only debate between Mondale and Coleman the day before the election, citing Moore's low poll numbers. In reaction Governor Ventura held an angry news conference during the debate, denouncing the two major parties and announcing his appointment of Independence Party stalwart Dean Barkley to fill the short-term vacancy created by Wellstone's death. Although directed at both parties, Ventura's pique, coming on the heels of his denunciation of the Wellstone memorial service, probably contributed to the anti-Democratic anger that motivated independents in the final days of the campaign. Green Party candidate Tricomo was not a factor in the race.

10. Panel discussion at the Minnesota Political Science Association meeting, November 9, 2002.

11. These estimates and those in the rest of the paragraph are based on data found at Center for Responsive Politics, "Congressional Races 2002: Minnesota," 2002 (www.opensecrets.org [January 2, 2003]).

12. Greg Gordon, "Costs of Senate Race Go Skyward," *Minneapolis Star Tribune*, October 16, 2002, p. 1B.

13. Greg Gordon, "Mondale Entry Sparked Dash for Cash," *Minneapolis Star Tribune*, November 12, 2002, p. 1B.

14. The Campaign Media Analysis Group (CMAG) count cited by Alliance for Better Campaigns (www.bettercampaigns.org [May 15, 2003]).

15. These counts are based on data provided by CMAG.

16. Since negative information is more attention-getting and memorable, it is possible that a small proportion of negative spots among many more positive

ads will still create an overall impression of negativity in a campaign. See Felicia Pratto and Oliver P. John, "Automatic Vigilance: The Attention-Grabbing Power of Negative Social Information," *Journal of Personality and Social Psychology,* vol. 61, no. 3 (1991), pp. 380–91.

17. Our analysis is based on data provided by CMAG. The Wisconsin Advertising Project, under the direction of Kenneth Goldstein, receives the CMAG data and codes the ads for a variety of characteristics, including the overall tone of the ad as either positive, negative, or positive-negative comparison. In the following analysis we treat positive-negative comparison ads as negative. The intent of these ads is to make one candidate look good and the other look bad. Usually the bad gets more emphasis than the good, hence our decision to count comparative ads as negative. Based on this coding, nine out of twelve of the Wellstone ads were positive, as were six out of eleven DFL Party ads, thirteen out of sixteen Coleman ads, and five out of nine Republican Party ads. For a more extensive analysis of the television advertising in the race, see William H. Flanigan and others, "The Television Campaign in the 2002 Minnesota U.S. Senate Race," paper prepared for the annual meeting of the Western Political Science Association, March 29, 2003, Denver, Colo.

18. LaCivita interview, November 7, 2002.

19. Quoted in Tom Webb, "Senate Campaign Wasn't All That Nasty, Professors Say," *St. Paul Pioneer Press,* February 4, 2003, p. 1A.

20. Nevertheless the Wellstone campaign aired more negative spots than did the DFL. See Flanigan and others, "The Television Campaign."

21. Tom Mason, Coleman for Senate campaign, interview by William H. Flanigan, St. Paul, Minn., November 20, 2002.

22. LaCivita interview, November 7, 2002.

23. We have no evidence from within Minnesota for this possibility. The evidence, if it exists, would be with the groups' national decisionmakers.

24. Mark H. Rodeffer, "Group Calls Wellstone 'Communistic,'" *National Journal,* August 14, 2002 (http://nationaljournal.com/members/adspotlight/2002/08/0815corad1.htm [January 14, 2003]).

25. www.coradpress.com. You can also listen to the rap hip-hop CD featuring "Gun Control Is Racist" and "Liberal Democrats Are Racist."

26. Bill Walsh, Republican Party of Minnesota, interview by William H. Flanigan, St. Paul, Minn., September 16, 2002.

27. Jeff Blodgett, Wellstone for Senate campaign manager, interview by William H. Flanigan, St. Paul, Minn., November 13, 2002.

28. Bill Walsh, interview by William H. Flanigan, St. Paul, Minn., November 15, 2002.

29. Scott Stoermer, communications director, League of Conservation Voters, interview by David Magleby and Jonathan Tanner, Washington, D.C., November 15, 2002.

30. Most independent polls showed Wellstone slightly ahead throughout. One exception was the respected St. Cloud state poll, which had Coleman ahead before the crash (untitled handout, Minnesota Political Science Association meeting, November 9, 2002). The private party polls invariably showed the party's candidate ahead.

31. For an excellent and lengthy account of the postcrash campaign, see Eric Black, "13 Days," *Minneapolis Star Tribune*, November 10, 2002, p. 1A.

32. Mason interview, November 20, 2002.

33. The *St. Paul Pioneer Press* reported a Mason-Dixon poll for these three days, which showed Coleman ahead, but the discrepancy can be accounted for by the poll's oversampling of Wednesday. Another poll by Zogby had the same margin as the Minnesota Poll (untitled handout, Minnesota Political Science Association meeting, November 9, 2002). See also "Minnesota Senate 2002: Head to Head Matchups," *National Journal*, 2002 (www.nationaljournal.com/members/polltrack/2002/races/sen/mn/mn_s_gen.htm#ZOGBY [January 14, 2003]); and Liz Fedor, "Different Polls, Different Results," *Minneapolis Star Tribune*, November 5, 2002, p. 15A.

34. Bill Amberg, state DFL, interview by William H. Flanigan, St. Paul, Minn., November 11, 2002; and Walsh interview, November 15, 2002.

35. Panel discussion at the Minnesota Political Science Association meeting, November 9, 2002. Such poll results may or may not exist, but no Republican is likely to want to be quoted as confirming them.

SIX   *Battle for the Bases:*
          The Missouri
          U.S. Senate Race

MARTHA KROPF

E. TERRENCE JONES

MATT McLAUGHLIN

DALE NEUMAN

THE 2002 U.S. SENATE race in Missouri lasted twenty-four and a half months, beginning with the tragic death of Democratic Governor Mel Carnahan on October 16, 2000, and ending with Jim Talent's Republican victory on November 5, 2002. Because this seat could have changed partisan control of the Senate, the race drew national attention and big money. Even under circumstances such as the 2000 election, winning elections in Missouri is about mobilizing base voters for each side, since elections are often competitive and the parties are fairly evenly divided, but the 2002 race also became a battle to demobilize or neutralize the other side's base. In the end, President Bush's political clout in the state may have tipped the balance in the Republicans' favor.

Governor Mel Carnahan died in a plane crash while on a campaign trip to southeastern Missouri in 2000. At the time, he was running for the Senate against incumbent John Ashcroft. The race was tight, but both sides regarded the Republican as having a slight edge. With the plane crash, the state was swept with emotions, which crystallized with the extensive coverage of Carnahan's funeral four days later. In an instant, Carnahan was transformed from a partisan candidate into a departed hero. But, under Missouri law, his death did not remove his name from the ballot.

Special thanks are due Amanda Baker, University of Missouri–Kansas City, for her research assistance.

137

The Democratic Party's core constituencies in Missouri—labor unions, African Americans, and pro-choice women—were quick to seize the moment. They urged Jean Carnahan, the late governor's widow, to stand in his stead and asked Governor Roger Wilson, the lieutenant governor who succeeded Carnahan, to commit publicly that, if Mel Carnahan won the election, Jean Carnahan would be appointed to serve his term until the 2002 general election. Meanwhile the Ashcroft campaign was paralyzed, not knowing how to navigate such politically uncharted waters.[1]

Jean Carnahan's campaign consisted of one sixty-second television spot. In it she talked about her grief but emphasized that her husband's commitment to children, family, and seniors could still prevail if citizens voted for him. The Carnahan campaign also paid for a letter to about 750,000 Democratic core voters, signed by numerous luminaries, including former Senator Thomas Eagleton. In contrast the Ashcroft campaign never recovered its bearings, and Carnahan won the seat, 50.5 to 48.4 percent.

By the 2002 campaign, Ashcroft had been appointed as U.S. Attorney General, and the GOP turned to former Congressman Jim Talent as the preferred candidate. Talent had represented part of suburban St. Louis before narrowly losing a bid for governor in 2000. His early informal entry into the 2002 contest, accompanied by the open blessing from national and state Republican leaders, meant he won the GOP nomination without significant opposition. The Bush administration showed its support early for Talent, visiting St. Louis in March 2002 and twice before that.[2]

The campaign remained close from start to finish, as can be seen from the numbers released by both media and campaign polls during 2002.[3] The polls show a Carnahan lead through September, with Talent moving ahead in mid-October and the race tightening in early November. Postelection interviews with the two state party executive directors found that the campaigns' tracking polls, each using a moving three-day average, revealed a somewhat similar trend.[4] Both parties' surveys had Carnahan narrowly ahead (by two to four points) until early October; then Talent opened up a lead in mid-October (by three to five points according to the Democrats, five to eight points according to the Republicans), with the contest moving toward a dead heat by the weekend preceding the election.

In the end, it was extremely close, with Jim Talent edging Jean Carnahan 49.8 to 48.7 percent. A mere 21,254 votes out of 1.8 million cast

Table 6-1. *Candidate Receipts and Expenditures, 2001–02*
Dollars

Source	Carnahan (D)	Talent (R)
From PACs	1,620,545	1,858,668
From individuals	9,943,621	6,803,449
From party	16,500	171,850
From candidate	0	0
Other contributions	735,659	597,636
Total receipts	12,316,325	9,431,603
Total expenditures	12,293,579	8,777,033
Cash on hand 12/31/02	22,746	655,317

Source: Federal Election Commission, "2001-02 U.S. House and U.S. Senate Candidate Info," December 31, 2002 (www.fecinfo.com/cgi-win/x_statedis.exe [June 8, 2003]).

separated Carnahan and Talent. Former Representative Talent won this election largely because he managed to define himself as the more experienced national legislator and the one best able to represent the interests of Missouri voters. In other words, he claimed the "incumbency" advantage. Party and interest group money helped ensure his core voters would vote. Furthermore, like Republicans all over the nation, Talent was able to capitalize on the campaigning of President Bush and his own support for the Republican version of the homeland security bill. However, this was hardly an easy win for Talent.

The Role of Money

Because of the importance of this race in determining the partisan balance of the Senate, both Jean Carnahan and Jim Talent received significant support from political parties and interest groups, who collectively rivaled the spending on the part of the candidates. In terms of candidate spending, the Carnahan-Talent race was the most expensive in Missouri history.[5]

The Candidates

Federal Election Commission (FEC) reports indicate that Carnahan raised and spent more money than Talent's campaign, an advantage she maintained throughout the campaign (see table 6-1). This fund-raising advantage allowed Carnahan to make a final television push the weekend before the election, which some say contributed to her closing the gap between her and Talent.[6]

Table 6-2. *National Party Committee Expenditures, Missouri Senate Race, 2001–02*
Dollars

Committee	Federal	Nonfederal	Total
Democratic Senatorial Campaign Committee	2,873,980	5,770,298	8,644,278
Democratic Congressional Campaign Committee	0	625,000	625,000
National Republican Senatorial Committee	2,180,067	5,567,365	7,747,432
National Republican Congressional Committee	25,000	125,000	150,000

Sources: Federal Election Commission, "Party Committees Raise More than $1 Billion in 2001–2002," press release, March 20, 2002 (www.fec.gov/press/20030320party/20030103party.html [April 29, 2003]); NRSC spending data: Chris LaCivita, NRSC political director, personal e-mail communication to Jonathan Tanner, January 3, 2003; NRCC spending data: Mike McElwain, NRCC political director, interview by David Magleby and Jonathan Tanner, Washington, D.C., December 2, 2002.

The Parties

Both state political parties made major television and modest radio buys. The Missouri Democratic Party spent $2,718,344 on television and $217,757 on radio. Its Republican counterpart came close to matching both amounts, purchasing $2,561,385 for television spots and $146,950 for radio buys.[7] The national parties made significant transfers to state and local party committees (see table 6-2), and the national parties spent significant amounts separately.

Interest Groups

Interest groups collectively had less of an electronic presence than the parties, spending only about $1.2 million. Labor unions were by far the biggest air-war participants, accounting for slightly more than half a million dollars. In addition the National Education Association (NEA) weighed in with another $111,970. On the Talent ally side, only Americans for Job Security broke into six digits, spending $208,130 (see table 6-3).

Interest groups targeting the African American community did play a role in this election, particularly the conservative Council for Better Government, based in suburban Kansas City.[8] Senior groups echoed the candidate and party themes of Social Security and prescription drug coverage. However, interest groups that had been involved in past elections did not play as great a role in 2002. For example, the abortion issue was one of the first to rise in 2000 but surfaced only toward the end of the 2002 campaign.[9] The gun control issue, also important in 2000, was blunted because Carnahan made a pre-emptive strike to avoid having

Table 6-3. *The Air War: Television and Radio Advertising Expenditures, Missouri Senate Race, 2002*[a]
Dollars

Type and organization	TV	Radio	Total spent	CMAG TV
Democratic allies[b]				
Candidates				
Jean Carnahan for Missouri Committee	4,953,844	77,317	5,031,161	3,844,562
Political parties[c]				
Missouri State Democratic Committee	2,718,344	217,757	2,936,101	3,404,339
Democratic Senatorial Campaign Committee	22,900	. . .	22,900	. . .
Interest groups[c]				
AFL-CIO	538,310	. . .	538,310	786,885
National Education Association	111,970	. . .	111,970	174,207
Law Enforcement Alliance of America	45,225	. . .	45,225	. . .
Sierra Club	2,300	21,000	23,300	38,940
Republican allies[b]				
Candidates				
Jim Talent For Senate	3,813,372	141,965	3,955,337	3,090,442
Political parties[c]				
Missouri Republican Party	2,561,385	146,950	2,708,335	3,094,281
National Republican Senatorial Committee	. . .	. . .	. . .	566,674
Republican National Committee	. . .	36,720	36,720	. . .
Interest groups[c]				
Americans for Job Security	184,130	24,000	208,130	235,458
United Seniors Association	63,325	. . .	63,325	297,580
Council for Better Government	12,745	36,960	49,705	. . .
The Seniors Coalition	41,320	. . .	41,320	. . .
Senate Majority Fund	33,974	. . .	33,974	. . .
GOPAC	12,800	9,300	22,100	. . .
Vitae Society	12,850	. . .	12,850	. . .
U.S. Chamber of Commerce	. . .	11,200	11,200	. . .
National Right to Life	. . .	7,650	7,650	. . .
Black America's PAC	. . .	5,600	5,600	. . .
Club for Growth	4,160	. . .	4,160	43,671
Nonpartisan				
Interest groups[c]				
AARP	. . .	28,000	28,000	. . .
Committee for the Advancement of Stem Cell Research	2,927	. . .	2,927	. . .

Source: Data compiled from David B. Magleby, J. Quin Monson, and the Center for the Study of Elections and Democracy, 2002 Soft Money and Issue Advocacy Database (Brigham Young University, 2002); and Campaign Media Analysis Group data.

continued on next page

Table 6-3. *The Air War: Television and Radio Advertising Expenditures, Missouri Senate Race, 2002*[a] *(continued)*

a. See appendix A for a more detailed data explanation. The ad-buy data collected for this study may contain extraneous data because of the difficulty of determining the content of the ads. The parties or interest groups that purchased the ad buys possibly ran some ads promoting House or Senate candidates or ballot propositions not in the study's sample but still within that media market. Unless the participating academics were able to determine the exact content of the ad buy from the limited information given by the station, the data may contain observations that do not pertain to the study's relevant House or Senate races.

For comparison purpose, CMAG data is included in the table. Because of the sheer volume of television and radio stations and varying degrees of compliance in providing ad-buy information, data on spending by various groups might be incomplete. This table is not intended to represent comprehensive organization spending or activity within the sample races. A more complete picture can be obtained by examining this table with table 6-4.

In blank cells, ". . ." reflects absence of collected data and does not imply the organization was inactive in that medium.

b. Certain organizations that maintained neutrality were categorized according to which candidates their ads supported or attacked or whether the organization was openly anti- or pro- conservative or liberal.

c. Totals for issue advertising (party and interest group spending) are underestimated due to our inability to collect ad-buy totals from the NBC, CBS, and FOX affiliates in St. Louis and the NBC affiliate in Springfield.

gun-owning labor union members defect to the GOP when she participated in a September skeet shooting contest.[10]

The Effects of Money: Ground War

The race broke all previous Missouri records for direct mail and get-out-the-vote allocations. Led by the two state parties and buttressed by interest groups and the candidate campaigns, each side's base was bombarded with messages.

The Candidates

The 2000 tragedy meant that Talent had to tread carefully. As one newspaper article noted, he had "to find a way to delicately undercut a sixty-eight-year-old grandmother who has been the object of bipartisan compassion."[11] Talent and the Missouri Republican Party ultimately emphasized his experience, his support for President Bush's agenda, and President Bush's support for him.

Talent also fought a gender gap by forming a group called Women for Talent, featuring prominent Republican women. As a part of several campaign events, national Republican women visited Missouri to stump for Talent; Laura Bush, Lynne Cheney, Karen Hughes, and Janet Ashcroft all campaigned for Talent. This effort illustrates Talent's effort to neutralize Carnahan's advantage with this key part of her base.

Talent also targeted women with mailers. A Missouri Republican Party mail piece highlighted issues in which the campaign thought women would be interested, such as education, support for families and faith-based organizations, and small-business support for women. He also highlighted having lost his mother to breast cancer, so he "knows how important it is to help women get better medical care."[12] Polls indicated that the efforts of Talent and the Republican Party to court female voters were reasonably successful. Polls taken early in the campaign had shown Carnahan with double-digit leads over Talent among women. However, according to a *Kansas City Star* poll taken the week before the election, Carnahan's lead among women had slipped to two points.[13] A Zogby International poll showed similar results in mid-October.[14]

In the Carnahan campaign, focus groups demonstrated that, while sympathy played a role in the 2000 victory of her husband, Carnahan would have to prove herself in the 2002 campaign. She was forced into a defensive position regarding her experience as well as her position on the Senate version of the homeland security bill. However, she still held an advantage on issues of interest to seniors, such as prescription drugs and Social Security. She also highlighted her support of labor. At least one poll, released by the Missouri AARP, indicated that 84 percent of people over forty-five listed Social Security as a very important issue to their voting decision. Other significant issues included the economy, at 80 percent, corporate responsibility, at 78 percent, and homeland security, at 76 percent.[15]

The Parties

Both state parties ran record direct mail programs, outnumbering the candidates themselves. The Missouri Democratic Party distributed thirty-six unique ads totaling 6 million pieces. The Missouri Republican Party sent approximately 3 million copies of fifteen different mailers. Together, the two organizations spent about $4 million on mail (see table 6-4).

Using both demographic profiling and voter identification files, Democrats targeted African Americans (message: the Democratic Party has historically been on your side), women (messages: Talent is weak on gun control and reproductive choice), and labor union members (messages: Carnahan will protect Social Security and jobs and fight corporate corruption). Understanding the key role that St. Louis County plays in the Democratic vote, the party sent about half the mail to voters in that jurisdiction.

Much of the Republican mail was intended to blunt Democratic attacks purporting that Talent was weak on education, health care, gun

Table 6-4. Number of Unique Campaign Communications by Organizations, Missouri Senate Race, 2002[a]

Type and organization[b]	Internet banner ads	E-mail messages	Surface mail pieces	Newspaper or magazine ads	Personal contacts	Phone calls	Radio ads	TV ads	Total
Candidates									
Jean Carnahan for Missouri Committee	1	11	2	7	1	1	3	12	38
Democratic allies[c]									
Political parties									
Missouri State Democratic Committee	...	13	36	4	3	12	5	7	80
Democratic National Committee	...	8	...	...	...	...	...	...	8
County Democratic Parties	...	1	1	1	...	...	...	...	3
Interest groups									
Labor[d]	...	...	21	3	4	2	...	1	31
National Women's Political Caucus	...	10	1	...	...	...	...	...	11
NARAL Pro-Choice America	...	4	4	1[e]	...	1	...	...	10
Planned Parenthood	...	3	6	...	...	1	...	...	10
National Education Association	...	...	6	1	...	...	...	1	8
Brady Campaign to Prevent Gun Violence	...	...	2	1	1[f]	1	...	...	5
Sierra Club	...	...	2	...	1	1	...	1	5
NAACP	...	...	1	1	1	1	...	...	4
Alliance for Retired Americans	...	...	1	...	1[g]	1[g]	1	...	3
Freedom, INC	...	...	1[h]	2	...	...	...	...	3
Human Rights Campaign	...	...	1	...	...	1[h]	...	...	2
Missouri Equal Rights Amendment PAC	...	...	...	...	1	...	...	...	1
Missouri Progressive Vote Coalition	...	...	1	...	...	...	...	...	1
National Organization for Women	...	...	1	...	...	...	...	...	1
People for the American Way	...	...	1	...	...	...	...	...	1

Republican allies[c]

	Republican allies[c]									
Candidates										
Jim Talent for Senate	1	19	3	3	1	1	…	1	9	37
Political parties										
Missouri Republican Party	…	5	15	…	1	1	14	1	10	47
Republican National Committee	1	3	…	…	…	…	…	…	…	4
National Republican Senatorial Committee	…	1	…	…	…	…	…	…	2	3
West County Republican Organization	…	…	1	…	…	…	…	…	…	1
Interest groups										
Council for Better Government	…	…	…	1	…	…	…	5	…	6
National Right to Life	…	…	3	1	…	1	…	1	…	6
Americans for Job Security	…	…	1	…	…	…	…	1	…	3
National Rifle Association	…	1	2	…	…	…	1	1[i]	…	3
Susan B. Anthony List Candidate Fund	1	…	1	…	…	…	…	…	…	3
60 Plus Association	…	…	1	…	…	…	1[j]	…	…	2
America 21	…	…	1	…	…	…	1	…	…	2
American Medical Association Political Education Fund	…	…	1	…	…	…	…	…	…	1
Americans Taxpayers Alliance	…	…	…	…	…	…	1	…	…	1
Cape County Farm Bureau	…	…	1	…	…	…	…	…	…	1
Club for Growth	…	…	…	…	…	…	…	…	1[k]	1
Common Sense Coalition	…	…	…	…	…	…	1	…	…	1
Eagle Forum PAC	…	…	1	…	…	…	…	…	…	1
Hunting and Shooting Sports Heritage Foundation	…	…	…	…	…	…	…	…	…	1
Knights of Columbus	…	…	1	1	…	…	…	…	…	1
Missouri Farm Bureau	…	…	1	…	…	…	…	…	…	1
Missouri Soybean Association	…	…	1	…	…	…	…	…	…	1
National Shooting Sports Foundation	…	…	1	…	…	…	…	…	…	1
National Federation of Independent Business	…	…	1	…	…	…	…	…	…	1
Seniors Coalition	…	…	1	…	…	…	…	…	…	1

continued on next page

Table 6-4. Number of Unique Campaign Communications by Organizations, Missouri Senate Race, 2002[a] (continued)

Type and organization[b]	Type of campaign communication								
	Internet banner ads	E-mail messages	Surface mail pieces	Newspaper or magazine ads	Personal contacts	Phone calls	Radio ads	TV ads	Total
United Seniors Association	...	...	...	...	...	...	...	1	1
U.S. Chamber of Commerce	...	...	...	...	...	1[l]	...	...	1
Other party allies									
Political parties									
Missouri Green Party	...	...	...	...	1	...	...	...	1
Nonpartisan									
Interest groups									
AARP	...	...	1	1	1	...	...	...	3
Missouri Citizen Education Fund	...	...	2	...	...	...	...	...	2
Vote Hemp	...	1	...	...	...	...	...	...	1

Sources: Magleby, Monson, and CSED 2002 Soft Money and Issue Advocacy Database.

a. See appendix A for a more detailed explanation of data. This table is not intended to portray comprehensive organization activity within the sample races. A more complete picture can be obtained by examining this table together with table 6-3. Data represent the number of unique pieces or ads by the group and do not represent a count of total items sent or made.

In blank cells, "..." reflects absence of colleted data and does not imply that the organization was inactive in that medium.

b. All state and local chapters or affiliates have been combined with their national affiliate to better render the picture of the organization's activity. For instance, the Missouri National Education Association data have been included in the NEA totals.

c. Certain organizations that maintained neutrality were categorized according to which candidates their ads supported or attacked or whether the organization was anti- or pro-conservative or liberal.

d. The Labor category includes the AFL-CIO and all labor groups not explicitly affiliated with the AFL-CIO, including such groups as the United Brotherhood of Carpenters and Joiners of America and the Service Employees International Union.

e. Kate Michelman, president, and Monica Mills, political director, NARAL Pro-Choice America, telephone interview by David B. Magleby, Quin Monson, and Nicole Carlisle Squires, December 19, 2002.

f. Margaret Conway, national political director, Sierra Club, telephone interview by David B. Magleby and Quin Monson, December 16, 2002.

g. Ed Coyle, executive director, Alliance for Retired Americans, telephone interview by David B. Magleby and Quin Monson, December 20, 2002.

h. Mark Perriello, PAC manager, Human Rights Campaign, telephone interview by David B. Magleby and Jonathan Tanner, January 17, 2003.

i. Glen Caroline, director, NRA Institute for Legislative Action, Grassroots Division, interview by David B. Magleby, Quin Monson, Jonathan Tanner, Nicole Carlisle Squires, and Stephanie Perry Curtis, November 14, 2002.

j. Jim Martin, president, 60 Plus Association, interview by Quin Monson and Jonathan Tanner, Washington, D.C., December 11, 2002.

k. Stephen Moore, president, Club for Growth, interview by David B. Magleby and Jonathan Tanner, Washington, D.C., December 2, 2002.

l. Bill Miller, political director, U.S. Chamber of Commerce, interview by David B. Magleby and Quin Monson, Washington, D.C., November 7, 2002.

control, Social Security, and women's issues. Other pieces stressed his legislative experience and his connections with President Bush; in fact, over half of all party mailers included presidential photos. In an effort to narrow the gender gap and be more consistent with one of Talent's messages, campaign materials included far more pictures of women than men.

Minorities make up a growing voting bloc in Missouri, and subsequently both parties courted the Latino vote, particularly in Kansas City.[16] Among Republicans, Bush had pushed that strategy prior to September 11, 2001, working to develop a relationship with Mexico's President Vicente Fox Quesada and suggesting that undocumented aliens of Latino descent be granted amnesty. However, the Republican effort was pushed aside in the wake of September 11.[17] In response, the Democratic Coordinating Committee mobilized in Kansas City, setting up an ad hoc group called Latinos for Carnahan and holding a fund-raiser. Six hundred and fifty people were invited, seventy-five attended, and $4,000 was raised. Democrats also advertised on Spanish-speaking radio, ran phone banks, and distributed bumper stickers. The Democratic Party also placed Spanish ads in the *Kansas City Hispanic News*.

The Missouri Democratic Party worked to earn or keep the African American vote. The objective of the program was to make the community aware of the election. Democratic volunteers made phone calls, and ads appeared in both the *Kansas City Call* and the *St. Louis American*. Democrats also sent direct mail to African Americans and placed phone calls from Bill Clinton, Congressman John Lewis (D-Ga.), prominent African American pastor Emmanuel Cleaver (Kansas City), and Congressman William Lacy Clay (D-Mo., St. Louis).[18] Mobilization of African Americans in Kansas City was also part of a larger Democratic get-out-the-vote (GOTV) effort.

The Democratic GOTV effort was unprecedented. One week before the election, teams held signs around Kansas City's Country Club Plaza, a large open-air mall in midtown Kansas City. Volunteers made phone calls and knocked on doors of potential voters who had a history of voting Democratic but who did not always turn out for midterm elections. Voters in high-performing districts were targeted based on their past voting records. Those who voted in every election or those who never voted were not likely to be contacted.[19]

On Election Day, the GOTV effort included poll checkers, poll runners, sandwich makers, volunteer cab drivers, callers, and "pull teams."

Poll checkers monitored the polls to find out whether certain targeted voters had made it to the polls; poll runners took the results to the phone center, where calls were made to the targeted voters. Sixty runners and "pullers" physically looked for the people who had not yet voted to remind them of their duty and encourage them to go vote. Volunteers also placed orange door tags that read "Protect Seniors and Working Families: Vote Democratic!" on the doors of those individuals who had not voted yet.

Republicans began organizing GOTV efforts in the summer. They started their ground-war campaign by studying the tactics long used by the labor unions in Missouri.[20] Thus the Missouri Republicans' 72 Hour Task Force was a "Cadillac" compared to GOP efforts in other states. The executive director of the Missouri Republican Party, John Hancock, noted that GOTV is a much greater challenge for Republicans than for Democrats, because their base is more rural and thus not as geographically concentrated. Because of that, some of the union techniques did not translate directly but could be modified. Republican consultant Curt Anderson noted, "The concept of having personal contact could be done. So in places like that we say to somebody who is willing to give their time and effort: 'Here are forty people who live in your county who we have reason to believe could be persuaded to vote for Talent. You need to contact them, whether you go see them, whether you run into them at a coffee shop, whether you call them.'"[21] For the first time, the Missouri Republican Party paid individuals to help with the GOTV effort because the number of volunteers did not meet staffing needs. This willingness to invest funds combined with two visits by President Bush late in the campaign, all targeted at Republican strongholds, contributed to making the Missouri GOTV one of the most successful in the nation.

Labor

The case of the Missouri AFL-CIO illustrates that interest groups have a wide variety of techniques to mobilize the electorate. It used phone and mail strategies to mobilize its almost 600,000 members on Jean Carnahan's behalf.[22] The first part of its strategy included twenty-one unique mailers, featuring seven distinct statewide mail pieces, each labeled "A Message from Your Union." They emphasized both bread-and-butter issues (Social Security, minimum wage, workplace safety, health care, corporate corruption), as well as the importance of voting.

Second was member-to-member phone appeals within individual locales, many using state-of-the-art predictive dialing operations. Both of these efforts used the first-rate member database the unions had created over the previous two years.

Beyond this collective push, many individual unions and allied groups added their own distinctive appeals. For example, the Coalition of Black Trade Unionists (CBTU) passed out leaflets ("Let Your Voice Be Heard!"), and the Service Employees International Union ran ads about gun control ("Jim Talent Is Dead Wrong about Guns") in suburban newspapers. The CBTU also placed ads about minority rights ("The NAACP Report Card Is Out: Jim Talent: Dead Last in His Class") in the African American press. The Missouri National Education Association (MNEA) weighed in with six mailings to its members. There was no coordinated message from the different unions, however.[23]

Sensitive to the possible concerns that some of its hunting members might have about Carnahan's support from groups like the Brady Campaign to Prevent Gun Violence,[24] more than one labor piece featured a picture of Senator Carnahan skeet shooting.[25] The Teamsters made a handout with the state's hunting schedule on one side and the skeet-shooting photo on the other.

Abortion

Both pro-life and pro-choice forces were involved in the campaign, each focusing on its identifiable constituency. National Right to Life did one mailing to a list developed through a voter identification program, ran radio spots during the last week on the leading Christian radio station in the St. Louis market, and placed a full-page ad in the *St. Louis Review*, the Catholic newspaper distributed free to almost 1 million parishioners in the St. Louis region.[26] Missouri Right to Life had its own mailing, also to its established list. As has been its custom the past several election cycles, Right to Life placed fliers on parishioners' windshields during the November 3 Sunday services at Catholic churches across the state. They gave special prominence to the U.S. Senate race in Missouri, using half the space to compare Talent and Carnahan on four issues: partial-birth abortion, abortion on demand, human cloning, and pro-life appointees. The Missouri Republican Party also devoted one of its direct mail pieces to abortion, sending it only to voters identified as pro-life. Some generic pro-life television ads created for the 2000 Missouri senate campaign by the Vitae Society also reappeared in 2002.

On the choice side, Planned Parenthood of St. Louis, Kansas City, and mid-Missouri each sent their supporters three mailings, including voter guides featuring the U.S. Senate contest. Their mailers hit about 170,000 Missouri households and targeted suburban, independent women.[27] NARAL Pro-Choice America sent at least four direct mail pieces and e-mailed people who had signed up for its Action Alert Network. In total NARAL sent 332,000 pieces of mail and coordinated twenty different letters to the editor. They also made approximately 184,000 phone calls in the state.[28] All these groups also employed e-mail directed to targeted populations.

Civil Rights and Minority Issues

The battle for base voters among civil rights and minority interest groups is clearly evident. Conservative groups, such as the Council for Better Government, placed phone calls in the Kansas City area to persuade African American voters to rethink voting Democratic, attempting to neutralize the Democratic base or capture those voters for Republicans.[29] More liberal groups put the issue bluntly. The Missouri Citizen Education Fund, for example, issued two pieces of mail: "Ever think some police believe that just being black is a crime? Enough is enough." Inside it read, "Stand up and be counted. Vote November 5th."[30] The NAACP played a role as well, sending direct mail, going door to door with fliers, making phone calls to targeted households, and placing a newspaper ad in the *Kansas City Call*.

Seniors' Issues

While the parties and candidates were busy attacking each other about who was "scaring Missouri seniors" more, interest groups advocating seniors' issues were active as well. Conservative organizations had at least a small role in the race. The Seniors Coalition mailer said: "While the liberals were talking, Jim Talent was voting for the first comprehensive Medicare prescription drug benefit." The United Seniors Association ran a television ad saying: "Find out about Jim Talent's plan to add prescription drug coverage to Medicare. Urge him to keep fighting for seniors." And the 60 Plus Association sent a mail piece stating: "Jim Talent is a Guardian of Seniors."[31] The 60 Plus Association sent out 319,255 mailers in support of Talent and made phone calls to targeted seniors in Missouri.[32]

In keeping with previous efforts, the AARP distributed a voter's guide and a guide explaining how to cast an absentee ballot in Missouri

("Vote without Ever Leaving Home").[33] Approximately 5,000 absentee ballot guides targeting homebound persons were distributed around the state to social service agencies such as Meals on Wheels.[34]

Business and the Environment

Business interests did not play a large role in this election, as is fairly typical in this relatively conservative state.[35] The U.S. Chamber of Commerce spent about $11,000 on radio in St. Louis, and the Kansas City Chamber limited their involvement to distributing voter guides online, with one ad in the business section of the *Kansas City Star* noting the existence of the voter guide and encouraging readers to vote.

The National Federation of Independent Business (NFIB) sent out a mailer emphasizing its support for issues important to small business. The piece of mail pictured a needle sucking blood out of a patient with the headline, "She is sucking the life blood out of your business." On the back, the mailer added, "Jean Carnahan has been sticking small business with the bill."

The environment was only a minor issue in this campaign. While the League of Conservation Voters promised to spend money in support of Jean Carnahan, this team found no evidence that they did. The Sierra Club sent two mailers.

The Effect of Money: Air War

As in other competitive contests in the United States, Missouri voters were inundated with information. During the last week of the election, Missouri voters reported seeing twelve to thirteen political ads a day.[36] The most significant advertisers were the parties, the candidates, and the labor unions (see table 6-3).

The Candidates

Initially all negative ads were aired by the parties; in October the candidate ads also went negative, which is consistent with other states and districts studied nationally. The first Talent campaign ads began in late summer in the various television markets in Missouri. His first ad emphasized his experience, consistent with one of his primary themes. It also noted that he supported a "bipartisan patients' bill of rights" and helped write the bill that moved "millions off welfare." Democrats challenged these claims, and Talent's campaign was forced to defend them.

The first Carnahan ads did not appear until the last week in August. Her ads criticizing corporate irresponsibility started running just as prosecutors issued indictments in the WorldCom case.[37] In her ad she said, "We cannot let dishonest people in corporate boardrooms get rich while the life savings of hard-working Americans dwindle away." The Republican Party responded to this ad, noting that Carnahan had accepted contributions from the former chief executive officer of Global Crossing. Carnahan's campaign defended itself by releasing names of prominent Republicans who had also accepted such contributions.

The Parties

Party-funded television and radio ads began early in this race, with Missouri Republicans in May in Springfield and Columbia and Missouri Democrats in July in Springfield, St. Joseph, Columbia, and Kansas City. The Missouri Democratic Party spent $2,936,101, and the Missouri Republican Party spent $2,708,335 on radio and television ad buys.

The response to a Missouri Democratic Party television ad set a defensive, negative tone for the race. In late July the party ran an ad crediting Carnahan with saving 12,000 Missouri jobs because of the TWA–American Airlines merger. Pilots' unions and Republicans cried foul, noting that Carnahan had little to do with the merger,[38] and Carnahan's campaign was forced to defend her.[39] A Missouri Republican ad in response told voters to "tell Jean Carnahan we're disappointed." For its part, the Missouri Democratic Party aired a series of ads with the same ending: "For the real truth about Jim Talent's record on [insert issue here], visit www.TALENTFACTS.com." The Missouri Republican Party responded with ads telling voters that "Jean Carnahan and her allies are at it again."

While Republican Party money was spent in every television market in Missouri, a great deal of the Republican money was targeted at the Springfield market area in order to shore up the Republican base, according to National Republican Senatorial Committee political director Chris LaCivita. The Republican messages especially questioned Carnahan's experience and ability. Many questioned her ability to understand the legislative process. According to political pundit Charlie Cook, there was "considerable anecdotal evidence from Missourians and inside-the-Beltway types of both parties that Carnahan sometimes seems lost in the Senate." As one Missouri Democrat who came to Washington to lobby Carnahan on a legislative issue said, 'I didn't expect for her to understand our issues, but she didn't understand the [legislative] process.'"[40] This report provided the grist for several Republican general attack ads emphasizing Carnahan's lack of experience.[41]

The Republican Party also hit Carnahan particularly hard for the position she took on Bush's version of the homeland security bill. According to LaCivita, "People couldn't understand why Jean Carnahan opposed the president on homeland security. I mean, people just couldn't understand that."[42] Accordingly the Missouri Republican Party aired television ads emphasizing this issue and invoking the image of John F. Kennedy, who also had to protect security and noting, "Jean Carnahan accepts thousands of dollars—rejects president's plan." Carnahan responded that she supported the development of the Department of Homeland Security and that Talent should not question her patriotism.

Labor

Labor also maintained a noticeable media presence throughout the state. The AFL-CIO spent well over half a million dollars on television advertisements in Missouri (see table 6-3). These ads, sponsored by "the working men and women of the AFL-CIO," emphasized such themes as corporate accountability, saving Missouri jobs, and health issues like prescription drug coverage; they also implicitly supported Jean Carnahan. One particular corporate accountability ad focused on WorldCom and noted, "In Congress, Jim Talent opened the door to such abuses by voting with the big corporations to weaken securities laws. Call Jim Talent and tell him his vote shattered lives."

Minority Interests

Party activity included mobilizing and persuading minority voters. Early on, GOPAC sponsored radio ads produced by Kansas City political activist Richard Nadler. GOPAC aired ads on minority-owned stations asserting that Social Security was nothing more than "reverse reparations." These early ads were quickly pulled because the state Republican Party did not want to be associated with them.

The Council for Better Government also placed ads on radio stations and in the African American weekly paper in Kansas City, the *Call*. The ads asserted that Democrats were taking the African American vote for granted and addressed themes such as faith-based initiatives and the African American church, anti-abortion themes ("Black babies are terminated at triple the rate of white babies. . . . Each year the abortion mills diminish the human capital of our communities by another 400,000 souls."), and school choice.[43] Attempting to protect their base, Missouri Democrats responded by noting that Carnahan had worked to protect the interests of seniors, particularly concerning prescription drug coverage and Social Security. While some charged that the Council for Better Government ads were designed to suppress minority votes for Democrats,[44] John Altevogt, president of the Council for Better Government, said in his defense that we "want those votes; they are there to be had."[45]

This strategy resulted in a barrage of advertisements on the minority-owned stations in Kansas City (with a total of about 212,000 listeners) as well as in St. Louis. Republican-allied groups spent about $50,000 on these ads, with a goal of fifteen one-minute spots each day.[46] Carnahan and the Democratic Party were forced to counter this effort with a series of ads on urban contemporary and hip-hop stations featuring luminaries such as Jesse Jackson Jr. and Emmanuel Cleaver. The Democratic Party also responded with attack ads ("Can you believe all them slick Republican ads?").

Conclusion

With such a scant margin of victory, many factors may have tipped the balance narrowly toward Republicans. Party and interest group money played a significant role in mobilizing voters. However, President Bush's campaigning on behalf of Jim Talent played an important role. According to survey data collected for this study, Bush had high favorables in Missouri: 67 percent of those who reported that they voted had a "favorable" or "very favorable" opinion of Bush. Homeland security was a major issue for Missourians, with 59 percent citing it as "one of the most important" or a "very important" issue. Talent and the Republican Party pressed their advantage on this issue, as did many Republicans across the nation. However, Social Security and Medicare were also important to voters, and these issues tended to benefit Carnahan, as did union turnout. Talent also managed to appear more experienced than did Carnahan.

Since such a race is about mobilizing voters, examining vote shares in 2002 compared to 2000 also sheds light on the election (see table 6-5).

First, relative turnout was down in the two Democratic central cities, more so in Kansas City than in St. Louis. Even though the partisan split

Table 6-5. *Turnout Share and Republican Percent of Vote,*
Missouri Senate Races, 2000 and 2002
Percent

Jurisdiction	2000		2002	
	Turnout share	GOP	Turnout share	GOP
Greene County	4.36	60.54	4.45	59.73
Jackson County (non-KC)	6.36	47.43	6.00	48.02
Kansas City	5.15	24.72	4.69	24.63
St. Charles County	5.42	55.60	5.65	57.95
St. Louis City	5.26	20.22	5.05	20.93
St. Louis County	20.70	45.54	20.92	48.05
Remainder of state	52.75	54.06	53.24	55.40

Source: Missouri Secretary of State, "Elections," 2002 (www.sos.state.mo.us/elections/ [December 5, 2002]).

in the state's urban core remained essentially the same, it constituted less of the overall total. Second, vote shares were up in all the Republican areas of Greene and St. Charles counties and the remainder of the state, giving them more weight in the overall outcome. On President Bush's last two campaign visits to Missouri, he stopped in Greene and St. Charles counties. Third, Talent ran two and a half percentage points ahead of Ashcroft in St. Louis County, an area that he formerly represented in the U.S. House. In sum, both the polling and the electoral data provide credible evidence that, in a nip-and-tuck contest, President Bush's popularity and personal campaigning made the difference.

Notes

1. Martha E. Kropf and others, "The 2000 Missouri Senate Race," in David B. Magleby, ed., *Election Advocacy: Soft Money and Issue Advocacy in the 2000 Congressional Elections* (Center for the Study of Elections and Democracy, Brigham Young University, 2001), pp. 75–91.

2. David Goldstein, "GOP Puts Muscle, Money behind Talent," *Kansas City Star,* March 19, 2002, p. A1.

3. Polls were conducted by American Viewpoint for the Talent campaign, by Garin-Hart-Yang for the Carnahan campaign, by Zogby for the *St. Louis Post-Dispatch* and KMOV-TV (St. Louis), and by Research 2000 for KSD-TV (St. Louis). The *Kansas City Star* conducted its own survey. All polls indicate that they screened so that only likely voters were included. The sample sizes range from 500 to 800.

4. John Hancock, executive director, Missouri Republican Party, interview by E. Terrence Jones, St. Louis, November 22, 2002; Michael Kelley, executive

director, Missouri Democratic Party, interview by E. Terrence Jones, St. Louis, November 22, 2002.

5. Matt Stearns, "Talent, Carnahan Campaigns Set State Record for Spending," *Kansas City Star,* December 6, 2002, p. A9.

6. Hancock interview, November 22, 2002.

7. These outlays underestimate radio purchases, because data on radio buys were only obtained for the major radio stations in the urban markets (St. Louis, Kansas City, and Springfield).

8. This group is coordinated by John Altevogt, former associate vice chair of the Kansas Republican State Committee, who according to ABC News "has written extensively on reaching out to the black community." See "Election Watchdogging," ABC News, 2002 (www.abcnews.go.com/sections/politics/DailyNews/TheNote.html [October 7, 2002]).

9. Kropf and others, "The 2000 Missouri Senate Race."

10. Carnahan's campaign formed a group called Sportsmen for Carnahan, which issued bumper stickers with a camouflage-style background in rural Missouri.

11. David Goldstein, "Talent Campaign Tactics Must Tiptoe Over Tragedy," *Kansas City Star,* August 19, 2002, p. A1.

12. This quote is from Congresswoman Jennifer Dunn (R-Wash.) in a Missouri Republican Party mailer.

13. Steve Kraske, "Latest Polls Show Talent Leading Carnahan," *Kansas City Star*, November 1, 2002, pp. A1, 6.

14. Steve Kraske, "New Statewide Poll Shows Talent Is Leading Carnahan," *Kansas City Star,* October 15, 2002, p. B3.

15. Christine Bechtel, "AARP 2002 Election Survey: Missouri" (http://research.aarp.org/general/2002_election_mo.pdf [July 23, 2003]).

16. There was no discernible effort to court Latinos in St. Louis.

17. Ana Melgoza, coordinator, Latinos for Carnahan, interview by Martha Kropf, Kansas City, Mo., October 17, 2002.

18. Kelley interview, November 22, 2002.

19. Scott Burnett, Democratic consultant, SGB Communications, interview by Martha Kropf, Kansas City, Mo., October 23, 2002.

20. Curt Anderson, The Anderson Group, press event, "The Last Hurrah? Soft Money and Issue Advocacy in the 2002 Congressional Elections," Center for the Study of Elections and Democracy, National Press Club, Washington, D.C., February 3, 2003.

21. Ibid.

22. Kelley interview, November 22, 2002.

23. Without exit polling data it is difficult to estimate whether there was an increase in mobilization over the 2000 election. However, both the Missouri

Republican and Democratic Party chairs noted an increase in union voting and volunteering over previous elections.

24. The NRA did not play a big role in Missouri, issuing just one relatively inexpensive mail piece.

25. In response, groups such as the Hunting and Shooting Sports Heritage Foundation issued a mailing noting that "Jean Carnahan has taken every opportunity to restrict your gun rights and sporting heritage." This mail piece shows Carnahan skeet shooting, as well, but highlights the fact that Handgun Control endorsed her.

26. The full-page ad ran in the *St. Louis Review* on November 1, 2002, p. 5. It is a picture of a twenty-one-week-old unborn baby reaching its hand out and grasping the finger of a doctor during an in-womb procedure. Below the picture are various slogans—"we all want to survive," "we want to be given a chance"—followed by encouragement to vote pro-life.

27. David Williams, director of Action Fund and PAC, Planned Parenthood, interview by David Magleby and Nicole Carlisle Squires, Washington, D.C., November 8, 2002.

28. Kate Michelman, president, and Monica Mills, political director, NARAL Pro-Choice America, telephone interview by David Magleby, Quin Monson, and Nicole Carlisle Squires, December 19, 2002.

29. John Altevogt, Council for Better Government, telephone interview by David Magleby and Jonathan Tanner, January 21, 2003.

30. This group is partially funded by the Proteus Fund, a group that makes grants to progressive organizations such as the Missouri Progressive Vote Coalition. See "State Strategies Fund: Grantees," Proteus Fund, 2002 (www.funder.org/grantmaking/ssf/grantees/ [January 6, 2003]).

31. According to table 6-3, the United Seniors Association spent more than $50,000 on television ads in Missouri.

32. Jim Martin, president, 60 Plus Association, interview by Quin Monson and Jonathan Tanner, Arlington, Va., December 11, 2002.

33. The Missouri voter guide appeared as an insert in the September issue of *Modern Maturity* magazine, September/October 2002.

34. Norma Collins, associate state director for advocacy, AARP Missouri Office, interview by Martha Kropf, Kansas City, Mo., November 13, 2002.

35. The amount of business involvement dropped only slightly from the 2000 race. One group, involved in 2000 in several battleground states, did not air ads in Missouri in 2002. See Kropf and others, "The 2000 Missouri Senate Race," pp. 75–91.

36. David B. Magleby and J. Quin Monson, "Campaign 2002: 'The Perfect Storm'" (Center for the Study of Elections and Democracy, Brigham Young University, November 13, 2002) (http://csed.byu.edu).

37. Libby Quaid, "Carnahan Takes on Corporate Vandals," *Springfield News Leader*, August 29, 2002, p. B3.

38. David Goldstein, "Senate Rivals Battle on the Airwaves," *Kansas City Star*, July 27, 2002, p. A4.

39. In defense of their questionable ad that claimed credit for saving TWA jobs, the Carnahan campaign again appeared to overreach, making it possible for Republicans to attack her even more. (Hancock interview, November 22, 2002)

40. Charlie Cook, "These Four Races Are Worth Watching," *National Journal*, July 6, 2002, p. 2039.

41. Chris LaCivita, political director, NRSC, interview by David Magleby, Quin Monson, Jonathan Tanner, and Nicole Carlisle Squires, Washington, D.C., November 7, 2002.

42. Ibid.

43. Council for Better Government, "Abortion Takes Lives," KPRS-FM, Kansas City, October 17, 2002.

44. See John B. Judis, "Soft Sell," *New Republic*, November 11, 2000, pp. 12–15.

45. Altevogt interview, January 21, 2003.

46. David Goldstein, "Talent Pursues Black Voters," *Kansas City Star*, October 4, 2002, pp. A1, A6.

SEVEN   *The More You Spend,*
         the Less They Listen: The
         South Dakota U.S. Senate Race

JOHN BART
JAMES MEADER

With control of the senate at stake, South
Dakota became a key battleground state in the 2002 race. President
Bush saw an opportunity to not only gain a seat but to deliver a political
blow to the Democrats in Majority Leader Tom Daschle's own state.
The president persuaded popular Republican Representative John
Thune to challenge incumbent Democratic Senator Tim Johnson. From
the beginning of the campaign, this election was characterized as a
proxy battle between Bush and Daschle. Both parties transferred a significant amount of money to the state, and the president made five campaign visits.

On a night when Republicans, led by a popular president, regained
the Senate, a primarily Republican state reelected Democrat Johnson by
524 votes in the most expensive election in South Dakota history. This
election lived up to the expectations set for it over the summer. Two
popular, well-funded incumbents, backed by two of the most powerful
people in Washington, faced off in an intense battle.

The election turned more on who best served the interests of the
state. Johnson effectively framed his campaign on local impact, while
Thune campaigned on the popularity of President Bush and larger
national issues.

This race was extraordinarily expensive. The candidates each spent
around $6 million—$12 million total, or $35.25 per vote (see table 7-1).

The authors wish to thank Heidi Bratland and Josh Thomas for research
efforts that made this project possible.

Table 7-1. *Candidate Receipts and Expenditures, 2001–02*
Dollars

Source	Johnson (D)	Thune (R)
From PACs	2,103,756	1,312,130
From individuals	3,315,113	3,573,720
From party	34,972	316,223
From candidate	0	0
Other contributions	118,210	312,153
Total receipts	5,572,051	5,514,226
Total expenditures	6,152,991	5,989,043
Cash on hand 12/31/02	14,430	7,716

Source: Federal Election Commission, "2001-02 U.S. House and U.S. Senate Candidate Info," December 31, 2002 (www.fecinfo.com/cgi-win/x_statedis.exe [June 8, 2003]).

Party and interest group expenditures added approximately another $12 million, for a total of $24 million, or $70.50 per vote. To place this in perspective, the candidates doubled the amount spent in 1996, the state's last competitive senate race. Expressed another way, had the amount per voter been applied to neighboring Minnesota's Senate race, that election would have exceeded $150 million in total expenditures.

The GOP viewed this race as the spearhead of its national strategy. The National Republican Senatorial Committee transferred $4.3 million to the state (see table 2-4), its highest per capita transfer. Thune was encouraged to run by the president and was promised party support. The race stayed extremely close. The NRSC knew that defending Johnson was a priority for Democrats, especially in Tom Daschle's home state. The Democratic Senatorial Campaign Committee transferred $6.5 million to the state (see table 2-4). Keeping the race competitive forced Democrats to funnel more money to South Dakota, siphoning money from other races. While Republicans had a legitimate chance to unseat Johnson, the party also knew that losing a close election would help the party in other states.[1]

This chapter examines the race, an election that supports the thesis that money follows competitive races. First, we set the stage by discussing the state's characteristics. Second, we review the air war, demonstrating that third parties spent more on air and used more negative campaigning than the candidates themselves. Third, we demonstrate that both sides waged an intense ground war that decided the election.

South Dakota at a Glance

South Dakota has a low population density. Census data estimate that the state has 9.9 people per square mile, compared with the national average of 79.6 per square mile. The population is 88.7 percent white, and Native Americans constitute the largest minority group, at 8.3 percent.

The state as a whole tends to be politically conservative. Republican registration outpaces Democratic registration, and the Republican Party has dominated the governorship since 1979. George Bush won 60 percent of the vote in 2000 and maintained a 70 percent job approval rating during 2002.

While there has been a distinct Republican advantage in the number of registered voters since 1970, voters have tended to elect Republican candidates to state office and Democratic candidates to federal office. Since the 1980 census, South Dakota has had one representative in the U.S. House, a position that has become a virtual "third Senator" in the sense that, like a senator, the representative serves the entire state and receives virtually the same media coverage.

In 2002 Representative John Thune loomed as the logical candidate to challenge incumbent Senator Tim Johnson. Having won his last election 73 percent to 25 percent and promising to limit himself to three terms in the House, the only question was whether Thune would run for governor or for senator. Had Thune run for governor, he would have faced little opposition in his party and an easy general election. However, pressure from the administration, and from President Bush personally, persuaded Thune to challenge Johnson.

Campaign Themes

The Bush-Daschle proxy fight had the potential to overshadow the campaign. Each campaign needed to walk a fine line between establishing the candidate and maintaining connections to national party resources and issues. While each candidate benefited from connections to powerful people (Daschle and Bush), each needed to demonstrate that he was an effective representative for the state. The campaigns differed in their approach to this dilemma.

The Johnson campaign chose to establish Tim Johnson as a candidate early, focusing on his ability to serve state interests as a member of the

Appropriations Committee. Tom Daschle kept a low public profile, working behind the scenes to raise money. Toward the end of the campaign, Democrats effectively used Daschle's position as majority leader in conjunction with Johnson's Appropriations Committee appointment to discuss how the two together could best deliver for the state.

The Thune campaign took the opposite approach. Rather than focus on what he had done for the state, Thune focused on national issues and campaigned on the president's agenda. In essence, his prairie values theme argued that electing Thune would allow President Bush to control the national agenda.

These divergent strategies continued throughout the campaign. Johnson's focus on the state rather than national party concerns was the most significant factor in his winning this election.

The Air War

Consistent with other races in this election cycle, third parties outspent the candidates over the air. The South Dakota Democratic Party and its allies spent over $3 million, compared to the candidates' (Herseth and Johnson) $2.2 million. The South Dakota Republican Party and its allies spent $4 million, compared to the candidates' (Janklow and Thune) $1.97 million. (See table 7-2.) The nature of the third-party ads was decidedly more negative than the candidate ads, using policy decisions to attack the candidates' character.

The Republican gubernatorial primary influenced the air war. In that race two prominent, well-funded front-runners waged an extremely negative campaign, attacking each other. One memorable ad emphasized a candidate's business interests in a company that purchased human skin and maximized profits by selling it for cosmetic surgery rather than making it available to burn victims. The voters were so turned off that they elected the third candidate, former State Senator Mike Rounds, because he had avoided the mudslinging. Ryan Nelson, Thune's political director, admitted that the primary raised the "antennae" of the average voter and made contrast ads appear more negative. He speculated that the Republican Party interjected humor into some of their ads to accommodate the public's rejection of all that seemed negative.

The senatorial campaign's first televised advertisements appeared in November 2001. By Election Day the candidates had produced a total of 100 different television spots.[2] Third-party ads by the state Demo-

Table 7-2. *The Air War: Television and Radio Advertising Expenditures, South Dakota Senate and Congressional Races, 2002*[a]
Dollars

Type and organization	TV	Radio	Total spent
Democratic allies[b]			
Candidates			
Tim Johnson for South Dakota	1,591,870	. . .	1,591,870
Herseth for Congress	682,265	. . .	682,265
Political parties			
South Dakota Democratic Party	2,731,865	. . .	2,731,865
Rapid City Democratic Party	173,790	. . .	173,790
Interest groups			
Sierra Club	86,270	. . .	86,270
League of Conservation Voters	2,336	. . .	72,336
Republican allies[b]			
Candidates			
John Thune for South Dakota	1,533,273	. . .	1,533,273
Janklow for Congress	439,855	. . .	439,855
Political parties			
South Dakota Republican State Central Committee	3,148,072	. . .	3,148,072
National Republican Congressional Committee	465,045	. . .	465,045
Interest groups			
Americans for Job Security	426,495	. . .	426,495

Source: David B. Magleby, J. Quin Monson, and the Center for the Study of Elections and Democracy, 2002 Soft Money and Issue Advocacy Database (Brigham Young University, 2002).

a. See appendix A for a more detailed explanation of data. The ad-buy data collected for this study may contain extraneous data due to the difficulty in determining the content of the ads. The parties or interest groups that purchased the ad buys possibly ran some ads promoting House or Senatorial candidates or ballot propositions not in the study's sample but still within that media market. Unless the researchers were able to determine the exact content of the ad buy from the limited information given by the station, the data may contain observations that do not pertain to the study's relevant House or Senate races. Because of the volume of television and radio stations and varying degrees of compliance in providing ad-buy information, data on spending by various groups might be incomplete.

This table is not intended to represent comprehensive organization spending or activity within the sample races. A more complete picture can be obtained by examining this table with table 7-3. Because ad-buy content was often nondescriptive and sometimes difficult to distinguish between the different races, data in this table are combined for all races studied in South Dakota. CMAG did not cover a market in South Dakota.

In blank cells, ". . ." reflects the absence of collected data and does not imply that the organization was inactive in that medium.

b. Certain organizations that maintained neutrality were categorized according to which candidates their ads supported or attacked or whether the organization was openly anti- or pro-conservative or liberal.

cratic and Republican parties began in January 2002.[3] Since there were no real challengers in the primaries, campaigning began in earnest in November 2001, and ads became a regular media fixture by February. Given the number of candidates in the gubernatorial and U.S. House primaries, the state was inundated with political advertisements for months—a deluge that only intensified during the general election.

Since South Dakota is a sparsely populated state, airtime is relatively inexpensive. During the general election alone over fifty thousand spots related to the House or Senate races were purchased. The candidates and third parties combined spent over $11 million on television spots (see table 7-2).[4] To put this in perspective, television expenditures for the Senate race cost $33 per vote. The frequency of the ads increased toward the end of the campaign, and over five thousand ads ran during the last ten days of the election. An executive at KOTA-TV in Rapid City informed us that, toward the end of the campaign, the station readjusted ad runs daily to ensure equal access to time. Requests for ad buys were so numerous that the station manager actually had to reject some. The overwhelming television presence made it virtually impossible for potential voters to ignore the campaign.

Candidates

The candidates' primary air war messages took divergent paths. Johnson focused on his ability to protect state interests.[5] Thune focused on national issues, attempting to demonstrate their potential impact on the state.[6] Each candidate portrayed his opponent as having lost touch with South Dakota.

Johnson produced a series of spots that emphasized his influence as a member of the Appropriations Committee. Each spot told a story: Johnson helped a family get medical care; his focus on water projects, hospitals, and school computers benefited communities; he assisted in statewide issues such as high-tech research centers, adoptions, and women's health. While the broader themes were the same, the examples targeted the specific markets of either East River (a more populated farming area east of the Missouri River) or West River (a less populated, more conservative ranching area west of the Missouri River). Toward the end of the campaign, clips from each of the ads were edited together to demonstrate the breadth of Johnson's influence. The campaign concluded with the only spot featuring Daschle. In it Daschle emphasized the clout that the state had with him as majority leader and Johnson on the

Appropriations Committee. Consistent with the message, Johnson ran character pieces that portrayed him as bipartisan. One ad claimed that Johnson voted in the interest of the state rather than following party lines. A second ad attacked Thune with the claim that neither party is always right and demonstrating that Thune voted party-line 93 percent of the time. The ad showed a marching toy soldier, while the voice-over talked about Thune's votes (for example, he voted for big oil over ethanol); the ad concluded by saying the state did not need a yes-man.

Thune employed a prairie values theme: decreased taxes, strong national defense, prescription drug benefits, decreased government waste, and stopping raids on Social Security. These ads were primarily broad position statements, leaving the Republican Party to attack Johnson on prescription drugs, military spending, and taxes. Thune also launched a major offensive on Social Security, tying Johnson to a 1996 plan for the government to invest Social Security money in the stock market. The most negative ad of the campaign, one that drew national attention, attacked Johnson's record on missile defense, displaying his picture with images of Saddam Hussein and al-Qaida leaders. The ad made no explicit connection between the issue and the images, but it led viewers to believe that Johnson opposed the Iraq resolution and the fight against terrorism.[7] Thune responded to Johnson's appropriations ads with an ad from President Bush, who endorsed Thune and used the example of drought relief to argue that "politicians point fingers. Leaders solve problems." Thune also ran an ad in which he argued that it was bad to "place all your eggs in one basket." He claimed that Daschle's position of power could bring in Democrats and that he could deliver the president. Together they could exercise a strong bipartisan voice for the state.

Thune's image on the air might have hurt him. Thune's family was prominent in the televised messages, along with his claim to support family and South Dakota values. Johnson-sponsored focus groups revealed that many voters were put off by the extensive use of his family for political gain.[8] The Thune campaign believed that family was essential to who Thune was and pointed out that Johnson used his family as well. Johnson used his son, who serves in the military, to fend off attacks on a weak military spending record; he also used his wife, a breast cancer survivor, in a breast cancer spot.[9] Thune's televised messages were filled with him walking across the prairie. All these images were of grazing areas rather than croplands, which tied him more to

West River than East River. Being labeled a West River candidate hurt Thune, because significantly fewer voters reside there.[10]

Political Parties

The party spots were more negative in tone than the candidate-sponsored spots. For example, the Democratic Party of South Dakota argued that Johnson was tough on corporate corruption and noted that Thune missed that vote to attend a fund-raiser. The South Dakota Republican Central Committee argued that Johnson voted against raising military pay but voted for raising his own salary. The party ads set a more character-based tone than the candidates' contrast ads, which focused more on voting records and issues. Because the public did not distinguish between candidate, group, and party ads, it held the candidates accountable for the negative party ads.[11]

The issues addressed by the parties were distinct from those addressed by the candidates. Rarely did the candidate's party and the candidate run ads on the same issues. For example, the Democratic Party of South Dakota attacked Thune on prescription drugs (saying he had been bought off by big drug companies) and corporate greed (he skipped the vote to attend a fund-raiser); they also defended Johnson on Social Security. Meanwhile the South Dakota Republican Central Committee criticized Johnson for taking expensive trips to exotic places paid for by corporate lobbyists. The party also took the lead on bolstering Thune on prescription drugs and military issues.

Interest Groups

While interest groups were heavily involved in the election, most chose to remain off the air. The nature of the issues (abortion, guns, education, unions) indicated that it was better to target messages via mail and phone rather than run broadcast ads, which could alienate people on the other side. Two exceptions to this rule were environmental groups (the Sierra Club and the League of Conservation Voters) and Americans for Job Security.

The Sierra Club and the LCV attacked Thune's environmental record early in the campaign and then pulled back. The LCV placed Thune on their "dirty dozen" list and ran a 3,000-point ad buy against him in both South Dakota media markets from June 7 to July 9.[12] Thune countered with an ad attacking the LCV. The LCV then backed off and relied only on earned media (free coverage on the local news and in newspapers) for the rest of the race.[13] The decision to withdraw might have also been influenced by the Johnson campaign. The campaign complained that the ads were potentially hurting their candidate.[14]

Americans for Job Security was the most active outside group, spending $426,000 in ad buys. The ad focused on Thune's leadership and praised him for having the courage to rise above politics and secure drought relief that did not increase the deficit. The spot looked like a candidate ad, because the organization purchased video from Thune's production company.[15] Johnson charged Thune with illegal coordination and raised the prospect of a Federal Election Commission claim. Thune maintained that Dirt Road Productions owned the video used in both spots and was free to sell the footage, denying any illegal cooperation.[16] The story lasted one news cycle and had no impact on the campaign.

The Ground War

Given the state's relatively small population, personal contact with voters is expected. It is therefore no surprise that South Dakota mirrored the rest of the nation in its reliance on a strong ground campaign.

In addition to television spots, mail deluged voters; some people in our reconnaissance network reported receiving six to ten pieces of political mail each day.[17] In the voter log survey conducted by the Center for the Study of Elections and Democracy, the average South Dakota registered voter received nearly nineteen pieces of political mail, of which nearly eight were related to the Senate race, during the last three weeks prior to the election.[18] Our data collection netted 176 unique direct mail pieces in the Senate race (see table 7-3). These were primarily visual, usually filled with babies, the candidate with his family, or distorted images of opponents. Most messages were brief enough to be read on the way to the trash can.

Phone calls were also a regular feature in the campaign. Republican voters received recorded messages from President Bush, Barbara Bush, Charlton Heston, Rudolph Giuliani, John Thune, and John Thune's mother. Democrats received recorded calls from Tom Daschle and Tim Johnson. Voters on both sides received up to five calls a day from various campaign workers.

The Candidates

Johnson developed an impressive ground-war strategy. He began by developing a registered voter database. Each entry contained voting

Table 7-3. Number of Unique Campaign Communications by Organizations, South Dakota Senate Race[a]

Type and organization[b]	E-mail messages	Surface mail pieces	Newspaper or magazine ads	Personal contacts	Phone calls	Radio ads	TV ads	Total
Democratic allies[c]								
Candidates								
Tim Johnson for South Dakota	18	13	4	4	2	9	25	75
Political parties								
South Dakota Democratic Party	4	39	…	1	5	14	12	75
Democratic National Committee	…	3	…	…	…	…	…	3
Democratic Senatorial Campaign Committee	…	1	…	…	…	…	…	1
Interest groups								
AFL-CIO	…	5	…	…	…	1[d]	…	6
National Education Association	…	5	…	…	1	…	…	6
Sierra Club	…	3	…	…	…	…	…	3
South Dakota Clean Water Action	…	…	…	2	…	…	…	2
Alliance for Retired Americans	…	1[e]	…	…	…	…	…	1
American Association of University Women	…	1	…	…	…	…	…	1
American Nurses Association PAC	…	1	…	…	…	…	…	1
Association of Trial Lawyers of America[f]	…	…	…	…	…	…	…	1
Farmers and Ranchers for Johnson	…	…	1	…	…	…	…	1
Humane USA PAC	…	1	…	…	…	…	…	1
Main Street USA	…	1	…	…	…	…	…	1
Planned Parenthood of South Dakota	…	1	…	…	…	…	…	1
Save Our Environment Coalition	…	1	…	…	…	…	…	1

	Republican allies[c]						
Candidates							
John Thune for South Dakota	32	6	1	…	5	11	55
Political parties							
South Dakota Republican State Central Committee	…	68	1	2	3	8	82
Republican National Committee	…	4	…	…	…	…	4
Minnehaha County Republican Party	…	1	…	…	…	…	1
Interest groups							
National Rifle Association	…	5	…	1	1	…	7
National Right to Life	…	4	2	…	…	…	6
Hunting and Shooting Sports Heritage Foundation	…	2	1	…	…	…	3
South Dakota Family Policy Council	…	2	1	…	…	…	3
U.S. Chamber of Commerce	…	2	…	…	1[g]	…	3
Americans for Job Security	…	1	…	…	…	1	2
Club for Growth	…	…	…	…	1	1[h]	2
National Federation of Independent Business	…	…	…	…	1[h]	1[h]	2
Catholic Voters for John Thune	…	1	1	…	…	…	2
Gun Owners for John Thune	…	…	1	…	…	…	1
Knights of Columbus	…	…	1	…	…	…	1
National Right to Work Committee	…	1	…	…	…	…	1
National Shooting Sports Foundation	…	1	…	…	…	…	1
South Dakota Sportsman's Alliance	…	…	1	…	…	…	1
United Seniors Association	…	1	…	…	…	…	1
Youth Pro-Life	…	…	1	…	…	…	1

continued on next page

Table 7-3. *Number of Unique Campaign Communications by Organizations, South Dakota Senate Race*[a] *(continued)*

Type and organization[b]	\multicolumn{8}{c}{Type of campaign communication}							
	E-mail messages	Surface mail pieces	Newspaper or magazine ads	Personal contacts	Phone calls	Radio ads	TV ads	Total
Interest groups								
Nonpartisan								
AARP	…	…	2	…	…	…	…	2
American Renewal	…	…	1	…	…	…	…	1
Committee for the Advancement of Stem Cell Research	…	…	1	…	…	…	…	1
Priests for Life	…	…	1	…	…	…	…	1

Source: Magleby, Monson, and CSED, 2002 Soft Money and Issue Advocacy Database.

a. See appendix A for a more detailed explanation of data. This table is not intended to portray comprehensive organization activity within the sample races. A more complete picture can be obtained by examining this table together with table 7-2. Data represent the number of unique pieces or ads by the group, not a count of total items sent or made.

In blank cells, "…" reflects the absence of collected data and does not imply that the organization was inactive in that medium.

b. All state and local chapters or affiliates have been combined with their national affiliate to better render the picture of the organization's activity. For instance, the South Dakota Education Association data have been included in the NEA totals.

c. Certain organizations that maintained neutrality were categorized according to which candidates their ads supported or attacked or whether the organization was anti- or pro-conservative or liberal.

d. Denise Mitchell, assistant to the president of public affairs, AFL-CIO, interview by Quin Monson and Jonathan Tanner, Washington, D.C., December 10, 2002.

e. Ed Coyle, executive director, Alliance for Retired Americans, telephone interview by David Magleby and Quin Monson, December 20, 2002.

f. Unspecified race involvement. Linda Lipsen, senior director of public affairs, Association of Trial Lawyers of America, telephone interview by David Magleby and Quin Monson, December 19, 2002.

g. Bill Miller, political director, U.S. Chamber of Commerce, interview by David Magleby and Quin Monson, Washington, D.C., November 7, 2002.

h. Stephen Moore, president, Club for Growth, interview by David Magleby and Jonathan Tanner, Washington, D.C., December 2, 2002.

records, demographics, and campaign contact information. This allowed the Johnson campaign to target both whom they called and the topic of the call. Johnson and his campaign workers visited as many households as they could, carrying nine different scripts that contained different issues. Before knocking on the door they knew something about the occupant and selected the script designed for that demographic profile.[19] Just as contemporary marketers attempt to reach consumers with a personal touch, the Johnson campaign applied these tactics to foster a relationship between candidate and voter.

Thune also executed an impressive ground war. Having learned the importance of a strong organization from past elections, the South Dakota Republican Party created the Victory Operation; it enlisted six thousand South Dakota volunteers on Election Day, compared to sixty in the past. The party had precinct captains in 842 precincts overseeing get-out-the-vote (GOTV) efforts. Thune also organized impromptu visits with voters in the downtown area, what he called "main street tours," and campaigned door-to-door extensively during the summer.[20]

South Dakota voters have a long tradition of personal relationships with their elected officials. Politicians are referred to by their first names, and people encounter them at local restaurants. In keeping with this tradition, Johnson organized a large number of "feeds," which invited voters to have a meal and a conversation with him. The campaign invited voters (Democrats, Republicans, and independents) through an automated phone call from Johnson himself, followed up by a call from a staffer. Recognizing that politics and politicians turn off the voting population, Johnson refrained from having political material on tables or posters on the wall. He would walk around the room meeting people and visiting while they ate. After the meal, he would make a brief statement and then allow people to ask him questions. In many ways, these events were a throwback to a time when politicians campaigned door-to-door. Historically South Dakota has been a populist state, and this type of campaign seemed to resonate with voters. The Feed South Dakota events were one of the reasons Johnson was able to get the crossover votes needed to win the close election.[21]

The success of these events was magnified by the backfired efforts of a group of college students, hired by the state Republican Party, called the Thunatics. The Thunatics, present outside all the Johnson feeds, would line the sidewalk holding handmade signs with negative comments about Johnson. Apparently neither the Thune campaign nor the Thunatics realized that the people attending were undecided independents, Republicans, and Democrats. The image of the Thunatics and their signs provided a negative first impression of Thune's campaign, and that image contrasted with the "nonpolitical" event inside.[22] Dave Kranz, a political reporter for the *Sioux Falls Argus Leader*, speculated that backlash to the Thunatics was a key factor in Johnson's win. Ryan Nelson, Thune's political director, believed that Johnson complained about them because he did not like them. However, the Thune campaign received no complaints about the Thunatics, and Nelson felt they brought energy to the party.[23]

Thune's voter gatherings focused primarily on his Republican political base.[24] He held ice cream socials in August but did not have the same type of large-scale events as Johnson.[25]

Johnson waged a better ground war. It is ironic that the large sums of money expended on mediated messages may have had little effect. The sheer volume of messages led voters to tune them all out. It was not uncommon to hear people say that they could not wait for the campaign to end, especially after the extremely negative gubernatorial primary. In many respects, the most important aspect of the air war was that both sides fought with equal sums of money. When comparing messages, a face-to-face meeting tends to have a more positive impact and focuses on issues in a more substantive manner than a thirty-second spot or a direct mail piece with a glossy picture and slogan. Johnson and his aides were able to reach more people directly; this may have also made a difference in this campaign.

The Political Parties

The South Dakota Republican State Central Committee produced sixty-eight discrete pieces of mail. While the volume was significant, many of the pieces carried the same messages if not the same text. The issues covered were consistent with interest groups operating on behalf of Republicans, including ten mailers on guns and thirteen mailers on abortion or cloning or both.

The South Dakota Democratic Party produced thirty-nine direct mailings that also corresponded with the issues raised on its behalf by outside interest groups. Unlike the Republican's mailings, the Democratic pieces were more distinct from each other. Six pieces targeted seniors (on prescription drugs and Social Security) and four targeted primarily women (on child care, women's health, and adoption). Three mailings focused on education and six on corporate corruption (Enron, tax havens, and corporate influence). The Democrats also did single mailings on issues such as gun control and ethanol and seven generic mailers promoting their full statewide ticket as a unified team.

Native American Voter Registration

Early in the campaign, Democrats knew that they would need to increase the number of Democratic registered voters if they were going to defeat John Thune. The state Democratic Party devised a strategy to increase registration and voter turnout among the Native American population. They accomplished this by hiring independent contractors to collect registration cards; a portion of the compensation was based on the number of people who registered. Four thousand Native Americans were registered in 2001–02.

Johnson would not have won without this intense effort to register Native Americans and get them to the polls. The three counties with significant Native American population—Dewey, Shannon, and Todd—showed an additional 3,298 people registered who declared themselves Democrats.[26] On Election Day Johnson received 5,251 more votes than Thune in those three counties. The results from Shannon County were among the last to be tabulated, and those votes put Johnson over the top. This strategy seemed to have made the difference in an election decided by just 524 votes.

While Native American registration was important for Johnson, it may have disguised weaknesses by both parties in getting out the vote in other parts of the state. In several precincts voter turnout was lower than in the rest of the state because the state Senate seat was uncontested.[27] The Republicans' biggest problem was in Pennington County, the second largest in the state, which includes Rapid City. This heavily Republican county's voter turnout was 6 percent below the rest of the state. Had this county experienced the same turnout as elsewhere, Thune likely would have had about 8,500 additional votes.[28] Some voters reported difficulty finding their polling places because of redistricting. Ellsworth Air Force Base, usually a Republican stronghold, held emergency training drills on Election Day, which also suppressed turnout.[29]

The Influence of National Politicians

The South Dakota Senate race drew both national and international attention because of its perceived closeness and because of the heavy involvement of President Bush and Majority Leader Daschle. The race was also nationalized by the heavy party investment and its allied interest groups.

The two campaigns differed in their relationships to their respective alliances. Johnson ran his campaign on his record and waited until the end of the campaign to introduce the Daschle factor. In contrast, Bush participated in the Thune campaign from beginning to end. In essence Johnson ran under the theme "Elect me and I can use the majority leader and my appointment to the Appropriations Committee to deliver for the state." Thune ran under the theme "Elect me and we can pass the president's agenda." The two approaches influenced the ways in which the campaigns played out.

Johnson effectively argued that his seat on the Appropriations Committee was important to the state. He also portrayed himself as a person who had access to power (Daschle and the Democratic majority) but was willing to part company with his party for the betterment of the state. These two arguments resonated with voters. Johnson also maintained that a vote for him was a vote to keep Daschle as majority leader. Consistent with this strategy, Johnson did not bring in outsiders to stump for him.[30]

Thune chose the Senate race over the gubernatorial race primarily at the president's urging and with a promise of presidential support. The president showed his support with five visits to the state (the first in 2001, a second in April 2002, and three others during the general election). Vice President Cheney, Lynne Cheney, Rudolph Giuliani, and Laura Bush also visited the state. However, the major draw was the president himself. President Bush is very popular across the state of South Dakota, where presidential visits are rare. Given the state's Republican majority, conservative leanings, and support for Bush, it appeared to be a good strategy.

Local stations covered presidential visits from landing to departure, which critics argued was inequitable free airtime. Anticipation of the visit, the visit, and the aftermath dominated local news coverage. KELO-TV even canceled the last Johnson-Thune debate, in part because they wanted to send all their crews to Aberdeen for the presidential visit. In essence, a presidential visit was most valuable for its ability to focus media attention on one candidate.[31]

Bush's second visit, in August, was to Rapid City. The Democrats helped create anticipation of the visit by speculating that Bush would bring a large drought relief package with him to help the state and Thune. However, when Bush told voters in Rapid City that he would not support additional relief for their drought-stricken region, Thune's presidential ties made voters question his commitment to South Dakotans, the most likely reason Thune lost the election.[32]

Voters were disappointed a second time by the Bush-Thune duo in Aberdeen on October 31, when many were turned away from an event for which they had been given tickets. An elementary school class was turned away from the event after waiting in the cold for hours. The Thune campaign believed it was a nonissue, because most of those turned away were loyal Republicans.[33] However, the media attention focused on the students, prompting Daschle to visit the students who were "left in the cold."

Bush's final visit was to Sioux Falls the Sunday before the election. The timing of the presidential visit meant that the Republican ground war for undecideds and GOTV was placed on hold, while they made preparations for the visit and watched the president. While Republicans were preparing for the visit, Democrats were on a bus tour of the eastern part of the state, going door-to-door for undecideds and doing GOTV. The president's visit was followed by equal airtime provided to the Democrats while they rallied in Vermillion. The television images of Republicans showed 3,500 people in an arena, dressed in suits, talking primarily about national issues on the president's agenda. In contrast, the Democrats were at a small gathering, dressed down, talking about the state and their concern for the people there.

Overall the Thune campaign felt that the president's visits helped energize their base.[34] The Johnson campaign realized that tying Thune to the president and national concerns created a contrast to the Johnson-Daschle ties that Democrats emphasized to South Dakota voters. However, Johnson's campaign believed the Bush visits helped Johnson, and Johnson's campaign manager, Steve Hildebrand, speculated that, had he been on the other side, he might have asked the president to skip the visits after the disaster in Rapid City.[35]

Interest Groups

The gun issue was pulled into the campaign by outside groups and magnified by the Republican state party's direct mail. The National Rifle Association supported Thune primarily through direct mail. Charlton Heston also made a visit to Sioux Falls and spoke at a local gun shop on Thune's behalf. Several sportsmen's clubs and hunters' groups also distributed direct mail attacking Johnson. The Hunting and Shooting Sports Heritage Foundation ran a widely circulated ad in *Field and Stream* magazine, calling on gun owners to finish the job begun in 2000 and replace Tim Johnson. This organization also did direct mail with the same message in two different mailings. The gun issue received a lot of attention in the media, because the state's most prominent hunting and fishing media personality, Tony Dean, voiced support of Johnson early in the campaign. Dean argued that Johnson's position on conservation was important to preserve wildlife and benefit state tourism and hunting. The media picked up on the story, because several gun groups urged their members to boycott Tony Dean's *Dakota Backroads* radio program and lobby to have it taken off the air. The controversy prompted Johnson to run an ad professing his support for hunting and gun ownership. In the ad Johnson is dressed in camouflage hunting gear and is shopping for a new rifle with Tony Dean. The Thune campaign and the Republican Party alluded to the issue in several ads that included the phrase "and he voted to take guns away from law-abiding citizens."

Anti-abortion groups conducted direct mail campaigns attacking Johnson and supporting Thune. Two of these groups distributed six direct mail pieces. When combined with the thirteen from the Republican Party, the direct mail barrage on this issue might have been so extensive as to be counterproductive. Johnson's campaign manager said, "They overplayed at all levels the right-to-life issue. They should have played it, but they played it too hard, and it turned some people off. It got so sickening for some pro-life voters that they said 'we're not voting for this guy because he's too extreme.'"[36]

Thune was the beneficiary of more interest-group activity than Johnson. Johnson actually requested that some interest groups not campaign against Thune or for him. His theory was that together he and the party had more than enough money to run an effective campaign. In a close election, he felt that complex strategies were needed and that outside groups might do more harm than good. The involvement of both the pro-life and gun groups might have worked against Thune. The state was already inundated with material, and the number of abortion and gun mailings could have been overkill. People sympathetic to both issues were turned off by the volume of messages, which in turn made Thune look more extreme on the issues than he actually was.[37]

Conclusion

The South Dakota Senate contest was one of the top races in the 2002 election. In a race this close, any number of factors could have influenced the final outcome. It could have been the large-scale strategies involving Bush and Daschle, or it could have been as simple as passing out too many tickets to a presidential visit and leaving elementary students literally out in the cold. It could have been the "feed South Dakota" events or the Thunatics with their hand-painted signs. Each of these factors was important, but none by itself can fully explain the outcome.

The election was a victory for the Daschle-Johnson team, with their promises of serving South Dakota's interests. They were able to cite large projects that delivered cash to the state. In contrast the Bush-Thune team focused on ideology rather than state benefits. South Dakota, because of its small population, is not a major player on the national political scene. The last time the state had national significance was McGovern's failed presidential bid in 1972. While many in the state might not agree with all of Daschle's positions, his ascension to power is a source of state pride. This played a role in the election's outcome. Ironically, when the night ended, Daschle had lost that leadership position due to elections in other states. Had South Dakotans known that before voting, they might have voted differently and changed the outcome of the election.

Given the population of the state, the amount of money expended during the 2002 South Dakota Senate election was astronomical. The state was inundated with television spots, phone calls, and direct mail. In the end, most voters probably tuned out the commercials, turned off the phone, and discarded the mail. One woman wrote and explained that she started watching public television and stopped answering the phone in the evening. Candidates are in a difficult position: If they back off on mediated messages, their opponent's voice will be heard, and they stand to lose the election. But with the huge sums expended on the messages, it is ironic that a return to traditional campaigning probably decided this election. It is hard to generalize from a low-population state, and it would be impossible for candidates in larger states to have the same level of personal contact with voters. It does demonstrate, however, the need for personal contact when the public turns off the air messages. Thus it remains to be seen whether the last hurrah of soft money will ground the air campaign.

Notes

1. Ryan Nelson, political director, John Thune for South Dakota, telephone interview by Quin Monson, Jonathan Tanner, James Meader, and John Bart, January 14, 2003.

2. Ibid.

3. FCC records at local television stations.

4. Ibid.

5. Steve Hildebrand, campaign manager, Tim Johnson for South Dakota, interview by James Meader and John Bart, Rapid City, S.D., November 26, 2002.

6. Nelson interview, January 14, 2003.

7. Saxby Chambliss ran a similar ad against Max Cleland in Georgia's Senate race in 2002. See Meg Kinnard, "Chambliss Ad Features Saddam, Osama," *National Journal Ad Spotlight*, October 15, 2002 (http://nationaljournal.com/members/adspotlight/2002/10/1015scga1.htm [July 30, 2003]).

8. Hildebrand interview, November 26, 2002.

9. Nelson interview, January 14, 2003.

10. Hildebrand interview, November 26, 2002.

11. Hildebrand and Nelson interviews.

12. A point equals 1 percent of a television market. The LCV ad would presumably be viewed by each household in the media market thirty times.

13. Scott Stoermer, political director, LCV, interview by David Magleby and Jonathan Tanner, Washington, D.C., November 15, 2002.

14. Hildebrand interview, November 26, 2002.

15. Mike Madden, "Business Organization Spends Millions to Help GOP, Attack Democrats," *Gannett News Service*, October 25, 2002.

16. Mike Madden, "Democrats Call Group Running Ads 'Shadowy,'" October 25, 2002 (www.southdakotaelections.com [January 13, 2003]).

17. Notes received while collecting direct mail pieces.

18. David B. Magleby, J. Quin Monson, and the Center for the Study of Elections and Democracy, 2002 Soft Money and Issue Advocacy Database [dataset] (Brigham Young University, 2002).

19. Hildebrand interview, November 26, 2002.

20. Nelson interview; Blaise Hazelwood, political director, RNC, telephone interview by David Magleby, Quin Monson, and Jonathan Tanner, January 17, 2003.

21. Hildebrand interview, November 26, 2002.

22. Ibid.

23. Nelson interview, January 14, 2003.

24. Hildebrand interview, November 26, 2002.

25. Nelson interview, January 14, 2003.

26. State of South Dakota Election Information, 2002 (www.state.sd.us/sos/ Elections%20home%20page.htm#2002%20Election%20Information [January 20, 2003]).

27. Bob Mercer, governor's press secretary, phone interview by James Meader and John Bart, December 13, 2002.

28. This number is based on the percentage of people who voted for Thune in Pennington projected out to a 71 percent voter turnout. It is probably an underestimate because Hildebrand said their numbers showed that Republican turnout was down 10 percent. More Republicans stayed home than Democrats.

29. Nelson interview, January 14, 2003.

30. Hildebrand interview, November 26, 2002.

31. Ibid.

32. Nelson interview, January 14, 2003.

33. Ibid.

34. Ibid.

35. Hildebrand interview, November 26, 2002.

36. Ibid.

37. Ibid.

EIGHT   *Strings Attached:*
Outside Money in
Colorado's Seventh District

DANIEL A. SMITH

I N E V E R Y G E N E R A L E L E C T I O N political pundits
select a handful of "toss-up" congressional races they deem too close to
call.[1] In 2002 Colorado's newly carved Seventh Congressional District
lived up to its competitive billing.[2] Despite being outpolled on Election
Day by 2,502 votes, Republican Bob Beauprez ultimately won the district by 121 votes over Democrat Mike Feeley.[3] Unlike other closely
fought congressional races, interest groups stayed above the fray, focusing their collective energy on Colorado's U.S. Senate race. Instead, most
of the heavy hitting in Colorado's Seventh was carried out by Republican and Democratic national congressional campaign committees. The
expenditures made by the two national parties—which dwarfed the
spending by the candidates—had a nationalizing effect, as the outside
money restricted the ability of the candidates to control the substantive
issues debated during the campaign. While alarmed by the vitriol of the
negative television ads and direct mail produced on their behalf, both
Beauprez and Feeley became increasingly beholden to the directives of
their respective congressional parties as the election neared.

Research for this chapter was conducted while I was on the faculty of the
University of Denver. Joseph Lubinski provided excellent research assistance,
and Andy Busch was an invaluable colleague. Josh Brodbeck and Kevin Opp
kept me abreast of the latest campaign developments. Helene Orr and my
department's work-study students helped with administrative tasks, and the candidates, their staff, and the consultants were generous with their time.

Although the use of outside money in federal campaigns is well documented, what is less known is the daily coordination that occurs between the candidates and the national parties. As stakeholders in the contest, the national congressional committees had a powerful incentive to ensure a yield on their investments—namely, that their candidate emerge victorious. In addition to making coordinated hard- and soft-money expenditures on behalf of the two candidates, both congressional campaign committees plied the candidates' staffs with pointed directives from their Washington perches. Reflecting on the campaign a month after the election, Congressman-elect Beauprez deadpanned, "The national party swung pretty hard."[4]

Inside the Seventh District

Shaped like an unlucky horseshoe encompassing Denver's older suburbs, the boundaries of the new district were established in January 2002 by a court ruling that approved a Democrat-sponsored redistricting plan. Although the district comprised roughly equal numbers of registered Republicans (120,009), Democrats (120,119), and "unaffiliated" voters (122,888), state Democratic Party leaders thought the district leaned their way. Of the precincts that would eventually compose the Seventh, Al Gore defeated George Bush by slightly less than 8 percent (about 2,000 votes) in 2000.[5]

The district resulted from a decade of explosive growth in Colorado, during which the state's population ballooned to 4.3 million.[6] The Seventh was the state's second most racially and ethnically diverse congressional district. In 2002 minorities accounted for more than 31 percent of the population, including 19.6 percent Hispanics and 5.8 percent African Americans. Nearly 40 percent of the residents were renters, and one in ten constituents was sixty-five years of age or older.[7]

The Candidates and Their Campaigns

As anticipated, the new district attracted several talented candidates in the primaries. On the Republican side, Beauprez, the sitting state party chairman, entered the race after receiving phone calls from White House political counselors Karl Rove and Ken Mehlman, as well as a visit by the National Republican Congressional Committee (NRCC) chair, Representative Tom Davis (R-Va.).[8] Although the front-runner, the fifty-four-year-old banker was not a shoo-in as the party's nominee. Indeed Beauprez failed to win the top line at the GOP's district assembly caucus in May. In the primary, his three opponents labeled him a carpetbagger (Beauprez and his wife resided north of the district) and accused him of conducting push polls and authorizing his bank to run favorable radio ads. Beauprez outspent his opponents, airing close to $150,000 worth of television and $40,000 of radio ads. The straight-laced Republican withstood the intraparty wrangling and held on to win the primary with 38 percent of the vote.[9]

State and national Democratic Party leaders, including the House minority leader, Representative Dick Gephardt (D-Mo.), lured Feeley, a former state senator, to run for the seat. Term-limited in 2000, Feeley had represented a predominately Republican constituency in Jefferson County for eight years. Upon his retirement from the state Senate, the forty-nine-year-old lawyer joined a Denver law firm, Baker and Hostetler. Due to some opportunistic lobbying in the private sector and overzealous support from organized labor, many party faithful initially shied away from Feeley.[10] Sensing rank-and-file dissent, Feeley eschewed the party's caucus in May and instead petitioned his way onto the mid-August primary ballot. During the signature-gathering process, the former Marine knocked on nearly 7,500 doors.[11] Feeley's gambit to circumvent the party caucus and take his campaign directly to the citizens—along with $37,125 worth of television ads—proved successful, as he defeated Dave Thomas, the Jefferson County district attorney, with 56 percent of the vote.[12]

Following their respective primary victories on August 13, both candidates endeavored to shape the agenda for the general election, with both camps vowing to run issue-based, positive campaigns.[13] On the hustings, the two candidates spoke passionately about the issues, though Beauprez was far more scripted than Feeley. Beauprez discussed the grave concerns about transportation and water in the district, as well as how he could draw on his banking and farming experience and provide fiscal responsibility in Washington. He identified himself closely with President Bush, backing his proposed tax cuts and crackdown against Saddam Hussein and terrorist networks. For his part, Feeley initially touted solutions to the water, growth, and transportation problems in the district and also addressed corporate accountability, the high costs of prescription drugs, and his opposition to the Bush tax cut.

The two men were cognizant, though, that if the race remained tight, their campaigns would likely morph beyond their control, with party leaders in Washington calling the shots. In early September, their worst fears were realized. The race quickly devolved into a mud-slinging battle, with most of the recriminating ads paid for with soft money flowing from the national congressional parties. As Election Day neared, Beauprez's campaign shifted gears, and the national party instigated a malicious "biographical campaign."[14] Feeley, under the direction of the Democratic Congressional Campaign Committee (DCCC), tried to differentiate himself from Beauprez on abortion, Social Security, and gun control. Beauprez quickly countered by moderating his neoprivatization stance on Social Security and, more significantly, by playing up the character issue.

Money: Candidates, Parties, and Interest Groups

In contrast to other tight congressional races in 2002, special-interest groups never became heavily involved in Colorado's Seventh. Rather it was the national congressional campaign committees that were largely responsible for the surprising amount of outside money spent in the race. While Beauprez and Feeley each raised respectable campaign chests, the two national parties far outpaced the candidates, spending nearly $3.5 million in the district.

Candidates

The candidates proved to be prodigious fund-raisers. Beauprez amassed only a slight fund-raising advantage, besting his Democratic foe by less than $300,000, excluding the candidates' personal loans and contributions from the parties. Both candidates kick-started their primary races by lending their campaigns money. Beauprez secured three banker's loans totaling $455,000, while Feeley lent his campaign $56,000, taking out a second mortgage on his home. The loans enabled both campaigns to run television ads in the primaries, increasing their name recognition. Interestingly the national parties viewed the candidates' personal antes differently. The NRCC badgered the Beauprez camp for being too profligate during the primary, while the DCCC encouraged Feeley to lend money to his campaign to demonstrate his commitment to run for Congress.[15]

Feeley's personal investment was rewarded by the DCCC, when it selected the race as its "top target." Just days after the primary, the national party conducted a "sniff test" at campaign headquarters. Like "a big stockbroker looking through a portfolio," the DCCC was convinced that Feeley could win, but it found the campaign to have "some problems"—from inadequate office equipment to poor message development.[16] To rectify these identified shortcomings, in mid-August the party assigned Erik Greathouse to head the campaign, effectively displacing Feeley's longtime confidante, Beth Minahan. Working in tandem with the DCCC midwest regional field director, who "spent lots of time on the ground" with the campaign, Greathouse formulated a strategic plan that included weekly conference calls with the DCCC and its media consultants. Feeley's staff drew heavily on the DCCC's "institutional knowledge," as the national party sent daily briefings to the campaign and helped the candidate gain command of the issues transpiring in Washington.[17]

The NRCC, while not directly involved in the primary, clearly wanted Beauprez to win the party nomination. Although it made no attempt to replace Beauprez's campaign manager—Sean Murphy, an experienced politico who had worked previously under Beauprez at the state party—the NRCC constantly monitored the campaign.[18] The national party told Murphy that it would be priming the campaign with the "largest amount of money given to any race in the country," unless the campaign committed "a catastrophic error." At times the NRCC's intrusions plainly peeved Murphy, who muttered that the party's hands-on approach was intrusive: "They crawl up our ass on a daily basis." The regional field office regularly badgered the campaign staff, asking, "What earned media did you get?" and "What's your cash on hand?" In addition the NRCC sent several members of Congress and the Bush administration to the district to stump for Beauprez, including individuals with little name recognition or perceived electoral value.[19]

The NRCC took full advantage of President Bush's popularity to raise money for Beauprez. In late September, Beauprez and the state GOP split $1.5 million raised at a $1,000-a-plate luncheon with the president; the campaign pocketed more than $600,000 of the total, with the balance going to the state party.[20] A month later, on October 28, Air Force One cruised into Denver just long enough for Bush to hold a Republican pep rally.[21] By the October 16 Federal Election Commission (FEC) reporting period, Beauprez had raised $1,013,310 (including his $380,000 loan), with an impressive $542,224 cash on hand, due largely

Table 8-1. *Candidate Receipts and Expenditures, 2001–02*
Dollars

Source	Feeley (D)	Beauprez (R)
From PACs	463,396	443,402
From individuals	542,597	899,776
From party	15,700	54,320
From candidate	56,000	455,000
Other contributions	82,799	303
Total receipts	1,160,492	1,852,801
Total expenditures	1,147,759	1,827,119
Cash on hand 12/31/02	12,732	14,430

Source: Federal Election Commission, "2001–02 U.S. House and U.S. Senate Candidate Info," December 31, 2002 (www.fecinfo.com/cgi-win/x_statedis.exe [June 8, 2003]).

to the star appeal of Bush (see table 8-1). In contrast, Feeley had $127,389 on hand for the final three-week push. The Democrat had raised $808,188 by mid-October (including his loan).[22] He was aided by a string of high-profile Democrats who stumped for him, including Gephardt, House Minority Whip Nancy Pelosi (D-Calif.), Senator Joe Lieberman (D-Conn.), and former Senator Bill Bradley (D-N.J.).[23]

Both candidates spent the bulk of their contributions on television advertising. In the final week, the two campaigns spent more than $230,000 on television.[24] During the general election, Beauprez paid National Media $646,330 to air three ads on Denver stations. Although Beauprez's camp wanted to broadcast more spots during the final week, the choice time slots were filled by other political candidates and ballot issue committees, so it instead paid National Media $35,855 to air three last-minute radio ads (see table 8-2).[25] Excluding a fund-raising invitation to the September 27 luncheon with Bush, Beauprez spent no money on direct mail after the primary. For its part, the Feeley campaign paid Armour Media $547,142 to produce and run three television ads in the general election. Feeley did no radio and little direct mail during the general election, as he "only [had] so much money for voter contact."[26]

Parties

It came as no surprise that the national parties' expenditures far outstripped the money spent by the two candidates. According to reports filed with the FEC and inquiries to the campaigns, the Republican state and federal parties spent roughly $2.5 million in the Seventh District,

Table 8-2. *The Air War: Television and Radio Advertising Expenditures, Colorado Seventh District Race, 2002*[a]
Dollars

Type and organization	TV	Radio	Total spent	CMAG TV
Democratic allies[b]				
Candidates				
Feeley for Congress	547,142	. . .	547,142	737,406
Political parties				
Democratic Congressional Campaign Committee / Colorado Democratic Party	621,704	. . .	621,704	1,128,908
Republican allies[b]				
Candidates				
Bob Beauprez for Congress	646,330	35,855	682,185	976,174
Political parties				
National Republican Congressional Committee / Colorado Republican Federal Campaign Committee	1,945,981	. . .	1,945,981	1,128,854
National Republican Congressional Committee / Republican State Central Committee of Colorado	58,000	. . .	58,000	463,236
Interest groups				
Council for Better Government	33,200	. . .	33,200	. . .
National Right to Life	0	. . .	. . .	. . .
Heritage Bank	0	. . .	. . .	. . .

Sources: David B. Magleby, J. Quin Monson, and the Center for the Study of Elections and Democracy, 2002 Soft Money and Issue Advocacy Database (Brigham Young University, 2002); and Campaign Media Analysis Group data.

a. See appendix A for a more detailed data explanation. The ad-buy data collected for this study may contain extraneous data because of the difficulty in determining the content of the ads. The parties or interest groups that purchased the ads possibly ran some ads promoting House or Senate candidates or ballot propositions not in the study's sample but still within that media market. Unless the participating academics were able to determine the exact content of the ad buy from the limited information given by the station, the data may contain observations that do not pertain to the study's relevant House or Senate races.

For comparison purposes the CMAG data are included in the table. Because of the volume of television and radio stations and varying degrees of compliance in providing ad-buy information, data on spending by various groups might be incomplete. This table is not intended to represent comprehensive organization spending or activity within the sample races. A more complete picture can be obtained by examining this table with table 8-3.

In blank cells, ". . ." reflects the absence of collected data and does not imply that the organization was inactive in that medium.

b. Certain organizations that maintained neutrality were categorized according to which candidates their ads supported or attacked or whether the organization was openly anti- or pro-conservative or liberal.

dwarfing the approximately $830,000 spent by the Democratic parties. Both national congressional campaign committees capitalized on the financial motivation to transfer money to the state parties, taking advantage of Colorado's favorable fixed ratio of hard to soft dollars.

The NRCC funneled nearly $2.4 million in combined hard and soft dollars into the Colorado Republican Federal Campaign Committee (CRFCC). The party paid for a barrage of television and direct-mail issue ads touting Beauprez and slamming Feeley. According to Alan Philp, executive director of the Colorado Republican Party, the NRCC specified what to do with its transferred money "down to the dollar."[27] With the NRCC's contributions to the state party coming in two parts—78 percent in soft dollars and 22 percent in hard dollars, Colorado's designated hard-soft match—the CRFCC paid Strategic Media Services $1.95 million to produce five televised issue ads. The NRCC also channeled approximately $200,000 in hard and soft money through the CRFCC to Targeted Creative Communications to do fourteen direct mail ads.[28] The NRCC also independently spent $200,000 to purchase ten direct mail ads.[29] Finally the NRCC contributed $38,000 (which was matched by the state GOP) to the state party's coordinated campaign; roughly $58,000 was used to run another television ad through Strategic Media Services, with the remaining $18,000 paying for one more targeted mailing.[30]

The DCCC also used its state party as a conduit to pay for television and direct mail issue ads criticizing Beauprez and venerating Feeley. Unlike the NRCC, the DCCC made no independent expenditures. Rather, the national party transferred its federal and nonfederal dollars directly to the state party's federal campaign fund.[31]

Federal Election Commission records and interviews with media consultants indicate that the party spent $47,577 to produce five television issue ads and $524,127 to air them.[32] The DCCC (via the state party) also spent $180,000 to produce and mail seven individual direct mail pieces, which were developed in consultation with the Feeley campaign.[33] Through the coordinated campaign, the party aired one late-running TV ad for $50,000, which the Feeley campaign authorized.[34] Finally, the Democratic National Committee (DNC) paid $38,000 via the state party to produce three narrowly targeted mail pieces to active voters (seniors, young Republican women, and Latinos) which were posted only days before the election.[35]

Interest Groups

National interest groups generally kept their distance during the campaign, concentrating the bulk of their attention on the U.S. Senate race between Republican incumbent Wayne Allard and Democrat Tom Strickland. Tellingly, special interests ran no television and only a few radio ads featuring the candidates contesting the Seventh.[36] National Right to Life bought limited radio time, and Beauprez's Heritage Bank ran radio spots during the primary and general elections.[37] Neither the campaign nor specific political issues were addressed in the Heritage Bank ads (which aired on Clear Channel stations), but the tone of each preached integrity and trust, with Beauprez speaking during the final fifteen seconds. Three 527 organizations, all fronts for the pharmaceutical industry, each sent out a direct mail piece, but overall, interest groups mailed less than half the total number of unique pieces sent by the parties.[38] Other interest groups, most notably the National Rifle Association (NRA), the Colorado AFL-CIO, the Colorado Education Association (CEA), and the Sierra Club, sent mailings to their members. While the amount spent on issue ads and internal communications is not disclosed, it is likely that less than $100,000 was spent in the Seventh District by outside groups.

The Effects of Money: Ground War

Waging an effective ground war is crucial to electoral success in Colorado. During the 1990s, campaigns became increasingly front-loaded, because county clerks were authorized to mail absentee ballot request forms to registered voters and open early voting centers (from October 21 to November 1) in an effort to trim voting queues on Election Day.[39] Beauprez, Feeley, and the state parties encouraged their core supporters to vote before the November election.[40] Early voting was especially pronounced in Jefferson County, with roughly half of those voting doing so with absentee ballots or at early voting stations.[41] Public opinion polls, including the third wave of the Center for the Study of Elections and Democracy (CSED) Perfect Storm Election Study, found that over 50 percent of Republicans and Democrats who said they voted did so by casting absentee ballots or voting early.[42] Early voting, though, appeared to benefit Beauprez, because more registered Republicans than Democrats voted early.[43] Feeley conceded that Beauprez and the state

GOP did "a terrific job" motivating supporters to vote early, putting his campaign in "a rather shallow hole that we couldn't climb out of."[44]

In terms of mail, the NRCC relied on independent expenditures to produce ten hard-hitting pieces, half of which slammed Feeley and made no mention of Beauprez.[45] (See tables 8-3 and 8-4). Postelection, Beauprez's campaign manager conceded that many of the ads were "pure, harsh hate."[46] In concert with the state party, the NRCC financed fifteen more targeted direct mail pieces. Although Beauprez sent no direct mail in the general election, his staff preapproved each coordinated NRCC–state party mailing, including (albeit belatedly) a highly controversial piece featuring side-by-side photographs of a cigar-chomping lobbyist and a rabid dog. The oversize postcard inveighed, "What happens when you cross this [cigar-chomping lobbyist] with this [rabid dog]?" "You get Mike Feeley. And he wants to be your Congressman?" The tagline read: "He's just out for himself. He's everything wrong with politics today."[47]

The "rabid dog" piece was clearly the nastiest direct mail piece of the campaign. Feeley was so enraged that he sent a copy of it to Beauprez's home with a curt note. After the election, Feely complained, "The Republican Party was pretty shameless. The distortion, the volume— that really wasn't attributable to Bob—was relentless."[48] Feeley did his best to make the caustic nature of the campaign an issue. The street-smart New Jersey native reasoned, "You can only sit back and let people smack you in the belly so many times. You don't go to a gun fight and bring a knife." While Beauprez admitted privately that he was personally concerned about the negative tone, he defended the NRCC's calculated campaign of character assassination, saying Feeley "would do what he had to [as a lobbyist] and take a shower the morning after."[49] Internal polling by the GOP suggested that the campaign in the Seventh did not approach the viciousness of the U.S. Senate race, so the party saw no reason to limit its negative attacks: "We could have put a flame-thrower in [Feeley's] ear," an NRCC direct mail consultant confided, "and we almost did!"[50]

For its part, the DCCC financed no independent expenditure direct mail ads and spent far less than Republicans in its coordinated efforts with the state party. Routing its hard-soft money split through the state party, the DCCC paid for seven glossy direct mail pieces, three of which assailed Beauprez for his stances on guns, abortion, and corporate corruption. One piece featured the same cigar-chomping lobbyist used by

Table 8-3. *Number of Unique Campaign Communications by Organizations, Colorado Seventh District Race, 2002*[a]

Type and organization	E-mail messages	Surface mail pieces	Newspaper or magazine ads[b]	Personal contacts	Phone calls	Radio ads	TV ads	Total
			Democratic allies					
Candidates								
Feeley for Congress	5	1	...	2	2	...	4	14
Political parties								
Democratic Congressional Campaign Committee/Colorado Democratic Party	...	7	...	2	...	1[c]	6	16
Democratic National Committee/ Colorado Democratic Party	...	3	...	...	...	...	...	3
Interest groups								
Colorado AFL-CIO	2	1	...	1	1	...	...	5
Colorado Education Association	...	2	...	...	...	...	...	2
Alliance for Retired Americans[d]	...	...	...	...	...	...	...	1
Gay Lesbian Bisexual Transgender Majority Vote Project	...	1	...	...	...	...	...	1
Members of the Romer Family	...	1	...	...	...	...	...	1
Planned Parenthood[e]	...	...	...	...	...	...	...	1
Rocky Mountain Chapter of the Sierra Club	...	1	...	...	...	...	...	1
Sierra Club	...	...	...	...	1[f]	...	...	1
America's Credit Unions	...	1	...	...	...	...	...	1
Jeffco Schools Credit Union	...	1	...	...	...	...	...	1
Public Service Credit Union	...	1	...	...	...	...	...	1

		Republican allies[b]				
Candidates						
Bob Beauprez for Congress	5	3	...	3	3	17
Political parties						
National Republican Congressional Committee/Colorado Republican Federal Campaign Committee	...	15	1	...	5	21
National Republican Congressional Committee	...	10	...	2	1	13
National Republican Congressional Committee/Republican State Central Committee of Colorado	...	2	2	...	4	6
Colorado State/Federal Victory 2002	...	1	2	...	...	3
Local Republican parties	...	2	...	...	...	2
Republican National Committee	...	...	1[g]	...	...	1
Interest groups						
Council for Better Government	...	...	...	...	24	24
National Rifle Association	...	4	...	...	...	4
60 Plus Association	...	2	...	1[h]	...	3
National Right to Life	...	1	...	2	...	3
Heritage Bank	...	...	...	2	...	2
Unknown Organization	...	...	2	...	...	2
America 21	...	1	...	...	...	1
Arapahoe Republican Men's Club and Aurora Republican Forum	...	...	1	...	...	1
Christian Coalition	...	...	1	...	...	1
National Federation of Independent Business	...	1	...	...	...	1
Seniors Coalition	...	1	...	...	...	1
U.S. Chamber of Commerce[i]	...	1	...	...	...	1

continued on next page

Table 8-3. *Number of Unique Campaign Communications by Organizations, Colorado Seventh District Race, 2002*[a]
(continued)

Type and organization	Type of campaign communication							
	E-mail messages	Surface mail pieces	Newspaper or magazine ads	Personal contacts	Phone calls	Radio ads	TV ads	Total
Other party allies								
Candidates								
Victor Good for Congress Committee	...	...	1	...	...	...	...	1

Source: Magleby, Monson, and CSED, 2002 Soft Money and Issue Advocacy Database.

a. See appendix A for a more detailed explanation of data. This table is not intended to portray comprehensive organization activity within the sample races. A more complete picture can be obtained by examining this table together with table 8-2. Data represent the number of unique pieces or ads by the group and do not represent a count of total items sent or made.

In blank cells, "..." reflects the absence of collected data and does not imply that the organization was inactive in that medium.

b. Certain organizations that maintained neutrality were categorized according to which candidates their ads supported or attacked or whether the organization was anti- or pro-conservative or liberal.

c. Mike Matthews, political director, DCCC, interview by David Magleby and Nicole Carlisle Squires, Washington, D.C., November 12, 2002.

d. Unspecified race involvement. Ed Coyle, executive director, Alliance for Retired Americans, telephone interview by David Magleby and Quin Monson, December 20, 2002.

e. Unspecified race involvement. David Williams, director of Action Fund and PAC, Planned Parenthood, interview by David Magleby and Nicole Carlisle Squires, Washington, D.C., November 8, 2002.

f. Margaret Conway, national political director, Sierra Club, telephone interview by David Magleby and Quin Monson, December 16, 2002.

g. Marc Racicot, RNC chairman, interview by David Magleby, Washington, D.C., December 6, 2002.

h. Jim Martin, president, 60 Plus Association, interview by Quin Monson and Jonathan Tanner, Washington, D.C., December 11, 2002.

i. Unspecified race involvement. Bill Miller, political director, U.S. Chamber of Commerce, interview by David Magleby and Quin Monson, Washington, D.C., November 7, 2002.

Table 8-4. *Direct Mail Expenditures by Parties, Colorado Seventh District Race, 2002*
Dollars

Type and organization	Amount
Democratic allies	
Political parties	
DCCC / Colorado Democratic Party	180,000
DNC / Colorado Democratic Party	38,000
Republican allies	
Political parties	
NRCC / Colorado Republican Federal Campaign Committee	200,000
NRCC	200,000
NRCC / Republican State Central Committee of Colorado	18,000

Source: FEC. See appendix A for a more detailed explanation of data. This table is not intended to represent comprehensive organization spending or activity within the sample races. A more complete picture can be obtained by examining this table with table 8-3.

the NRCC in its infamous rabid dog piece. Another negative piece depicted a match lighting a copy of the Constitution on fire, with the tagline reading, "Bob Beauprez Wants to Ban All Abortion—EVEN in Cases of Rape and Incest."[51]

Get-out-the-vote (GOTV) efforts in the district fell under the umbrellas of the state parties, which were bolstered by soft money transferred from the national parties. Beauprez participated in the state Republican party's ninety-six-hour program—outlasting the Republican National Committee's national 72 Hour Task Force—which was run out of Governor Bill Owens's campaign headquarters. Aided by a $250,000 soft money contribution from the RNC, the state party's ninety-six-hour program paid "volunteers" $200 for their efforts and included 114 Oral Roberts University students bused in from Oklahoma.[52] During literature drops, the students were seen talking on cellular telephones provided by the party and driving cars courtesy of a John Elway dealership.[53] The NRCC also spent $14,559 in hard money to target Latinos in a late surge of "robo-calls" strafing Feeley's legislative and lobbying record.[54]

The state Democratic Party ran its traditional "ninety-six-day" campaign in an effort to turn out its base. With more than eighty paid staff, the party mobilized over 5,000 volunteers statewide on Election Day, including more than 1,000 union members. Although it fell short of its $3 million goal, the state party paid for generic absentee ballot request forms, GOTV literature, and phone banks imploring "lazy Dems" to vote. The party also expanded its Latino voter outreach, which included running Spanish-language radio and TV spots aimed at "lazy Democratic Latinos."[55] The party's coordinated campaign was "pay to play," with candidates, national parties, interest groups, and the proponent of a ballot measure anteing up to participate.[56]

Shying away from the expensive Denver television market, interest groups concentrated their electioneering efforts on the ground war but not nearly to the degree that many observers had expected. Targeting likely Republican voters, unaffiliated women, and especially seniors, several conservative groups sent oversize postcards highlighting issues at the heart of the campaign. National Right to Life mailed a small express advocacy postcard that placed a red heart next to Beauprez's staunch pro-life position. In addition to holding a political rally in Aurora in late October that featured Charlton Heston, the NRA sent four mailings (with a bumper sticker in one) to its Colorado members expressly supporting Beauprez because of his defense of the Second Amendment.[57] While the National Federation of Independent Business (NFIB) and the U.S. Chamber of Commerce endorsed Beauprez, any electioneering activities they conducted fell well below the radar screen. The Colorado Christian Coalition was also a nonfactor, distributing candidate slate cards to evangelical churches but issuing no other mailings.

More significantly, three sister 527 organizations—each a known shill for the pharmaceutical industry—used direct mail to counter Feeley's effort to criticize Beauprez's neoprivatization stance on Social Security and his ambiguous plan to rein in the rising costs of prescription drugs. The Seniors Coalition, America 21, and the 60 Plus Association collectively inundated the homes of older Republicans and independent voters with oversize postcards. None of these pieces mentioned Feeley. Clearly the groups were not coordinating their efforts with the Republican candidate; each praised "Beuprez" (misspelling his name) for his work on behalf of seniors, with the 60 Plus Association even giving the Republican an "Honorary Guardian of Seniors Award." With military service a latent issue during the campaign, America 21, in a piece filled with images of World War II servicemen, praised "Beuprez's [sic] Commitment to Seniors," and his willingness to "stand up for the Greatest Generation."[58]

Excluding organized labor, liberal interest groups were not as active on the ground as conservative groups. No national group surfaced to offset the mailings touting Beauprez's support of seniors. Organized labor contacted its members door-to-door, over the phone, and via e-mail; it also provided manpower for the Democrats' GOTV campaign. The CEA sent letters supporting Feeley to its members, and the Sierra Club sent an environmental scorecard to its members. The environmental group maintained a low profile, perhaps sensing that its endorsement of Feeley over the Green Party candidate, Dave Chandler, may have turned some voters away from the Democratic candidate.[59] On the periphery, local credit unions mailed postcards to their members supporting Feeley.[60] Finally, although it endorsed Feeley, NARAL Pro-Choice America focused its resources on the U.S. Senate race, sending no mailings in support of Feeley.[61]

The Effects of Money: Air War

Despite the nearly $4 million pumped into television ad buys in the Beauprez-Feeley contest, the spots were often drowned out by airwaves chock full of spots for other campaigns and ballot measures. An overwhelming number of ads were dedicated to the U.S. Senate melee, the reelection bids of Governor Owens and Attorney General Ken Salazar, and the particularly dyspeptic "No on 31" ballot issue campaign against the elimination of bilingual education. The barrage of negative ads on the airwaves clearly turned off voters and likely contributed to lower than expected statewide turnout.[62] The CSED survey revealed that 70 percent of respondents thought the race for the Seventh District was "more" negative "compared to other recent political contests," with 77 percent of respondents saying they "stopped paying attention" to the campaign ads.[63]

The viciousness of the air war, however, was not attributable to special interests, as they ran no television spots naming either Seventh District candidate. While party insiders anticipated that outside interests—labor, pro-choice, and environmental groups backing Feeley, and the NRA, anti-abortion, and pharmaceutical companies supporting Beauprez—would storm the airwaves with negative ads, it never happened. Only the Council for Better Government, a 527 political organization, ran television ads reaching voters in the district. The Kansas-based group spent $33,200 to run two dozen non-candidate-specific ads targeting Latinos and blacks and encouraging voters to back the GOP.[64] (See table 8-2).

The preponderance of money (roughly $2.5 million) spent on television ads originated from the national parties, with most of it redirected through state party organizations. The DCCC spent $621,704 on six issue ads supporting Feeley and trashing Beauprez; the NRCC tripled the amount of its Democratic foe, spending $1.946 million on six issue ads hammering Feeley and lionizing Beauprez. As Feeley noted ruefully in mid-September, "I think we're getting a god-awful amount of television."[65] Although some were deemed slanderous by the candidates, no ads were taken off the air by the stations.[66] The parties spent considerably more than the candidates on TV: Beauprez ran three ads for $646,330, and Feeley ran four ads for $547,142.

Half of the six issue ads underwritten by the NRCC and the state party were pure attack ads. While the NRCC ran a few positive ads beginning in mid-September, they took a decisively negative turn by early October. The GOP's most spiteful TV spot opened with a black background and a spray of question marks dotting the screen. A grainy silhouette emerged, with the narrator asking, "What kind of person works for a group that wants to force people to pay rent in a nursing home up to ninety days after they die?" A grainy image of Feeley gradually appeared, with the narrator blasting the Democrat for lobbying on behalf of drug companies and nursing homes. The thirty-second ad closed by asking viewers to "call Mike Feeley" and ask, "What kind of person are you?" Another of the NRCC's six issue ads, which began running in October, slammed "lobbyist Mike Feeley" for pushing a bill backed by "a powerful drug industry group" that would have made "medicine by mail more expensive" and hurt seniors "who have to choose between food and medicine." The spot was a clear indication that the GOP wanted to neutralize any courting of seniors by the Democrats.

The half dozen ads paid for by the DCCC (and coordinated with the state party) were nearly all negative, assailing Beauprez's "extreme views" on abortion and gun control. Feeley's internal polling found that both issues provided the Democrat with traction among Republican women and unaffiliated voters in the district.[67] DCCC money also partially funded the most ruthless assault against Beauprez, an ad produced by Armour Media titled, "Protect."[68] The ad accused the Republican of opposing a ban on so-called "cop-killer" bullets and broader controls on guns. The coordinated ad, which was authorized by the Feeley campaign, began running on October 29, a week before the election. Feeley "unveiled" the ad at the state capitol, accompanied by Representative Bob Menendez (D-N.J.) and several gun control activists and police officers.[69]

Of Beauprez's three television ads, his last, which ran the final week of the campaign, was perhaps the most effective. Titled, "That Smell," the spot was a ray of hope in an increasingly dark campaign, the first positive ad of the campaign to air in nearly two months. In the testimonial, Beauprez addressed the camera directly in his deliberate, plain-spoken manner. He lamented how a lot of negative things were said about him, and how, as a former dairy farmer, he recognized the smell. The ad closed with Beauprez asking voters for their support. Produced by National Media, the footage was actually shot in early September in a Denver city park, not in the district. At that time, the Beauprez camp was accentuating to the public how it would wage a clean campaign, eschewing negative attacks. Clearly, though, Beauprez's staff (and the NRCC media consultants, who were also shooting footage that day) had the clairvoyance to anticipate how bitter the campaign would become.

The Feeley campaign was absolutely "flabbergasted" by the "That Smell" spot after Beauprez's campaign of "character assassination."[70] In response to Beauprez's uplifting finale, Feeley dearly wanted to run a positive ad of his own in which he would "go to [the] camera and make [a] personal appeal," but the Democrat did not have "$250,000" to run an ad. His staff opted instead to keep airing an uncompromising pro-choice ad.[71] Following the election, Beauprez said he thought his last-minute positive spot put him over the top: "I think that resonated with people, I think that they wanted to hear from the candidate and not third parties."[72]

Radio ads were infrequent during the campaign. The parties essentially did not use the medium, and only a couple of interest groups aired ads. Beauprez ran three radio ads on Clear Channel stations during the last week of the campaign, turning to radio after they were unable to buy more television airtime.[73] One of Beauprez's scripts was lifted directly from the NRCC's television ad that criticized Feeley for lobbying on behalf of nursing home operators and against seniors.

Conclusion

In tight races, congressional candidates may have great difficulty running their own campaigns. The race for Colorado's razor-close, delicately reapportioned Seventh District exhibits how Washington party insiders are able to exert tremendous pressure on congressional candidates because of the national parties' potent elixir of soft and hard money. Both the Beauprez and Feeley campaigns were financed, albeit indirectly, by their respective national parties. But the money came with strings attached. Accompanying the staggering amount of outside money supplied by the NRCC and the DCCC were their tightly orchestrated campaign plans. The parties' external influence had the dual effect of distorting the local issues the two candidates initially had touted and inflaming the candidates' campaign rhetoric, making it more personal and spiteful. More worrisome, the parties' outside money contributed to the widening disconnect between the constituents residing in the district and the candidates who tirelessly campaigned to represent them.

Notes

1. "CQ's House Race Ranking Update," *CQ Daily Monitor*, July 15, 2002, p. 22; "Competitive House Races," *New York Times*, September 27, 2002, p. A21; and Peggy Lowe, "Feeley Closes Gap against Beauprez," *Rocky Mountain News*, October 30, 2002, p. A20.

2. Floyd Ciruli, "Close Races Were Challenge to Polling," *Denver Post*, November 24, 2002, p. E1.

3. Although Feeley won more votes cast on Election Day, Beauprez bested Feeley in early voting and absentee balloting. When the polls closed on November 5, Beauprez led Feeley by 386 votes. It took three county clerks two weeks to count the more than 1,900 valid provisional ballots cast on Election Day in the district. Following the tabulation of provisional ballots on November 21, Beauprez led Feeley by 122 votes—81,520 to 81,408—out of more than 170,000 votes cast. On December 10, following a mandatory recount, Beauprez emerged victorious, winning with 81,789 votes to Feeley's 81,668. Michele Ames, "Court May Settle Race in Seventh," *Rocky Mountain News*, November 15, 2002, p. A5.

4. Michael Janofsky, "Colorado Awaits Result of Electoral Photo Finish," *New York Times*, December 4, 2002, p. A20.

5. Feeley's own polling firm found that the new district leaned slightly Republican in terms of *likely* voters—those registered voters who cast ballots in the 1998 primary and general elections or who voted in the 2000 general and 1999 or 2001 off-year general elections. Chris Keating, research director, Harstad Strategic Research, interview by Daniel Smith, Denver, Colo., November 13, 2002.

6. Colorado's population rose from 3.3 million in 1990 to 4.3 million in 2000. U.S. Bureau of the Census, "Ranking Tables for States," 2000 (www.census.gov [September 2, 2002]).

7. Burt Hubbard, "New 7th District Is Middle-Class," *Rocky Mountain News*, January 26, 2002, p. B3.

8. Julia Martinez, "Feeley, Beauprez for the 7th," *Denver Post*, August 14, 2002, p. A1.

9. Feeley accused Beauprez of conducting push polls in the general election, though it was likely phone calls paid for by the NRCC. Peggy Lowe, "GOP Hopeful Blasted; 'Push Poll' Claimed," *Rocky Mountain News*, September 25, 2002, p. A28.

10. Ellen Golombek, president of the Colorado AFL-CIO, spoke passionately for Feeley in February at the Jefferson County Democratic Party's Jackson Dinner. According to the Colorado AFL-CIO's political director, it "was not a question" that labor would support Feeley. Tyler Chafee, political director, Colorado AFL-CIO, interview by Daniel Smith, Denver, Colo., November 7, 2002.

11. Bob Ewegen, "Where Politics Is Clean and Fun," *Denver Post*, September 7, 2002, p. B23.

12. Martinez, "Feeley, Beauprez for the 7th." Primary television ad totals are derived from the candidates' ad buy sheets on file with metro Denver TV stations.

13. Erik Greathouse, campaign manager, Feeley campaign, interview by Daniel Smith, Lakewood, Colo., September 9, 2002; Sean Murphy, campaign manager, Beauprez campaign, interview by Daniel Smith, Aurora, Colo., October 12, 2002. Both candidates remained cordial throughout the campaign. M. E. Sprengelmeyer, "Capitol Hill's Odd Couple May Deserve an Oscar," *Rocky Mountain News*, November 13, 2002, p. A4.

14. Sean Murphy, telephone interview by Daniel Smith, December 5, 2002. Ironically fellow Republicans had criticized Beauprez harshly on the character issue during the primary. Bill Scanlon, "Funding Feud in District 7," *Rocky Mountain News*, August 5, 2002, p. A14.

15. The NRCC was "upset with Bob's tight fight" in the primary and chided Murphy, asking why he was "spending so much money" and telling him he needed to "manage [his] margin of victory." Murphy interview, October 12, 2002; Greathouse, telephone interview by Daniel Smith, December 5, 2002.

16. Greathouse interview, September 9, 2002.

17. Matt Mosley, communications director, Feeley campaign, telephone interview by Daniel Smith, November 13, 2002.

18. In 1996 Murphy ran Representative Bob Schaffer's successful campaign in Colorado's Fourth District; two years later, he managed Bob Greenlee's unsuccessful bid to win Colorado's Second District. Murphy then served as executive director of the state Republican Party under Beauprez.

19. Murphy interview, October 12, 2002.

20. Murphy interview, December 5, 2002. Some of the tickets for the Bush event sold for far less than the advertised $1,000. Lynn Bartels, "$1,000 Tickets

to GOP Fund-Raiser Sold at a Discount to Some Guests," *Rocky Mountain News*, September 28, 2002, p. A8.

21. Karen Hughes, Bush's former presidential advisor, also flew into Denver to hold a $100-a-ticket rally for Beauprez. Arthur Kane, "Bush Adviser Rallies for Beauprez," *Denver Post*, October 23, 2002, p. B2.

22. Ibid.

23. Ryan Morgan, "House Races Join Millionaire's Club," *Denver Post*, October 16, 2002, p. B2; Trent Seibert, "Stars to Come Out in Colorado," *Denver Post*, September 20, 2002, p. A14.

24. Beauprez spent $166,070 on 151 TV spots, and Feeley spent $69,325 on 68 spots in the final week. Burt Hubbard and Katie Kerwin, "Onslaught of Political Ads Will Hit Airwaves," *Rocky Mountain News*, October 25, 2002, p. A8.

25. Murphy interview, December 5, 2002.

26. Feeley also paid the Strategy Group $36,519 to do nine direct mailings in the primary. Steven Stenberg, partner, Strategy Group, telephone interview by Daniel Smith, December 12, 2002.

27. Alan Philp, executive director, Colorado Republican Party, interview by Daniel Smith, Denver, Colo., September 24, 2002.

28. Dan Hazelwood, president, Targeted Creative Consulting, telephone interview by Daniel Smith, December 3, 2002.

29. Mike South, production manager, Arena Communications, telephone interview by Daniel Smith, December 3, 2002.

30. The NRCC and state party each put $38,000 into the coordinated campaign; the state party then transferred the money to the NRCC. Most of the money, around $58,000, was spent on a television ad; the remainder was put into a scathing direct mail piece that dovetailed with the NRCC's soft money TV ad. Hazelwood interview, December 3, 2002.

31. In the words of the Colorado Democratic Party's executive director, the state party's accounting is "legal fiction," with the party creating separate financial accounts every election cycle to facilitate independent and collective decisionmaking by candidates and state and national party officials. Mike Melanson, executive director, Colorado Democratic Party, interview by Daniel Smith, Denver, Colo., October 8, 2002.

32. Kyle Osterhout, vice president, Media Strategies and Research, telephone interview by Daniel Smith, December 10, 2002.

33. According to Feeley's campaign manager, the NRCC already had sent three or four direct mail pieces by October 7 to the DCCC's one piece. Greathouse interview, December 5, 2002. The DCCC contracted with Mammen-Pritchard but was paid by the state party. Amy Pritchard, partner, Mammen-Pritchard, telephone interview by Daniel Smith, October 17, 2002.

34. Mark Armour, president, Armour Media, telephone interview by Daniel Smith, December 10, 2002.

35. Stenberg interview, December 12, 2002.

36. In early September, Minahan stated that "every day I get on my knees and pray" that unions and pro-choice organizations will run issue ads on behalf of Feeley. Beth Minahan, chair of Feeley campaign, interview by Daniel Smith, Lakewood, Colo., September 9, 2002.

37. Republican opponents in the primary asked Beauprez to cancel his bank's ads, but Beauprez's campaign manager claimed that the ads were taped and scheduled well before he entered the race. Bill Scanlon, "Campaign Ads Stir Cries of Foul," *Rocky Mountain News*, July 11, 2002, p. A21. The Heritage Bank ads never surfaced as a salient issue during the general election; however, the Feeley campaign did file an unsuccessful complaint with the FEC. Greathouse interview, December 5, 2002.

38. National Right to Life spent approximately $20,000 on its AM radio spot that supported Beauprez and Senator Wayne Allard.

39. By mid-October, Jefferson County had mailed 85,000 absentee ballots to voters (44,054 to Republicans, 26,910 to Democrats, and 13,815 to unaffiliateds), accounting for 39 percent of active GOP voters, 30 percent of active Democrats, and 20 percent of unaffiliateds. Lynn Bartels, "Early to Ballot Box," *Rocky Mountain News*, October 17, 2002, p. A28.

40. The candidates and parties checked daily with the county clerks to see who had voted and get a sense of whether Republicans, Democrats, or unaffiliateds were casting ballots. "The universe of actual likely voters shrinks every day from now through Election Day," Philp said in mid-October, as "candidates [and] both parties will try to avoid contacting Coloradans who have already voted." Bartels, "Early to Ballot Box." Purging those who voted early from direct-mail lists, however, was not always smooth, because the county clerks were sometimes slow to provide updated voting records so the consultants could do "match-backs." Stenberg interview, December 12, 2002.

41. Berny Morson, "Early Votes Coming in 'Briskly,'" *Rocky Mountain News*, October 30, 2002, p. A19.

42. David B. Magleby and J. Quin Monson, "Campaign 2002: 'The Perfect Storm'" (Center for the Study of Elections and Democracy, Brigham Young University, November 13, 2002) (www.csed.byu.edu [July 23, 2002]). A poll conducted for Feeley by Harstad Strategic Research in August found that 62 percent of likely voters would vote early; of those early voters, 56 percent said they would mail in an absentee ballot, with another 6 percent saying they would vote at an early voting center. Minahan interview, September 9, 2002.

43. Magleby and Monson, "Campaign 2002: 'The Perfect Storm.'" An independent poll by Talmey-Drake Research and Strategy found that early voters

were more likely to be Republicans (45 percent) than Democrats (32 percent) and that the average age of early voters was nearly ten years greater than Election Day voters (55 to 46 years old). John Sanko, "Many Loyal Voters Won't Line Up Today," *Rocky Mountain News*, November 5, 2002, p. A4.

44. Peggy Lowe and Lynn Bartels, "Beauprez Grows Used to Close Calls," *Rocky Mountain News*, November 23, 2002, p. A4.

45. Arena Communications, which produced the independent expenditure ads, allegedly never spoke with the Beauprez camp during the campaign and was "totally isolated" from the NRCC's field representatives. South interview, December 3, 2002.

46. Murphy interview, December 5, 2002.

47. Hazelwood interview, December 3, 2002.

48. Lowe and Bartels, "Beauprez Grows Used to Close Calls."

49. Arthur Kane, "It's Down, Dirty in 7th District," *Denver Post*, October 30, 2002, p. A17.

50. Hazelwood interview, December 3, 2002.

51. The abortion piece and another on Social Security were mailed to the twenty-eight-year-old wife of Beauprez's campaign manager, even though she is an active Republican. Murphy interview, October 12, 2002. Hazelwood also heard of the DCCC's outreach to staunch Republican voters, prompting him to comment that their direct mail was "either very sophisticated or they used very sloppy, outdated registrations." Hazelwood interview, December 3, 2002.

52. Steve Truebner, organization director, Owens 2002, interview by Daniel Smith, Golden, Colo., November 7, 2002.

53. Chafee interview, November 7, 2002.

54. Michele Ames, "Wanted: Hispanic Vote," *Rocky Mountain News*, August 27, 2002, p. A14; Michael Riley, "Program Aims to Coax Hispanics to Voting Booths," *Denver Post*, October 30, 2002, p. A16.

55. Melanson interview, October 8, 2002. The DNC conducted a poll and focus groups in August that found running issue ads on Spanish-language TV was not effective. As Feeley's primary election campaign manger put it, Latino voters "don't watch Spanish TV." Minahan interview, September 9, 2002.

56. The committee in support of Amendment 30, the Election Day registration initiative, was the only ballot-issue committee to participate in the Democrats' coordinated campaign. Congressional candidates Diana DeGette and Stan Matsunaka also participated in the coordinated campaign. The DCCC sponsored Feeley's $25,000 "buy-in." An individual close to the Feeley campaign also gave the state party $50,000 earmarked for Feeley, with the donor informally telling the party that "Feeley's a good guy." Greathouse interview, December 5, 2002.

57. Peggy Lowe, "Heston's Visit May Sway Tight Races," *Rocky Mountain News*, October 24, 2002, p. A36. Despite Beauprez's strong pro-gun stance, his

staff did little to publicize the rally because many residents in the district found the NRA too extreme. Beauprez was not featured at the rally, and he arrived just as it was ending. Murphy interview, December 5, 2002.

58. Feeley served in the Marine Corps; Beauprez never served in the military because of a medical exemption (bleeding ulcer). Though both candidates supported Bush's war on terror and action in Iraq, Feeley stressed that the House needed another Marine and even crashed a Beauprez function featuring veterans. Peggy Lowe, "Rhetoric Heats up in 7th Race," *Rocky Mountain News*, October 14, 2002, p. A14. Feeley also vowed to unveil "every chicken-hawk Republican running for office." Peggy Lowe, "Bush's Iraq Remarks Leave Feeley Furious," *Rocky Mountain News*, September 26, 2002, p. A6.

59. Chandler, who raised virtually no money for his campaign, was reprimanded by the national Sierra Club after he publicly voiced his displeasure for being overlooked. Following the rebuke, Chandler asked rhetorically, "Is the club even more aligned with the Democrats than I suspected?" Peggy Lowe, "Sierra Club Gives Officer Ultimatum," *Rocky Mountain News*, October 12, 2002, p. A23.

60. The involvement by credit unions was clearly an attempt to mitigate the Heritage Bank radio ads, as well as Beauprez's role as past chairman of the Independent Bankers of Colorado. Arthur Kane, "Beauprez Accused of Coercion," *Denver Post*, October 22, 2002, p. A12.

61. George Merritt, "Pro-Choice Democrats Rally on Capitol Steps," *Denver Post*, October 8, 2002, p. A10.

62. Chris Frates, "Negative Ads Irritate Some," *Denver Post*, October 31, 2002, p. A20; Ryan Morgan, "Turnout Was High in Pockets of State," *Denver Post*, November 8, 2002, p. B1; Susan Greene, "Low Turnout of Minorities, Poor Splits Dems on Tactics," *Denver Post*, November 10, 2002, p. A1.

63. Magleby and Monson, "Campaign 2002: 'The Perfect Storm.'"

64. All the ads were aired on two Spanish-language stations in Denver, though a few were broadcast in English. KCEC-TV/KTFD-TV, Denver, facsimile transmittals from Access Advertising to Paul Chavez, September 19, 2002, in the station's FEC public file.

65. Peggy Lowe, "GOP Airs First Ads in Crucial Contest," *Rocky Mountain News*, September 18, 2002, p. A14.

66. Trail Dust, "Beauprez Campaign Lambastes Feeley Ethics," *Denver Post*, October 23, 2002, p. A19.

67. Keating interview, November 13, 2002. According to the CSED poll, abortion was the major issue for 12 percent of likely voters by Election Day. A poll by Ciruli and Associates revealed that 15 percent of voters said they supported Feeley for his pro-choice stance, but 13 percent of voters supported Beauprez for his pro-life stance. Arthur Kane, "Near Tie in Race for 7th District," *Denver Post*, October 18, 2002, p. B1.

68. Armour interview, December 10, 2002.

69. John Sanko, "Gun Ad Hits Beauprez," *Rocky Mountain News*, October 29, 2002, p. A22.

70. Greathouse intreview, December 5, 2002.

71. Mosley interview, November 13, 2002.

72. Paola Farer and Susan Wells, "Beauprez Officially Declared Winner of 7th Congressional District," *9News* (www.9news.com/storyfull.asp?id=9222, [December 11, 2002]).

73. Murphy interview, December 5, 2002.

NINE   *Incumbent vs.*
Incumbent in
Connecticut's Fifth District

SANDRA M. ANGLUND
SARAH M. MOREHOUSE

TWO INCUMBENTS FOUGHT for their political lives
in the 2002 House race in Connecticut's newly redrawn Fifth District,
spending more than any other congressional race in state history. The
state had lost one seat in the House because of slow population growth,
and after intense negotiations, the bipartisan Reapportionment Committee merged the Fifth District, held by Democrat James Maloney, and the
Sixth District, held by Republican Nancy Johnson. Both sides generally
agreed that the process that created the new Fifth District resulted in a
"fair fight."[1] The Johnson campaign knew that the redrawing of District
Five "had to be," and neither campaign challenged the results.[2]

The Johnson-Maloney race was unique in two ways; it also illustrates
several of the themes of this book. The race was unique because it was
one of only four incumbent-versus-incumbent races in the nation and
presented a quandary for some interest groups as they faced two moderate House members who had been helpful in the past. It was also unique
because the battle had to be fought according to Connecticut rules,
which forbid soft money, including national party transfers of soft
money to the state parties. However, the race also shared several characteristics with other battleground contests:

—The tone of the campaign was negative. The air war was noted for
attack advertising by both candidates, their congressional campaign
committees, and the AFL-CIO.

—National parties spent soft money on issue ads, and interest groups
engaged in election issue advocacy. These ads could not be coordinated

with the candidates, and some of them backfired. Among the advertisers were at least one front group and an anonymous organization that paid for phone calls.

—Both parties and several allied groups waged expanded ground-war campaigns. The Republicans invested a much higher level of resources in the ground war than they had before.

The Race: District, Candidates, and Results

Maloney and Johnson each brought about half of their current constituents with them into the new district, which reaches from central Connecticut to the New York border. Registration as of October 22, 2002, was 26 percent Republican, 30 percent Democrat, and 43 percent unaffiliated.[3] The new district is one of contrasts. It includes the well-to-do suburbs of Hartford and affluent towns in the rolling hills of western Connecticut as well as three of Connecticut's poorest cities—Meriden, New Britain, and Waterbury.[4] The district's minority population, consisting of about 20 percent, is concentrated in the small cities.[5]

Johnson is from New Britain, and although Democrats have a four-to-one registration advantage, the city has often gone for Johnson as their "hometown girl." Danbury is Maloney's home, and Democrats there have a sixteen-point edge in party registration.[6] As the campaign for the Fifth District began, the Johnson team reminded observers that Republicans are generally more likely to vote than Democrats. Maloney forces believed they could make inroads into Johnson's base in New Britain, while Johnson's campaign staff argued that they could cut into Maloney's base in Waterbury and appeal to the Republican-leaning voters in three Fairfield County towns in the south.

The Candidates: Moderates Attacked Each Other

Johnson, in her tenth term, and Maloney, in his third, had both survived tough fights in the past.[7] Johnson came within 1,587 votes of losing her seat in the 1996 anti-Gingrich backlash but had won comfortably since.[8] Maloney won his seat in 1996 by beating three-term Republican Gary Franks, 53 to 46 percent. In 1998 he squeaked by Republican State Senator Mark Nielson, but he won handily when Nielson mounted another challenge in 2000.[9]

The importance of candidate experience with difficult races cannot be overemphasized. In contrast to Johnson, George Gekas, the ten-term

Republican who lost the match between incumbents in Pennsylvania Seventeen, had enjoyed so many easy elections that he lacked campaign savvy. The candidates in Connecticut both had campaign savvy. They both employed professional campaign managers who had past experience working with the congressional campaign committees. They both had experience with negative campaigns and both went negative in this campaign.

In their six shared years in the House of Representatives, Maloney and Johnson were never far apart in their views. Johnson, the fourth most senior Republican on the powerful Ways and Means Committee and chair of a subcommittee on health, was praised by groups such as Planned Parenthood and the League of Conservation Voters (LCV). Maloney, a member of the Armed Services Committee and the Financial Services Committee, supported repeal of the estate tax and the marriage penalty tax.

Because the two incumbents were not far apart on policy, they had to differentiate themselves on effectiveness in office. Issues ranged from number of bills enacted and volume of projects brought home to their old districts to committee assignments. In their frenzy to produce evidence of their own effectiveness and attack the claims of their opponent, personality also became an issue. Character attacks were not far from the surface. James Maloney, fifty-four, is a large, open, tough-talking graduate of Harvard College and Boston University Law School. Nancy Johnson, sixty-seven, is a small, energetic, personable graduate of Radcliffe College. Although she has been referred to as a "political pit bull in pearls"[10] and, by the White House director of political affairs, as "a political machine,"[11] photos portray her as a caring grandmother who wants to make children and seniors healthy and comfortable. This image served her well in this race.

The Results: A Strong Win for Johnson

In the final week of the campaign, a University of Connecticut poll showed that Nancy Johnson enjoyed a seventeen-point lead, 53 percent to Maloney's 36 percent among likely voters. Ten percent of likely voters remained undecided. The poll results had not changed since the poll three weeks before.[12] The results were closer than expected, but Johnson defeated Maloney by eleven points.

Johnson did better among her party's identifiers than Maloney did among his. She also drew more Democrats than Maloney drew Republicans. In the last wave of the survey sponsored by the Center for the Study of Elections and Democracy (CSED), 20.2 percent of Democrat identifiers and leaners reported voting for Johnson, while only 14.4 percent of Republicans chose Maloney. Pure independents split, with 50 percent for Johnson and 46.4 percent for Maloney.[13] Maloney won in Danbury, Waterbury, and Meriden, but the margins were not enough to overcome Johnson's domination of the suburban towns in the district. The "hometown girl" even held onto New Britain by 150 votes.[14] Turnout was 58.42 percent, which was two percentage points higher than average turnout within the state's five districts.[15]

Money: Johnson and Allies Outspent Maloney and Allies

On election night of the most expensive U.S. House race in Connecticut history, Representative James Maloney conceded to Representative Nancy Johnson, saying: "Mrs. Johnson had a fourteen-year head start in terms of tenure. She had a million dollars more in money. There were just too many resources on the other side." Meanwhile, Nancy Johnson, who spent more than any candidate elected to the House in 2002, condemned the influence of interest groups and the national parties that paid for many of the ads.[16]

Candidates: Johnson Raised $1.3 Million More

Johnson raised $3.4 million in the 2002 cycle. Of this, 50 percent came from political action committee contributions, with business PACs dominating the field (81 percent) (see table 9-1).[17] A sponsor of the Republican prescription drug bill, Johnson received more from the pharmaceutical and health products industries than any other member of Congress—$204,817.[18]

Maloney raised $1.3 million less than Johnson, in spite of fundraising help from Bill and Hillary Clinton, Al Gore, Richard Gephardt, and others (see table 9-1). Maloney started behind. His 2000 race was one of the most competitive in the country, and he entered the 2002 cycle with debt and only $8,158 cash on hand.[19] Johnson, who won easily in 2000, entered the 2002 cycle with $452,143 cash on hand.[20]

One factor that hurt Maloney's ability to raise funds in Washington was a pledge he made in 1998 to the U.S. Term Limits organization to serve no more than four terms.[21] Johnson's campaign made much of the pledge, to emphasize Maloney's inability to develop long-term influence

Table 9-1. *Candidate Receipts and Expenditures, 2001–02*
Dollars

Source	Maloney (D)	Johnson (R)
From PACs	1,153,808	1,677,167
From individuals	812,988	1,546,989
From party	10,951	35,513
From candidate	2,300	0
Other contributions	90,221	146,189
Total receipts	2,070,268	3,405,858
Total expenditures	2,075,621	3,752,161
Cash on hand 12/31/02	2,705	105,840

Source: FEC, "2001–02 U.S. House and U.S. Senate Candidate Info," December 31, 2002 (www.fecinfo.com/cgi-win/x_statedis.exe [June 8, 2003]).

in the House.[22] Johnson's seniority, her position in the House, and her record as a moderate were also strikes against Maloney. Even though Maloney neared the top of the list of labor PAC recipients,[23] labor contributions to his campaign were roughly the same as the 2000 level, and ideological and single-issue PAC receipts were also almost even.[24] Proceeds from most types of business PACs were down, as race-specific factors joined a general shift toward Republicans.[25]

Political Parties: Connecticut Soft Money Ban Hurt Democrats

Connecticut law prohibits state parties from raising soft money and from receiving soft money from national committees. Therefore the national committees could transfer only hard money to Connecticut parties. However, in 2002 the national parties could buy advertising within the state with soft money, and they did.

Table 9-2 shows our estimate for National Republican Congressional Committee (NRCC) television buys, based on data in public files. This is consistent with the $900,000 reported by the NRCC in an interview.[26] Two NRCC issue ads ran throughout October on the four major television stations. The NRCC, which reported spending $1.1 million for Johnson overall, was authorized by Connecticut Republicans to spend their quota on coordinated expenditures.

The Republican National Committee (RNC) transferred $920,500 in hard money to Connecticut Republicans and paid for three mail issue ads.[27] National Republicans emphasized get-out-the-vote (GOTV) programs, and the state party developed comprehensive grassroots plans. Chris Santasiero, the executive director of Connecticut Republicans,

Table 9-2. *The Air War: Television and Radio Advertising Expenditures, Connecticut Fifth District Race, 2002[a]*
Dollars

Type and organization	TV[b]	Radio	Total spent	CMAG TV
Democratic allies[c]				
Candidates				
Maloney for Congress	700,000[d]	. . .	700,000	353,390
Political parties				
Democratic Congressional Campaign Committee	1,163,008	0	1,163,008	1,388,413
Interest groups				
AFL-CIO	519,225	0	519,225	346,054
Republican allies[c]				
Candidates				
Nancy Johnson for Congress	1,600,000[e]	. . .	1,600,000	1,598,111
Political parties				
National Republican Congressional Committee	821,700[f]	0	821,700	500,449
Interest groups				
United Seniors Association	546,374[g]	0	546,374	492,890
60 Plus Association	0	109,830[h]	109,830	. . .
COMPASS	72,462	0	72,462	. . .
Business Roundtable	64,179	0	64,179	. . .
Republican Leadership Council	36,833	0	36,833	. . .
Council for Better Government	0	10,000	10,000	. . .
Republican Main Street Partnership	9,687	0	9,687	. . .
Latino Coalition	0	600	600	. . .
Nonpartisan				
Interest groups				
Connecticut AARP	0	4,610	4,610	. . .

Sources: David B. Magleby, J. Quin Monson, and the Center for the Study of Elections and Democracy, 2002 Soft Money and Issue Advocacy Database (Brigham Young University, 2002); Campaign Media Analysis Group data.

a. See appendix A for a more detailed explanation of data. The ad-buy data collected for this study may contain extraneous data due to the difficulty in determining the content of the ads. The parties or interest groups that purchased the ads possibly ran some ads promoting House or Senatorial candidates or ballot propositions not in the study's sample but still within that media market. Unless the researchers were able to determine the exact content of the ad buy from the limited information given by the station, the data may contain observations that do not pertain to the study's relevant House or Senate races.

For comparison purposes, the CMAG data are included in the table. Because of the volume of television and radio stations and varying degrees of compliance in providing ad buy information, data on spending by various groups might be incomplete. This table is not intended to represent comprehensive organization spending or activity within the sample races. A more complete picture can be obtained by examining this table with table 9-3.

In blank cells, ". . ." reflects the absence of collected data and does not imply that the organization was inactive in that medium.

b. Certain organizations that maintained neutrality were categorized according to which candidates their ads supported or attacked or whether the organization was openly anti- or pro-conservative or liberal.

continued on next page

Table 9-2. *The Air War: Television and Radio Advertising Expenditures, Connecticut Fifth District Race, 2002*[a] *(continued)*

c. Television stations covered include major network affiliates and cable systems serving the district. Television buys for WVIT-TV (NBC), which does not provide financial information on issue ad buys in its public files, were estimated on the basis of one-half the buy made by the same group at WFSB-TV (CBS). This rule of thumb was adopted based on input from both candidate campaign managers (David Boomer, Johnson campaign manager, interview by Sarah Morehouse, November 18, 2002, New Britain, Conn.; and Jason Linde, Maloney campaign manager, interview by Sandra Anglund, November 12, 2002, Waterbury, Conn.) and an expert on buying political advertising in Connecticut media (Ed Katz, principal, Cashman and Katz, telephone interview by Sandra Anglund, November 15, 2002).

d. Joe Musante, "Yankee Duel: How Congressional Incumbent Nancy Johnson Defeated Incumbent Jim Maloney in Connecticut 5," *Campaigns & Elections*, vol. 32, February 2003. The Johnson campaign estimated that Maloney (excluding allies) spent $577,000 on television (Johnson for Congress, "TV Spending Equal between Maloney-Johnson Camps," press release, November 2, 2002).

e. The Johnson campaign announced that Johnson (excluding allies) spent $1.3 million on television ads (Johnson for Congress, "TV Spending Equal between Maloney-Johnson Camps"). Others estimated Johnson television ad expenditures as higher—$1.6 million.

f. The NRCC reported spending $0.9 million on television in support of Johnson. Total spending was $1.1 million (Mike McElwain, political director, NRCC, interview by David Magleby and Jonathan Tanner, Washington, D.C., December 2, 2002).

g. During the fall campaign season United Seniors Association ran issue ads in support of both Johnson and the Republican House candidate in another district on the same television stations. While this was not apparent from materials in public files, the stations were rotating spots. It was thus assumed that just one-half the amount indicated on contracts was for Johnson ads.

h. 60 Plus Association radio expenditures are incomplete because WTIC-AM, which was used heavily, does not provide dollar amounts for issue ads in its public files. Ad buys at other stations totaled $109,830, and the group may also have made buys at a few stations in small towns that were not monitored. One source puts 60 Plus total radio expenditures at $159,229.

explained that Democrats had traditionally had a ground troop advantage, but in 2002 "we met them toe to toe."[28]

Connecticut Republicans also spent about $150,000 on six targeted mail pieces for Johnson. One mailer used a comparison repeated over and over in many media settings: Johnson had written twenty-three laws in the previous six years, while Maloney had written only one. The Republican direct mail illustrates how parties can provide a counterweight to interest groups focused on one or a few issues. Additional topics covered by the mailers included Social Security, prescription drugs, education, children's health, pensions, taxes, and job creation.[29]

On Maloney's side, the Democratic Congressional Campaign Committee (DCCC) spent an estimated $1.1 million on seven television advertisements. Even though Maloney fell behind in the polls, the DCCC stuck by him. In the words of its political director, they had made a commitment to Maloney, so they stayed the course.[30] Two ads attacked Johnson, and the rest promoted Maloney. In one ad, paid for jointly with the candidate's campaign as a coordinated expenditure, a father recounted how Maloney had fought for the release of his student son, Jack Tobin, from a Russian jail. The others were issue ads. Topics included military pay, taxes, trade, and health maintenance organizations.

The DCCC also paid for persuasion phone calls to seniors the day before the election and two rounds of GOTV phone calls to Democratic households on Election Day. The Maloney campaign manager said that the relationship was good, that the DCCC did not try to micromanage. He objected to DCCC lawyers, however, and said, "We could never attack her [Johnson] as hard as we wanted because of the DCCC lawyers."[31]

The DCCC's involvement in the phone GOTV program, a project often handled by state parties, points out the plight of Connecticut Democrats. The Democratic National Committee (DNC) transferred only $101,808 in hard money to the Connecticut Democratic Party.[32] Maureen Grieco, executive director of Connecticut Democrats, said this money helped the party with voter file costs and conventions.[33] The state's U.S. senators raised money for the party, and they and other officeholders donated excess campaign funds. Still, the absence of soft money severely limited what the state party could do for its candidates. The DCCC, while pitching in with television advertisements and phone calls, could not handle local organizing.

By the 2002 election, Connecticut Democrats were no longer the mighty party of John Bailey, who headed the state party from 1946 to 1975 and chaired the DNC under President Kennedy. The party had not held the governorship since 1990 and had experienced a series of leadership struggles. The chair in 2002, John Olsen, was also head of the Connecticut AFL-CIO, which provided ground-war support for Maloney, as it had in 1998 and 2000. According to national AFL-CIO political director Steve Rosenthal, "The AFL-CIO has never aspired to be the Democratic Party's ground organization."[34] However, the unions have certainly filled that role in Connecticut, and national party committees rely on union help in places where they are strong.[35]

In summary, the cash shortage of the Connecticut Democrats, in part due to the state's soft-money ban, meant that, outside of the DCCC phone calls, there was no broad GOTV campaign on Maloney's side. Labor unions targeted members, not the larger mass that is the party constituency.

Interest Groups: More Groups Campaigned for Johnson than Maloney

Table 9-3 lists the major interest groups campaigning for Johnson and Maloney. Of the sixteen groups allied with Johnson, five focused on senior citizens and senior issues. These included the United Seniors Association, funded in part by the pharmaceutical industry, which made the largest television buy, at $546,374. Also extremely active was the 60 Plus Association, which ran newspaper, mail (to 28,000 seniors), and radio campaigns.[36] The frequency of 60 Plus radio spots was so high it became the topic of radio talk show hosts and newspaper columnists.[37] Other participating interest groups included America 21, the Seniors Coalition, and the Coalition for the Modernization and Protection of America's Social Security System (COMPASS), which counted the Business Roundtable and the United Seniors Association among its members.[38] In addition, an unknown organization was behind anonymous phone calls, presenting what one respondent described as "a rant against Maloney" on the Social Security issue.[39]

Maloney did not have as many allies as Johnson, and with two exceptions their campaigns were bland and limited. The exceptions were the AFL-CIO and the Connecticut Education Association (CEA). The AFL-CIO paid $519,225 for two television issue ads attacking Johnson, and both labor groups conducted multifaceted member-oriented ground campaigns. However, labor failed to influence many of its own members in this election. Despite the AFL-CIO's support for Maloney, almost 40 percent of the CSED survey respondents from union households said they voted for Johnson.

Turning to the more limited interest group campaigns, the League of Conservation Voters' (LCV) direct mail consisted of a membership newsletter with a scorecard showing Johnson not far behind Maloney. This was a major disappointment for Maloney, as LCV ran a large independent expenditure campaign for him in 2000. The Save Our Environment Coalition mailer asked voters to keep the environment in mind when voting and mentioned no candidates.

Noticeably absent on the Maloney side were U.S. Term Limits, whose pledge Maloney had signed in 1998, the Sierra Club, and the National Education Association (NEA). The Sierra Club, like the LCV, had actively campaigned for Maloney in 1998 and 2000. But since Johnson's environmental credentials were solid, the Sierra Club endorsed both Johnson and Maloney and sat out this election. The NEA, which had actually endorsed Johnson in a few previous elections, endorsed Maloney and made the maximum PAC contribution, but this was nothing compared to the campaigns waged for Maloney in 1998 and 2000. In 2002 CEA mounted a major mail and phone campaign targeting mem-

Table 9-3. *Number of Unique Campaign Communications by Organizations, Connecticut Fifth District Race, 2002*[a]

Type and organization	Type of campaign communication					
	Surface mail pieces	Newspaper or magazine ads	Phone calls	Radio ads	TV ads	Total
Democratic allies[b]						
Candidates						
Maloney for Congress	31[c]	1	1[c]	1	5	39
Political parties						
Democratic Congressional Campaign Committee	...	...	3	...	7	10
Interest groups						
Connecticut AFL–CIO	3	...	3	...	...	6
Connecticut Education Association	4	...	1	...	...	5
Alliance for Retired Americans	1[d]	...	1[e]	...	...	2
AFL–CIO	...	...	...	...	2	2
Agencia Nacional de los Lideres Hispanos	...	1	...	...	...	1
Connecticut Citizen Action Group	1	...	...	...	...	1
League of Conservation Voters	1	...	...	...	...	1
National Committee to Preserve Social Security and Medicare	...	...	1	...	...	1
Save Our Environment Coalition	1	...	...	...	...	1
Republican allies[b]						
Candidates						
Nancy Johnson for Congress	7	1	...	11	11	30
Political parties						
Connecticut Republicans	6	...	3	...	...	9
Republican National Committee	3	...	...	...	...	3
National Republican Congressional Committee	...	...	...	...	2	2

Interest groups

60 Plus Association	2	1	...	1	...	4
America 21	2	...	1	...	...	3
Seniors Coalition	2	...	1	...	...	3
United Seniors Association	...	...	...	...	3	3
U.S. Chamber of Commerce	1	...	2	...	2	3
Council for Better Government	...	...	...	2	...	2
Latino Coalition	1	...	...	1	...	2
American Taxpayers Alliance	...	...	1	...	...	1
Business Roundtable	...	...	...	...	1	1
COMPASS	...	...	...	...	1	1
Kidney Cancer Association	1	1	...	...	...	1
NARAL Pro-Choice America	1[f]	...	...	...	...	1
National Association of Homebuilders	1	...	...	...	...	1
National Association of Manufacturers	...	...	...	...	...	1
Republican Leadership Council	...	...	...	...	1	1
Republican Main Street Partnership	...	...	...	...	1	1

Nonpartisan

Interest groups						
AARP	1	...	1[g]	...	...	2
Connecticut AARP	...	...	..[g]	1	...	1

Source: Magleby, Monson, and CSED, 2002 Soft Money and Issue Advocacy Database.

a. See appendix A for a more detailed explanation of data. This table is not intended to portray comprehensive organization activity within the sample races. A more complete picture can be obtained by examining this table together with table 9-2. Data represent the number of unique pieces or ads by the group and do not represent a count of total items sent or made.

In blank cells, "..." reflects the absence of collected data and does not imply that the organization was inactive in that medium.

b. Certain organizations that maintained neutrality were categorized according to which candidates their ads supported or attacked or whether the organization was anti- or pro-conservative or liberal.

c. Maloney volunteers made 47,000 phone calls. Based on issues identified, follow-up mail included candidate comparisons on one of 30 issues.

d. This is a proxy for a billboard.

e. Ed Coyle, executive director, Alliance for Retired Americans, telephone interview by David Magleby and Quin Monson, December 20, 2002.

f. Kate Michelman, president, and Monica Mills, political director, NARAL Pro-Choice America, telephone interview by David Magleby, Quin Monson, and Nicole Carlisle Squires, December 19, 2002.

g. Two respondents reported receiving pro-Maloney phone calls from AARP on November 2. One said they were asked to vote for Maloney because of his stand on Social Security; the other said the caller was refuting a claim that Maloney favored privatizing Social Security. Connecticut AARP received similar reports according to Ed Dale, associate director (personal communication, January 2, 2003). We do not know the source of these calls. Dale said the state group had not done any phoning, and he doubts the chapters would have broken the association's nonpartisanship rules. National AARP paid for recorded GOTV calls to those in the district who are part of its grassroots database.

bers, but the NEA did not even send a staff member to help.[40] Jack Polidori, NEA political affairs specialist, acknowledged its hesitancy to back Maloney, explaining that Johnson was "the sponsor of our biggest legislation—a school modernization bill—with Rangel."[41]

Absent on the Johnson side were Associated Builders and Contractors (ABC) and the National Federation of Independent Business (NFIB). Johnson, who was actually endorsed by a few unions, did not meet ABC's merit shop criteria.[42] While Johnson announced her NFIB endorsement with fanfare, the small-business group did not actively campaign on her behalf. According to Sharon Wolff, campaign services and PAC director, the race was on the NFIB's list for extra attention until September. When it looked like Johnson would win, they moved their resources to other districts.[43]

Issues: Economy Not Stressed

A noteworthy feature of the interest-group campaigns was the issues addressed. The United Seniors Association and 60 Plus dwelled on prescription drugs in their intense radio and television campaigns, but only 4 percent of the respondents in the third wave of the CSED panel study ranked it as the most important problem.[44] Either the ads muted the importance of the issue, or voters had different priorities than the groups. The Social Security issue was well muddied by the various participants. Each side accused the other of wanting to privatize Social Security, but "privatize" had many unstated meanings. Employment was the most important problem to 39 percent of the voters and should have worked to the advantage of the Democrats. Although the AFL-CIO touched on jobs in its July ad, Maloney's television ads never stressed the economy.

Effects of Money: Who Controls Whom?

After the campaign was over, neither Johnson nor Maloney considered outside money a good thing. David Boomer, Johnson's campaign manager, said he wished Johnson could have run her own campaign without other groups spending money for her. He felt that she should have been in control.[45] Jason Linde, Maloney's campaign manager, expressed particular concern about groups that threatened candidates with the promise to withhold support or campaign against them if they did not sign a pledge.[46]

Air War: Some Attack Ads Backfired

The air war was noted for attack advertising. It began in July when the AFL-CIO ran an ad attacking Nancy Johnson for supporting fast-track legislation. Johnson responded with an ad claiming that Maloney was running a negative campaign: He and his "special interest friends" were attacking "our respected congresswoman." The next ad, originally scheduled for the last week of August, was pulled by the AFL-CIO. According to Maloney's campaign manager, the Maloney forces saw the ad and objected to it, because it attacked Johnson for a vote on Medicare that Maloney himself had also made.[47] But did the Maloney team actually see the ad on television? Johnson's campaign manager suspected inappropriate coordination between the labor group and Maloney's campaign.[48]

In the last two weeks of September, the AFL-CIO ran another ad attacking Johnson for a vote they claimed helped Enron. The ad became major news and one station pulled it, but the AFL-CIO made minor changes and placed the ad back on the air.[49] Johnson responded by charging Maloney and his "special interest friends" with attacking again. On October 8 the Center for Survey Research and Analysis at the University of Connecticut announced survey results indicating that Maloney was viewed as a negative campaigner, even though the first Maloney campaign ads did not go on TV until the survey was completed.[50] People blamed Maloney for ads over which he had no control. However, Maloney could have disavowed the ads at a major press conference and did not.

Also joining in attack advertising were the NRCC, the DCCC, and the candidates. Maloney ran three attack ads out of five total ads, and Johnson ran five attack ads out of eleven total. Johnson's higher number of positive ads—thanks to her financial advantage—may have contributed to the public view that she was the more positive candidate.

The ads of Johnson's group allies also helped her avoid the negative campaigner label. Johnson's interest-group allies avoided negative ads. All but the Republican Leadership Council (RLC) ran positive ads, and the RLC made a relatively small buy.

In the words of the executive director of the state Democrats, the election results suggested that voters believed, "That big guy is against our grandmother!"[51] However, Johnson may not have been immune to attack and public dislike of attack ads. Although she was seen more favorably than Maloney, her favorability ratings declined as the campaign progressed.[52]

Ground War: Republicans Won with New Grassroots Campaign

Ground tactics, which allow tailoring messages for different subsets of the population, are particularly advantageous in the Fifth District because of its demographic heterogeneity and presence in multiple expensive media markets. Maloney and allies were major users of ground-war tactics in the prior two elections. In 2002 the Republican candidate and her allies successfully placed an emphasis on the ground war. As shown in table 9-3, national Republicans and interest group allies helped with direct mail and phone calls, but the real street fighting was handled by the state party and candidate.

The Connecticut Republican grassroots program was coordinated by a fifteen-member field staff and included campaign training, absentee ballot distribution and follow-up phone calls to all Republicans, minority outreach, volunteer phoning from regional headquarters, and a massive GOTV program. Called the "feet on the street" campaign by the party's GOTV director, it included door-to-door literature drops the weekend before the election as well as phone calls and other activities.[53] Voter histories were provided to volunteers so they could seek out the people most likely to vote.

Meanwhile the Johnson campaign targeted ground efforts at the nine towns in the south of the new Fifth District that had not been in Johnson's district before and that contained half the new district's population.[54] The campaign sent representatives to Republican town committees, held town meetings with the candidate, went door-to-door each weekend, and mailed three personalized letters to each new constituent.

Given the Maloney campaign's financial problems, its strategy emphasized the ground war. It hired twenty-three field staffers from Strategic Consulting Group of Chicago and assigned them to campaign headquarters in nine towns in the district. Field staff and volunteers made 47,000 phone calls and followed up with letters and one of thirty different issue pages, based on the interests of the person contacted.[55]

The source of inspiration for contemporary grassroots campaigns, the AFL-CIO was Maloney's chief ground ally. The Connecticut unit sent three mail pieces produced by the national office to over 40,000 members in the district. Volunteers phoned members each weekend in September and October. In addition, union affiliates were urged to make at least two additional contacts with their members. On Election Day, the AFL-CIO continued GOTV efforts with phone calls and visits, and they provided about 600 volunteers statewide.[56]

Conclusion

The political party campaigns in Connecticut's Fifth District race were shaped by the state's ban on soft money. Because Connecticut parties could not receive soft money, the national committees, rather than the state parties, were the source of party issue ads. The national Republicans transferred significant sums of hard money to the state party, but the national Democrats were not forthcoming, so the state Democrats could do little to support their candidates. Both national parties spent heavily on the race, but the two incumbents, particularly Nancy Johnson, were seasoned fund-raisers, so party involvement was not as great as it was in some other races.

Interest group campaigning was heaviest on the Johnson side. Johnson's status in the House as well as the incumbency and the moderate positions of both candidates help explain the imbalance in the group lineup. Faced with two moderate House members who had helped them in the past, some groups that had once been strong Maloney backers sat out the race.

The tone of the campaign was negative and noted for attack advertising by both candidates, their party congressional campaign committees, and some interest groups. The expectation is for parties and interest groups to attack the opposition so the candidate can stay above the fray. Instead in this race the candidates themselves, both of whom had previous experience with negative campaigns, were very much in the fray. They joined the parties and some groups in running attack ads. In an extremely important turn, however, most interest groups advertising on Johnson's behalf used positive messages. Meanwhile, the only Maloney interest-group ally to advertise on television, the AFL-CIO, attacked Johnson, and the ads backfired. Ultimately the voters saw Maloney as more negative than Johnson, even before his own campaign ran any advertising.

The party soft-money-funded issue ads and interest group issue ads aired in the race could not be coordinated with the candidate. The consequences of the lack of coordination are well illustrated by the AFL-CIO's Enron ad and the ad, cancelled on the first day of the schedule, attacking Johnson for a vote that Maloney had also made. The inability to coordinate may also have resulted in lost opportunity. The DCCC ran seven television ads, but none stressed unemployment, which should have worked to the advantage of the Democrat.

One of the sixteen groups allied with the Johnson campaign was the United Seniors Association, which was funded in part by pharmaceutical companies. United Seniors spent an estimated $546,374 on television ads, the largest interest group media buy in the race. But voters did not know who was behind the ads. As noted in chapter 3, 58 percent of voters had an unfavorable impression of drug companies, but only 5 percent had a negative impression of United Seniors.

The ground war was extremely important in this election. Candidates themselves waged major ground campaigns of their own, in part because sections of the district were new for each. State Republicans followed the national Republican lead to emphasize a new grassroots GOTV program targeting people most likely to vote Republican. The state Democrats, lacking funds for a ground engagement, left the field open for the AFL-CIO and other unions, but the labor campaigns focused only on members. Had the party been a viable participant, it doubtlessly would have undertaken a broader mobilization.

The state's soft-money ban and the cash shortage of the Connecticut Democrats clearly hurt Maloney, but it can also be argued that it hurt the general public and the democratic cause as well. Democracy benefits when voter information addresses the multiplicity of important issues and mobilization efforts are widespread. It is political parties and not interest groups that are most likely to undertake such efforts.

Notes

1. Maloney was the only member of the Connecticut congressional delegation to assign a campaign staffer to the redistricting process. The campaign also purchased the same software that the Reapportionment Committee was using and organized grassroots support for Maloney positions, including generating a few petitions. Jason Linde, manager, Maloney Campaign, interview by Sandra Anglund, Waterbury, Conn., November 12, 2002.

2. David Boomer, manager, Johnson Campaign, interview by Sarah Morehouse, New Britain, Conn., November 18, 2002.

3. Connecticut Secretary of the State, "Registration and Party Enrollment Statistics as of October 22, 2002," p. 11.

4. Mike Swift, "Poverty's Web Widens," *Hartford Courant,* May 22, 2002,

p. 1. Cities are defined as municipalities with 50,000 or more people. Cities with an 11 to 16 percent poverty rate were termed poor.

5. "Connecticut: New Congressional Districts for 2002," National Committee for an Effective Congress, 2002 (www.ncec.org [July 31, 2002]).

6. Connecticut Secretary of the State, "Registration and Party Enrollment Statistics," pp. 3, 6.

7. The race also included two third-party candidates. Walter Gengarelly, a retired advertising executive, ran on the Libertarian ticket. Joseph Zdonczyk, who also ran two years ago, represented the Concerned Citizens Party.

8. Diana Evans, "Johnson versus Koskoff: The 1998 Campaign for Connecticut's Sixth District," in James A. Thurber, ed., *The Battle for Congress: Consultants, Candidates and Voters* (Brookings, 2000), pp. 45–80.

9. Sandra Anglund and Clyde McKee, "The Connecticut Fifth Congressional District Race," in David B. Magleby, ed., *Outside Money: Soft Money and Issue Advocacy in the 1998 Congressional Elections* (Lanham, Md.: Rowman and Littlefield, 2000), pp. 153–69; and Sandra Anglund and Joanne M. Miller, "Interest Group and Party Election Activity: A Report on the 2000 Connecticut Fifth Congressional District Race," in David B. Magleby, ed., "Outside Money," *PS: Political Science and Politics* online e-symposium, June 2001 (www.apsanet.org/PS/june01/outsidemoney.cfm [July 25, 2003]).

10. Jennifer A. Peyton, "Johnson, Rowland Energize Supporters in Waterbury as GOP Hopeful Gather," *Waterbury Republican American*, November 3, 2002, p. 1B.

11. Kenneth B. Mehlman, deputy assistant to the president and director of political affairs, interview by David Magleby and Jonathan Tanner, Washington, D.C., November 15, 2002.

12. "Johnson Maintains Strong Lead over Maloney in Final UCONN Poll of 5th Congressional District," press release, Center for Survey Research and Analysis, University of Connecticut, November 1, 2002.

13. See appendix A for survey methodology details.

14. Connecticut Secretary of the State, "November 05, 2002 General Election Results, Representative in Congress, Congressional District 5," 2002 (www.sots. ct.us [November 30, 2002]).

15. The number of absentee ballots voted was 10,544. Both turnout and absentee ballot statistics from Connecticut Secretary of the State, "November 05, 2002 General Election Results."

16. Center for Responsive Politics, "Election Overview, 2002 Cycle, Who Spent the Most" (www.opensecrets.org [April 9, 2003]). Johnson spent $3.75 million. Four candidates for the House actually spent more than Johnson, but they did not win.

17. Federal Election Commission, "Campaign Finance Info: Johnson, Nancy L." (www.fecinfo.com/cgi-win/x_candpg.exe?DoFn=H2CT06014*2002 [January 10, 2003]).

18. Center for Responsive Politics, "Pharmaceuticals/Health Products: Top 20 Recipients, 2002 Election Cycle" (www.opensecrets.org [January 4, 2003]).

19. Center for Responsive Politics, "Representative Jim Maloney 2000 Election" (www.opensecrets.org [November 21, 2002]).

20. Center for Responsive Politics, "Representative Nancy L. Johnson 2000 Election" (www.opensecrets.org [November 21, 2002]).

21. Sandra Anglund and Clyde McKee, "The 1998 Connecticut Fifth Congressional District Race," in Magleby, *Outside Money*, p. 162.

22. Linde interview, November 12, 2002.

23 Center for Responsive Politics, "Labor: Top 20 Recipients, 2002 Election Cycle" (www.opensecrets.org [January 4, 2003]).

24. Center for Responsive Politics, "Top Sectors: 2000 Race, Connecticut District 5" and "Top Sectors: 2002 Race, Connecticut District 5."

25. Thomas B. Edsall, "Big Business's Funding Shift Boosts GOP," *Washington Post*, November 27, 2002, p. A01.

26. Mike McElwain, political director, NRCC, interview by David Magleby and Jonathan Tanner, Washington, D.C., December 2, 2002.

27. FEC, "Party Committees Raise More than $1 Billion in 2001–2002," press release, March 20, 2003 (http://fecweb1.fec.gov/press/20030320party/20030103party.html [April 29, 2003]).

28. Chris Santasiero, executive director, Connecticut Republicans, interview by Sandra Anglund, Hartford, Conn., November 14, 2002, and telephone interview, December 2, 2002.

29. Santasiero said the direct mailers were nonallocable expenditures or "exempt activities" for party building because volunteers were involved in the production.

30. Mike Matthews, political director, DCCC, interview by David Magleby and Nicole Carlisle Squires, Washington, D.C., November 12, 2002.

31. Linde interview, November 12, 2002.

32. FEC, "Party Committees Raise More than $1 Billion."

33. Maureen Grieco, executive director, Connecticut Democrats, interview by Sarah Morehouse, Hartford, Conn., November 14, 2002.

34. Steve Rosenthal, political director, AFL-CIO, press event, "The Last Hurrah? Soft Money and Issue Advocacy in the 2002 Congressional Elections," Center for the Study of Elections and Democracy, National Press Club, Washington, D.C., February 3, 2003.

35. According to Andrew Grossman, DSCC executive director, "And depending on where they're strong . . . there is an absolute reliance upon the AFL-CIO as an active player in the overall effort." Press event, "The Last Hurrah?"

36. Jim Martin, president, 60 Plus Association, interview by Quin Monson and Jonathan Tanner, Washington, D.C., December 11, 2002.

37. Michele Jacklin, "Who's Behind Those Annoying Radio Ads?" *Hartford Courant*, September 8, 2002, p. C3.

38. Meg Kinnard, "Coalition Calls for Social Security Reforms," *National Journal Ad Spotlight*, October 3, 2002 (www.nationaljournal.com [October 6, 2002]).

39. A reporter from the *Waterbury Republican American* received one of these calls and asked the caller whether she worked for the Johnson campaign. The telemarketer said she didn't know and was reading from a script and confirmed that she works for a private company in Tennessee. Cara Rubinsky, "Johnson, Maloney Swap More Gripes," *Waterbury Republican*, October 20, 2002, p. 1B.

40. Don Ciosek, political coordinator, Connecticut Education Association, telephone interview by Sandra Anglund, November 21, 2002.

41. Jack Polidori, political affairs specialist, NEA, interview by Sandra Anglund, Washington, D.C., February 3, 2003. Polidori noted that he had less money for campaigning than in prior years, and all of it was spent on Senate races. However, reflecting the moderation and education credentials of both candidates in the Connecticut Fifth District race, he said, "If I had been told to put money in House races, which I wasn't, I would not have known what to do."

42. Ned Monroe, Associated Builders and Contractors, interview by Quin Monson and Jonathan Tanner, Washington, D.C., December 9, 2002.

43. Sharon Wolff, NFIB campaign services and PAC director, telephone interview by Sandra Anglund, November 15, 2002.

44. See appendix A for survey methodology details.

45. Boomer interview, November 18, 2002.

46. Linde interview, November 12, 2002.

47. Ibid.

48. Boomer interview, November 18, 2002.

49. See chapter 3 for a discussion of station monitoring of political ads. The AFL-CIO Enron ad was a cookie-cutter ad, which met a different fate at the stations in other districts. In Mississippi's Third District, for example, the ad was pulled by five stations. See David A. Breaux, "The Mississippi 3rd Congressional District Race," in David B. Magleby and J. Quin Monson, eds., *The Last Hurrah? Soft Money and Issue Advocacy in 2002 Congressional Elections*, monograph version (Center for the Study of Elections and Democracy, Brigham Young University, 2003), p. 248.

50. "Johnson Increases Lead over Maloney to 15 Points in 5th Congressional District Race," press release, Center for Survey Research and Analysis, University of Connecticut, October 8, 2002.

51. Grieco interview, November 14, 2002.

52. David B. Magleby and J. Quin Monson, "Campaign 2002: 'The Perfect Storm'" (Center for the Study of Elections and Democracy, Brigham Young University, 2002) (http://csed.byu.edu [January 18, 2003]).

53. Nancy Matthews, GOTV director, Connecticut Republicans, telephone interview by Sarah Morehouse, December 3, 2002.

54. Aimee Malenfant, director of field operations, Johnson Campaign, interview by Sarah Morehouse, New Britain, Conn., November 20, 2002.

55. Linde interview, November 12, 2002.

56. Tom Carusello, education director, Committee on Political Education, AFL-CIO, interview by Sandra Anglund and Sarah Morehouse, Rocky Hill, Conn., November 20, 2002. Jason Linde estimated that the AFL-CIO provided 160 volunteers on Election Day (interview, November 12, 2002).

TEN   *When Incumbents Clash,*
            Fundamentals Matter:
            Pennsylvania Seventeen

STEPHEN K. MEDVIC

MATTHEW M. SCHOUSEN

IN 2002 PENNSYLVANIA'S Seventeenth Congres-
sional District was one of four races nationally in which two incumbents
faced off as the result of redistricting.[1] This race should have been relatively safe for the Republicans. Instead it was the most competitive of
the member-versus-member House races, at 51 percent to 49 percent,
and the only one in which a Democrat won. Spending by both parties
and at least half a dozen interest groups, in addition to candidate spending, made this race one of the three most expensive races in the country—in a district that does not contain a large media market![2]

Though the candidates and their allies spent an enormous amount of
money in this race, it was the parties, particularly Republicans, that
drove spending to such astronomical heights. Obviously both Democrats and Republicans were extremely interested in a competitive race
involving two incumbents. The intensity of the parties' interest, coupled
with what may have been the last election cycle in which unlimited soft
money could be spent in congressional campaigns, produced the
extraordinary level of activity from noncandidate groups in this district.

To a significant extent, party and interest group efforts created the
message environment in which the campaign took place. But unlike so
many other races in which the highest spenders carry the day, in Pennsylvania Seventeen the loser and his allies substantially outspent the winner.

The authors would like to thank Michael DeGrande for his assistance in collecting and entering data for this chapter.

The lesson from this case study, then, is that spending does not always determine the outcome of elections and, perhaps more important, that candidates—and what is said and done in their campaigns—still matter.

The District and the Candidates

Sixty percent of the new Pennsylvania Seventeenth consists of the old Seventeenth District, which was represented by ten-term incumbent Republican George Gekas. The rest comes from the old Sixth District, where five-term Democrat Tim Holden was the representative.[3] Though the Republican state legislature could have drawn Holden into a northeastern district with another Democratic incumbent, it chose to put him in a district where voter registration favored Republicans by over 50,000 and where President Bush received an estimated 57 percent of the vote in 2000.[4] An analysis of the race in March by Republican political consultant Keith Naughton found "Holden in a no-win situation."[5]

The district is located in eastern central Pennsylvania and includes the state capital of Harrisburg and the surrounding Dauphin County, Gekas's home turf, as well as Holden's base in Schuylkill County. Though Schuylkill tends to be Democratic, the district—like most of central Pennsylvania—is quite conservative, particularly with respect to social issues such as gun control and abortion. There are, however, working-class pockets in the district, and, as a result, economic populism also resonates with many voters in the Seventeenth District.

Given the district's makeup, it should be no surprise that Tim Holden is generally moderate though socially conservative. His ideological rating from the liberal Americans for Democratic Action (ADA) was 55 (out of 100) in 2000. A member of the centrist "Blue Dog" Democrats, he is anti-abortion and anti-gun-control. He also voted against the North American Free Trade Agreement and fast-track trade authority.

George Gekas had never faced a serious electoral challenge in his twenty years in Congress. Though on occasion Gekas shows an independent streak, he has been consistently conservative during his tenure in the U.S. House; in 2000 his ADA rating was 0.

Money

With total spending by candidates and allied groups surpassing $10 million, the race for the House seat in the Seventeenth Congressional District

Table 10-1. *Candidate Receipts and Expenditures, 2001–02*
Dollars

Source	Holden (D)	Gekas (R)
From PACs	784,522	770,245
From individuals	538,275	496,417
From party	160,749	66,276
From candidate	0	10,000
Other contributions	24,661	7,602
Total receipts	1,508,207	1,350,540
Total expenditures	1,714,892	1,427,486
Cash on hand 12/31/02	25,803	8,566

Source: Federal Election Commission, "2001-02 U.S. House and U.S. Senate Candidate Info," December 31, 2002 (www.fecinfo.com/cgi-win/x_statedis.exe [June 8, 2003]).

of Pennsylvania was one of the three most expensive in the 2002 election cycle (see table 10-1).[6] Taking advantage of the relatively inexpensive media market (Nielsen Media Research reports that the district includes the forty-seventh most expensive television market in the nation), the candidates, political parties, and interest groups saturated the airwaves, stuffed mailboxes with literature, and phoned thousands of potential voters (see table 10-2 and table 10-3).[7] At least one estimate suggests that Gekas and his allies spent in excess of $6.37 million, and that Holden and his allies spent more than $4.27 million during the campaign.[8]

In many ways, the Seventeenth District is a prime example of the role outside money plays in congressional elections. This member-versus-member race illuminates three of this book's principal themes. First, outside money dominated the race, with outside groups spending more money than the candidates themselves. Second, each of the national parties spent more money than its candidate did, and on the Republican side, the national party also contributed nonmonetary resources, including a full-time political strategist who had access to weekly polling data. Finally, the Seventeenth District also highlights the important contributions outside groups made, not only in the air but also on the ground. In addition to flooding the airwaves, outside groups led the direct mail and get-out-the-vote efforts. On the Republican side, the party led the effort to mobilize voters, a role played on the Democratic side by the AFL-CIO.

Candidate Spending

The Gekas and Holden campaigns had fund-raising operations that together netted nearly $3 million. Holden raised $1.5 million, with just

Table 10-2. *The Air War: Television Advertising Expenditures,*
Pennsylvania Seventeenth District Race, 2002[a]
Dollars

Type and organization	TV	CMAG TV
Democratic allies[b]		
Candidates		
Friends of Congressman Tim Holden	784,385	743,656
Political parties		
Pennsylvania Democratic Party	408,640	719,346
Interest groups		
AFL-CIO	180,280	228,680
League of Conservation Voters	57,510	148,626
Pennsylvania State Education Association	3,975	. . .
Republican allies[b]		
Candidates		
Gekas for Congress	697,820	571,044
Political parties		
Republican State Committee of Pennsylvania	734,820	758,732
Republican National Committee	92,200	. . .
National Republican Congressional Committee	82,475	303,438
Interest groups		
United Seniors Association	697,640	668,407

Source: David B. Magleby, J. Quin Monson, and the Center for the Study of Elections and Democracy, CSED 2002 Soft Money and Issue Advocacy Database (Brigham Young University, 2002); and Campaign Media Analysis Group data.

a. See appendix A for a more detailed explanation of data. The ad-buy data collected for this study may contain extraneous data due to the difficulty in determining the content of the ads. The parties or interest groups that purchased the ad buys possibly ran some ads promoting House or Senatorial candidates or ballot propositions not in the study's sample but still within that media market. Unless the researchers were able to determine the exact content of the ad buy from the limited information given by the station, the data may contain observations that do not pertain to the study's relevant House or Senate races.

For comparison purposes the CMAG data are included in the table. Because of the volume of television and radio stations and varying degrees of compliance in providing ad-buy information, data on spending by various groups might be incomplete. This table is not intended to represent comprehensive organization spending or activity within the sample races. A more complete picture can be obtained by examining this table with table 10-3.

In blank cells, ". . ." reflects absence of collected data and does not imply that the organization was inactive in that medium.

b. Certain organizations that maintained neutrality were categorized according to which candidates their ads supported or attacked or whether the organization was openly anti- or pro-conservative or liberal.

over half that money coming from political action committee contributions.[9] Labor PACs took the funding lead and were followed by ideological and single-issue PACs. Smaller but significant contributors also included PACs from agribusiness, law, and health care.[10] Of the individuals who contributed $200 or more, the Center for Responsive Politics reports that about three-quarters of the donors came from Pennsylvania and that most of those individuals were within Holden's former or current congressional district.[11]

Table 10-3. *Number of Unique Campaign Communications by Organizations, Pennsylvania Seventeenth District Race, 2002*[a]

	Type of campaign communication				
Type and organization	Surface mail pieces	Phone calls	Radio ads	TV ads	Total
Democratic allies[b]					
Candidates					
Friends of Congressman Tim Holden	4	. . .	. . .	5	9
Political parties					
Pennsylvania Democratic State Committee	5	. . .	. . .	1	6
Pennsylvania Democratic Party	. . .	. . .	. . .	2	2
Interest groups					
AFL-CIO	1	. . .	. . .	3	4
Alliance for Retired Americans	1[c]	1[c]	1[c]	. . .	3
Pennsylvania State Education Association	2	. . .	. . .	. . .	2
AFSCME	1	. . .	. . .	. . .	1
League of Conservation Voters	. . .	. . .	. . .	1[d]	1
Republican allies[b]					
Candidates					
Gekas for Congress	. . .	. . .	. . .	2	2
Political parties					
Republican Federal Committee of Pennsylvania–Victory 2002	12	. . .	. . .	. . .	12
National Republican Congressional Committee	9	. . .	. . .	. . .	9
Republican State Committee of Pennsylvania	3	. . .	. . .	1	4
Interest groups					
United Seniors Association	. . .	. . .	. . .	3	3
Republican Main Street Partnership	2	. . .	. . .	. . .	2
60 Plus Association	1	. . .	. . .	. . .	1
America 21	1	. . .	. . .	. . .	1
Business Roundtable	. . .	. . .	. . .	1	1
National Federation of Independent Business[e]	. . .	. . .	. . .	. . .	1
Seniors Coalition	1	. . .	. . .	. . .	1
U.S. Chamber of Commerce[f]	. . .	. . .	. . .	. . .	1

Source: Magleby, Monson, and CSED, 2002 Soft Money and Issue Advocacy Database.

a. See appendix A for a more detailed explanation of data. Data represent the number of unique pieces or ads by the group and do not represent a count of total items sent or made. This table is not intended to portray comprehensive organization activity within the sample races. A more complete picture can be obtained by examining this table together with table 10-2.

In blank cells, ". . ." represents uncollected data and does not imply that the organization was inactive in that medium.

b. Certain organizations that maintained neutrality were categorized according to which candidates their ads supported or attacked or whether the organization was anti- or pro-conservative or liberal.

c. Ed Coyle, executive director, Alliance for Retired Americans, telephone interview by David Magleby and Quin Monson, December 20, 2002.

d. Scott Stoermer, communications director, and Amy Kurtz, campaign director, LCV, interview by David Magleby and Jonathan Tanner, Washington, D.C., November 15, 2002

e. Unspecified race involvement. Sharon Wolff, campaign services and PAC director, Dennis Whitfield, senior vice president, Political and Media Communications, and Kristen Beaubien, NFIB, interview by David Magleby and Quin Monson, Washington, D.C., November 8, 2002

f. Unspecified race involvement. Bill Miller, political director, U.S. Chamber of Commerce, interview by David Magleby and Quin Monson, Washington, D.C., November 7, 2002.

Gekas raised $1.34 million for his 2002 race, with PAC contributions representing 58 percent of total revenue.[12] Ideological and single-issue PACs led the way, followed by PACs representing insurance, real estate, and financial interests.[13] A clear majority of individual donors (73 percent) came from Pennsylvania, most from within Gekas's congressional district.[14] But, while Holden raised more money than Gekas, candidate funding alone does not begin to tell the story of money's role in this campaign.

Political Parties

The national parties, primarily through the Democratic Congressional Campaign Committee (DCCC) and the National Republican Congressional Committee (NRCC), dominated the race, pouring more than $6 million into the Seventeenth District. In this case, party spending was not evenly divided between the candidates. The Republicans funneled $4 million through the state party, while the Democrats injected only $2 million into the race through the Pennsylvania Democratic Party.[15]

Clearly the two major political parties played very different roles in the campaign. Almost immediately the national Republican Party made the district a high priority. In addition to pumping millions of dollars into the race, the NRCC dispatched one of its election specialists to the district.[16] Jerry Morgan, district director for Congressman Don Sherwood in Pennsylvania's Tenth District, described himself as a "magic man"[17] and "work[ed] out of Gekas's headquarters and over[saw] all aspects of his campaign."[18] Morgan was paid by the NRCC, and his office space in the Gekas campaign headquarters was paid for by the Republican Federal Committee of Pennsylvania–Victory 2002, a federal PAC set up by the Republican Party of Pennsylvania.[19] Morgan moved into the district in early spring and stated that he was spending seven days a week, twenty-four hours a day, working on behalf of the Gekas campaign.[20]

Although Morgan claimed that he did not coordinate with the Gekas campaign, he did tell us that he had dinner every night with Gekas's campaign manager, Wendell Packard, and two full-time campaign workers. When asked whether they talked about the campaign over dinner, Morgan literally winked at us and said that they never mentioned the campaign because that would be coordination.[21] Bruce Andrews, Holden's campaign manager, was incensed by the close relationship between Morgan and the Gekas campaign. According to Andrews, the idea that Morgan was not working with the Gekas campaign defied logic, and he tried to get Brett Lieberman, a journalist covering the race for the *Patriot-News*, to report on the connection. Lieberman refused to write the story, however, telling us that even though it looked liked coordination, there was no tangible proof that they were sharing information. Nevertheless Lieberman states that Morgan never objected to being characterized as "overseeing all aspects of the Gekas campaign."[22] Morgan not only controlled the $2.4 million the NRCC spent on television ads, but he also ran the ground campaign, orchestrating the roughly twenty separate mailings that were sent to voters and organizing a GOTV drive targeted at specific areas in the district. In addition, Morgan received weekly polling data from the national party and on Election Day organized and paid for phone banks that made 75,000 calls on Gekas's behalf.[23]

But Morgan was not the only "magic man" the Republican Party sent to the district. During the election Vice President Dick Cheney, House Speaker Dennis Hastert, and former President George H.W. Bush visited the district and campaigned with Gekas. In addition President George W. Bush joined Gekas in Harrisburg during the last week of the campaign. Wendell Packard told us that on the Sunday night before the election, Karl Rove, the president's own political strategist, called to ask whether there was anything more the White House could do to help Gekas. Packard responded by saying no, the White House and the NRCC had done more than enough.[24] Clearly the Republican Party made the Seventeenth District a top priority early in the election cycle and continued to make the race a priority through the election.[25]

The Democratic Party did not provide as much support to Holden. According to Holden's campaign manager, Bruce Andrews, the DCCC did not make the race a priority. Andrews likened the set of congressional campaigns in 2002 to "playing fifteen simultaneous poker games. The Republicans came in and said, 'Here's money on fifteen games—call or fold.'"[26] When we interviewed Andrews in early October, he suggested that Democrats would essentially have to fold in a number of those games, including his. The Holden campaign, he said, was not expecting much help from the DCCC.[27] On the other hand, Michael Matthews, the DCCC's political director, described the Seventeenth District as one in which the DCCC was active from beginning to end.[28] In fact the DCCC did fund $2 million worth of television ads to help elect

Holden—spending more money than the Holden campaign was able to raise by itself. Whether Andrews was being disingenuous or the DCCC was not communicating with the campaign is unclear, but Andrews was adamant in stating that the campaign and the DCCC did not communicate, because they firmly believed that such coordination would be a violation of the law.[29]

Interest Groups

In terms of overall expenditures, interest groups spent over $1 million, which is well below the level of spending of both the parties and the candidates. Pro-Gekas groups pumped as much as $1 million into the race, while pro-Holden groups spent considerably less.[30] As in a number of races, including Connecticut Five (see chapter 9), the single dominant interest group was the United Seniors Association, which spent at least $1 million on television ads in support of Gekas.[31] The Business Roundtable spent more than $100,000, primarily on pro-Gekas radio ads, and while the National Federation of Independent Business (NFIB) participated actively, much of its work focused on mobilizing its members to get out the vote on Gekas's behalf. At least one other group was active on behalf of Gekas. The 60 Plus Association ran radio spots thanking Gekas for his support of Medicare, placed 60,000 phone calls, and bought newspaper ads.[32]

Holden was the beneficiary of $300,000 worth of television ads paid for by the AFL-CIO.[33] Nevertheless the Gekas campaign manager cited the AFL-CIO as the most effective group in this race because of their GOTV effort on Holden's behalf.[34] The AFL-CIO has more than 40,000 members in Pennsylvania's Seventeenth District, and the organization's national field representative estimated that each member was contacted between seven and eleven times. Members were contacted in a variety of ways, including letters in business envelopes from their local union president, phone banks, work site leafleting, and labor-to-labor walks.[35]

The League of Conservation Voters (LCV) also supported Holden, spending $250,000 on television ads.[36] Scott Stoermer and Amy Kurtz, communications director and campaign director, respectively, for LCV, said they targeted Pennsylvania Seventeen because Gekas is on their "dirty dozen" list.[37] Though the district did not show up on a list of targeted races for the National Education Association (NEA),[38] Steve Dunkle, assistant director of government relations for the Pennsylvania State Education Association (PSEA), told us that NEA "designed and originated" (that is, paid for) the three mailings that PSEA authorized for use in the Gekas-Holden race.[39] PSEA also made advocacy and GOTV phone calls to targeted PSEA members.[40] Although interest groups spent less money in this race than did the national parties or candidates, some of their efforts, particularly the GOTV efforts of Holden's allies, played a significant role in the outcome of the election.

Generally speaking, however, interest groups were not as active in this race as one may have anticipated, given the importance of the race to both parties. Part of the explanation for their relative absence could be that both contestants were incumbents. Interest groups might not have wanted to risk losing access to the eventual winner if they were to get involved on only one side of the race. A more likely reason, as in the cases of Connecticut Five and Utah Two (see chapters 9 and 11), is the ideological similarity between Gekas and Holden, at least on issues about which the most active interest groups care. For example, the National Rifle Association (NRA) promised to stay out of the race in Pennsylvania Seventeen and its magazine gave ratings of A+ and A to Gekas and Holden, respectively.[41]

Effects of Money

Republicans and their allies clearly spent more than Democrats in Pennsylvania's Seventeenth District. Though table 10-2 indicates only a slight edge for Gekas, our interviews and media accounts of the race indicate that the Gekas side outspent Holden and his allies by more than $2.4 million. Despite being outspent and the district's Republican leanings, Holden won the race with 51 percent of the vote to Gekas's 49 percent. At first glance, then, it might appear as though the Republican money was wasted. But Gekas campaign manager Wendell Packard insists, "If the party hadn't been as involved as it was, the race wouldn't have been as close as it was."[42] What explains Gekas's loss despite a number of crucial factors working in his favor? As a *Patriot-News* postmortem put it, the Gekas loss was the result of "a candidate rusty from years of easy re-election wins and out of touch with changing constituencies, a bitter division between Gekas and the team brought in to help him, and a strategy that careened futilely from one tack to another."[43]

Gekas's less-than-able performance as a campaigner meant that someone had to be brought in from the outside to control the campaign. That decision apparently did not sit well with the congressman, who was "used to being the commander-in-chief" and believed he had "the right way to do the campaign," according to NRCC operative Jerry Morgan.[44] But Morgan told the *Patriot-News*, "There are so many ways to do a campaign, and the strategy never meshed between the participants."[45]

The Republican Party, which spent more on television and sent more pieces of mail than any other actor in this race, clearly set the agenda for Gekas. Their message was simple: Tim Holden is too liberal for the Seventeenth District of Pennsylvania. Many of the direct mail pieces sent by the NRCC included the line, "Tim Holden is far more liberal than you think." The proof of that claim often rested on Holden's alleged record of raising taxes. In one piece, the cover of a bifold brochure said, "Tim Holden treats *everyone* the same." On the inside cover the piece continued, "High taxes for *everyone*." Another piece stated, "The world can be a dangerous place." It then informed the reader that "Tim Holden voted against funding to protect America." The obvious conclusion, once again, was that "Tim Holden is more liberal than you think."

The Holden-as-liberal argument meshed nicely with the Gekas campaign's goal of reminding voters in this Republican district that Gekas was the Republican candidate. What might have appeared to be a coordinated message was, on the contrary, simply "happenstance" according to Wendell Packard.[46] Nevertheless Packard admitted that the convergence of messages "worked out well" and added, "Intelligent people will come to the same conclusion" about how to run a race.[47]

Though the Republican Party displayed "message discipline" throughout the campaign, there were times when it appeared that the Gekas forces were working at cross-purposes. The campaign's "message convulsed between attacking Holden to trying to convince voters that Gekas had a strong record of legislative accomplishments to clinging to President Bush's popularity."[48] Yet the candidate himself made it difficult to convey any message whatsoever. To begin with, Congressman Gekas never had to work to secure an incumbency advantage during his twenty years in office. Thus he had begun to take reelection for granted. As just one example, he neglected to get involved with state legislators during redistricting and thus failed to secure a safe district.[49] In addition Gekas was a poor campaigner. He and his wife often campaigned alone and would fail to inform campaign aides of their whereabouts. At one point, Mrs. Gekas set up campaign offices in one county and installed a campaign coordinator in another without telling anyone in the party or the campaign. And Gekas failed to follow through with the 60 Plus

Association when the organization tried to present him with its Guardian Award.[50] Together, the Gekases' efforts were described as "random and ineffective."[51]

In the end, there were three entities campaigning for George Gekas (not including interest groups): the Republican Party, the Gekas campaign, and Representative and Mrs. Gekas themselves. This created an image of a disconnected campaign. As one state representative active in the campaign concluded, "We're all trying to reach the same goal, but we're on a different page."[52]

The Gekas campaign primed voters according to partisanship, while the Republican Party emphasized ideology. The problem with the latter strategy, which, as we stated earlier, dominated the campaign agenda, was that it was not credible to many voters who were aware of Holden's decidedly nonliberal record. And Holden reminded them of that record. In fact, he answered the "liberal" charge preemptively, by defining himself as a conservative early in the campaign. And, despite what he said about the DCCC's lack of involvement, Holden's campaign manager told us that the state Democrats helped to define Holden as a conservative as early as the end of August.[53] Holden and Democratic Party ads routinely referred to him as a "conservative," often flashing the word across the screen. Some Holden ads pictured him with a hunting rifle and noted that he wanted "to ban desecration of the American flag."

Ultimately, the Holden campaign hoped to "lock in Democrats" early in the race and then target independents and moderate Republicans.[54] After accomplishing the first goal, the campaign sent its first round of direct mail to Republicans in Berks and Schuylkill Counties, areas that were amenable to Holden's candidacy.[55] State Democrats, on the other hand, sent their first round of mail to Democrats and independents in the Gekas territories of Dauphin and Lebanon Counties. The party's second round of mail reinforced the Holden campaign's efforts in Berks and Schuylkill Counties.

In some ways, the most important element of this race was turnout. Both candidates had a base from which to work, though Holden's was considerably smaller than Gekas's. For Republicans, Victory 2002, the state party's federal PAC, ran all aspects of the GOTV effort, though the national party's 72 Hour Task Force did assist by bringing volunteers into the district to help mobilize voters.[56] Jerry Morgan figured that if Gekas got 97,700 votes, he would win the election; in the end, he got

97,540.[57] Since Republicans almost hit their mark in terms of turnout, why did Gekas lose? It was probably because Holden and his allies mobilized more of their voters than Morgan and the Republicans expected. The Holden campaign used forty volunteers a week for door-to-door efforts before Labor Day and eighty a week subsequently.[58] Coupled with the efforts of the Democratic Party and particularly the AFL-CIO, the Holden mobilization effort was extensive and ultimately helped Holden win.

Finally, the campaign stops on behalf of Gekas by national Republican figures influenced this race. In particular, the efforts of President Bush are noteworthy. Indeed, much analysis of the midterm elections in 2002 focused on the impact of the president on Republican candidacies in close contests.[59] President Bush included Pennsylvania's Seventeenth District as part of his campaign tour around the country, stumping for Gekas on the Friday before Election Day. As with Republican Party efforts generally, it might appear that the president's appearance in the district had little impact, given that Gekas lost. In fact President Bush tightened what would have otherwise been an easy win for Holden. Bruce Andrews claims that two weeks before the election, Holden held a ten-point lead in the polls, as he had throughout virtually the entire campaign. Eleven days out, Vice President Cheney visited the district, as did House Speaker Dennis Hastert the following day. Those visits, combined with news of the president's national travels, cut Holden's lead to three points just eight days out. After the president's visit, the race was a statistical dead heat, and Holden won by just two points.[60] Thus the party's efforts, and particularly those of President Bush, on behalf of Gekas probably made a close race out of a potentially noncompetitive contest.

In the end, the 2002 congressional race in Pennsylvania's Seventeenth District can be summed up as follows: The Republican Party controlled the campaign agenda with a message that was not believable and did not resonate with a sizable portion of the electorate. While Gekas's campaign manager may be partially right when he says the loss was due to "internal problems with our campaign," clearly the Republican Party might not have helped Gekas as much as it could have had it pursued a different communication strategy.[61] On the other hand, the Holden campaign was effective at deflecting the "liberal" charge and at mobilizing its base. As Bruce Andrews put it, Holden won because he "was a better candidate, had a better message, and was better organized."[62]

Conclusion

The congressional race in Pennsylvania's Seventeenth District stands out in the 2002 midterm election cycle for a number of reasons. First, it ranks as one of the most expensive races in the nation. Second, it is the only member-versus-member race in which the Democrat won, bucking the general trend toward Republican victories in 2002. Third, though Republican Party spending helped Gekas make the race competitive, in the end this race may be an exception to the rule that money determines the outcome of congressional elections. As an article in the *Patriot-News* put it, money "can't always buy you a seat in Congress."[63] Candidates still matter, as do campaigns that emphasize the fundamentals, such as voter mobilization. After all the money had been spent, old-style grass-roots politics prevailed in Pennsylvania Seventeen in 2002.

Notes

1. For another incumbent-versus-incumbent race, see chapter 9 of this volume.

2. Lara Jakes Jordan, "$10 Million Gekas-Holden Race Was One of Nation's Most Costly," Associated Press, December 5, 2002 (www.pennlive.com [December 5, 2002]).

3. A very small portion of the new district (part of Perry County) had previously been in the Ninth District. Charles E. Cook, "House Update Part 4," *Cook Political Report*, May 28, 2002 (www.cookpolitical.com/display.cfm?edit_id=34 [July 12, 2002]).

4. Keith Naughton, "Re-election of Congressman Gekas," memo to Pennsylvania Republican Opinion Leaders, March 5, 2002 (www.politicspa.com/FEATURES/031202gekasmemo.htm [August 20, 2002]). The estimated Bush vote for 2000 is taken from Cook, "House Update Part 4."

5. Naughton, "Re-election of Congressman Gekas."

6. Jordan, "$10 Million Gekas-Holden Race."

7. "Local Universe Estimates," Nielsen Media Research, September 21, 2002 (www.nielsenmedia.com [December 13, 2002]).

8. Lara Jakes Jordon, Associated Press, telephone interview by Stephen Medvic, December 10, 2002. We consider Jordan's estimates reliable because they are based on her reporting on the Seventeenth Congressional District race and on interviews she conducted with party and interest group actors close to the race. They were confirmed, more or less, by at least one other journalist in an interview. Brett Lieberman, *Patriot-News* reporter, telephone interview by Stephen Medvic, December 10, 2002. According to Jordan, on the Republican

side, the Gekas campaign spent $1.37 million, national Republicans $4 million, and United Seniors $1 million, for a total of $6.37 million. On the Democratic side, the Holden campaign spent $1.72 million, national Democrats $2 million, the AFL-CIO $300,000, and the LCV $250,000, for a total of $4.27 million. These figures are higher than the dollar amounts cited in table 10-2 because they come from a different source and take into account total spending (not just television buys).

9. "Total Raised and Spent, Pennsylvania District 17," Center for Responsive Politics, January 6, 2003 (www.opensecrets.org/races/summary.asp?ID=PA17& cycle=2002&special=N [January 7, 2003]).

10. "Business/Labor/Ideological Split in PAC Contributions, Pennsylvania District 17," Center for Responsive Politics, January 6, 2003 (www.opensecrets.org/races/blio.asp?ID=PA17&cycle=2002&special=N [January 7, 2003]).

11. "In-State vs. Out-of-State, Pennsylvania District 17," Center for Responsive Politics, January 6, 2003 (www.opensecrets.org/races/instate.asp?ID=PA17&cycle=2002&special=N [January 7, 2003]).

12. "Total Raised and Spent," Center for Responsive Politics.

13. "Business/Labor/Ideological Split," Center for Responsive Politics.

14. "Total Raised and Spent," Center for Responsive Politic.

15. Our estimates of total party spending are based on a newspaper report (Jordan, "$10 Million Gekas-Holden Race.") and a telephone interview with Jordan (December 10, 2002). The Republican numbers are, it should be noted, higher than the estimate provided by Mike McElwain for table 2-5. McElwain's estimate of $2.6 million in NRCC spending in the Seventeenth District is lower than the total NRCC transfers to the entire state of Pennsylvania ($3.4 million), as also shown in table 2.5. Jordan's estimate of $4 million in Republican spending is for "national Republicans," which presumably includes other party organizations, such as the Republican National Committee.

16. Similarly the DCCC provided a staffer to run the Mike Feeley campaign in Colorado Seven (see chapter 8 of this volume).

17. Jerry Morgan, election specialist, NRCC, interview by Stephen Medvic and Matthew Schousen, Harrisburg, Pa., October 2, 2002.

18. Brett Lieberman, "Election-Bureau Visits by GOP Draw Flak," *Patriot-News*, October 31, 2002 (www.pennlive.com [October 31, 2002]).

19. Wendell Packard, manager, Gekas Campaign, telephone interview by Stephen Medvic, December 13, 2002.

20. Morgan interview, October 2, 2002.

21. Ibid.

22. Lieberman interview, December 10, 2002.

23. Jerry Morgan, telephone interview by Matthew Schousen, November 7, 2002.

24. Packard interview, December 13, 2002.

25. One might wonder why the GOP stayed committed to this race, given that some polls showed Gekas down by nearly ten points for most of the campaign. We can only speculate, but at least three reasons seem plausible. First, of course, Gekas was an incumbent and parties place high priority on the survival of their incumbents. Second, the NRCC put Jerry Morgan in charge of overseeing the campaign. Morgan's prior success may have given them confidence that Gekas would prevail in the end. Finally, the Republicans were so flush with money that they could afford to fund this campaign, even without a sure win in sight.

26. Bruce Andrews, manager, Holden Campaign, interview by Stephen Medvic and Matthew Schousen, Harrisburg, Pa., October 2, 2002.

27. Ibid.

28. Mike Matthews, political director, DCCC, interview by David Magleby and Nicole Carlisle Squires, Washington, D.C., November 12, 2002.

29. Andrews interview, October 12, 2002.

30. Total spending by interest groups is greater than the amount listed in table 10-2 because it includes television ad buys, mailings, and money spent on GOTV efforts.

31. Morgan interview, October 2, 2002; Jordan, "$10 Million Gekas-Holden Race."

32. Amy Noone Frederick, executive vice president, 60 Plus Association, telephone interview by Matthew Schousen, January 8, 2003.

33. Jordan, "$10 Million Gekas-Holden Race."

34. Packard interview, December 13, 2002.

35. Paul Lemmon, national field representative, AFL-CIO, telephone interview by Stephen Medvic, January 7, 2003.

36. Jordan, "$10 Million Gekas-Holden Race."

37. Scott Stoermer, communications director, and Amy Kurtz, campaign director, League of Conservation Voters, interview by David Magleby and Jonathan Tanner, Washington, D.C., November 15, 2002.

38. Jack Polidori, NEA political affairs specialist, interview by David Magleby and Jonathan Tanner, Washington, D.C., November 15, 2002.

39. Steve Dunkle, assistant director of government relations, PSEA, telephone interview by Stephen Medvic, December 13, 2002.

40. Ibid.

41. Brett Lieberman, "NRA Gives Gekas an A+," *Patriot-News*, October 21, 2002 (www.pennlive.com [October 21, 2002]).

42. Packard interview, December 13, 2002.

43. Brett Lieberman, "What Went Wrong?" *Patriot-News*, November 7, 2002 (www.pennlive.com [November 7, 2002]).

44. Quoted in ibid.

45. Ibid.

46. Packard interview, December 13, 2002.

47. Ibid.

48. Lieberman, "What Went Wrong?"

49. Ibid.

50. Frederick interview, January 8, 2003. According to Frederick, most candidates jump at the opportunity to receive the Guardian Award because of the free media exposure. For example, in the Colorado Seventh race, 60 Plus gave the award to Republican Bob Beauprez, who accepted the honor (see chapter 8 of this volume).

51. Lieberman, "What Went Wrong?"

52. Ibid.

53. Bruce Andrews, telephone interview by Stephen Medvic, November 22, 2002.

54. Ibid.

55. Ibid.

56. Wendell Packard, telephone interview by Stephen Medvic, April 29, 2003.

57. Morgan interview, November 7, 2002.

58. Andrews interview, November 22, 2002.

59. See, for example, R.W. Apple Jr., "President's Risks Are Rewarded at Polls," *New York Times*, November 6 2002, p. A1; and Terry Neal, "Bush the Campaigner Delivers," *Washington Post*, November 6, 2002 (www. washingtonpost. com/ac3/ContentServer?pagename=article&articleid=A17844-2002Nov6&node=politics/elections/2002/archive [November 11, 2002]).

60. Andrews interview, November 22, 2002.

61. Packard interview, December 13, 2002.

62. Andrews interview, November 22, 2002.

63. Brett Lieberman and Peter L. DeCoursey, "Spending Doesn't Do Much for Gekas," *Patriot-News*, November 9, 2002 (www.pennlive.com [December 5, 2002]).

ELEVEN   *When Redistricting Means*
Never Having to Say You're
Sorry: Utah's Second District

KELLY D. PATTERSON

THE STORY OF THE 2002 RACE in Utah's Second
Congressional District reads like a mystery thriller, complete with plot
twists and a surprise ending. Going into the 2002 election cycle, most of
the national punditry, including the *Cook Political Report* and *Campaigns and Elections*, identified the Second District as a race to watch.[1]
With control of the House of Representatives up for grabs, it appeared
that the parties and interest groups would vigorously contest this race.[2]
Pundits were right about the competitiveness but wrong about the intensity. First-term incumbent Jim Matheson barely won reelection; however,
the race exhibited few characteristics normally associated with an ostensibly competitive race. First, the national parties seemed mostly unconcerned about the race. Second, only a small number of interest groups
participated in the campaign. Finally, those groups that did participate
dedicated unexpectedly small amounts of time and few resources. In this
race, Republicans and their allies missed a golden opportunity to pick up
another seat.

The story of the 2002 Second District race begins in 1980, when Utah
received a third congressional district. The legislature created an "urban"
district that included most of Salt Lake County. In contrast to the Second
District's distinctly urban composition, the other two districts incorporated massive rural tracts. The two rural districts leaned heavily Republican. However, the competition between Democrats and Republicans
became so fierce in the Second that it sent four different representatives
to Congress during the 1990s, and during that period the seat changed
party hands three times.

Matheson won the seat in 2000 by easily defeating Derek Smith, the Republican candidate who defeated incumbent Merrill Cook in the primary. However, in 2001 the Utah State Legislature redrew the district's boundaries. Republican leaders argued that all three districts should incorporate urban and rural elements so that each district would become "a healthy way to blend city and county interests."[3] This meant dividing Salt Lake County among the three congressional districts.

The new Second District moves eastward out of central Salt Lake City to encompass the rural northeastern counties. It then moves south and west to incorporate the rural and Republican enclaves of Kane, Iron, and Washington counties. The district grew in size from 250 square miles to over 50,000. There were Democratic enclaves in parts of Salt Lake, Emery, and Carbon counties, but the new boundaries took enough Republican voters from the other two districts to make the new district about 55 percent Republican.[4]

With a majority of Republican voters in the new district, most observers anticipated a hard-fought campaign for Matheson. He eventually won reelection by less than 1 percent of over 200,000 votes cast. Furthermore, he lost eleven of the sixteen counties and seemed to benefit from an initiative on the ballot that energized prospective voters concerned about the environment. However, despite the apparent competitiveness of the campaign, the two national parties and many interest groups decided mainly to watch from the sidelines. Their reasons for not getting more involved in the campaign reveal the extent to which the political parties and interest groups increasingly make decisions in a national context that may obscure critical local factors.

The Candidates and Their Campaign

The new Second District poses formidable problems for any Democratic candidate. Even in its previous incarnation, the Second District gave George W. Bush 57 percent of the vote.[5] Voters in the new district boundaries gave Bush 63 percent of the vote. Matheson understands these challenges and charts a moderate course in the House. He broke with his party to vote for some of the Bush tax cut plan and stresses fiscal conservatism. He belongs to the Blue Dogs, a moderate group of Democrats in the House that stresses bipartisanship. Matheson also assiduously avoids mentioning the Democratic Party in his campaigns. The Democratic label is nowhere to be found on his website or in his campaign literature.

Representative Matheson is the son of Scott Matheson, a popular two-term governor who served from 1976 to 1984. Governor Matheson was quite active in the Utah Democratic Party but enjoyed broad support in the state. He had a reputation as an independent and pragmatic governor who fought hard for Utah. Representative Matheson has not been afraid to tap into his father's lingering popularity and the family's southern Utah roots. In his 2000 campaign he ran ads that used the image of his father fading into the image of the candidate. In 2002 he recycled his campaign theme from 2000 and from his father's successful gubernatorial campaigns: "Matheson Makes Sense." Indeed, the prominence of the Matheson name in southern Utah may have led some groups and parties to overestimate support for Matheson and to discount the importance of party. However, in a sign of the problems with such a calculation, a barber from a small town in southern Utah purportedly said that he "really liked the boy [Matheson] but that he belonged to the wrong party."[6]

Matheson was not oblivious to the challenge. Throughout the campaign, he asserted his independence from interest groups and parties. He often made statements such as the following: "I look at the issue, and I can honestly say I don't vote for a party or special-interest group. I do what I think is the right thing."[7] Part of doing the right thing meant attempting to associate himself with President Bush, the most popular political figure in Utah.[8] Matheson carried a letter in his suit coat pocket from President Bush. The letter praised him for his "courage" to vote for the President's tax plan. Even the Democratic Congressional Campaign Committee (DCCC) used the letter and a photograph of President Bush when it produced and ran ads in the Second District for Matheson.

State Representative John Swallow took a different approach. The three-term state legislator from Sandy, Utah, a conservative suburb in southern Salt Lake County, touted his party affiliation whenever he could. His television ads and campaign literature included the party symbol and often used scenes of him walking outside the White House with President Bush. Swallow strove hard to persuade voters that the district needed more than an independent in Washington; it needed a person who would support President Bush. This was the core message of the campaign, and it found success with voters.[9] Swallow argued further that representatives vote to choose party leadership and committee chairs. Therefore, a vote for him meant a vote for Speaker Hastert and the rest of the Republican team. The first radio ad run by the Swallow campaign featured Representative Jim Hansen, the eleven-term Republican from the First District, talking about the importance of having more Republicans in the House and telling how Jim Matheson voted to replace him and all the other committee chairs and leaders in the House. One of only three television ads produced by the Swallow campaign was entitled "First Vote" and had the candidate making the same argument Hansen made in the radio spot.

Both candidates knew the critical role southern Utah would play in the final outcome. Matheson ran a television spot that showed him walking through a cemetery to illustrate the family roots, six generations deep, that the Mathesons have in southern Utah. Swallow reached out to southern Utahns in his ad "Public Lands," in which Swallow walks toward a horse while discussing how public lands are used and how to guarantee access to them. He then unties the horse, climbs on, and rides off. The ad directly addressed the sensitive issue of federal management of federal lands in Utah. Environmentalists normally side with the federal government and want strict control to ensure preservation and manage recreation. Most local residents have doubts about federal management of these lands and want more access to them for economic development. However, the issue did not stir many voters. Only 3 percent of voters in the Second District said that the environment was one of the issues that mattered most in helping them decide how to cast their vote in the congressional election.[10]

The candidates differed on several issues that mattered to Utah voters. Both candidates supported the Bush tax cuts. However, Matheson wanted to make only some of the tax cuts permanent. He also stressed fiscal conservatism in his arguments dealing with the tax cuts. Swallow favored the tax cuts and wanted to make all of them permanent. He tried hard to make voters understand that Matheson may have voted for the tax cuts in the final vote, but he did not support President Bush on many of the earlier votes. The two candidates also clashed over education. Again President Bush's legislative agenda became an issue. Matheson voted for the president's education bill. Swallow agreed with elements of the bill, but questioned the extent of federal control of local schools. Matheson convinced educators and received the endorsement of the National Education Association (NEA) and the Utah Education Association (UEA). Because of the differences between the two candidates, the NEA and UEA campaigned hard for Matheson and even sent out several mailings at the end. As illustrated by the KBYU–Utah Colleges exit poll, the candidates chose their issues wisely. When asked, "Which one or two issues mattered most in deciding how you would vote for your representative?" 29 percent of the voters in the Second District said education; another 21 percent cited taxes.[11]

The two candidates argued most over abortion. In 2002 Matheson cast a vote against outlawing the practice of partial-birth abortion. Swallow used that vote to try to paint Matheson as a liberal, pro-abortion candidate. Matheson explained his vote by saying that the law lacked a provision to allow the procedure in the event that a pregnancy jeopardized a mother's health. He also stated that the law against which he voted was inconsistent with federal law.[12] Swallow did his best to portray Matheson as out of touch with Utah values on this and other moral issues. Yet the effort appeared to be largely unsuccessful. Only 3 percent of the voters identified abortion as an issue that helped them decide how to cast their votes.[13]

The candidates also had to contend with a ballot initiative. Initiative 1 sought to increase taxes on low-level nuclear waste stored in Utah and prohibit higher levels of nuclear waste from being stored in the state. The issue gave both candidates a perfect opportunity to reach core constituencies. Matheson supported Initiative 1 and emphasized his opposition to the Yucca Mountain Project, which would mean more nuclear waste being shipped through the state. In a television ad he mentioned how his father died of throat cancer, possibly caused by downwind exposure to the nuclear testing that used to occur in Nevada. His opposition to nuclear waste of all types probably strengthened his standing among voters concerned about the environment. Swallow, on the other hand, opposed Initiative 1 and stressed that the initiative unfairly taxed a particular business. Overall 46 percent of the individuals who voted for Jim Matheson also voted for Initiative 1, while 76 percent of Swallow voters voted against it.[14] The message seemed to work for Matheson. Thirty-nine percent of voters in the Second Congressional District said that he would protect the environment, while only 20 percent said that Swallow would.[15]

Political Party Activity

With a newly drawn district in a conservative state, the Second Congressional District seemed poised for a highly competitive contest. And as various chapters in this volume argue, funds from parties and interest groups flow to those contests perceived to be competitive. Yet an influx of money from the Republican Party did not materialize until the end, and then it was too late for the Swallow campaign. Support from the Democratic Party for Matheson did not come in great amounts either. Why did party money not flow to a race in which the margin was so close? Three factors account for the lack of interest from the national parties. First, the National Republican Congressional Committee (NRCC) had a strategy to protect incumbents first, assist open-seat candidates second, and support challengers third. Swallow fell into the third category. Second, Swallow's campaign did not appear to be a good investment early in the campaign cycle. Conversely, Matheson's campaign seemed poised for victory. However, the Matheson campaign was just as wary of party activity as the Swallow campaign was eager for it. And finally, poll results at strategic points in the campaign cycle reinforced or undermined, depending on the candidate, the effects of the first two factors.

Political parties have one primary purpose: win as many seats as possible.[16] With limited resources to accomplish this goal, parties must prioritize to allocate their resources efficiently. Early in the election cycle, the NRCC decided to spend money to protect its lead in the House; this decision generally meant allocating resources to incumbents, particularly endangered incumbents like Representative Morella in Maryland's Eighth District, where the NRCC spent nearly twice as much as it did in the Swallow campaign.[17] Furthermore, open seats are much easier to win than incumbent-challenger races. If a party is going to protect and even expand its margin, it makes more sense to expend its resources in open-seat contests. Only under the best of conditions will parties invest heavily in incumbent-challenger races.[18] Yet the favorable redistricting scheme for Republicans in Utah's Second District should have made the NRCC rethink this strategy much earlier.

Political parties reconsider their general strategies and adapt to unique circumstances as the campaign develops and Election Day approaches.[19] Certain developments in the Swallow campaign probably made it difficult for the NRCC to alter its strategy for this particular campaign. First, the Swallow campaign emerged deeply in debt from a bruising primary battle. According to Swallow's campaign director, the NRCC wondered what had happened to the money. When it saw the debt-ridden campaign and a weak fund-raising organization, it decided it could better spend its money elsewhere.[20] The Swallow campaign, on the other hand, expected the party to push money in its direction to alleviate its financial woes. Yet the party regarded those same woes as reasons not to get more involved. A disagreement over control only compounded the situation. Apparently the NRCC did not like the media consultants hired by the Swallow campaign. However, the Swallow campaign refused to fire the consultants or use those favored by the NRCC.[21] What little party support arrived came in the form of mail. The Utah Republican Party sent out twelve unique pieces of mail for Swallow, and the Republican National Committee (RNC) sent out seven. The Swallow campaign sent out two pieces, while the NRCC did not send out any. However, the Utah state party probably received its money for the mailings from the NRCC.

While unwilling to make any significant financial investments, the Republican Party recognized the potential in the Second District and committed some resources by sending Vice President Cheney to Utah in August to hold a fund-raiser. The event brought in $250,000 but was not enough to alleviate the campaign's financial challenges, especially after expenses and donations to other candidates.[22] The campaign started with the Hansen radio ad and went on television shortly thereafter. Financial problems caused the campaign to cancel television ad buys during a one-week period toward the end of the campaign. Its financial woes may have also resulted in a series of financial dealings in which the Utah Republican Party traded soft funds for hard funds. For example, Utah sent $12,000 in soft money to North Dakota for $10,000 in hard money. The state party donated the hard money to the Swallow campaign. With the hard money, the Swallow campaign received the infusion it needed to conduct the last few weeks of the campaign more vigorously. The "shuffle" with the other states raised $140,000.[23] The transfers occurred at the instigation of the Swallow campaign because the national party generally avoids involvement.[24] The NRCC spent a total of $178,875 on television ads to aid the Swallow campaign (see table 11-1), but this seems like a paltry sum when compared to the amount spent in races to protect incumbents whose chances of winning likely did not exceed Swallow's chances.

The Matheson campaign took just the opposite approach. It was wary of the outside assistance provided by the political party because the campaign's overriding goal was to maintain tight control of the message.[25] When parties and interest groups get involved in campaigns, their activities can dilute the strength and influence of the candidate's

Table 11-1. *The Air War: Television and Radio Advertising Expenditures, Utah First and Second District Races, 2002*[a]
Dollars

Type and organization	TV	Radio	Total spent	CMAG TV
	Democratic allies[b]			
Candidates				
Matheson for Congress	353,471	12,259	365,730	1,211,094
Committee to Elect Dave[c]	227,922	21,280	249,202	402,990
Political parties				
Utah Democratic Party	305,815	13,860	319,675	282,617
Democratic Congressional				
Campaign Committee	18,250	. . .	18,250	. . .
	Republican allies[b]			
Candidates				
John Swallow for Congress	293,394	28,369	321,763	549,278
Robert Bishop for Congress[c]	144,462	20,185	164,647	213,438
Utah Republicans for Rob Bishop[c]	9,100	. . .	9,100	. . .
Political parties				
National Republican Congressional				
Committee	178,875	. . .	178,875	111,819
Utah Republican Party	15,900	. . .	15,900	8,403
Interest groups				
United Seniors Association	. . .	. . .	. . .	67,348

Source: David B. Magleby, J. Quin Monson, and the Center for the Study of Elections and Democracy, 2002 Soft Money and Issue Advocacy Database (Brigham Young University, 2002); and Campaign Media Analysis Group data.

a. See appendix A for a more detailed explanation of data. The ad-buy data collected for this study may contain extraneous data because of the difficulty in determining the content of the ads. The parties or interest groups that purchased the ads possibly ran some ads promoting House or Senatorial candidates or ballot propositions not in the study's sample but still within that media market. Unless researchers were able to determine the exact content of the ad buy from the limited information given by the station, the data may contain observations that do not pertain to the study's relevant House or Senate races.

For comparison purposes the CMAG data are included in the table. Because of the volume of television and radio stations and varying degrees of response in providing ad-buy information, data on spending by various groups might be incomplete. This table is not intended to represent comprehensive organization spending or activity within the sample races. A more complete picture can be obtained by examining this table with table 11-2. Because ad-buy content was often nondescriptive and sometimes difficult to distinguish between the different races, data in this table are combined for all races studied in Utah.

In blank cells, ". . ." reflects absence of collected data and does not imply that organization was inactive in that medium.

b. Certain organizations that maintained neutrality were categorized according to which candidates their ads supported or attacked or whether the organization was openly anti- or pro- conservative or liberal.

c. These were the only amounts documented for the Utah First Congressional District Race.

desired message. Voters may even attribute negative advertisements to the candidates when they actually come from outside sources not controlled by the candidate.[26] In fact, in a debate Matheson said, "This nameless, faceless, unidentified, unregulated amount of money can come in and dilute or even pollute the dialogue between candidates and voters. We have been rather fortunate not to see so much soft money this year as we did two years ago."[27] Therefore, the Matheson campaign initially did not want help from the DCCC. The DCCC field staff worked hard to build enough trust with the Matheson campaign that it would feel comfortable with what little the party decided to do.[28]

The DCCC spent a little over $18,000 on television ads and transferred a little over $300,000 to the state Democratic Party, which spent the money on mailers and other communication efforts (see table 11-1). However, as table 11-2 shows, most of the activity in the campaign came from Matheson's organization. Part of the reason for the lack of Democratic activity can be attributed to the weakened condition of the Utah Democratic Party. In the opinion of the Matheson campaign, the party organization had very little infrastructure for voter identification and turnout.[29] Only three unique mail pieces came from the Utah State Democratic Party, while the Matheson campaign sent out ten unique pieces on its own. The discrepancy between what the party does and what the candidate does only reinforces the responsibility of a Democratic candidate in Utah to staff and manage all campaign functions. For example, the Democratic candidates in the other two districts received even less support from the state and national Democratic Parties. Those two races were not nearly as competitive and struggled to attract interest from outside sources.[30] Finally, because Matheson was perceived as the front-runner from the beginning, the DCCC did not need to commit any resources until the NRCC did.

Early public opinion polls seemed to confirm the original decision of the Republican Party not to get too involved in the campaign. Swallow's campaign manager said, "All along the poll numbers in the campaign did not help."[31] A Swallow campaign poll in late August showed Swallow trailing by twelve points. An NRCC poll later showed him down by eighteen points.[32] NRCC chair Representative Tom Davis visited Utah in mid-October, but even after visiting with the Swallow campaign, he chose not to commit party resources. At the time of his visit, an NRCC poll showed Swallow behind by thirteen points. This poll, however, was taken on Sunday. By most indicators, Utah is a religious state, so many

Table 11-2. *Number of Unique Campaign Communications by Organizations, Utah Second District Race, 2002*[a]

	Type of campaign communication					
Type and organization[b]	Surface mail pieces	Personal contacts	Phone calls	Radio ads	TV ads	Total
Democratic allies[c]						
Candidates						
Matheson for Congress	10	. . .	3	1	4	18
Political parties						
Utah State Democratic Committee	3	1	1	. . .	1	6
Democratic Congressional Campaign Committee	. . .	. . .	. . .	. . .	1	1
Interest groups						
National Education Association	7	. . .	2	. . .	. . .	9
Unknown Organization	. . .	. . .	3	. . .	. . .	3
AFL-CIO	1	. . .	. . .	. . .	. . .	1
Planned Parenthood of Utah	1	. . .	. . .	. . .	. . .	1
Sierra Club	1	. . .	. . .	. . .	. . .	1
Republican allies[c]						
Candidates						
John Swallow for Congress	2	4	4	1	3	14
Political parties						
Utah Republican Party	12	. . .	. . .	. . .	. . .	12
Republican National Committee	7	. . .	. . .	. . .	. . .	7
National Republican Congressional Committee	. . .	. . .	. . .	. . .	1	1
Interest groups		. . .		. . .		
National Right to Life	1	. . .	1	. . .	. . .	2
Business Roundtable	1	. . .	. . .	. . .	. . .	1
Club for Growth	. . .	. . .	. . .	1	. . .	1
Eagle Forum PAC	1	. . .	. . .	. . .	. . .	1
National Right to Work Committee	1	. . .	. . .	. . .	. . .	1
U.S. Chamber of Commerce[d]	. . .	. . .	. . .	. . .	. . .	1
Unknown Organization	. . .	. . .	1	. . .	. . .	1
Nonpartisan						
Interest groups						
America's Credit Unions	1	. . .	. . .	. . .	. . .	1
League of Women Voters	1	. . .	. . .	. . .	. . .	1

Source: Magleby, Monson, and CSED, 2002 Soft Money and Issue Advocacy Database.

a. See appendix A for a more detailed explanation of data. This table is not intended to portray comprehensive organization activity within the sample races. A more complete picture can be obtained by examining this table together with table 11-1. Data represent the number of unique pieces or ads by the group and do not represent a count of total items sent or made.

In blank cells, ". . ." reflects absence of collected data and does not imply that the organization was inactive in that medium.

b. All state and local chapters or affiliates have been combined with their national affiliate to better render the picture of the organization's activity. For instance, the UEA data have been included in the NEA totals.

c. Certain organizations that maintained neutrality were categorized according to which candidates their ads supported or attacked or whether the organization was anti- or pro-conservative or liberal.

d. Unspecified race involvement. Bill Miller, political director, U.S. Chamber of Commerce, interview by David Magleby and Quin Monson, Washington, D.C., November 7, 2002.

potential voters, especially the more conservative ones, would have been hard to reach on Sunday. The NRCC realized the mistake and commissioned another poll just a week later which showed Swallow behind by just one point and Republicans leading in the generic ballot question by eighteen points.[33] With this new information, much of the earlier reluctance to participate in the campaign quickly dissipated. After Swallow narrowed Matheson's lead in the polls, the NRCC helped pay for mail from the state party and aired television and radio ads featuring Senator Orrin Hatch.

The Swallow campaign laments what could have been. The influx of money at the end from the party and other sources made the campaign more competitive, but it did not come soon enough to invest in activities and infrastructure that might have produced a Republican victory. For example, had the campaign had more money, it would have hired more field coordinators for other parts of the sprawling district. It had only enough money to work the rural southwest part of the district, where Swallow won by impressive margins. Swallow beat Matheson handily in Washington and Iron counties (southwest), for example, but he only won half of the rural vote in Wasatch and Duchesne counties (northeast). Matheson's early and impressive fund-raising capability allowed the campaign to put field coordinators in all the counties. Matheson's campaign manager said, "It was the perfect campaign, and we still only won by 1 percent."[34] Republicans might say, "It was a much less than perfect campaign, and we only lost by 1 percent." This alone demonstrates the monumental miscalculation the Republican Party made by largely ignoring the Second District in 2002.

Interest-Group Activity

Interest groups seemed to follow the lead of the political parties. Groups that had participated actively in previous Second District campaigns generally sat on the sidelines. The strategic thinking of the outside groups mirrored the parties, with one important exception: Some of the normally Republican-allied groups genuinely liked Matheson. While the Republican Party and other groups may have underestimated the competitiveness of the district, and there is every reason to believe they did, some groups cited Matheson's record and personality as reasons not to get involved. The U.S. Chamber of Commerce, which spent money to defeat him in 2000, endorsed him in 2002 "because of how good he was to business."[35] When pressed to explain why the Chamber had changed its mind, Bill Miller, political director, said:

> Quite frankly he voted the right way. We didn't believe in him when this was an open seat. We went after him with a lot of money. . . . He came to Washington and literally a week after he was sworn in called us at the Chamber and said, "Look, I realize you went after me. I realize you don't want me to be here. I am here. I am going to be a pro-business vote for you on the Democratic side. I want to form a partnership whereby you tell me what you need on votes that are significant votes to the business community, and I'll be there for you."[36]

The National Rifle Association also moderated its attitude toward Matheson. Swallow received an A rating from the NRA, while Matheson only received a B. However, the NRA did not get involved because the race did not appear to be "competitive with good-versus-evil candidates."[37] The NRA typically has a policy of endorsing incumbents who have been friendly to their cause, but since Matheson had accepted a campaign contribution from the Brady Campaign in 2000, the NRA did not feel it could endorse him. However, during his first term in office, Matheson sponsored a bill for the NRA, so the organization did not feel it could endorse Swallow either.[38] Even the abortion debate did not generate serious activity. Planned Parenthood sent out one mailer on behalf of Matheson, and National Right to Life contributed a mailing and phone call for Swallow (see table 11-2). The Swallow campaign readily admitted how likable Matheson could be and how effectively he had worked to pacify groups such as the Chamber of Commerce and the NRA.[39] In a further demonstration of how groups strategically allocate their resources, Republican candidates in the other two congressional races in Utah received even less attention from the interest groups.[40]

The one group that ratcheted up activity in the Second District was the Club for Growth. The CFG came in at the end of the campaign and ran radio ads attacking Matheson as a "tax-and-spend liberal." It also acknowledged that it should have entered the race much sooner. In a postrace interview, the political director for the CFG said:

> That race, out of all the races in the country, that race breaks my heart more than any one. Because John Swallow really ran a very

strong campaign and nearly knocked off an incumbent Democrat in a year when incumbents very rarely lost. . . . Why did we get in so late? When I think about mistakes that we made this past year, I think one of our biggest mistakes is that we didn't get behind John Swallow earlier. EMILY's list has the right formula. Early money *is* like yeast. If we had put money behind him earlier, I think he might have won. I think it was just a strategic mistake we made.[41]

In the end, the CFG pumped about $95,000 into the Swallow campaign during the last Federal Election Commission reporting period (October 17 through November 25). According to Swallow's campaign director, the support came at a critical time. The bundled contributions from CFG members and the ads run by the CFG helped the campaign make a serious run at Matheson in its last two weeks, but earlier money probably would have helped Swallow win.

The NEA endorsed Matheson and worked hard for him. It sent out seven different pieces of mail and made at least two phone calls on his behalf. This endorsement was important because the UEA is a particularly powerful political force in Utah. Matheson's campaign commercials also prominently featured schoolchildren and commitments to support education. However, in the minds of voters he did not enjoy the same advantage in education that he did on the environment. When voters were asked which candidate "would improve education in Utah," 30 percent said Matheson, 26 percent said Swallow, 32 percent said "both," and 11 percent said "neither."[42] Like candidates in other districts in this study, the candidates and the interest groups focused on the issues of education and taxes (see table 1-6).

Excluding the CFG and the NEA, very little interest-group activity occurred in Utah's Second District. The groups took their cue from the national parties. As with the parties, interest groups believed polling that indicated that Matheson would win regardless of their involvement in the race. Matheson's effectiveness at painting himself as a conservative-to-moderate representative helped add credibility to the polling and reinforced that conclusion. The parties and groups also pointed to his family name and the roots the Matheson family had in southern Utah as reasons he would be difficult to beat, even in the new district.

In spite of little assistance from outside groups and parties, and with serious financial constraints, Swallow was able to wage a campaign so competitive that voters seemed to place it on equal footing with Mathe-

Table 11-3. *Candidate Receipts and Expenditures, 2001–02*
Dollars

Source	Matheson (D)	Swallow (R)
From PACs	642,457	154,488
From individuals	638,727	660,333
From party	155,189	180,922
From candidate	0	171,000
Other contributions	28,240	844
Total receipts	1,464,613	1,167,587
Total expenditures	1405,199	1,163,612
Cash on hand 12/31/02	120,837	3,975

Source: Federal Election Commission, "2001-02 U.S. House and U.S. Senate Candidate Info," December 31, 2002 (www.fecinfo.com/cgi-win/x_statedis.exe [June 8, 2003]).

son's campaign. When asked who spent more money in the campaign, 32 percent said Swallow, 21 percent said Matheson, and another 45 percent did not know.[43] Contrary to voters' perceptions, Matheson eventually did outspend Swallow by about $300,000 (see table 11-3). Twenty-nine percent of voters also thought that Swallow received more assistance from outside groups, while only 18 percent said Matheson received more. Consistent with the findings in the previous question, 46 percent of voters did not know.[44]

Conclusion

The Utah State Legislature created a competitive district when it redrew congressional boundaries. The Second District is now indisputably Republican. Most voters still reside in Salt Lake County, but the district now encompasses more suburban and rural voters. Both tend to be staunchly conservative in Utah. A politically savvy Democratic incumbent had to run a perfect campaign to retain his seat. Many of the objective indicators point to an evenly matched campaign with ample resources on both sides. The final spending totals for both Swallow and Matheson are impressive. Even the totals for the national parties and some interest groups look impressive. But Republicans (and probably some allies) now admit that they misread this seat. The botched polling by the NRCC and the reluctance of the CFG to enter early meant support and funds did not arrive in time to permit the development of a top-notch campaign organization. The incumbent had access to funds early and used them to build an efficient campaign structure. Final spending and vote totals suggest a competitive campaign; however, the timing and amount of support indicates that parties and interest groups thought otherwise. The Second Congressional District will be competitive for the foreseeable future. As researchers continue to assess the effect of outside money in this and other congressional campaigns, it is important not only to consider the amount but the timing. Interest groups and political parties should be wiser for the opportunity they missed in 2002.

Notes

1. See, for example, Charlie Cook, "2002 Competitive House Races," *Cook Political Report*, October 4, 2002, p. 51; Ron Faucheux, "50 Hot Races to Watch Nov. 5," *Campaigns and Elections*, vol. 23 (October/November 2002), p. 22.

2. The district received a great deal of attention from the parties and outside groups in both 1998 and 2000. See, for example, Jay Goodliffe, "The 1998 Utah Second Congressional District Race," in David B. Magleby, ed., *Outside Money: Soft Money and Issue Advocacy in the 1998 Congressional Elections* (Lanham, Md.: Rowman and Littlefield, 2000), pp. 171–86.

3. Patty Henetz, "Democrats to Republicans: Beware Unintended Redistricting Consequences," Associated Press (Salt Lake City, Ut.), November 29, 2001.

4. Percentages are from the 2002 KBYU–Utah Colleges exit poll, November 5, 2002.

5. Michael Barone with Richard E. Cohen, eds., *Almanac of American Politics 2002* (Congressional Quarterly Press, 2001), p. 1536.

6. "Election 2002," KBYU Television, November 4, 2002.

7. Bob Bernick Jr., "Chamber Is Now Matheson's Friend," *Deseret (Utah) News*, October 9, 2002, p. B2.

8. According to the 2002 KBYU–Utah Colleges exit poll, President Bush had an average favorability rating in the Second District of 3.87 on a scale of 1 (very unfavorable) to 5 (very favorable). Matheson's rating was also quite high for a Democrat (3.3) and higher than John Swallow's (3.07).

9. Dave Hansen, director, Swallow Campaign, interview by Kelly Patterson, Salt Lake City, Utah, November 8, 2002.

10. 2002 KBYU–Utah Colleges exit poll, November 5, 2002. The question was, "Which one or two issues mattered most in deciding how you would vote for your representative? Mark one or two."

11. Ibid.

12. Bob Bernick Jr., "Swallow Attacking Matheson on Abortion," *Deseret (Utah) News*, October 29, 2002, p. B1.

13. 2002 KBYU–Utah Colleges exit poll, November 5, 2002. The question is the same as in endnote 10.

14. Ibid.

15. Ibid. The question was, "Below is a list of phrases. Please mark whether the phrase correctly describes John Swallow, Jim Matheson, both or neither: Would protect the environment." Percentages are based on 224 respondents to this particular question.

16. Paul S. Herrnson, *Congressional Elections: Campaigning at Home and in Washington*, 3d ed. (Congressional Quarterly, 2000), p. 84.

17. Mike McElwain, political director, NRCC, interview by David Magleby and Jonathan Tanner, Washington, D.C., December 2, 2002.

18. Herrnson, *Congressional Elections*, p. 92.

19. Ibid.

20. Hansen interview, November 8, 2002.

21. Ibid.

22. Kenneth B. Mehlman, deputy assistant to the president and director of political affairs, interview by David Magleby and Jonathan Tanner, Washington, D.C., November 15, 2002.

23. Lee Davidson and Bob Bernick, "Money Shuffling Aiding Utahn," *Deseret (Utah) News*, October 31, 2002, p. A1.

24. Hansen interview, November 8, 2002. Ed Brookover confirmed this in an interview with David Magleby and Nicole Carlisle Squires, Washington, D.C., November 12, 2002.

25. Robyn Matheson, director, Matheson Campaign, interview by Kelly Patterson, Salt Lake City, Utah, November 13, 2002.

26. For a discussion of the impact on voters, see David B. Magleby, ed., *Election Advocacy: Soft Money and Issue Advocacy in the 2000 Congressional Elections* (Center for the Study of Elections and Democracy, Brigham Young University), p. 48; and David B. Magleby and J. Quin Monson, "Campaign 2002: 'The Perfect Storm'" (Center for the Study of Elections and Democracy, Brigham Young University, November 13, 2002) (http://csed.byu.edu).

27. Dan Harrie, "Matheson, Swallow Race Noted for Its Cleanliness," *Salt Lake (Utah) Tribune*, October 29, 2002.

28. Mike Matthews, political director, DCCC, interview by David Magleby and Nicole Carlisle Squires, Washington, D.C., November 12, 2002.

29. Matheson interview, November 13, 2002.

30. For a discussion of the resources that parties provided to the other two congressional races in Utah, see Kelly Patterson, "The Utah 2nd District Congressional Race," in David B. Magleby and J. Quin Monson, eds., *The Last Hurrah: Soft Money and Issue Advocacy in the 2002 Congressional Election*, monograph version (Center for the Study of Elections and Democracy, Brigham Young University, 2003), p. 306–20.

31. Hansen interview, November 8, 2002.

32. The poll numbers come from the author's interview with Hansen. They have not been independently verified.

33. Tom Davis, chair, NRCC, interview by Paul S. Herrnson, Washington, D.C., February 27, 2003. The generic ballot question asks possible voters if they are more likely to vote for the Republican or Democratic candidate in the congressional election. It does not mention the names of the candidates.

34. Matheson interview, November 13, 2002.

35. Bill Miller, political director, U.S. Chamber of Commerce, interview by David Magleby and Quin Monson, Washington, D.C., November 7, 2002.

36. Bill Miller, press event, "The Last Hurrah? Soft Money and Issue Advocacy in the 2002 Elections," Center for the Study of Elections and Democracy, National Press Club, Washington, D.C., February 3, 2003.

37. Chuck Cunningham, director, federal affairs, NRA Institute for Legislative Action, interview by David Magleby, Quin Monson, Jonathan Tanner, and Nicole Carlisle Squires, Washington, D.C., November 7, 2002.

38. For a description of the way in which the NRA chooses to support and endorse candidates, see Kelly D. Patterson and Matthew M. Singer, "The National Rifle Association in the Face of the Clinton Challenge," in Allan J. Cigler and Burdett A. Loomis, eds., *Interest Group Politics*, 6th ed. (Congressional Quarterly Press, 2002), pp. 67–68.

39. Hansen interview, November 8, 2002.

40. For a discussion of the resources that parties provided to the other two congressional races in Utah, see Kelly Patterson, "The Utah 2nd District Congressional Race," in Magleby and Monson, *The Last Hurrah*, monograph version, pp. 306–20.

41. Stephen Moore, political director, Club for Growth, press event, "The Last Hurrah? Soft Money and Issue Advocacy in the 2002 Elections," Center for the Study of Elections and Democracy, National Press Club, Washington, D.C., February 3, 2003.

42. Results are from the 2002 KBYU–Utah Colleges exit poll. Percentages are based on 227 respondents to the same question cited in endnote 14.

43. Ibid. The question was: "Please indicate which candidate in your U.S. House election you believe spent the most money." There were 259 respondents to this question.

44. Ibid. The question was: "Please indicate which candidate in your U.S. House election had the most money spent by outside groups to assist in the election." There were 266 respondents to this question.

TWELVE

The Consequences of
Noncandidate Spending,
with a Look to the Future

DAVID B. MAGLEBY

J. QUIN MONSON

OUTSIDE MONEY HAS CHANGED the dynamics of campaigns and elections in competitive congressional elections. Unlike most candidate-centered congressional elections, much of the campaigning in a competitive race falls outside the control of the candidate. Political parties and interest groups do not all share the same agenda, and some have resources well beyond those of the candidates. Instead of seeing an election as a race between two major party candidates, we now need to consider the campaigns mounted by the party committees and interest groups as part of the overall campaign. In an extremely competitive South Dakota Senate race, nearly forty groups communicated with voters, compared to the noncompetitive New Mexico Senate race, where fewer than ten messengers communicated with voters. These noncandidate groups have also changed the volume and tone of competitive congressional elections, making them more intense and negative.

Candidates continue to play an important role, even when substantial outside money is invested in a race. They remain the focal point, even while they have less control over defining themselves and their opponents, because noncandidate spending typically also focuses on the candidates. This is ironic because most of the noncandidate activity is by political parties, yet party soft-money-funded messages rarely even mention the party. The importance of candidates is well understood by the parties, who invest heavily in candidate recruitment in potentially competitive races. As noted in chapter 1, President George W. Bush and the White House political staff gave this added emphasis in 2002. When a candidate fails to remain competitive, party soft money and issue advocacy spending in that race tends to fade. For example, the Mississippi Third Congressional District race between Republican Chip Pickering and Democrat Ronnie Shows, both incumbents, was initially expected to be competitive and attracted substantial noncandidate money. However, "as the campaign wore on, and polls showed that Shows was not going to be able to offset the advantages held by Pickering, interest in the race evaporated and [the parties and interest groups] took their money elsewhere."[1]

In 2002 party soft money was again the most important source of outside money. As in 1998 and 2000, it was spent strategically in the competitive races and largely invested in voter persuasion and mobilization. The Republicans invested more of their soft money than before in voter mobilization through the 72 Hour Task Force, but both parties continue to spend large amounts of their money on broadcast communications.

Two factors converged in 2002 to make the impact of soft-money expenditures especially heavy. First, because 2002 was billed as the "last hurrah" for soft money, donors were especially motivated to give. As detailed in chapter 1, compared to the previous midterm election, soft money soared in 2002 and very nearly rivaled soft-money spending in the 2000 presidential election. Second, these soft dollars were spent in a small number of congressional races, in large part because most federal contests in 2002 were not competitive, especially because redistricting in 2002 tended toward incumbent protection and produced fewer competitive seats than anticipated. Additionally the few competitive Senate races in 2002 tended to be in less populated states with less expensive media markets. Cheap media markets and sparse populations in South Dakota, Arkansas, and New Hampshire permitted the parties and interest groups to stretch their soft-money dollars more than they would have if the battlegrounds had been New Jersey, Florida, California, or New York.

Our research in 2002 reinforces our earlier findings that the two parties have different strategic advantages. Republicans clearly have a hard-money advantage, something Democrats could counter in 2002 with soft money but which, under the Bipartisan Campaign Reform Act, gives the GOP a substantial head start in the now more important hard-money game. In 1998 and 2000 Democrats had a large ground-war advantage. This was due in part to the strength and expertise of their large membership-based interest-group allies. In 2002 the Republicans took major steps toward closing the gap on their ground-war deficiency. How the Democrats do in mounting a ground war without soft money and whether the Republicans have really "gotten religion" on spending hard money for the ground operation are questions to be explored in future studies.

As discussed in chapter 3, interest-group issue advocacy, while still a factor in several contests in 2002, did not grow in importance as soft money did. This is in part because donors seemed to invest more of this fungible money in the parties in 2002. The economy also appeared to limit some of the very large donors who had bankrolled some of the largest issue advocacy campaigns in 2000. For example, Citizens for Better Medicare, Planned Parenthood, and the NAACP National Voter Fund all benefited from large donors in 2000 that did not contribute at the same level in 2002

Voters see party, most issue advocacy, and candidate communications as equally intended to influence their vote for or against a particular candidate. This simple fact is part of the attraction of soft money and issue advocacy to donors. Soft money and issue advocacy provide individuals and groups desiring to influence an election with two unlimited mechanisms to accomplish that purpose.

Noncandidate campaign activity is concentrated in competitive races, and the contrast between contests with outside money and those without is dramatic. As shown in chapter 1, competitive U.S. House and Senate races in our study saw between nine and ten times as many noncandidate television ads compared to control races, which, like most congressional elections, were not competitive. A stark difference is also apparent in campaign mail; the mail sponsored by noncandidate groups was about five times more frequent in battleground races than in control races.

Substantial expenditures of outside money have important implications for candidates, interest groups, and parties. Candidates have found that the kinds of soft money and issue advocacy campaigns described in this book and in our prior research are "two-edged swords."[2] Outside money has the potential of helping you and hurting your opponent, but it can backfire on you as well. Outside money can help keep candidates visible when they are short on campaign resources, and it also has the potential to force your opponents to discuss issues they might prefer not to raise. But outside money sometimes lacks sensitivity to local circumstances and can be overly negative. When this happens, it can often harm the intended beneficiary. For example, in the Connecticut Fifth Congressional District race in 2002, Republican Nancy Johnson's campaign successfully branded Democrat Jim Maloney as a negative campaigner after the AFL-CIO began running ads attacking Johnson. Respondents in an independent survey conducted before the Maloney campaign ran a single ad viewed his campaign as negative because they associated it with the AFL-CIO ads.[3] At the same time, candidates can benefit from the virtually unlimited arsenal that soft money and issue advocacy provide. This arsenal can be used to respond to attacks on one candidate, often by raising even more shrill attacks on the other candidate.[4]

Outside money creates uncertainty in campaigns, forcing candidates to anticipate what the opposing party and its allied groups will do. Facing outside money also motivates candidates to raise as much money as they can for their own campaigns. In some cases, it may also influence legislative behavior to attempt to minimize the chances of facing a group funded by outside money.[5] Candidates sometimes even find themselves disagreeing with tactics used by their allies seeking to attack their opponents.[6]

One of the most important consequences of outside money has been a decline in candidate accountability for campaigns. Until the advent of soft money and issue advocacy, the public and the media assumed the candidates were responsible for the content of campaigns. Those assumptions are still valid in noncompetitive races. But as we have shown, in competitive races in 2002, there was often twice as much campaign communication from party and interest groups as from the candidates. Political consultants consciously attempt to see that voters blame candidates when the tone of a race is unacceptable or when one candidate appears untruthful. Ironically, when ads funded by soft money or issue advocacy groups are forced off the air, the party or interest groups on the other side are quick to blame the candidate for the inaccuracy, knowing full well that the ad did not come from the candidate.

The absence of candidate control over the content of a campaign leads to more attack or negative advertising, and candidates are even quicker to claim that the tone is not their fault. Our research has shown, however, that voters do blame the candidates for this increasing negativity of campaigns.

In light of the data we present in this book and in our past research, the conventional view of political parties, at least in competitive elections, should be revised. Parties are in reality networks or alliances with interest groups, operating in a semiautonomous way on behalf of candidates. In the past, parties and interest groups were seen as operating through candidates, largely through campaign contributions or coordinated expenditures. Parties and their interest group partners can powerfully influence the relatively few elections they enter, but in a Congress where there are such slim majorities this can have a tremendous policy impact.

Outside money likely influenced the outcome of several races in 2002. For example, activity by the National Republican Senatorial Committee (NRSC) was clearly important to the election of John Sununu in New Hampshire. Sununu won an expensive primary, unseating incumbent Bob Smith. Republican soft money transferred to the New Hampshire Republican Party funded a series of ads attacking Democratic candidate Jeanne Shaheen, until the Republican nomination was settled in early September and Sununu could replenish his campaign accounts.[7]

For groups and individuals wanting to spend money on electoral politics in contests critical to determining which party controls one or both houses of Congress, outside money is an attractive option. As we show in chapter 3, the presence or absence of a wealthy individual can alter by several million dollars the issue advocacy budget of an interest group. Well-funded groups can also spend unlimited amounts of money through independent expenditures, but these must be fully disclosed. A major reason most groups have adopted issue advocacy as their preferred mode of electioneering is to avoid disclosure. In fact, even organizations funded by industry groups seek to mask their identity by adopting neutral-sounding names like United Seniors Association or Citizens for Better Medicare, both largely funded by the pharmaceutical industry. For unions and corporations, soft money and issue advocacy has the additional advantage of permitting them to spend unlimited amounts from their treasury funds on electing and defeating candidates. This is something they are expressly forbidden to do in any other way. States with an active initiative and referendum process have also seen groups masquerade behind innocuous group names. Michigan, in an effort to help voters know who was actually funding ads, required the names of the principal donors to the group to be revealed in the ad's tag line.

Hence an ad paid for by money donated by Michigan public utilities would say the utilities paid for the ad, rather than the campaign committee named Citizens for Jobs and Energy. This disclosure provision was declared unconstitutional by the District Court for the Eastern District of Michigan, Southern Division, and was not appealed to the U.S. Supreme Court.[8]

The Impact of Noncandidate Spending on Voters

Past research has largely overlooked the impact of noncandidate spending on voters. The paucity of information on this topic is of particular interest because one of the justifications that the Supreme Court gave in *Buckley* v. *Valeo* upholding the limits on donations was the potential impact that the appearance of corruption could have on public confidence in democracy and the electoral system. As the Court noted in *Buckley*, "of almost equal concern as the danger of actual quid pro quo arrangements is the impact of the appearance of corruption stemming from public awareness of the opportunities for abuse inherent in a regime."[9] In *CSC* [U.S. Civil Service Commission] v. *Letter Carriers,* the Court explicitly raised the public confidence concern, saying Congress could legitimately conclude that the avoidance of the appearance of improper influence "is also critical . . . if confidence in the system of representative Government is not to be eroded to a disastrous extent."[10] Some recent work presents conflicting analysis of the link between public trust in government and levels of soft-money expenditures, in an attempt to predict the effects of BCRA.[11] We take a different approach, by presenting evidence of the more immediate impact of noncandidate spending on the public's perceptions of the tone of campaigns, as well as the public response to the high levels of campaign intensity.

For the first time in 2002, the Center for the Study of Elections and Democracy conducted polling to ascertain how the public reacts to the intense candidate and noncandidate campaigning that is now part of competitive races.[12] We used two complementary methodologies to gather these data. First was a three-wave telephone panel survey, in which a random sample of self-identified registered voters was selected and interviewed and then reinterviewed during the campaign and soon after the election. The panel design enables us to learn the extent of exposure to all forms of electioneering and to assess voter reactions to the campaign over time. The panel survey was conducted with five separate samples; four of these were in competitive U.S. House or Senate contests, and the fifth was a national sample intended as a baseline for comparison. The four competitive contests were the Connecticut Fifth Congressional District race, the Colorado Seventh Congressional District race, the Arkansas Senate race, and the Missouri Senate race.

The second survey was a campaign communication voter log survey, in which we asked respondents sampled from voter registration lists to forward to us their political mail and list in a log book political phone calls and personal contacts they received during a three-week period prior to Election Day. This survey was conducted statewide in four U.S. Senate campaigns in Arkansas, Minnesota, New Mexico, and South Dakota. Three of the four U.S. Senate races were competitive contests, and the fourth, New Mexico, had competitive races in two of its three congressional districts. Appendix A provides a detailed description of the design of both surveys.

Respondents in both surveys reported high levels of exposure to campaign advertising, mail, and other forms of communication. In the most competitive races they became overwhelmed by the volume and suffered from "election fatigue," wishing for the return of more benign used-car ads and junk mail. Election fatigue makes it more difficult for voters to effectively sift through the barrage of information; it also means that the effectiveness of traditional ads is diminished. Voters look away from the campaigns to more trusted sources (such as family and friends, newspaper articles or endorsements, and organizations they belong to) for signals about the election.

Exposure

The data in previous chapters clearly demonstrate that candidates, parties, and interest groups saturated voters with advertising in competitive contests. But how much are potential voters exposed to this advertising? The answer is, a lot. Using the panel survey data, in figure 12-1, we contrast the proportion of respondents in wave three who reported having "seen, read, or heard anything" about their House or Senate race in our four competitive contests with our national baseline sample. Respondents in the battleground races were much more aware of the contest. Nationally 68 percent of respondents were aware of the congressional contest. In the competitive races this ranged from 88 percent in the Connecticut Fifth Congressional District race, the least competitive race we surveyed, to 92 percent in the Colorado Seventh Congres-

Figure 12-1. *Level of Awareness of Political Races, 2002*

Percent

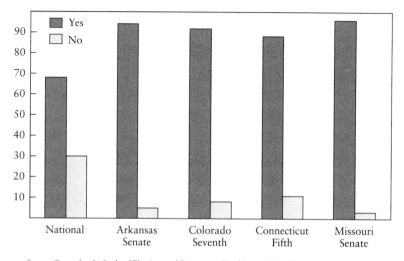

Source: Center for the Study of Elections and Democracy, Panel Survey, Wave Three.
Question: "Have you seen, read, or heard anything about the campaign for U.S. Senate/House of Representatives between _____ and _____, including information from the candidates, political parties, or other groups?"

sional District race, 94 percent in the Arkansas Senate race, and 96 percent in the Missouri Senate race.

Much of the campaign activity in battleground races in 2002 continued to be on television. We asked respondents in the panel survey to estimate how many television ads they saw in their competitive House or Senate race "on an average day during the past week." The means for the five contests in the panel survey across all three waves are presented in figure 12-2. Nationally wave-three respondents saw a mean of 7.6 ads per day in the week leading up to the election. During this same time period, respondents in the Colorado Seventh District and Arkansas and Missouri Senate races all reported seeing between 12 and 13 ads per day, a significant increase from the levels observed in wave one. In the Connecticut Fifth District, where the campaign was less competitive than the others after Labor Day, the ads also declined in intensity, with a mean of about 8.7 ads per day during the last week.

A similar pattern occurs in the panel survey with political mail. Figure 12-3 presents the mean number of pieces of mail respondents reported receiving on an average day in the congressional race by contest and wave. Our national baseline sample received on average 2.5

Figure 12-2. *Number of Political Television Advertisements,*
Contest and Wave, 2002

Mean

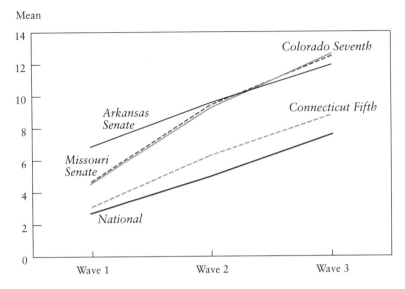

Source: CSED, Panel Survey.
Question: "On an average day this past week, how many television ads about the U.S. Senate/House of Representatives race did you see?"

pieces of political mail a day in the last week of the campaign. In the
Connecticut Fifth District, the average per day was 3.6 pieces of mail, in
Arkansas it was 3, in the Colorado Seventh District it was 4.2, and in
Missouri it was 3.9. It is important to note that the question referred
specifically to the House or Senate race and not all political mail. Our
panel study design also permits us to assess when the different modes of
communication occurred. Political mail, for example, rose from an average of 1 piece a day in early September in Missouri, to 1.7 pieces a day
in the last two weeks of October, to 3.9 pieces of mail a day in the Senate race alone during the last week of the campaign. Similar patterns
emerge in the other contests. It is also important to note that these figures are for the average voter, not groups of undecided or swing voters,
who are generally even more heavily targeted by campaigns and groups.

   In our voter log survey, where we asked voters to collect and forward
their mail, we also detected high levels of campaign activity. Table 12-1
contains the average number of pieces of political mail received by our
survey respondents in each state for all races, as well as for the U.S. Sen-

Figure 12-3. *Number of Political Mailings Received, by Contest and Wave, 2002*

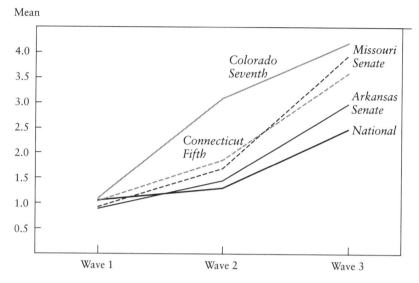

Source: CSED, Panel Survey.
Question: "On an average day this past week, how many pieces of mail about the U.S. Senate/House of Representatives race did you receive?"

ate during the last three weeks of the campaign. Registered voters in South Dakota and Minnesota received about twice as much political mail as those in Arkansas and New Mexico. The numbers vary predictably according to the competitiveness of the elections in each state. In South Dakota, where there were competitive races for U.S. Senate and House as well as for governor, the average for our respondents was 18.68 pieces of mail overall and 7.57 for the Senate race. Respondents in Minnesota, with competitive races for U.S. Senate and governor and at least two competitive House races, averaged 18.15 pieces of mail overall and 4.10 for the Senate race.[13] In New Mexico, with a noncompetitive Senate race and two of the three House races competitive, respondents received an average of 10.41 pieces of mail overall and only 2.19 for the Senate race. Finally, in Arkansas, where the Senate race began competitively but was not close at the end, respondents received 8.85 pieces of mail overall and 4.62 for the Senate race. Again, it is worth noting that these figures do not separate out swing or undecided voters.[14] There are some respondents in each Senate race who received

Table 12-1. *Number of Pieces of Political Mail during Last Three Weeks of Campaign, 2002*

State	All races		U.S. Senate race	
	Average	Maximum	Average	Maximum
Arkansas	8.85	47	4.62	31
Minnesota	18.15	80	4.10	20
New Mexico	10.41	48	2.19	21
South Dakota	18.68	60	7.57	32

Source: CSED voter log survey.

at least one piece of mail about the race *every day* during the three-week period. One Minnesota respondent sent in 80 distinct pieces of political mail from both state and federal races collected during the three-week period.

Tone

Outside-money campaigns are often characterized by their level of negativity. Several factors appear to account for this. Some party lawyers in 1996 and 1998 advised that ads that were critical were less vulnerable to legal challenge. There are practical reasons as well. Even though it is possible to create a positive issue ad that praises a candidate's work on an issue, the consultants view it as much easier and more effective to use a negative message. In addition, because ads from the party and interest groups are not controlled by the candidate, there is a certain amount of plausible deniability—if the ad backfires the candidate can disavow the content and deny responsibility.

A majority of our national sample found the tone of the 2002 campaign to be about the same as in other recent campaigns. But in three out of four of our battleground races, most respondents saw the 2002 campaign as more negative than other recent races. In the Connecticut Fifth District, nearly half of all respondents said the contest was more negative, while 57 percent in Arkansas said the 2002 Senate race was more negative. In the Colorado Seventh District, however, 70 percent of respondents said the race was more negative than other recent races. Because it was a newly created congressional district, the Colorado Seventh had not previously experienced a highly competitive election environment. The perceived negativity in the Seventh District is consistent with the characterization of that race in chapter 8. Respondent percep-

Figure 12-4. *Perceived Responsibility for Negativity of Political Messages, 2002*[a]

Percent

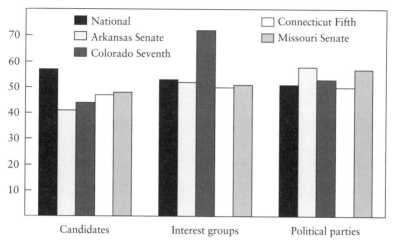

Source: CSED, Panel Survey, Wave Three.

a.Question: "Do you believe the campaign for U.S. Senate/House of Representatives this year was more negative, less negative, or about the same compared to other recent political contests?" [If more] "I'm going to read a list of groups. For each one, please tell me how responsible you think they are for the increased negativity? A great deal, some, not too much, or not at all. The candidates' campaigns, the interest groups, the political parties." Figure shows share of respondents answering "a great deal."

tions of negativity in Colorado contrast with the Missouri Senate race, where only about four in ten respondents saw the 2002 campaign as more negative than recent contests, while a majority thought it was about the same. Given the intensity of the 2000 presidential and senatorial races in Missouri, this is not surprising.

We asked those respondents who saw 2002 as more negative than past campaigns who they thought was responsible for the increased negativity. As figure 12-4 shows, respondents in our national sample apportioned the majority of the blame evenly to the candidates (57 percent), parties (53 percent), and interest groups (51 percent). But in our battleground contests, respondents were much more likely to lay "a great deal" of the blame on the parties or interest groups. In the Arkansas and Missouri Senate races, respondents gave "a great deal" of the responsibility to the parties (58 and 57 percent), and only 41 percent to the candidates in Arkansas and 48 percent in Missouri. In the Colorado Seventh District race, 72 percent gave "a great deal" of the blame for the increased negativity to interest groups.

Figure 12-5. *Share of Respondents Stating They Received Too Much Mail and Advertising, 2002*[a]

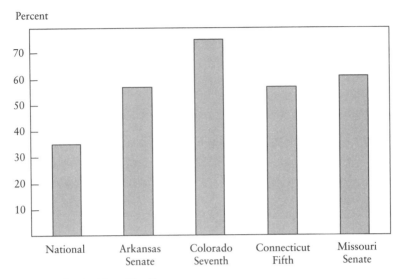

Percent

Source: CSED, Panel Survey, Wave Three.

a. Question: "Which of these statements best summarizes your view of the U.S. Senate/House of Representatives campaign? There was too much mail and advertising. There was about the right amount of mail and advertising. There was too little mail and advertising."

Voter Reaction to the Torrent of Information

One of the questions we sought to answer with our surveys was how voters deal with the large volume of information they receive in competitive races with substantial noncandidate expenditures. Figure 12-5 presents the results of a question in the panel survey, in which we asked respondents whether the amount of advertising was too much, about the right amount, or too little. Nationally 34 percent said there was "too much mail and advertising" in their U.S. House race. And not surprisingly, in our four sample races, between 57 and 75 percent gave this response—57 percent in Arkansas and the Connecticut Fifth District, 61 percent in Missouri, and 75 percent in the Colorado Seventh. The two contests with the highest percent saying they received too much mail and advertising are also the two highest in terms of average mail pieces received or television ads viewed each day during wave three of the survey.

In our voter log survey we asked respondents to respond to the following question after the election. "Which of the following statements best summarizes your experience during the election campaign? 'After all the advertising and mail, I stopped paying attention'; or 'There was a lot of advertising and mail, but I kept paying attention throughout.'" The modal response to this question in all four states was "After all the advertising and mail, I stopped paying attention." Respondents agreeing with this statement ranged from 51 percent in Minnesota, where all campaigning came to a halt for five days, to 61 percent in South Dakota. The response was the same in the panel survey, where 56 percent nationally compared to 77 percent in the Colorado Seventh District said they "stopped paying attention."

Many of the respondents to our log survey in South Dakota, after observing a campaign that had been waged at high intensity for several months, wrote lengthy comments on the backs of their survey booklets. Some of them expressed disappointment and frustration with the campaign. One said, "I cannot make an informed decision about a candidate from advertising. I only care about their ideas, beliefs, and values. . . . The TV ads and mail ads don't tell me anything." Another commented, "The length of time spent campaigning, and the amount of money spent was absolutely ridiculous. . . . The TV ads were so numerous and repetitive, you eventually tune them out entirely." Finally, one voter wanted "to see [a] campaign not longer than 4 months. . . . I start getting bored and uninterested by election time." A study conducted among a group of undecided women voters by the Garin-Hart-Yang Research Group during the 2000 campaign for EMILY's List found similar results. It concludes, "By the last week of the campaign, even the most earnest and thoughtful panelists suffer from severe 'election fatigue' that wears them down to the point that they are unwilling to or incapable of actively engaging in the messages and issues that dominate the final days of the campaign."[15]

What do voters do when confronted with too much information? They turn to trusted or "objective" sources, like newspapers and television news. In our log survey, roughly one in four respondents in all four states said that news coverage in newspapers or on television was very important. Ironically, local broadcast news coverage of congressional campaigns is relatively small, compared to the number of television ads. An analysis of a random sample of local news broadcasts in 2002 estimates the ratio of political ads to campaign news stories at 3.6 to 1. The majority of local news broadcasts do not contain any stories about the campaign, especially not congressional races.[16] Voters also value unfiltered exposure to candidates. This would lend support to those who advocate giving free airtime so candidates can break out of the mold of thirty-second campaign ads and sound bites.[17] Similar proportions of respondents in Arkansas, New Mexico, and South Dakota said direct contact with the candidates was very important in such an election. Finally, 28 percent of respondents in Arkansas and New Mexico listed family, friends, or coworkers as very important sources of information about the election they were a part of. Similarly, the EMILY's List study concludes, "The frustration that panelists express in accessing information that they feel will help them make informed choices on Election Day leads them to be highly skeptical of any information coming directly from candidates and political parties and, instead, pushes them to place a great deal of weight on news or other more 'objective' accounts of the candidates and the issues."[18]

The data summarized here demonstrate that these competitive contests, with high levels of candidate and noncandidate spending, have measurable effects on voters. They end up with "election fatigue," concerned about the negative tone of the campaign, and less satisfied with the workings of electoral democracy. This is especially evident when they experience a highly competitive election for the first time, as the voters in Colorado's Seventh District did in 2002. Potential voters reach a point of frustration with the volume of political communication. The challenge for campaigners is to know when that point arrives and time their campaigns accordingly. But in campaigns with substantial noncandidate electioneering, the candidates do not control much of the information flow. In some very competitive situations, spending by noncandidates takes on an arms-race mentality. Each side spends in order to match the opposition; both sides know that the additional spending will win them very few votes, but they think that not spending would be disastrous. The differential impact of the information flow on voters also deserves study. Some voters may have a higher tolerance for saturation advertising than others. It is conceivable therefore that information flow itself could be a tool of vote suppression.

The Last Hurrah? A Look to the Future

Whether 2002 will be a harbinger of future elections depends in part on what sections of BCRA survive constitutional challenge, and the interpretation of provisions of the law by the Federal Election Commission. If the soft-money ban in BCRA is upheld, we anticipate more issue advocacy by interest groups, both in the number of groups advocating and the volume of communications. If the soft-money ban is declared unconstitutional, both parties have clearly indicated that they will continue to utilize soft money as a strategic resource for competitive races. The most likely scenario is that parts of BCRA will be found constitutional and parts will not. The future of campaign finance will depend on the interplay of these components.

If the soft-money ban is upheld and issue advocacy limits, including the use of corporate and union treasury funds, are struck down, we can anticipate a substantial surge in issue advocacy. Even if the source limits are upheld, it is likely that there will be more issue advocacy should the soft-money ban be upheld. Some and perhaps most soft money can be expected to shift to issue advocacy. This is because none of the motives that prompted donors to give soft money to the parties or issue advocacy money to interest groups have gone away. The partisan control of Congress remains at play, and the policy consequences of controlling the presidency have not diminished. Given the comprehensive nature of BCRA, these interaction effects make predicting the future of campaign finance difficult.

The rule-making of the Federal Election Commission and the Federal Communications Commission will significantly influence how the 2004 elections are financed. The FEC rules can shape the scope and reach of BCRA, in ways that are inconsistent with the legislative intent, by issuing regulations that narrowly define organizations or activities restricted under BCRA, thus opening loopholes to circumvent the law. It is worth remembering that the origin of soft money was in advisory opinions issued by the FEC that allowed for some exceptions to the newly enacted contributions limits under the Federal Election Campaign Act. Early FEC rule-making on BCRA was seen by the chief legislative sponsors of the act as inconsistent with legislative intent, and they prompted a legal challenge.[19] Christopher Shays and Marty Meehan were not alone; several reform groups also were critical of the FEC rule-making.[20] One of the glaring omissions of BCRA is that it did nothing to remedy the problems with the Federal Election Commission. As rule-making under BCRA has already demonstrated, the FEC is willing to assert broad regulatory powers to interpret the law in ways inconsistent with the intent of those who wrote the law. But neither party is willing to give the other a tie-breaking power, and the leadership in both parties has shown a desire to keep the FEC as docile as possible.

Individuals

We can say with confidence that the increased individual contribution limits, both to candidates and to the parties, will withstand constitutional challenge. Congress effectively doubled individual contribution limits, from $2,000 per candidate per cycle to $4,000 per candidate per cycle. Authors of the reform legislation saw individual contributions as more broadly democratic than contributions by interest groups. Further evidence for the desired elevation of individual donors in relation to political action committees is that BCRA did not increase PAC contribution limits.

Reformers hoped that raising individual contribution limits would help challengers in congressional elections.[21] They assumed that individuals are more likely to contribute to challengers than are parties or PACs. Whether individuals will actually give more to challengers remains to be seen. What is more likely is that groups that "bundle" individual contributions from similarly minded individuals will have expanded power and influence. Interest groups like EMILY's List and the Club for Growth, who bundle individual contributions, will now be able to appeal to their supporters for greater support and hence increase aggregate contributions from group members to candidates. Individuals who bundle contributions to a single candidate, like the Bush Pioneers in 2000, will also have expanded influence.

Parties

Both major parties have become increasingly dependent on soft money in recent years. This dependency has been most acute for the Democrats. In 2002 soft money accounted for more than half (53 percent) of all funds raised by the Democrats, up from 47 percent in 2000. Republicans, while less dependent on soft money, still have received over a third of all their contributions via soft money in the past three election cycles. As we know from chapter 2, Republicans actually raised more soft money in 2002 than the Democrats. However, the proportion of soft money raised by Republicans is lower than that of the Democrats, because Republicans raise so much more hard money.

The Republican hard-money advantage is substantial and is even more consequential in a world without soft money. The success of the Bush Pioneers in hard-money fund-raising will be repeated in 2004, except that in 2004 the hard-money donors can contribute twice as much. But the GOP hard-money head start is not isolated to the RNC. As we show in this book, the NRCC clearly adopted this strategy in 2002. Whether Democrats can develop a hard-money base that permits them to compete under BCRA is unclear and will be a major part of the story of campaign finance in 2004 and beyond. Developing a stronger hard-money base is essential to a competitive Democratic Party, but the party can also hope that its interest-group allies continue to be as effective as they were in recent election years in mobilizing voters.

Passage of BCRA provides political scientists with an opportunity to monitor the behavior of individuals, candidates, interest groups, and political parties under a new regulatory regime. How will the players adapt to the new rules? What will soft-money donors do should the soft money ban be upheld? Will different types of interest groups behave differently under BCRA? It is not clear that BCRA will reduce the total amount of money invested in federal elections, although the reformers certainly sold the legislation on this premise. How much citizens and scholars will be able to know about money in federal elections depends on how BCRA is interpreted and applied. But it is certainly possible that we may end up knowing less about the behavior of large donors under this law than we knew under the Federal Election Campaign Act (FECA). This is because under FECA, soft-money donors disclosed their contributions to the parties. These same donors may avoid disclosure under BCRA if the issue advocacy provisions are declared unconstitutional.

Under BCRA it is predictable that in the short term overall national party budgets will be smaller. With soft money unavailable, parties will be much less likely to transfer large amounts of hard money to state parties for competitive races. Rather the strategic decision will be how best to target and spend hard money. One possibility is to expand independent expenditures. This option, declared constitutional in *Colorado Republican Federal Campaign* v. *Federal Election Commission,* may lead to party independent expenditures supporting or opposing particular candidates.[22] Another possibility is for individuals and groups to invest much more in quasi-party shadow organizations whose disclosure requirements are limited. Almost certainly, all groups will spend more on mail, telephone, and personal contact—what we have called the ground war.

BCRA allows limited individual soft-money contributions to state and local party committees for voter registration and mobilization purposes. These provisions, sometimes called the Levin Amendment after the amendment's sponsor, Senator Carl Levin (D-Mich.), permit donors to contribute up to $10,000 to any state or local party committee for voter registration or get-out-the-vote efforts. BCRA prohibits federal officeholders from raising Levin Amendment funds, which may make raising these funds more difficult. But more fundamentally, donors may choose to write one check to an interest group to accomplish these similar purposes rather than writing several checks to state and local party committees. Such a decentralized effort is also inherently inefficient. BCRA includes new rules intended to alter the ability of groups to overtly coordinate campaign messages. Until 2002 Democrats had a clear advantage in voter mobilization. Republicans made major strides in this area in 2002 with largely soft-money-funded activity. The GOP hard-money edge may give them enough resources to fund mobilization with hard dollars. Democrats and their allies, particularly the labor unions, may also benefit from the use of "Levin fund" soft money for voter mobilization allowed under BCRA.

Finally, it is unclear whether the key elements of soft money are really on their way out. Will party committees encourage the creation of quasi-party interest groups to whom soft-money donors can continue to contribute and which can continue to spend unlimited amounts of money in competitive races? This is a predictable scenario and one that already appears to be under way. The latitude these interest groups will have with regard to issue advocacy depends in part on how the FEC defines *political committee* and otherwise implements BCRA in light of McConnell *v.* FEC. If the courts strike these BCRA issue advocacy provisions while upholding the BCRA soft-money ban, a substantial surge in issue advocacy is likely. This spending would lack the current disclosure of large soft-money donors and party spending-transfer disclosure. It is quite possible that the aggregate levels of outside money will not diminish in 2004 and beyond.[23]

Interest Groups

BCRA did not legislate away the factors that motivate interest groups to invest in electing or defeating candidates. Groups will continue to use their PACs to help ensure the election of candidates friendly to their cause. In 2002 party spending once again significantly exceeded spending by interest groups. But in a world without soft money, there is every reason to believe that issue advocacy will grow dramatically.

The track record of elections since 1996 also makes clear that we will see groups with names not previously active in federal elections in the post-BCRA world. As noted in chapter 2, some of the new groups in 2004 will be spin-offs of the current party committees, but others will simply be a new intentionally unrecognizable name for an interest previously active under a different name. The possibility that Section 501(c)4 groups will also be active means that there may be even more new groups active in 2004 than in 2002 or 2000.

Air and Ground Wars under BCRA

One constraint on interest groups under BCRA will be the ban on the use of corporate or union treasury funds for soft-money contributions or election issue advocacy campaigns. For groups that can make electioneering communications, such as individuals and unincorporated associations, BCRA requires disclosure of the communication if more than $10,000 is spent. The definition of electioneering communications was hotly contested in the initial judicial consideration of the act. Its definition of electioneering communications covers only broadcast, cable, or satellite advertisements that refer to a clearly identified candidate within sixty days of a general and thirty days of a primary election and are targeted to a population of 50,000 or more people in a candidate's district or state. As under FECA, it is a critical definition, and it will greatly influence where the money goes and how it is spent.

One predictable growth area in post-BCRA campaigning will be the ground war. In part because it is increasingly viewed as effective, the ground war grew in importance in 2002, and the focus on ground-war activities will not diminish in 2004, with or without BCRA. Republicans are likely to build on their 72 Hour Task Force in 2004, and Democrats will have to decide on the right mix of reliance on interest-group allies and independent party-funded efforts. It is likely that ground-war efforts will continue to be a major priority in both parties; voters in competitive contests in 2004 can expect to see the same high volume of mail, telephone calls, and personal contacts we observed in 2002.

One enduring lesson of past campaign finance reform efforts is that unintended consequences arise which themselves become major problems. It should not be forgotten that the origin of soft money can be traced back to an effort to rework FECA in 1979. The uses to which soft money has been put in recent cycles were not the intent of those who wanted the parties to be able to conduct generic party-building efforts. Campaign finance reform is an iterative process. This was clearly the case with FECA in 1971 and the subsequent amendments in 1974 and 1979. Typically there will be legislative modifications in the period after major reform is implemented. It will be important to carefully assess how BCRA actually works so that future legislative and administrative policymakers will have the benefit of a careful assessment of the new law as it is interpreted and practiced. The study of congressional campaigns and campaign finance is a moving target, and the potential effects of BCRA should provide researchers with ample fodder for years to come.

Past reform episodes have had a period of legislative amendment in the four or five years after the initial act was passed. There is good reason to believe that Congress will revisit campaign finance reform, to respond either to the BCRA Court decision or to the experience of the first election cycle or two under new rules. Democrats may well have buyer's remorse about having voted away soft money, Republicans may favor further increases to individual contribution limits, and both may want to do something about issue advocacy, including interest-group ground-war tactics. Furthermore Congress may seek to alter disclosure requirements or restrictions on fund-raising appearances that are deemed overly broad. This is only a partial list of reasons to continue to observe and evaluate this vital aspect of how our democracy actually works.

Notes

1. David A. Breaux, "The 2002 Mississippi Third Congressional District Race," in David B. Magleby and J. Quin Monson, eds., *The Last Hurrah? Soft Money and Issue Advocacy in the 2002 Congressional Races*, monograph version (Center for the Study of Elections and Democracy, Brigham Young University, 2003), p. 251.

2. This analogy was drawn by Lily Eskelsen, Democratic candidate in Utah's Second Congressional District in 1998. See David B. Magleby, ed. *Outside Money: Soft Money and Issue Advocacy in the 1998 Congressional Elections* (Lanham, Md.: Rowman and Littlefield, 2000), p. 217.

3. See chapter 9 of this volume.

4. In the South Carolina Senate race, the NRSC waited for opponents to attack Republican Lindsey Graham on the issue of Social Security and, in response, launched a counterattack on the issue of flag burning. Chris LaCivita, political director, National Republican Senatorial Committee, press event, "The Last Hurrah: Soft Money and Issue Advocacy in the 2002 Congressional Elec-

tions," Center for the Study of Elections and Democracy, National Press Club, Washington, D.C., February 3, 2003.

5. For example, see chapter 11 for a description of Utah Democrat Jim Matheson's overtures to the National Rifle Association and the U.S. Chamber of Commerce after they both actively worked to defeat him in 2000. In 2002, as a result of Matheson's efforts to convince them he was an ally, the NRA did not get involved, and the Chamber actually endorsed him.

6. In 2002 this was most notable in the Iowa Second Congressional District race where Republican Jim Leach disavowed ads run by the NRCC. Although apparently sincere, he was unable to convince the NRCC to change their tactics. See David Redlawsk and Arthur Sanders, "The 2002 Iowa House and Senate Elections: The More Things Change . . .", in David B. Magleby and J. Quin Monson, eds., "The Noncandidate Campaign," *PS: Political Science and Politics* online e-symposium, July 2003 (www.apsanet.org/PS/july03/magleby.pdf [July 30, 2003]).

7. J. Mark Wrighton, "The New Hampshire Senate and 1st Congressional District Races," in Magleby and Monson, *The Last Hurrah,* monograph version, pp. 144–55.

8. *Michigan State Chamber of Commerce* v. *Austin* 637 F.Supp 1192 (E.D. Mich. 1986).

9. *Buckley* v. *Valeo* 424 U.S. 1, p. 27 (1976).

10. *CSC* v. *Letter Carriers* 413 U.S. 548, p. 565 (1973).

11. See Robert Y. Shapiro, "Public Attitudes toward Campaign Finance Practice and Reform"; Mark Mellman and Richard Wirthlin, "Public Views of Party Soft Money"; Whitfield Ayres, "The Reform Act Will Not Reduce the Appearance of Corruption"; Robert Y. Shapiro, "Rebuttal to Ayres"; and David M. Primo, "Campaign Contributions, the Appearance of Corruption, and Trust in Government," in Anthony Corrado, Thomas E. Mann, and Trevor Potter, eds., *Inside the Campaign Finance Battle: Court Testimony on the New Reforms* (Brookings, 2003).

12. In 1998 and 2000 some polling done in competitive races provided important insights for us in the design of our 2002 surveys. See Jay Goodliffe, "The 1998 Utah Second Congressional District Race," in Magleby, *Outside Money*, pp. 171–86; and Craig Wilson, "The Montana 2000 Senate and House Races," in David B. Magleby, ed., *The Other Campaign: Soft Money and Issue Advocacy in the 2000 Congressional Elections* (Lanham, Md.: Rowman and Littlefield, 2003).

13. The higher average in Minnesota may also be partially explained by Minnesota's system of public financing, which allows a higher proportion of candidates the resources to pay for political mail.

14. One Republican direct mail consultant described how they targeted women over forty in one county in a House race. Dan Hazelwood, president,

Targeted Creative Communications, interview by David Magleby, Quin Monson, and Jonathan Tanner, Washington, D.C., November 14, 2002.

15. "The Women Voters' Journal Project," memorandum to Democratic leaders and interested parties from EMILY's List and Peter D. Hart Research and Associates, March 12, 2001; personal communication to Quin Monson from Sheila O'Connell, political director, EMILY's List, January 17, 2003.

16. The Lear Center Local News Archive, "Local TV Coverage of the 2002 General Election" (The Norman Lear Center at the University of Southern California Annenberg School and the Wisconsin News Lab at the University of Wisconsin, Madison) (www.localnewsarchive.org/pdf/LocalTV2002.pdf [July 29, 2003]).

17. Free airtime for candidates has been advocated by the Alliance for Better Campaigns. See www.bettercampaigns.org.

18. "The Women Voters' Journal Project."

19. *Shays* v. *FEC*. Complaint for Declaratory and Injunctive Relief. (www.campaignlegalcenter.org/attachment.html/SHAYS+V.+MEEHAN+COMPLAINT+FINAL+1+0+8+0211.pdf?id+88 [May 17, 2003).

20. For more information on the ongoing court challenge, see the Campaign Legal Center, www.campaignlegalcenter.org/cases.html.

21. Norman Ornstein, resident scholar, American Enterprise Institute, interview by David Magleby, Washington, D.C., March 18, 2003.

22. *Colorado Republican Federal Campaign Committee* v. *Federal Election Commission*, 116 S.Ct. 2309 (1996).

23. John Bresnahan, "Labor's New 527? Rosenthal Seeks $20 Million to Aid Candidates in '04," *Roll Call,* January 9, 2003, p. 1.

Studying the Noncandidate Campaign: Case Study and Survey Methodology

J. QUIN MONSON

STEPHANIE PERRY CURTIS

THE METHODOLOGY EMPLOYED in this research is designed to draw upon multiple sources of information (both quantitative and qualitative) to investigate noncandidate campaign activity in congressional elections. Using a set of case studies that employ multiple methods of data collection, we sought to systematically investigate the causes and consequences of campaign spending "within its real-life context."[1] We believe this method provides the richest, most feasible, and most accurate method of understanding the phenomenon of campaign spending by noncandidate entities in congressional elections.[2] Beyond providing the details of our methodology, this appendix also provides a rationale for the design, so that others embarking on similar projects can learn from the strengths and weaknesses of this approach.

The research reported here builds on similar projects the Center for the Study of Elections and Democracy (CSED) organized to study the 1998 and 2000 federal elections. During those elections, colleagues within competitive states or districts monitored thirty-eight congressional contests or presidential primaries.[3] In 2002 we monitored a total of forty-three races—twenty-six competitive races and seventeen control races.

Case Study Methodology

The research design for the case studies is based on three assumptions. First, noncandidate campaign activity is most likely to occur in competitive races. In the 2002 study we added seventeen noncompetitive races to our study as a control group, in part to test this assumption. We found overwhelming evidence that the vast majority of outside money is spent in competitive races.[4] Second, because much of noncandidate campaign activity is not disclosed, it is best uncovered and understood by someone with knowledge of the local context. To understand the full impact and reach of noncandidate activity, academics knowledgeable about the competitive race were recruited to systematically monitor each campaign. The academics in each competitive race oversaw the collection of campaign communications, including the extent of mail, telephone, and personal contact; they also collected as much information as possible on broadcast advertising. They monitored voter mobilization efforts conducted by candidates, parties, and interest groups. Data on campaign communication in the states or congressional districts were enhanced by a network of informants organized by the local academics. The informants agreed to collect their political mail and keep a record of other campaign activities that they encountered.[5] Our third assumption is that political professionals would be willing to be interviewed and discuss their decisionmaking and funding allocation strategies. Elite interviewing helps connect the dots of our data collection efforts, both by validating what is discovered in the data collection efforts of the academics and by providing new information. Each case study is also enhanced by interviews with informed elites and campaign professionals from the interest groups, political parties, and candidate campaign staff active in the district or state. All interviews for this study were conducted on the record, and with few exceptions the information from those interviews is fully attributed in this book. Appendix B contains a list of more than 130 interviews conducted at the national level by CSED.

Case Selection

The sampling pool of competitive races we monitored was developed based on a combination of lists of competitive races published in the early spring of 2002 by the *Cook Political Report*, the *Rothenberg Political Report*, and *Congressional Quarterly Weekly Report*. This list was enhanced by interviews with current and former party and interest group professionals, reporters, and other political experts who helped identify contests in which outside money was most likely to be present.[6] We listed eighty potentially competitive races mentioned by at least one of these sources in April 2002. In the final stages of sample selection in the early summer of 2002, we quantified the input from our contacts and published sources by computing an additive score for each race. Each score was composed of a combination of the ratings in the published reports, together with the likely competitive races named by the Republicans and key allied groups, as well those named by the Democrats and key allied groups. Once scored, the list was sorted in rank order and divided into quintiles. Eleven of the fifteen races in the top quintile and seven of the sixteen races in the second quintile are included in our sample, as well as one from the third quintile.[7] Except for two races, Pennsylvania's Fourth and Sixth Districts, our control races were not included on the full list of potentially competitive districts.

While largely based on the potential for a competitive race, the case selections took other considerations into account as well, in order to assure a broad range in the number and type of noncandidate groups observed. We made an effort to stratify the sample in terms of incumbent and open-seat races and for contests that would permit us to capture a wide variety of interest group and party communications and strategies. This was done by compiling a short demographic profile of each district, as well as listing the races where the experts from a variety of interest groups indicated that they or others were likely to become involved. Thus we were able to select cases so we had variation in geographic location, level of minority population, and the number and type of interest groups likely to become involved. The last step of the case selection involved finding academics willing to participate in the project. The academics recruited to monitor the contests were selected based on their scholarly reputations and knowledge of state electoral politics.

We added seventeen noncompetitive control races in 2002 to test some of the assumptions about where noncandidate money is spent, thus establishing a baseline against which to compare the competitive races.[8] Many of our control races were selected because they are adjacent to the competitive races being sampled. In addition to being more efficient for the academics covering multiple races, covering adjacent races provided a chance to compare noncandidate campaigning between two races in the same media market, sometimes with constituencies having similar demographic characteristics. We also selected some control races in states that had competitive races in the 2000 election, in order to contrast the role of outside money in the same state or district over time. The full list of U.S. House and Senate races sampled is in table 1-1. Examples of adjacent control races we monitored in 2002 include Arkansas First, Colorado Fourth, Connecticut First, Maryland Fifth,

Mississippi Second, New Mexico Senate and Third, North Carolina Ninth, New Hampshire Second, Pennsylvania Sixth, and Utah First and Third. The Pennsylvania Sixth Congressional District contest, which we selected as a control race, eventually became competitive. Examples of control races in 2002 that we previously monitored include the California Twenty-Ninth District (formerly the Twenty-Seventh), Delaware Senate, Michigan Senate, Montana Senate and at-large House seats, and the Pennsylvania Fourth District.

In sum, we believe that the procedures followed to select the cases for this study achieve an appropriate balance between maximizing the observable variance and minimizing bias, while at the same time keeping the research costs at an acceptable level. In addition, nonrandom case selection in a small-n study helps to ensure that one does not exclude an important case.[9]

Elite Interviews

In addition to interviews conducted by academics at the local level, we conducted over 130 interviews in Washington. A list of interviews conducted for this study at the national level is found in appendix B. In some instances, individuals were interviewed multiple times throughout the election cycle. These interviews were expressly "on the record," and the postelection interviews were tape-recorded. Information from the interviews is frequently cited throughout this book. Data gathered from these interviews concerning organization involvement in a particular race were incorporated into the respective case studies. The interviews were also supplemented with materials provided by the interview subjects, analysis of the websites of the groups we were interviewing, a careful reading of national print media sources, National Journal's Hotline (an online daily political news briefing), information from e-mail lists of the national party committees, and from activities that were disclosed to the Federal Election Commission or the Internal Revenue Service. There were a few groups who, despite repeated efforts to set up interviews, refused our request or were not responsive. In 2002 this list included National Right to Life; United Seniors Association; and the American Federation of State, County, and Municipal Employees (AFSCME).

CSED 2002 Soft Money and Issue Advocacy Database

Each group of academics was responsible for collecting and cataloging campaign-related communications produced and distributed by candidates, political parties, and interest groups in their respective races.

They recorded these observations in a database through a password-protected website interface. The data can be divided into two major groups: unique communications observed in various media and ad-buy data collected from television and radio stations.

It is infeasible to consistently gather and quantify the exact breadth and depth of each organization's activity in terms of total number of mailings sent or phone calls made in any given race over the course of an entire campaign. However, it is possible to track and estimate an organization's number of unique communications (that is, how many unique mailers they created for distribution). The academics recorded activity in the following media: mail pieces, television advertisements, radio advertisements, telephone calls, person-to-person contacts, newspaper and magazine advertisements, e-mails, and banner ads on the Internet.

In order to monitor their races, the academics set up reconnaissance networks to help collect unique ads and conducted elite interviews with consultants and party and candidate operatives. Efforts were made by the researchers to include people in the reconnaissance network who represented a broad range of groups including: pro-choice and pro-life supporters, labor union members, senior citizens, National Rifle Association members, small-business owners, ethnic and racial minorities, environmental activists, and religious group members. We also received help from Brigham Young University alumni, local university alumni, students, League of Women Voters, and Common Cause members in our sample. At their best, these networks included a range of informants across the partisan and ideological spectrum.

The academic investigators in our races were data scavengers and were often very creative in their data collection efforts. In addition to the efforts of their reconnaissance networks, they joined party and interest group mailing, e-mail, and fax lists. They also scrutinized campaign, party, and interest group websites and analyzed Federal Election Commission and Internal Revenue Service data for their races. Participating academics also used their elite interviews to ask questions about campaign communications in their races. Data from the CSED 2002 Soft Money and Issue Advocacy Database are summarized in each of the respective case studies.

Broadcast Television Data

To gather cost information on television advertising for the case studies, we relied upon two complementary sources. First, the academics contacted local network affiliates and cable companies to collect ad-buy information, which stations must make available to comply with Federal Communication Commission regulations.[10] These data were part of the CSED 2002 Soft Money and Issue Advocacy Database. Second, for contests in our sample within the top 100 media markets, we also relied on data collected by the Campaign Media Analysis Group (CMAG). Using both of these methods, a more complete picture was drawn of the use of television advertising in the races we monitored. Researchers also obtained information on what organizations actually spent in a race from elite interviews. This information was compared with the ad-buy data gathered from stations and the CMAG data and then incorporated into the case studies.

AD-BUY METHODOLOGY. Participating academics visited radio and television stations in their races to retrieve ad-buy data (the number of spots run by a given group and the cost of those spots). Although some stations were unwilling to cooperate, refusing to provide data on groups other than candidates, this study constitutes the most complete existing tally of money spent by interest groups and parties in the races we sampled. When complete, using the dollar amounts in the actual ad buys of various organizations is better than using estimates. Unlike the CMAG data, the ad-buy data also include radio and television stations outside the largest 100 media markets.

The ad buys gathered from television and radio stations have limitations. It is usually not possible to determine from an ad buy the content of the ads run, including whether the ad was pure issue, electioneering, or express advocacy. We are also unable to disaggregate the data for specific races. We can only ascertain how much money was spent by a group at a particular station and how many spots they purchased. We cannot know from the ad-buy data whether ads sponsored by a political party or interest group were run on behalf of one or more candidates. This becomes especially problematic when tracking ad buys made by state party committees in states with more than one competitive race, such as South Dakota in 2002.

The ad-buy data are limited to the stations that our researchers were able to visit and that were willing to provide us with the relevant information from their public interest and political files. Before the passage of the Bipartisan Campaign Reform Act (BCRA), stations were required to share ad-buy information on candidates but not on ads purchased by parties or groups. Also, in some states there are so many television and radio stations that it is not feasible to visit them all. In other states the stations are geographically spread out, so the time and cost required for data collection is increased. When the stations did not fully cooperate or the number or location of stations exceeded the capacity of the academics to collect ad-buy data, we assume that the data that were collected are representative of what happened in the locations where they were not.

CMAG METHODOLOGY. The CMAG data are gathered using software that recognizes the electronic seams between television programming and advertising. Analysts then code the advertisements into particular categories—by product for commercial clients and by candidate or sponsor for political clients—and tag them with unique digital fingerprints. Thereafter the system automatically recognizes and logs that particular commercial whenever it airs.[11] The result is a dataset containing a record of individual broadcast ads aired during the election campaign. When the system encounters a new unique sound pattern, the new commercial spot is recorded. CMAG monitors the transmissions of the six national networks (ABC, CBS, NBC, FOX, UPN, and WB) and twenty-six national cable networks (such as CNN, ESPN, and TBS) in the country's top 100 markets.[12] Table A-1 shows the media markets for which we have obtained the CMAG data for the 2002 election cycle for our sample of competitive races. Combining the CMAG data with the data we collected directly from stations provides a more comprehensive picture of television advertising for our races.

In 2002 we coordinated our efforts with Kenneth Goldstein's Wisconsin Advertising Project at the University of Wisconsin–Madison, to obtain the CMAG data during the course of the election.[13] Two types of data were provided. First, for each political advertisement produced and aired, we received a storyboard. Storyboards include a full audio transcript and still shots of every four seconds of video. These storyboards were coded by students at the University of Wisconsin to analyze ad content on a wide range of topics. The second set of data that CMAG provided was the day-to-day tracking of the political ads in the top 100 media markets. For each airing of a unique ad, the data include information on the time the spot was aired, the length of the spot, the station the spot aired on, the program the spot aired on, and a cost estimate of a commercial during that time period. This targeting information was merged with the coded content from the storyboards to produce a single, comprehensive database.[14] The cost estimates of commercials during specific time periods were calculated based on the time slot, media market, and latest industry spending data, as well as CMAG historical data.

Table A-1. *Media Markets Monitored by CMAG in Our Sample Races*

Race	Media market
Arkansas Senate, First, Fourth	Little Rock-Pine Bluff, Shreveport, Springfield, Memphis
Arizona First	Phoenix, Albuquerque–Santa Fe
California Twenty-Ninth	Los Angeles
Colorado First, Seventh	Denver
Connecticut First, Fifth	Hartford-New Haven, New York
Delaware Senate	Philadelphia, New York
Iowa Senate, First, Second, Third, Fourth	Des Moines–Ames, Omaha-Council Bluffs, Cedar Rapids–Waterloo–Dubuque, Quad Cities (Davenport–Rock Island–Moline)
Indiana Second	Chicago, South Bend–Elkhart, Indianapolis
Maryland Fifth, Eighth	Washington–Hagerstown, Baltimore
Michigan Senate	Detroit, Flint-Saginaw–Bay City, Grand Rapids–Kalamazoo–Battle Creek, Toledo, South Bend–Elkhart
Minnesota Senate, Second	Minneapolis–St. Paul
Missouri Senate	St. Louis, Kansas City, Springfield, Omaha–Council Bluffs, Paducah (Cape Girardeau–Harrisburg–Mt. Vernon)
Mississippi Second, Third	Memphis, Jackson, Baton Rouge, New Orleans
Montana Senate, At-Large	None
North Carolina Eighth, Ninth	Charlotte, Greensboro–High Point–Winston-Salem, Raleigh-Durham (Fayetteville)
New Hampshire Senate, First, Second	Burlington-Plattsburgh, Boston (Manchester), Portland–Auburn
New Mexico Senate, First, Second, Third	Albuquerque–Santa Fe, El Paso
Pennsylvania Fourth	Pittsburgh
Pennsylvania Sixth, Seventeenth	Harrisburg–Lancaster–Lebanon-York, Philadelphia, Wilkes-Barre–Scranton
South Dakota Senate, At-Large	None
Utah First, Second, Third	Salt Lake City

The CMAG data were particularly helpful in our ad-buy data retrieval efforts from stations. The storyboards supplemented the researchers' efforts to monitor their races because they were an additional means to identify new ads in each race. They provided a listing of ads run, which prompted queries of station advertising managers about ad-buy data for various groups, permitting us to request information from stations on those advertisers.

While the CMAG data are a valuable addition to our study, they are not perfect. The data are limited to ads run in the top 100 media markets. In addition to the lack of coverage in small markets (such as South

Dakota), occasionally we learned from our academics about ads in the top 100 markets and on the national networks that were not captured by CMAG. For example, in table 3-3, CMAG did not record ads from several groups listed in ad-buy data.

Because of the substantial volume of ads tracked by their system, there are bound to be some coding errors in the CMAG data. A notable difficulty with the CMAG data lies with the use of so-called cookie-cutter ads, mostly by interest groups. Often a group will run an identical ad in multiple races and media markets, altering only the final few seconds and mentioning a different candidate in each version. Because of the fingerprint technology used to code the ads, cookie-cutter ads were coded in the CMAG data for the race in which they first appeared, and subsequent appearances of a similar ad in a different race were miscoded. In 2002 cookie-cutter ads were run by the United Seniors Association, the AFL-CIO, Club for Growth, Business Roundtable, Sierra Club, and various party committees. The data were checked and cleaned by looking at what markets the ads aired in and then correcting the candidate for whom the ad should have been coded. Sometimes it was obvious which race the ad should have been assigned to, but other times it was not. We used our knowledge of competitive races in and out of our sample where the advertising is most likely to occur, as well as media accounts and elite interview information, to help the Wisconsin Advertising Project accurately recode cookie-cutter ads whenever they were identified as such.

CMAG's estimates of the likely cost of an ad aired during a particular time slot also have limitations. CMAG uses a model based on average rates for each media market and not for individual stations. The differences between the cost of an average ad in a particular media market and the actual rate charged by the stations in that market vary according to market share and other circumstances. CMAG's cost estimates typically underreport actual costs. These estimates also do not include any costs beyond media buys, such as production costs or parameters in which buys were made (placement lead times, media packages, special negotiations, and so forth) and do not include all media markets. In addition these estimates may not accurately reflect the inflated rates that are charged when the market is saturated with political advertising as Election Day nears. Because television stations reserve the right to preempt advertisements at the last minute and without warning, groups often pay premium prices to ensure that their ad will run during specific time slots. These premiums ensure that an ad will not be preempted by another buyer.[15] This sometimes led to discrepancies in the CMAG data and what we gathered from television stations. In the 2002 election cycle, CMAG made some adjustments in their model to account for an increase in some issue advertising costs.[16] In some cases CMAG cost estimates were adjusted as often as every ten days. This was done by surveying their clients in the most competitive campaign environments and adjusting the estimates to match current market conditions.[17] Our researchers thought the CMAG frequency data were useful for overall summaries, especially for the groups and parties and for totals by station. When there was a big discrepancy, the researchers usually relied upon the ad-buy data they gathered; however, the CMAG data provided quick counts and the storyboards contain information about the content and tone that the ad-buy data do not.

Explanations for Tables Using CSED 2002 Soft Money and Issue Advocacy Database

The two categories of data gathered by the academic researchers in our sample races are summarized in two types of tables. The tables on the number of unique campaign communications highlight the communications observed in various media, and the tables on the air war summarize the ad-buy data collected from television and radio stations and the CMAG data. Each case study chapter has both types of tables for the races involved. Summaries of these tables for all the races can be found in chapters 1, 3, and 4. These tables summarize the involvement of all candidates and political parties and the most active interest groups in our sample races. The air war and unique communications tables are not intended to represent comprehensive organization spending or activity. The most complete picture of the level of activity by a party or interest group can be obtained by examining the air war and unique communications tables together.

The air war tables summarize the ad-buy data gathered from television and radio stations in our sample races. In the states where CMAG data were available, these data are also included as a comparison to our television ad-buy data. Due to the sheer volume of television and radio stations in any given race and varying degrees of compliance in providing ad-buy information, data on spending by various groups might be incomplete. Because ad-buy content was often nondescriptive and sometimes difficult to distinguish among different races, the data occasionally combine information regarding all races studied in a single state.

The number of unique campaign communications tables represent the number of distinct pieces or ads by a group that we gathered but do not necessarily represent a count of all distinct items sent or made. In other words the absence of a group in a unique communications table does not necessarily mean that the group was not active in the race, only that we did not find evidence of any activity. The candidate and party categories in the unique communications tables in chapters 1, 3, and 4 are complete counts of what we monitored in our races. However, the interest group category summarizes only the data from the most active organizations in our races.

ALLIED INTEREST GROUPS. Interest groups have been classified as Democratic or Republican allies or as nonpartisan. In many cases, organizations are openly supportive of a certain party and its candidates. Some organizations, such as the National Education Association (NEA) and the National Rifle Association (NRA), publicly maintain neutrality and occasionally support candidates of both parties. Upon closer examination of their communications, it was usually possible to categorize the groups as partisan allies, based on which candidates they generally supported or attacked.

AFFILIATE CONSOLIDATION. Data that are collected from multiple races contain observations from state-level organizations and their national affiliates. In our sample-wide totals (such as in table 4-2), some state and local chapters or affiliates have been combined with their national affiliate to better depict the organization's overall activity. For instance, the Iowa State Education Association data have been included in the NEA totals. The labor category listed in the air war and unique communications tables consists of all labor groups, including the AFL-CIO and affiliates, such as local AFL-CIO chapters, other state labor organizations, and organizations whose election activities are not directly connected with the AFL-CIO, such as AFSCME and the Service Employees International Union (SEIU).

Survey Methodology

We conducted two survey projects in 2002. The first used a three-wave panel design in competitive election contexts to examine public opinion dynamics in races that had substantial levels of noncandidate spending. The second project was a voter log survey, where registered voters tracked their contacts through the mail, telephone, and in person, with the candidate and noncandidate campaigns.

Three-Wave Panel Survey

Our 2002 project included for the first time a systematic effort to assess public opinion toward elections and campaigns in contests with substantial candidate, party, and interest group spending. Among the issues we explore with these data are the level of exposure to broadcast, mail, phone, and personal contact; the reaction to the tone and content of the candidate and noncandidate campaign; and overall assessments of disclosure, accountability, and other key dimensions. Panel studies are well suited to our research purposes because the same respondents are reinterviewed at different points in time throughout the campaign, permitting us to assess change because of events or stimuli. For each wave of the panel survey, we interviewed registered voters in each of four campaigns—Senate races in Arkansas and Missouri, House races in Connecticut's Fifth and Colorado's Seventh Congressional Districts, and a national sample. The national sample provides a baseline of comparison for our four competitive races.

We managed the project and oversaw the data collection. Throughout the process we closely consulted with a panel of prominent national political pollsters, who helped in the design of the research, the selection and wording of questions, and the analysis of the data. To avoid any conflict of interest with our consultants and their work for other clients, the actual data for all three waves of research were not shared with them until after the election on November 5, 2002. The participating pollsters were Linda Divall, Bob Carpenter, and Randall Gutermuth of American Viewpoint; Ed Goeas and Brian Tringali of the Tarrance Group; Mark Mellman of the Mellman Group; and Fred Yang of Garin-Hart-Yang Research Group. We commissioned Western Wats Center, a large data collection firm based in Provo, Utah, to conduct the actual interviewing. A report summarizing these data was previously released at the National Press Club on November 13, 2002, and at the U.S. Capitol on November 14, 2002.[18]

We began interviewing in August 2002, in an effort to measure opinion before most election advertising began in earnest. The initial sample for wave one was a random digit dial (RDD) sample generated by GENESYS Sampling Systems, using their MOD1 method of generation with the measure of size set to total households. Respondents were selected within each household using the most-recent-birthday method of respondent selection. We completed interviews only with selected respondents who said they were registered to vote. Interviewing for the first wave began August 25 and ended September 15. In wave one we completed interviews with 1,000 registered voters in each of the five samples. Second-wave interviewing occurred over a two-week period from October 14 to 27, during which we reinterviewed 600 of the original respondents in each of the five samples. The third wave of interviewing occurred on November 5, 6, and 7—election night and the next two days. We recontacted 500 respondents in the postelection stage, except for the national sample (481) and the Connecticut Fifth District sample (452). Finally, to check for possible panel effects, we added a fresh sample of new respondents who were interviewed in wave three, using an abbreviated questionnaire. This fresh sample equaled 300 in each of the five settings. In the end, these data represent nearly 12,000 interviews with 6,500 survey respondents.[19]

Campaign Communication Voter Log Survey

We also conducted a mixed-mode mail and telephone survey of registered voters in four states: Arkansas, Minnesota, South Dakota, and New Mexico. Respondents were asked to keep a log of their political contact during the three weeks before Election Day. Respondents were asked to track their political mail, e-mail, phone calls, and personal contacts, and to send their political mail to us. We contracted with the Social and Economic Sciences Research Center (SESRC) at Washington State University (WSU) for the fieldwork. At WSU Don Dillman, well known in the survey research field for his expertise with mail and mixed-mode survey designs,[20] consulted on the research design of the project, and Ashley Grosse managed the implementation of the field-work efforts.[21] Our efforts were inspired by a similar study conducted by Peter D. Hart Research for EMILY's List during the 2000 election cycle, in which a group of undecided women voters were recruited to write about their reaction to campaign communications in diaries during the three weeks leading up to the general election.[22]

Respondents were contacted six times by telephone or mail in the four-week period leading up to Election Day to request their participation, answer questions, and remind them to diligently collect the necessary information. This included an advance letter, a questionnaire packet sent by Priority Mail with a $5 incentive and an endorsement letter from the League of Women Voters, a supportive telephone call near the beginning of the three-week period, a reminder postcard, a letter during the second week with an additional log booklet and business reply envelope, and a thank you letter that arrived just before the election together with a free pen. After the election, respondents answered additional survey questions in the log booklet in which they had noted the political communications they received. They provided information on their reactions to the tone and conduct of the campaign, information about group memberships, and answers to demographic questions. Two additional telephone calls were made to respondents after the election. The first involved a brief list of additional survey questions especially about their voting decision, early and absentee voting, and influences on their decision to vote or not. A second postelection call was made to ask forgetful respondents to mail back the booklet and other materials. The booklets were returned together with the political mail received during the three weeks before Election Day.

Respondents were sampled from lists of registered voters. These were purchased from the secretaries of state in Minnesota, New Mexico, and South Dakota. Arkansas does not maintain a centralized voter file, and so a sample of registered Arkansas voters was purchased from a vendor, Voter Contact Services. Initially we drew a sample of 900 in each state.[23] In Minnesota and South Dakota, high-quality voter files combined with the generally cooperative nature of people in the upper Midwest led to well over 500 respondents in each state participating by returning the log booklet. The overall number of respondents was lower in New Mexico and especially low in Arkansas, in part because the voter files contained outdated address information for many of the names sampled, and so the survey materials never reached their destination.[24]

Notes

1. Robert K. Yin, *Case Study Research: Design and Methods,* 3d ed. (Thousand Oaks, Calif.: Sage Publications, 2003). Using multiple methods of data collection helps to enhance the validity of our conclusions. See Gary King, Robert Keohane, and Sidney Verba, *Designing Social Inquiry: Scientific Inference in Qualitative Research* (Princeton University Press, 1994).

2. Our methodology is similar to that followed by other research in congressional elections that uses case studies. See James A. Thurber, "Case Study Framework and Methodology," in James A. Thurber, ed., *The Battle for Congress: Consultants, Candidates, and Voters* (Brookings, 2001), pp. 239–46.

3. The 1998 data are summarized in David B. Magleby and Marianne Holt, eds., *Outside Money: Soft Money and Issue Ads in Competitive 1998 Congres-

sional Elections (Center for the Study of Elections and Democracy, Brigham Young University, 1999). The 2000 presidential primary data are summarized in David B. Magleby, ed., *Getting Inside the Outside Campaign: Issue Advocacy in the 2000 Presidential Primaries* (Center for the Study of Elections and Democracy, Brigham Young University, 2000). The 2000 general election case studies are in David B. Magleby, ed., *Election Advocacy: Soft Money and Issue Advocacy in the 2000 Congressional Elections* (Center for the Study of Elections and Democracy, Brigham Young University, 2001). Some of the 1998 case studies and expanded analysis of the broader trends in the election can be found in David B. Magleby, ed., *Outside Money: Soft Money and Issue Advocacy in the 1998 Congressional Elections* (Lanham, Md.: Rowman and Littlefield, 2000). Expanded versions of the 2000 presidential primary and general election case studies were part of an electronic symposium published by the American Political Science Association in David B. Magleby, ed., "The e-Symposium: Outside Money in the 2000 Presidential Primaries and Congressional General Elections," *PS: Political Science and Politics,* online e-symposium, June 2001 (www.apsanet.org/ps/june01/ [July 31, 2003]). This was followed by a book with expanded analysis of competitive congressional contests in 2000 with selected case studies; see David B. Magleby, ed., *The Other Campaign: Soft Money and Issue Advocacy in the 2000 Congressional Elections* (Lanham, Md.: Rowman and Littlefield, 2003).

4. See the discussion of competitive and noncompetitive races connected to table 1-2.

5. We gratefully acknowledge the participation in this data collection effort of local members of the League of Women Voters and Common Cause, as well as many others recruited by the local researchers.

6. Among others, we acknowledge the assistance in this effort of Karen Ackerman, Matt Angle, Damon Ansell, Bob Bennenson, Ed Brookover, Bernadette Budde, Martin Burns, Charlie Cook, Chuck Cunningham, Mike McElwain, Greg Giroux, Andy Grossman, John Guzik, Tom Hofeller, Chris LaCivita, Mike Matthews, Bill Miller, Stuart Rothenberg, Scott Stoermer, Deanna White, Derrick Willis, and Sharon Wolff.

7. In some cases we selected races because we were already studying another race in the same state and because we wanted to achieve varying levels of competitiveness in our sample. The following are the races in the top three quintiles that were sampled or not: In quintile one, races sampled were Arizona First, Colorado Seventh, Connecticut Fifth, Iowa Third and Fourth, Indiana Second, Maryland Eighth, Mississippi Third, North Carolina Eighth, New Mexico Second, and Utah Second. Not sampled in quintile one were Alabama Third, Kentucky Third, Ohio Third, and West Virginia Second. In quintile two, races sampled were Iowa First and Second, Minnesota Second, New Hampshire First, New Mexico First, Pennsylvania Seventeenth, South Dakota at-large. Not sam-

pled in quintile two were California Eighteenth, Connecticut Second, Florida Fifth, Georgia Third, Illinois nineteen, Minnesota Sixth, North Dakota at-large, Nevada Third, and Tennessee Fourth. In quintile three, the race sampled was Arkansas Fourth. Those not sampled were Georgia Eleventh, Indiana Seventh and Eighth, Kansas Third, Kentucky Fourth, Louisiana Fifth, Maine Second, Michigan Ninth and Tenth, Pennsylvania Thirteenth, Fifteenth, and Eighteenth, Texas Fifth and Twenty-Third, and Washington Second and Third.

8. On this point we are especially indebted to Janet Box-Steffensmeier, Richard Fenno, and other panel participants who provided feedback on our methodology as part of a panel titled "Getting Inside the Outside Campaign: Using Collaborative Fieldwork to Study Soft Money and Issue Advocacy" at the 2002 annual meeting of the American Political Science Association.

9. See Gary King, Robert Keohane, and Sidney Verba, *Designing Social Inquiry: Scientific Inference in Qualitative Research* (Princeton University Press, 1994), especially chapter 4, for a comprehensive discussion of the issues involved in qualitative case selection. They provide an especially good discussion of why a random sample is not always an acceptable method of case selection in small-n case study research. Our nonrandom case selection method uses a key explanatory variable (competitiveness) to drive the case selection of our focus and control races, while also using other available prior information to increase the range of values across our dependent variable (noncandidate campaign activity).

10. Sherrie Marshall and Trevor Potter, *What You Need to Know about Political Advertising: A Practical Guide for Candidates and Citizens to Enforcing Broadcast Rights and Obligations* (Washington, D.C.: Campaign Legal Center, 2002).

11. The technology was originally developed by the U.S. Navy to track Soviet naval vessels, primarily submarines, during the cold war. It did so by measuring and cataloguing the unique sound patterns of the propellers and screws of Soviet warships.

12. For a more complete explanation of CMAG data, see www.politicsontv. com, and Craig B. Holman and Luke P. McLoughlin, *Buying Time 2000: Television Advertising in the 2000 Federal Elections* (New York: Brennan Center for Justice, 2001). Although there are more than 200 media markets in the United States, over 80 percent of the population lives in the top 100 markets.

13. See the Wisconsin Advertising Project, http://polisci.wisc.edu/tvadvertising/.

14. Ken Goldstein and Paul Freedman, "Lessons Learned: Campaign Advertising in the 2000 Elections," *Political Communication*, vol. 19 (2002), pp. 5–28.

15. Holman and McLoughlin, *Buying Time 2000,* p. 20.

16. Evan Tracey, chief operating officer, TNSMI/Campaign Media Analysis Group, personal e-mail communication to Stephanie Curtis, February 27, 2003.

17. Evan Tracey, interview by David Magleby, Quin Monson, and Kelly Patterson, Philadelphia, Pa., August 28, 2003.

18. David B. Magleby and J. Quin Monson, "Campaign 2002: 'The Perfect Storm'" (Center for the Study of Elections and Democracy, Brigham Young University, November 13, 2002) (http://csed.byu.edu).

19. Using the American Association of Public Opinion Research (AAPOR) Response Rate 3, the average response rate for the five samples in wave one is 12 percent. This was calculated assuming that the proportion of cases of unknown eligibility that are actually eligible (or "e") equals 0.61. For further details on the formula, see *Standard Definitions: Final Dispositions of Case Codes and Outcome Rates for RDD Telephone Surveys and In-Person Household Surveys* (AAPOR, 2000) (www.aapor.org/pdfs/newstandarddefinitions.pdf). The response rate for wave one is lower than we desired. However, it seems to be within the range for campaign surveys routinely administered by this firm, and we were not aware of the response rate until it was too late. After consultation with our panel of campaign pollsters about the survey results, we have no reason to believe that our results were unduly biased by the response rate. The average response rate for wave two, calculated as the proportion of wave one respondents successfully reinterviewed, was 62 percent. The average response rate for wave three, calculated as the proportion of wave two respondents successfully reinterviewed, was 82 percent. Full details regarding the calculation of response rates for each of the five samples is available from the authors.

20. Don A. Dillman, *Mail and Internet Surveys: The Tailored Design Method*, 2d ed. (Wiley, 2000).

21. We are also indebted to Paul Lavrakas of Nielson Media Research for his advice on our research design. Our effort to have respondents keep a log of their political contacts is similar to the diary methodology used by Nielsen Media Research to gather data on household television viewing habits.

22. "The Women Voters' Journal Project," memorandum from EMILY's List and Peter D. Hart Research and Associates, March 12, 2001; personal communication from Sheila O'Connell, EMILY's List political director, January 17, 2003. Since our methodology was significantly different from the EMILY's List study, we conducted a full pilot test in the South Dakota primary election in June 2002 to ensure that the proposed methodology would work. It worked well, and the same methodology used in the pilot study was adjusted only slightly for the general election.

23. In Minnesota and South Dakota the voter files contained voting information from prior elections. In order to maximize the number of respondents who would be contacted by political campaigns, we stratified the sample by those who had participated in a midterm election from 1994 forward. They were then oversampled at a higher rate compared to the rest of the sample. A similar pro-

cedure was followed by Voter Contact Services with the file that they provided. New Mexico does not include prior vote in their voter file; thus we did not over-sample recent midterm voters. In the end, a very small number of respondents from the nonmidterm voter group actually participated in the survey. This hampered efforts to weight the data back to the voter file proportions.

24. The overall response rate, or the ratio of completed cases (defined as those with both a returned diary and a completed postelection telephone interview) to the number of potential respondents in all four states was 44 percent. The response rate was 35 percent in Arkansas, 40 percent in New Mexico, 49 percent in Minnesota, and 53 percent in South Dakota. Response rates for the telephone portion only averaged 66 percent, while response rates for the more time-consuming diary portion averaged 47 percent. Further details about response rates are available from the authors.

Interviews Conducted by CSED Researchers

Name	Title	Organization	Dates
Jim Martin	president	60 Plus Association	12/11/02
Martin Burns	legislative representative, grassroots and elections	AARP	4/12/02, 10/22/02
Kevin Donnellan	director of grassroots and elections	AARP	12/2/02
Karen Ackerman	political director	AFL-CIO	4/18/02, 12/2/02
Mike Podhorzier	assistant director, political department	AFL-CIO	12/2/02, 5/8/03
David Boundy	assistant director, political department	AFL-CIO	12/2/02
Denise Mitchell	assistant to the president for public affairs	AFL-CIO	12/10/02
James Chiong	analyst	AFL-CIO	12/2/02, 5/8/03
Ellen Moran	campaign operation analyst	AFL-CIO	12/2/02
Paul Taylor	executive director	Alliance for Better Campaigns	1/24/02, 5/6/03
Ed Coyle	executive director	Alliance for Retired Americans	12/20/02
Linda DiVall	president	American Viewpoint	11/12/02
Robert Carpenter	vice president	American Viewpoint	7/11/02
Grover Norquist	president	Americans for Tax Reform	4/22/02
Damon Ansell	vice president for policy	Americans for Tax Reform	4/22/02
Curt Anderson	consultant	The Anderson Group	5/8/03
David Krantz	political reporter	*Argus Leader*	7/25/02

Name	Title	Organization	Dates
Ned Monroe	director of political affairs	Associated Builders and Contractors	5/8/02, 12/9/02
Linda Lipsen	senior director of public affairs	Association of Trial Lawyers of America	12/19/02, 5/6/03
Earl Bender	president	Avenel Associates	5/10/02
Gregory Casey	president	BIPAC	12/11/02
Bernadette Budde	senior vice president	BIPAC	1/22/02, 10/24/02, 11/6/02
Darrell Shull	vice president, political operations	BIPAC	12/11/02
Roger Hickey	co-director	Campaign for America's Future	5/8/02
Curtis Gans	director	Center for the Study of the American Electorate	5/7/03
Roberta Combs	president	Christian Coalition	3/13/02
Stephen Moore	president	Club for Growth	12/2/02
John Altevogt	president	Council for Better Government	1/21/03
Hal Malchow	political consultant	Crounse, Malchow, Schlackman & Hoppey	4/22/02, 12/9/02
Michael Matthews	political director	DCCC	2/22/02, 11/12/02
Matt Angle	executive director	Democratic Caucus	2/21/02, 9/16/02, 12/2/02
Rob Engle	executive director	Democratic Legislative Campaign Committee	3/13/02, 9/17/02
Gail Stoltz	political director	DNC	1/23/02, 11/13/02
Andy Grossman	political director	DSCC	11/8/02
Mike Gehrke	research director	DSCC	1/23/02, 11/8/02
Sheila O'Connell	political director	EMILY's List	12/11/02
Laurie Moskowitz	principal	FieldWorks	2/21/02, 10/30/02
Sara Zdeb	legislative director	Friends of the Earth	9/17/02
Fred Yang	partner	Garin-Hart-Yang Research Group	7/11/02, 5/7/03
Alan Quinlan	president	Greenberg Quinlan Rosner Research	12/23/02
Ed Brookover	chairman, political practice	Greener & Hook	4/11/02, 9/17/02, 11/12/02
Judith Kindell	tax law specialist, exempt organizations	IRS	2/22/02
Bobby Zarin	director of customer education and outreach	IRS	2/22/02

Name	Title	Organization	Dates
David Bositis	political analyst	Joint Center for Political and Economic Studies	5/8/03
Martin Hamburger	partner	Laguens, Hamburger, Stone	11/6/02
Scott Stoermer	communications director	LCV	3/15/02, 9/16/02, 11/15/02
Andrew Schwartzman	president and CEO	Media Access Project	9/18/02
Mark Mellman	CEO	Mellman Group	7/12/02
Greg Moore	executive director	NAACP National Voter Fund	1/17/03
Tiffany Adams	assistant vice president of public affairs	NAM	5/8/02
Kate Michelman	president	NARAL Pro-Choice America	12/19/02
Monica Mills	political director	NARAL Pro-Choice America	12/19/02
Lisa Friday Scott	senior public advocacy representative	National Association of Realtors	1/24/02
Jack Polidori	political affairs specialist	NEA	5/9/02, 9/17/02, 11/15/02
Randy Moody	federal policy and politics manager	NEA	9/17/02
Dennis Whitfield	senior vice president, political and media communications	NFIB	11/8/02
Sharon Wolff	campaign services and PAC director	NFIB	3/13/02, 4/22/02, 11/8/02, 5/5/03
Kristen Beaubien	campaign services assistant	NFIB	3/13/02, 11/8/02, 5/5/03
Charles Cunningham	director of federal affairs	NRA	2/21/02, 11/7/02
Glen Caroline	director, Institute for Legislative Action grassroots division	NRA	11/14/02
Mike McElwain	political director	NRCC	4/11/02, 7/11/02
Chris LaCivita	political director	NRSC	1/23/02, 7/12/02
Ben Ginsberg	attorney	Patton Boggs	5/6/03
Robert Bauer	election lawyer	Perkins Coie	3/15/02
Marc Elias	election lawyer	Perkins Coie	3/15/02
Rachel Lyons	director of action fund and PAC	Planned Parenthood	3/15/02

David Williams	director of action fund and PAC	Planned Parenthood	3/15/02, 11/8/02
Karin Johansen	senior vice president	Precision Communications	12/20/02
Michael Lux	president	Progressive Strategies, LLC	2/21/02, 1/9/03
Bill McInturff	partner	Public Opinion Strategies	7/11/02
Marc Racicot	chairman	RNC	12/6/02
Jack St. Martin	director of grassroots development	RNC	1/23/02
Blaise Hazelwood	political director	RNC	1/17/03, 5/8/03
Timothy Teepell	deputy political director	RNC	1/23/02
Tom Hofeller	redistricting director	RNC	2/21/02
Charles Spies	deputy counsel	RNC	2/22/02
Tom Josefiac	election lawyer	RNC	2/22/02
Jim Dyke	press secretary	RNC	1/23/03
John Powell	senior vice president and chief operating officer	Seniors Coalition	11/14/02
Margaret Conway	national political director	Sierra Club	12/16/02
Deanna White	deputy political director	Sierra Club	3/14/02
Dan Hazelwood	president	Targeted Creative Communications	1/22/02, 11/14/02
Ed Goeas	president, CEO	Tarrance Group	11/12/02
Brian Tringali	partner	Tarrance Group	8/7/02, 11/12/02
Anita Benjamin	executive director	United Seniors PAC	9/16/02
Bill Miller	political director	U.S. Chamber of Commerce	4/27/02, 11/7/02, 5/5/03
Kenneth Mehlman	deputy assistant to the president and director of political affairs	The White House	11/15/02
Jan Baran	election lawyer	Wiley, Rein, & Fielding	2/22/02
John Guzik	vice president	Williams Mullen	4/11/02, 11/13/02
Chris Glaze	analyst	Winning Connections	12/11/02
Gary Teal	independent consultant		12/11/02
Heather Booth	independent consultant		5/8/02

Contributors

Sandra M. Anglund
University of Connecticut

John Bart
Augustana College

Stephanie Perry Curtis
Brigham Young University

William H. Flanigan
University of Minnesota

E. Terrence Jones
University of Missouri–St. Louis

Martha Kropf
University of Missouri–Kansas City

Matt McLaughlin
University of Missouri–St. Louis

James Meader
Augustana College

Stephen K. Medvic
Franklin & Marshall College

Joanne M. Miller
University of Minnesota

Sarah M. Morehouse
University of Connecticut

Dale Neuman
University of Missouri–Kansas City

Kelly D. Patterson
Brigham Young University

Matthew M. Schousen
Franklin & Marshall College

Nicole Carlisle Squires
Brigham Young University

Daniel A. Smith
University of Florida

Jonathan W. Tanner
Brigham Young University

Jennifer L. Williams
University of Minnesota

Nancy H. Zingale
University of St. Thomas

Index

305